Elisabeth Schumann

A BIOGRAPHY

Elisabeth Schumann

A BIOGRAPHY BY

GERD PURITZ

Edited and translated by

JOY PURITZ

ANDRE DEUTSCH

First published 1993 by
André Deutsch Limited
105 – 106 Great Russell Street, London WC1B 3LJ

ISBN 0 233 98794 0

Printed in Great Britain by
St Edmundsbury Press, Bury St Edmunds, Suffolk

CONTENTS

ACKNOWLEDGMENTS

Elisabeth Schumann made some biographical notes with me before she died (which were particularly useful for the early years). My father, Walther Puritz, also gave me much valuable information about my mother. Apart from these, many people have been very helpful, not least my wife Biddy, who did a certain amount of advising and editing until ill-health made this no longer possible.

For much useful information I also have to thank John Amis, Trude el Bedell, Anita Bild, Mary Bok, Lisl Bontemps, Franz, Gustl and Käthe Breuer, Ruth D'Arcy-Thompson, Gitta Deutsch, Harry Goddard Owen, Hubert Greenslade, Winifred Hall, Peter Heyworth, Lene Jung, Rudolf Klein, Lotte Klemperer, Trudchen Koch-Lissauer, Walter Legge, Lotte Lehmann, Dorothy Maddison, Bernard Miles, Gerald Moore, Ivor Newton, Maria Olszewska, Lisa Reitler, Suze Rueff, Erna and Jacques Samuel, Desmond Shawe-Taylor, Alice and Franz Strauss, Annelise Tchounikine-Bontemps, David Thaw, Emmy Tillett, Claire Watson, Karl Wisoko, the Archives Department of the Royal Opera House Covent Garden and the Curtis Institute of Music in Philadelphia.

For advice and encouragement in finding a publisher, both I and my daughter Joy wish to thank Patrick Carnegy, Mr and Mrs Frank Cutler, Mark Hamilton, Elizabeth and David McDowall, Joyce Rathbone, Clare Stevens and Tom Stacey.

We are also most grateful to Paul Richards for his help with computer-related matters.

G.P.

CHAPTER 1

Childhood

IN MERSEBURG, an old town of the German kingdom of Saxony, in a house not far from the cathedral, Elisabeth Schumann was born on June 13 1888.

Music came first in the Schumann household, although just at that time Alfred and Emma, Elisabeth's parents, had to spend more time on other things. He had to teach reading, writing and arithmetic in school, a rather tedious and exacting occupation, which he, a serious-minded and conscientious man, endured with patience. She had to care for her husband and children, and had to make sure that the housekeeping money lasted, which was often difficult.

"Frau Lehrer", approaching thirty, with her crown of thick brown hair streaked with white, was well known by most people in Merseburg. With little Frieda, Elisabeth's elder sister, holding her hand, she could often be seen doing the round of the shops and market. Not only was she admired for her singing in cathedral concerts, she was also much liked for her cheerful nature and her sympathy and understanding.

Alfred, who at first only assisted as organist in the massive early Gothic cathedral, was often to be seen practising at the splendid console: a rather slight bearded man, of medium height, soberly dressed. These were happy hours for him, compared to the drudgery of teaching untalented pupils to play the piano. Unfortunately the piano lessons were necessary, since his salary as a school teacher was small.

His love of music and gift for making it did not have to be limited to the home and to standing in as organist occasionally. He was also chorus master of the "Liedertafel [Choral Society] Merseburg", and conducted oratorios in the cathedral performed by a small orchestra together with the "Liedertafel". Emma sang solo soprano parts. On one occasion the famous violinist Joseph Joachim heard Emma singing in the cathedral. At the end of the concert he expressed the wish to be introduced to the soprano, "this born singer".

When this was done he said: "You must study singing! You must!" He pressed her to come to Berlin, to his college. It was a happy moment for Emma, but all she could say was: "How can I, a mother of two children, just go off to Berlin?"

It did not worry her unduly that she was unable to follow his advice. Admittedly, when she was a girl she would very much have liked to have had singing lessons, but she was an orphan and money was lacking. Musical activity at home with Alfred and at the occasional concert in the cathedral or in the grand restaurant in the castle gardens, the Schlossgartensalon, seemed to satisfy her musical needs.

The first signs of Elisabeth's musicality came to light when she was just nine weeks old. The scene was remembered many years later by Elisabeth Wintzer, a friend of Emma: the baby girl was being wrapped in swaddling clothes (as was still the custom in those days). She was staring with big eyes into the round, chubby face of her mother, who was singing. Alfred was accompanying Emma on the piano. They were studying Liszt's oratorio *Heilige Elisabeth* together, and this practising meant so much to Emma that not even maternal duties might interrupt it. Elisabeth (or Lies, as she was called), instead of indulging in her usual kicking about, lay completely still, spellbound by these new sounds.

Still as a baby, she would crawl beneath the piano and her father's stool when her mother was practising. Judging by her excited little squeaks, she was a very appreciative audience.

One day one of her squeaks was longer than usual and was on the same note as her mother was just singing, and then on the next note she did the same, and the next, until she had followed several bars of music.

Her parents were amazed, and this occurrence made a great impression on Alfred.

Elisabeth never forgot those early impressions. Almost sixty years later she could still remember: "I am sitting on the floor. Above me, on the keys, are hands playing. My mother is towering above me, singing. I keep hearing songs again and again, so of course I sing along too."

In the summer of 1892, as happened every year, there was a

2

charity concert in the Schlossgartensalon. When the official part was over, everyone always took refreshment at the grand coffee table. This time the Schumanns had brought their daughters, Frieda, who was now nine years old, and four-year-old Elisabeth.

If anyone felt inclined to boost the takings in aid of the charity by showing off his or her talents, this was the moment for it: the big collection plate would go round after the performance. So an ageing actor recited a poem by Schiller; a juggler threw spoons, forks, cups and plates wildly through the air, missing disaster by a hair's breadth; and a dashing youth played the mouth organ, which Lies obviously loved, for once or twice she sang a few notes along with him. The people around her laughingly suggested that she might want to perform too; perhaps she could sing something?

What then happened Elisabeth Schumann remembered all her life: "I am wearing my Sunday best. Around me there are masses of people in a huge room. Suddenly I feel myself being lifted up and put on the table. 'Sing, Lies, sing us a nice song!' And I sing to all those faces: 'My lover is a weaver...'"

A love song! Sung with such expression by a small child! Everyone forgot their coffee and cake, clapped wildly and clamoured for more. So Lies sang a song by Schubert and finally two by Robert Franz. The money was piling up on the collection plate: it was the largest sum of the afternoon.

Alfred now realized that in Lies there might be a future singer, and he was determined that she should be well prepared for it. Already he was speaking of piano and music-theory lessons, which he wanted to give her soon, so that when she started having singing lessons, at the age of sixteen or seventeen, she would know the theory backwards. Although Emma warned him not to burden the child too early, she agreed that Lies must not be musically illiterate, the way so many singers were who only had a beautiful voice. She would have a voice, perhaps a great one, but she would also be musical through and through.

At that time, of course, Elisabeth was still too young for theory, but she could be gradually introduced to the piano. Now Alfred would often ask his wife or Frieda to bring Lies with them when they fetched him from his organ-playing. Then the little girl would climb on all fours up the creaking, narrow stairs to the organ, as quickly as possible, in order to see Father playing – on the "big, big piano" with all those keys on top of one another. When the music echoed powerfully through the long cathedral, a shiver went down her spine. . . .

But Elisabeth's greatest pleasure in these early years was the summer holidays – spent at her grandparents' farm in Orlishausen. The first wonderful thing about those holidays would be at the railway station at Cölleda: there stood the big rack-wagon made of light-coloured wood, with the oxen in front. Next to it her grandfather would be waiting. Lies would always ride on top while Frieda and her parents walked a little way behind. Only out on the country road would they join her in the wagon. Her father always said: "You won't catch me being pulled by oxen through Cölleda!"

Once arrived at the farm of Wilhelm Heinrich Schumann, the hayloft was the first place to visit. It was like heaven playing there – leaping off the great haystack as if one were flying. Again and again, after just a quick "hallo" to her grandmother. Dorothea Schumann always found it difficult to say no to her little grand-daughter. Lies, with her silvery voice, had sung her way into the heart of the old lady, who could do nothing more severe than give words of warning: "It doesn't become a little girl to be romping around up there like that. In God's name, don't fall the wrong way!"

Whether becoming or not, for Elisabeth, the tomboy, everything enticingly new and strange was to be eagerly tried out. How she secretly laughed when her grandmother, clinging to her old ways, watched suspiciously while running water was laid on in the house, and then said, shaking her head: "They'll be wanting water plumbed straight into their noses next!"

Soon – too soon – the first day of school drew near and farewells had to be said. The grandmother's eyes were moist as she hugged the girls and said: "It's a coming and a going."

Then Orlishausen was just a memory and dreamy thoughts – during the dreary arithmetic class, in which such dreams were shattered by the bang of the teacher's ruler hitting his desk top; or during the frightful afternoons filled with homework.

Orlishausen was forgotten only when Elisabeth practised the piano, at least during the first hour; concentration during the second was harder, and frequently she would stop and listen to hear whether her mother was still bustling about next door or whether she had at last gone out. When finally she heard the front door, she would rush upstairs to Hänschen, the sweet canary, and to Friedchen who was cleaning up or sewing. She could only ever help her sister with housework in secret, since her father always said: "Lies has other things to do!"

Just a few minutes with Hänschen on her shoulder taking breadcrumbs from her lips – that did not keep her long from practising, and trying to imitate the bird's sweet trill was after all a kind of music-making.

Elisabeth took every opportunity to have secret "singing lessons" from her canary. Whistling through her teeth was already pretty close to the sound; it was the trill that was the problem. But one day a loose top milk tooth fell out, and by whistling through the gap the trill just seemed to happen. At first when they heard it, her father and mother thought that Hänschen had got down to the ground floor during one of his daily exercise breaks.

From then on two little birds were fluttering about the house. However, Alfred Schumann would have preferred to see his daughter devote herself as eagerly to her harmony studies as to her trilling. He had no idea that one day she would delight people with it at parties and on records.

He was, however, pleased with her progress. She rapidly mastered everything practical and learnt songs and piano pieces without any trouble. On the other hand she was not very interested in theory and sometimes had problems grasping it. It took her a long time to understand the relationships between keys. Writing out music by hand was not much fun either. Alfred, full of ambition for his daughter, set a fast pace; he thought that with her musical gift she would grasp everything at once. He would often cry "Wrong!", and sometimes broke off the lesson in anger. Tears then flowed.

But soon everything would be all right again and her father might call upstairs: "Lies, will you work the bellows for me?" Immediately she would run on ahead to the cathedral, unlock the blower room and start pumping, ready for him to start playing at once.

The serious side to life in Merseburg was hardly ever in evidence, and Elisabeth had too happy a disposition to be cast down for long. Besides, there were often wonderful things to look forward to – perhaps the rehearsal of a cathedral concert when she would be allowed up in the gallery. To one side, crouching behind the balustrade with her head between the balusters, she would listen intently and could clearly see the musicians blowing, bowing, beating and singing – some of them made such funny faces when they sang. Her mother never did. Her father's baton would go down, its tip quivering, and up again – stab at the tenors who came in forte and whom the quivering stick did not release until it began to sweep in great arcs and then change to a swinging motion, like a metronome. Everyone followed, made a great effort to perform as their conductor wanted it, for he knew what the composer had intended. Elisabeth often thought how wonderful it must be to conduct.

There was great excitement when Emma was to see *Tannhäuser* in Halle, and this time the seven-year-old Lies could go with her. Lies felt that opera, theatre with music, must be an enchanted world. Eleven long days to wait. At least there was the consolation of her mother telling her a lot about this opera, especially about the Shepherd Boy who had such a charming little role.

Elisabeth sat spellbound in the theatre. When the first act was over, her mother asked her: "Well, Lies, didn't you think the Shepherd Boy was sweet?"

Elisabeth had neither heard nor seen him, she had been completely enthralled by the transformation of the Venusberg into the Wartburgtal.

At her second visit to the opera, months later, at *The Merry Wives of Windsor*, there was a lady who sang in such a way, a way which touched Elisabeth strangely – it was not like listening to her mother. One moment there was a great bubbling of joy and rippling laughter, the next she was enchanted by sweet, melting tones. *That* was what people meant when they spoke of "a great singer". To be great was to sing like this, like Erika Wedekind at the Court Opera in Dresden. . . .

Elisabeth Schumann often said later: "From the moment I knew what a singer was, that was all I wanted to be."

Soon the urge to get a taste of what it was like became irresistible: to feel, to experience how it was to play-act and sing, to act out a fairytale, to get a group of children together and perform it with them, in costume, as in a real theatre. After all, her mother had so many interesting robes and shawls in a big chest. Friedchen could be orchestra cum conductor at the piano. Tickets would cost five or ten pfennigs. And one of the old patched sheets in the linen cupboard could serve as a curtain.

Sometimes it was almost like real opera, especially singing the *Freischütz* aria, "Through the forest and o'er the meadows" – actually meant for a tenor, but it was such a good one to sing. The other children and their parents made a storm of applause every time, and at the end they sometimes put extra money into the plate, money that filled the costumes kitty for the next show.

Her father hardly ever let Elisabeth go to the opera in the Tivoli, because the performances always seemed to start at her bedtime. Yet the touring companies were always from big cities and the performances were very good. Although the (by now) ten-year-old had great respect for her father, she would, if circumstances were favourable, act with the greatest temerity. "Favourable circumstances" meant her parents were making music or had gone to visit neighbours. As soon as it was all clear she quickly got dressed again and crept downstairs, shoes in hand, to the back door, leaving Friedchen in a frenzy of anxiety.

Even though she often arrived late at the Tivoli, her friend at the door helped her out: the dear old music-loving usher, who always wanted to know in the interval how she was liking the performance. Every time he listened very seriously to what the devoted little "musician" had to say, so in a way it was in his interest to save a hidden seat for her. She would probably have won the old man over anyhow, for Elisabeth captivated people with her sparkling nature: her gaiety, her liveliness and her love of pranks, combined – when it came to music and her longed-for career – with seriousness and an unusual determination. Her appearance achieved the rest, particularly her large, expressive, brown eyes.

The way she would look at her teacher when she had forgotten what he had just taught her was not embarrassed or guilty, but was full of sorrowful regret at having to disappoint him once again. That made it hard to be strict with her, although in school there was often good reason for strictness. It was true that Elisabeth shone when it came to singing, also that she loved learning poetry and understood what it meant without any trouble; but the other subjects bored her.

She had a devoted friend, Anni – a punctuality fanatic, who knew how to inspire Elisabeth with a sense of duty and even some ambition when they did their homework together. Books under arm, Anni would position herself at the front door at two minutes to four. As soon as the clock chimes began to ring out from the church towers, she raced up the steps and stood triumphantly in the room on precisely the fourth stroke. To her the thought that Elisabeth might have to stay down a year at school was unbearable. So she put every effort into pulling her through. "Think of your singing training," she would say, "if you stay down you'll have to start it a whole year later."

Anni's reproaches had an effect on Lies, but the warnings and scoldings of her teachers did not. When one of them for the umpteenth time criticized her poor achievements, she observed in a matter-of-fact tone of voice: "Sir, it doesn't matter a bit, I am going to be a singer."

In the summer of 1900 an opera company came to Merseburg again, this time from Düsseldorf – and in the holidays. Alfred considered that Dörner was an excellent producer – he tended to bring good up-and-coming people with him. There was a chance that they might go to several performances, not just one, because it might be some time before Alfred was well enough for the journey to Orlishausen. Every morning Dr Linke had to come to try to relieve his asthma. For Elisabeth that nearly always meant a ride in the pretty coupé behind the doctor's sleek dapple-grey.

One day he announced that he was going to the Tivoli to look down the singers' throats and see if they were fit to sing. After that he would listen to a bit of a rehearsal. Did Elisabeth want to come too?

Elisabeth leapt at the chance.

But at the Tivoli her enthusiasm was dampened. No orchestra, just a rattling old piano, and the singers were only "marking" – singing quietly to save their voices. Dr Linke explained that it was a blocking rehearsal: they went through the movements and positions on stage.

Now she often went to rehearsals. The best was *Der Freischütz*, with Fräulein Risch as Agathe. Herr Schreiner simply called her Liddi, addressed her with the familiar "du". Elisabeth wondered if she could get her autograph.

But it was not just a question of a signature and polite thanks. A proper conversation arose between the singers and the twelve-year-old, who soon forgot her shyness, listened intently, every now and then making a brief comment, or giving a decided opinion of her own.

Ten years later Elisabeth was to meet Liddi Risch and Emmerich Schreiner again, but this time as a fellow-singer; and they, who were by then married and well known, still remembered vividly the little girl at the Tivoli in Merseburg.

At these guest performances of the Düsseldorf company in the summer of 1900 Elisabeth experienced something else. The coloratura soprano had become unwell, and when the music-loving doctor arrived at the Tivoli with his little opera-crazy friend, he was asked to take a look at her.

Immediately there was only one thought in Elisabeth's mind: she was going to see that lady who looked simply heavenly in her costume and headdress. She was going to see her grand house and peep for a moment through her bedroom door to catch a glimpse of her lying in her four-poster bed, dressed in silk and lace.

The dapple-grey stopped outside a crooked house in the old part of town. A sloppy woman led them up the worn steps. The door at the top creaked open into a dark, musty little room. Instead of the radiant lady Elisabeth had seen on stage there was a pale creature with straggly hair, wearing a fustian nightdress buttoned right up to the neck. The bedstead was rusty, with a dress hanging on the bedpost; petticoats and stockings lay strewn over the floor. Over in the corner dirty cups and plates were stacked. Was this how singers lived?

Later, when Dr Linke had driven off to see other patients and she was walking home, she came to a firm decision: that she would never live like that. "One day I'll have a lady's maid."

She had no idea how close her life would come to being "like that".

Alfred Schumann was gradually coming to the conclusion that soon he would have no more that he could teach his daughter, and that for instruction in harmony she should now go to a respected music teacher, Professor Otto Reubke in Halle. That meant letting Elisabeth travel there alone; but at fourteen she was quite capable of taking care of herself in a large, busy town, and the journey to Halle which she had to do every week for over a year was perfectly to her taste.

Professor Reubke immediately brought her down to earth. He was extremely knowledgeable, he made her feel very small. Each lesson began with that awful moment when she had to hand over her homework for him to glance over. But sometimes he told wonderful stories. When he told of the composer Robert Franz, with whom he had been friends until his death in 1892, she could positively relive how this or that song had come into being. Another time she would feel that she was in an orchestra, right among the players or – and that was the best – she felt that she herself was the conductor.

CHAPTER 2

Finding a Teacher

ONLY ONE THING WAS CERTAIN ABOUT Elisabeth's singing studies: they could not start for another nine months, when she would have finished school. Otherwise there was no definite plan, not where to study, nor with whom.

Her parents acted as though they could foresee no problems: "Just wait until you have a good final report from school, then everything will work out." Basically they did not know how to go about it. Preferably Lies should go to a conservatoire, which would guarantee a solid and not too expensive training. But where?

Alfred Schumann, whose work extended no further than in and around Merseburg, had no contact with important musicians who might have given him advice. Even the Tivoli seemed to him to be part of the big wide world of which he had little knowledge.

The final school report turned out to be quite reasonable. Elisabeth's grandfather sent some money as a reward, and she was allowed to spend eight days in the charming Thuringian town of Gotha with the family of her father's old student friend Geutebrück.

It was heavenly to have school behind her for good and to stroll through the streets of Gotha with the two Geutebrück daughters, wearing a hat and long dress, and almost fifteen years old!

These were carefree days, even the big question as to how the training would work out did not seem so tricky. She discussed with the Geutebrücks what one could, should or must do, like singing to an expert perhaps, a well-known singer who could criticize seriously and give advice as to where to study.

Frau Geutebrück thought that the wife of Dr Obenberger had been a singer and still performed occasionally. Pia von Sicherer! Elisabeth had heard of her: soprano at splendid oratorio performances and beautiful recitals. That she was here in Gotha seemed like a sign from heaven.

Her heart was in her mouth when she announced herself and made her request for an audition. Many years later she noted down what happened:

> I was almost fifteen but looked even younger. When I approached Frau von Sicherer-Obenberger in her music room she was of course laughing inwardly and first gave me a long lecture: "My dear child, you simply cannot believe what a difficult career it is and how many singers there are, and how few good ones."
>
> I sat there humbly and listened to all of it. . . She asked me what I wanted to sing and was astonished when I said: "The aria from Haydn's *Creation*, 'With verdure clad the fields appear'."
>
> She was a good musician and accompanied me herself. After the first chord of the recitative and my three words "And God said" she turned round and asked how old I was. Then I warbled my way up to the B♭.
>
> Pia von Sicherer said: "You must study at once!" She recommended Fräulein Orgeni in Dresden to me, a world-famous singer and teacher.

After that there was nothing to keep Elisabeth in Gotha any longer and she raced back to Merseburg sooner than intended to talk things through.

To have lessons with Fräulein Orgeni suddenly seemed the most important thing in the world. Wedekind, who had impressed Elisabeth so much in her singing of *The Merry Wives of Windsor*, had studied with Fräulein Orgeni. Aglaja Orgeni: she was a star at the Berlin Court Opera. Frau von Sicherer was to write to her and could perhaps find Elisabeth lodgings in Dresden, in a nice little boarding house run by Fräulein Neuhaus.

Overjoyed and even relieved though her parents were, they had to give much thought to whether she should go to Dresden or not. First they would have to find out whether Orgeni taught at the conservatoire, for private tuition would be too expensive. And the boarding house – that, too, might be too dear.

That same evening Elisabeth wrote to Frau von Sicherer and waited for good news, in suspense but confidently: signs from heaven did not come for nothing. She could barely stop thinking about her future studies in Dresden, where the great teacher would eliminate all her failings with a few tips and exercises. She was already imagining herself in the splendid royal theatre, hearing the sound of the orchestra, and the voices of the famous. And every morning, still in her nightdress, she would look for the letter amongst the post, only to be disappointed.

Saturday June 13 approached, her fifteenth birthday – if only the postman could give her the best present of all: news that Fräulein Orgeni was at the conservatoire and that the boarding house was within their means.

He did not. But instead, on her birthday table lay a guitar! From her dear grandparents. She had been longing for it, and now at least she had something to distract her. She practised and practised the main fingerings with great enthusiasm.

Then all of a sudden, the letter from Gotha arrived.

21 June 1903

Dear Fräulein!

...I should like to say that your pretty voice has awakened my interest in you, and I wish you the very best for your future. – How happy I am for you that you are to be able to study in Dresden. Frl. Neuhaus, whom a friend of mine spoke to on your behalf, will be glad to take you in and will reduce her normal monthly charge by a third. But would 100 marks perhaps still be too much for you? Perhaps you could find a good place which is even cheaper. Unfortunately I do not know Frl. Orgeni personally, at any rate I'm afraid you misunderstood about a recommendation. However, if you would like to take with you a letter from me, I would be glad ... to say a few favourable words. I'm afraid I do not know whether Frl. Orgeni teaches at the conservatoire, but that is easily discovered. Frl. Neuhaus lives in Uhlandstrasse and has many conservatoire pupils; she is the sister-in-law of the composer Professor Draeseke in Dresden and is musical herself. – When will you begin your studies? Surely not before September?

Elisabeth was not really much the wiser about anything – except the awful boarding house charge. There seemed to be no hope now. Her father really had not expected such a high price. On top of that there would be fees, the cost of music, pocket money, quite apart from everyday necessities. Dresden now seemed a castle in the air; to study with the great Orgeni, a beautiful dream.

Her mother's outlook was not so gloomy. There would surely be some cheaper accommodation in Dresden. Perhaps her grandfather would contribute something. It was true he was very careful with money, but he had quite enough. And Lies was his favourite. When they went to Orlishausen for the Golden Wedding Alfred could explain to his father how things were.

By the time the Schumanns arrived in Orlishausen Elisabeth and

Frieda could have performed the song standing on their heads, Beethoven's "I love you, as you love me, at evening and at morn. There was no day when you and I did not share our sorrows." Luckily there was just enough time for a final rehearsal in the church.

Elisabeth wondered whether stage fright would always be as bad as it was now. She was only glad that the special Golden Wedding service was being held early in the morning, so that it would all be over quite soon.

The next day, the Golden Wedding day, all of Orlishausen spoke of the beautiful "concert in the church", and Elisabeth and Frieda were the pride of their grandparents. Thus it was not too difficult for Alfred Schumann to speak to his father about their plans and difficulties. The old man cried: "Lies can have as much as she needs. It would be a crime not to develop such a talent."

This house, which had already seen a great deal of girlish high spirits in its time, now witnessed enthusiasm of quite a different order: Elisabeth – dancing, prancing and twirling through rooms and along corridors, dragging Frieda with her, cheering and shouting with joy – "Dresden! Dresden! In the autumn it's Dresden, here I come!" Wherever Elisabeth went or stood in the next few days, her head was in the clouds with the yet unknown Dresden shimmering like a heavenly mirage before her eyes.

July came to an end, August began, they returned to Merseburg, but nothing was yet certain except that it was now too late to enrol for September at the conservatoire, where, as Elisabeth now knew, Fräulein Orgeni did, in fact, teach.

It was not long before Frau von Sicherer wrote that she had heard from Fräulein Orgeni. Unfortunately she would teach no one under seventeen, only in very special cases sixteen-year-olds. Also, due to overwork, she was unable to take on anyone new for the present. As soon as there was a vacancy she would let her know.

Emma Schumann did the best she could to help Lies over this big disappointment. Basically she was relieved. It did seem to her better that her "little one" should grow a bit older before she went to the big city on her own. The interim could be used profitably if Lies followed Frau Sicherer's closing advice:

It would be very good, if for the time being you would concentrate hard on your piano and language studies. It will then be easier for you

13

at the conservatoire. I believe that if you go on singing the way you have been without straining at all, you will not harm your very sound voice, on the contrary you could only do it good. . . .

By the spring of 1904 Elisabeth had written to Fräulein Neuhaus about the possibility of accommodation and about the uncertainty as to when she would be able to start studying.

Then something unexpected happened. Fräulein Neuhaus replied, saying that as she had gathered from Pia von Sicherer that this was a case of unusual talent, her brother-in-law, Professor Draeseke, would be glad to put in a good word to Fräulein Orgeni, whom he knew from having himself been active at the conservatoire for many years.

So at last the great moment had come – almost a year after the audition in Gotha – and Elisabeth, outside Pension Neuhaus, climbed into the hackney-carriage, ordered to be on the safe side. It was terribly extravagant, but to get lost in the big city and then to arrive late and exhausted into the presence of the great teacher did not bear thinking about! After a restless night, the young pupil was looking quite peaky in her dark blue Sunday best. The wide-brimmed hat with all its leaves and flowers, which was supposed to make her look older, almost overwhelmed her little face. Her mind was going round and round imagining the test which she must soon undergo in front of the celebrated lady.

But first she had to wait, sitting all alone on a monster of a chair – perfectly straight and of course modestly perched on the edge – in a high-ceilinged room with massive, dark furniture and heavy, half-drawn curtains. On top of it all a deathly quiet, broken only occasionally by the sounds of a contralto voice, coming from a distance as if through many walls.

Suddenly the sound of the door, and someone approached rapidly. Elisabeth started – a thin elderly lady stood before her. The eyes, embedded in countless crowsfeet, quickly and closely examined her, and a bony hand was thrust in greeting towards Elisabeth, who was speechless and could only bob a curtsey.

Aglaja Orgeni did not seem to notice and was at the window in two strides, closing the curtains completely. Out of the darkness a voice croaked: "Take your dress off." Intimidated, Elisabeth did as she was told and then jumped as she felt sharp fingers poking her body.

"No need to be so prudish! I just want to see if you are wearing a corset with bones."

14

It was no use denying it or drawing back, the hard hands went on fumbling until Fräulein Orgeni had found out for herself.

After these abominable goings-on, and with a great lump in her throat, Elisabeth was expected to sing. So this time after the first three words of the recitative there was no astonished enquiry as to her age. Nor, at the end, did Fräulein Orgeni cry "You must study at once!" Far from it. She pronounced: "Typical coloratura voice. But still not old enough to study, young lady." At the earliest Elisabeth should come back the following year. On no account before that. And then for the first six months she would learn with her assistant.

Like a whipped dog Elisabeth left the house and made her way to the Uhlandstrasse. If Orgeni thought she had to be drilled in coloratura, she was very much mistaken, thought Elisabeth. Happy singing, laughing with the voice, yes! But there was poetry which had to be expressed too, all those feelings which lay in lieder and arias, not just acrobatics. What manners that lady had! And *she* had once been a star of the Imperial Opera in Berlin!

Fräulein Neuhaus proved to be a good counsellor in this suddenly completely altered and apparently hopeless situation; she was also indignant at Fräulein Orgeni's behaviour, but advised Elisabeth not to leave immediately and not to tell her parents for the time being. First she should sing to Professor Draeseke. He would know of another teacher she could go to.

And who indeed could have been a better adviser than the respected, almost seventy-year-old poet, composer and theory teacher who, in recognition of his works and his advancement of musical education in Dresden, had had the titles Professor and Privy Councillor conferred upon him?

The "most feared contrapuntalist of his time" did not, however, behave in the least condescendingly as he strode briskly up in his black velvet jacket with a lavish pale grey bow tied around his shirt collar, and warmly spread out his arms in greeting to Elisabeth.

He spoke immediately of the "incident" as he called it. He commiserated with Elisabeth about her ordeal, but tried to explain the misguided behaviour of his "estimable colleague": she was overworked and had been unwell. He pointed out that in later life one realized that such setbacks had sometimes been a good thing: when he thought of his first years as a musician – dear God! "Now let's have some music and then we'll discuss your problems."

Thus began the audition, which soon became the most enjoyable music-making. It was a joy to have Felix Draeseke accompanying; he was obviously warming to the task, often nodding his head in approval. He seemed not to be able to have enough, for he found other arias, went on to several lieder, during the last of which he broke off in the middle of the postlude as if he could not keep it to himself any longer and had to congratulate this, as he said, exceptional talent which promised great artistic achievements. And as for Fräulein Orgeni, she should most certainly have recognized this talent. Naturally Elisabeth would not study with her. Dresden also had Natalie Hänisch, a singing teacher of outstanding repute. It was true that she did not teach at the conservatoire, but Elisabeth's father would be in agreement when he heard how the pupils flocked to her. (Perhaps he would remember her outstanding portrayal of Elisabeth* in Bayreuth.)

The professor promised to make enquiries with Fräulein Hänisch. What was most important was her fee and when to start. That would certainly not be before September, since there were only a couple more weeks before the summer holidays.

Professor Draeseke gave Elisabeth a letter for her father. In exchange he begged of her one favour: that she should take part in his family concerts.

*In Wagner's *Tannhäuser*.

CHAPTER 3

Dresden

THIS TIME THERE REALLY WAS no reason to be afraid of meeting her teacher, for Natalie Hänisch was kindness itself. She had been prepared to take on Elisabeth immediately, without having heard or even met her. At the first singing lesson, with almost motherly kindliness, she did not ask Elisabeth to sing a song to her straight away (having heard what she had been through at her last audition). The exercises which she gave her instead were child's play. And Fräulein Hänisch praised her – "fine, very pretty" – and made no other comments (except possibly to her little pug, Prinzchen, who was always present at lessons, lying on a silk cushion).

Thus in the first days of September 1904 the "big time" had begun: study. Three times a week half an hour's lesson and daily the "homework"; that meant practising diligently, for which there was ample opportunity. Fräulein Neuhaus loved and fostered music. So for her music-student guests she kept two attic rooms with pianos.

Every day Elisabeth spent almost an hour up there. When she had done half of it she had to have a rest, otherwise she would sometimes get a tightening feeling in her abdomen which occasionally grew worse and lasted quite a long time. Besides, a gulp of hot tea was good; the kitchen maid often had half a pot left over. With it she sometimes had some slices of delicious home-made sausage from Orlishausen. It was well worth eating a lot of this for another reason too: in almost every sausage her grandfather stuffed a golden twenty-mark piece, and that had to be brought to light as soon as possible otherwise there would be no chance of opera tickets; and a week without opera was no week at all.

She would queue at the box office very early in the morning for a cheap unnumbered ticket for the "gods". In the evening she would wait with beating heart until the liveried doormen opened the doors

17

to the upper galleries, then she would fly up the four or five flights of stairs to gain a place in the front row.

Elisabeth found the auditorium breathtaking. Each time the interior of the Semper* building looked so spectacular. The wide sweeping tiers in white and gold, the bright red upholstery; with it the lovely warm light of the new electric candlesticks: this was festiveness, the big world, a place of sublime art. Next to it the Tivoli seemed like a barn, and even the theatre in Halle seemed paltry. The director of music, Ernst von Schuch, conducted magnificently. The dynamics were subtle, there were no excessive crescendi or forti which were too loud for the singers to compete with – although these seemed able to compete with anything, like the tenor Karl Burrian, for instance, and especially Karl Scheidemantel with his heroic baritone voice. Or Marie Wittich, whose dramatic soprano voice penetrated every tutti and forte. Elisabeth was becoming ever more aware of how much there was to learn.

Fräulein Hänisch seemed very satisfied, and the lessons always seemed to be over quickly. But then Fräulein Hänisch always stopped right on the stroke of the clock, even if "our next one" was late.

A few weeks before Christmas she told Elisabeth about the pupils' concert they always gave in the winter semester. This time it was to be held on February 17 and she considered Elisabeth ready to take part. It would be rather like a test, and gentlemen of the press were invited, among them the music correspondent of a German-American paper. So it could be quite important for her future career.

Elisabeth protested that she could hardly sing in front of critics after only three months of lessons.

To her objections Fräulein Hänisch replied with uncharacteristic firmness: "Else, *you* won't let us down. And you should sing something which shows off your top notes."

Professor Draeseke dismissed her misgivings with a smile and the comment that with her great musicality she already counted as an advanced student.

Elisabeth often came to tea with the Draesekes and would help serve it to the other guests. Each time she pushed the tea trolley into the green drawing room, through the double doors with their heavy curtains, it was like appearing on stage. Everyone looked up, took

*Gottfried Semper, 1803–1879, German architect of the opera house.

note of what was being served, and many a gaze would then remain on the young girl in the frilled dress, who passed round tea and cake very gaily but also with a certain charming shyness.

On the first occasion everything had seemed intimidatingly grand, but Frau Frida had pulled her straight into the social mêlée, telling this and that guest who she was and what she was doing. Half jokingly she would add flattering comments such as: "Fräulein Schumann convincingly demonstrates how musical singers can be! . . . We have high hopes of her success . . . It certainly won't be long before we hear a lot of her. . . ."

With the approach of winter the social life in the Draeseke household intensified. Leading figures in Dresden's cultural scene took tea there – the conductor Ernst von Schuch, for instance, and also the director Count Nicolaus von Seebach.

Gone were Elisabeth's days of being a tomboy. This was the real adult world: now she was called "young lady".

However, after the Christmas holidays at the beginning of 1905, the pleasure in her newly found social status was dampened by the occurrence of more frequent and stronger pains in her abdomen. Sometimes she also suffered nausea, so Fräulein Neuhaus, unable to persuade Elisabeth not to sing in the concert, insisted that she should see a doctor as soon as it was over.

It was not really a problem, Elisabeth decided. She would survive that one little aria she had to sing, "Batti, batti" from *Don Giovanni*, even if it hurt a little. Later in her career, she would not be able to cancel every time she felt a twinge somewhere. And especially now – to miss being heard by critics – that was out of the question.

February 17 was a Friday. Fridays could be tricky sometimes. Of course that stabbing in her stomach was there again. And the artists' room, with its dark, heavy door, made her feel as if she were waiting for her execution. Sometimes it must really be a kind of execution. The long room was so cold and bare that she did not feel like sitting down. Either standing still or pacing to and fro she listened to as much as could be heard of the "sacrifice" that was going on out there, also, with some trepidation, to the whispering around her: renowned Dresden musicians were said to have accepted the concert invitation, even Hermann Kutzschbach, the young conductor from the Opera – he had surely been instructed to listen for new talent.

The gloomy portal opened, the usher was bringing back the pupil who was before her. He looked at his bit of paper and said, looking around: "Fräulein Schumann," and beckoned.

Now was the moment to go before all those faces, with that terrible beating in her breast . . . the curve of the grand piano was at her elbow . . . it seemed as if her voice came from far, far away. Then something curious happened: no sooner had she uttered the first three words than Elisabeth felt that she was on a completely solid base: the music, the aria. Despite those terrible nerves, the music had become a firm path along which she now surely and happily strode.

The applause was enthusiastic and there were cries of "bravo!" Later the correspondent of the American paper wrote:

> The very first among Dresden's vocal teachers presently is no doubt Natalie Haenisch whose pupils on February 17th came off with flying colours. Madame Haenisch has many good voices to train, scarcely any, however, of such great promise in future as that of little Else [the name Natalie Haenisch had suggested instead of Elisabeth] Schumann, a young girl yet in her teens, but a future Sembrich,[*] the owner of a deliciously warbling soprano voice of the true coloratura singer, who gave the Zerlina aria to the perfect delight of the hearers.

But a few days later this all seemed unimportant, for the result of the doctor's examination of Elisabeth was a diagnosis of appendicitis. The surgeon who was called advised an operation as soon as possible. Parental consent had to be obtained and in the meantime the patient should keep to her bed, have ice-bags on her abdomen and eat only a light diet.

To Elisabeth the carving up of her stomach seemed a disaster. How might it affect her strenuous breathing exercises which were supported by those stomach muscles? And the cost – would her father's sickness insurance cover everything? But worst of all: possibly to have to stop singing for several months.

In response to a telegram to her father, her mother appeared late in the evening, ready to see to everything in her calm, circumspect and indefatigable way: the deliveries of ice, the diet and the arrangement of hospital fees and accommodation: a room with two beds, second class. As a singer herself her chief concern was about any lasting effect the scars might have, and she would give her consent to the operation only when she had been convinced that

[*]Marcella Sembrich, 1858–1935, renowned Polish coloratura soprano.

this was the only way to insure against the possibly dangerous consequences of the inflammation, and that the scars would in no way hinder the singing career, provided the patient took it easy immediately after the operation.

Waking up from the operation was ghastly – not only the nausea, but – much worse – the dreadful burning sensation in the throat caused by the chloroform; it seemed at first as if the throat would be no good for anything any more. Elisabeth might have become very apprehensive had not the rather attractive young house doctor come and banished her worries with a few soothing words; the burning got better like magic. Her tender stomach made it necessary to avoid laughing which was quite a problem.

And soon the burning throat and laughing pains were all a thing of the past, and Elisabeth's kind grandfather could breathe easily again – for he had written to her parents:

> You must be thinking I'm no longer alive. I wasn't able to write for grief. But now, how is Lieschen? Will she soon be better? It was a terrible blow for me, but God willing, He will go on helping. . . .

Soon one could hear Fräulein Schumann's guitar around the wards. At first only reticent plucking could be heard coming from the corner of a corridor; inexplicably the trill of a canary could also be heard from that quarter. To Elisabeth's surprise the matron encouraged her to carry on cheering up the patients – it made a change from the usual mouth organ, she said.

As all had gone well since the operation, permission to start singing was obtained. But she was only allowed to sing carefully, and her stomach muscles felt like jelly.

It was a great relief to be free of her appendix. She was aware of this all the more when she was back in Merseburg. It was wonderful to be able to move freely, spring down the stairs, without feeling as if she had a weight in her belly. Life would be a joy if it were not for the interruption to her studies.

The Geutebrücks wrote: there was to be a huge student festival in Gotha at Whitsun. Would not one of the girls like to come? Unfortunately they did not have room for both as they were putting up a student.

Friedchen was to have gone, but on the Saturday morning she had such a bad migraine that she could only groan: "You go, Lies, you go."

The venerable town of Gotha seemed rejuvenated, almost unrecognizable. The railway station and its square were covered with flags in black, white and red. Every train brought hordes of young men, and older ones too, all wearing small, colourful peaked caps on their heads, and the coloured ribands of the fraternities across their chests. It seemed that the festival was to be a big occasion. Flags hung out of windows too, and high over the streets fluttered the ribbons and pennants of the student fraternities. Even the Geutebrücks had hung out flags and decorated the house with flowers. There was no sign of their other guest.

Early on Whitsunday morning the weather was as if ordained by the Kaiser: bright sunshine and little puffs of cloud. Down the stairs danced Elisabeth, trilling a little song as she went.

There was already someone in the dining room. It was a student, who stood up immediately, gave a quick bow and introduced himself. There was a fresh scar across his cheek and nose – he had been duelling! He had blue eyes, a narrow face with a strong, well-shaped and straight nose, beneath it lips which were markedly curved, in fact he was a good-looking chap. He gave his name, Walther Puritz – a strange-sounding surname – and she also heard him say that he was studying architecture.

The young student had immediately been struck by Elisabeth's appearance and personality. How prettily she had come into the room! And that lovely voice too! He had never met a girl quite like her before.

During the whole festival he hardly strayed from her side. Often in the company of the Geutebrück girls he escorted her to coffee afternoons and other formal gatherings, and sometimes they simply walked round the town, stopping occasionally so that he could make sketches of buildings which interested him. Every now and then he would slip in a cheeky drawing of one of the girls and make them laugh. When she felt she knew him well enough, Elisabeth asked Walther about the scar on his face. Had it hurt a lot? Was it not frightening? Why not wear a mask – was getting injured supposed to be the passing of a test?

The pain was just a smarting for a couple of days or so. The fear consisted of butterflies before the duel, but during it you had to concentrate too much to be afraid. Walther admitted he got satisfaction out of proving his courage; besides, it was honourable to fight for one's fraternity. Only sometimes did someone get a more serious injury; but then the doctor stopped the fight immediately. His own wound was not deep, soon it would hardly be visible. Some fellows put salt in their wounds so that later they could impress people with their wide scars. But for him that was not the point of a duel.

Elisabeth felt sure that it was not. And the fact that he admitted a certain amount of fear impressed her. He was turning out to be a friendly mentor, and actually it was rather flattering that he was paying her so much attention.

The climax of the stay was the big final ball. Elisabeth went, of course, as Walther's partner, after he had reassured her that her lack of dancing experience would be no impediment. No doubt her feet would prove as musical as other parts of her had done!

After a few tentative steps it seemed as if they had always danced together. All too soon it became light outside, and the band played the last number. At least there was the compensation of a hearty breakfast of clear chicken soup, rye bread and smoked ham at the Geutebrücks.

The ball had been the most wonderful part of the visit to Gotha. In the train back to Merseburg Elisabeth wondered whether she would ever see the architect student again. To judge by the eager assurances when they exchanged addresses, yes. Walther's parting words before dashing from the breakfast table to catch his train were: "I'll build you an opera house! I'll design one and you can be my expert adviser!" He seemed rather a crazy young man. But a nice one.

In Merseburg there was fun to be had too, especially at the concert which the Schumanns gave in a local village. A pastor, who was a friend of Alfred Schumann, had asked him if he would make music with his wife and daughters on a Sunday afternoon for the local church social club. Before the event the pastor announced from the pulpit that "artists" were coming from Merseburg to brighten up their afternoon.

When Elisabeth, with her parents and Friedchen, entered the dance room of the village inn, she was amazed at the large number of people in the audience.

Alfred and Frieda were on top form at the piano, and Emma and Elisabeth were in good voice too. The walls shook with the enthusiastic applause of the friendly country folk. Afterwards there was coffee and cake in the garden; then Alfred Schumann said to a couple of farmers that there seemed to be a lot of musical people around there – coming in droves to their concert! Whereupon out of the honest mouth of one of the farmers came the innocent words: "Well y'see, we thought we were gettin' tightrope walkers."

After summer holidays in Orlishausen, in September 1905, it was time to return to Dresden.

It was lovely to see her friends and fellow students again, and despite some misgivings about her studies Elisabeth threw herself into them enthusiastically. But nothing changed. As always it was a case of just singing arias and lieder; there were hardly any exercises, and if there were any, they were for the top of the voice. The way she was singing now was the way she had always been able to sing, except that before it had been easier; now singing was always such an effort. This seemed like a waste of time and of Grandfather's money. But where was the right teacher? It would not be that easy to change teachers, especially as Felix Draeseke had got her together with Fräulein Hänisch, and Elisabeth did not want to hurt the old man's feelings.

Another thing happened around this time which did not make life in Dresden any easier. In 1905 the rehearsals for *Salome*, the new opera by Richard Strauss, were in full swing at the Court Opera. At the time Richard Strauss was very controversial as an opera composer, and Ernst von Schuch, who was coaching the new work, had to cope with quite a lot of overt and covert opposition among his team. At the first sing-through all the singers except Burrian wanted to give up.

Elisabeth, who had learnt several lieder by Richard Strauss, was particularly interested in the *Salome* rehearsals. She came out of the first orchestral one quite inspired, and enthused about the music – "These colours, this transparency! Heavenly!" Even at the Draesekes she spoke of how impressed she was, although she had heard that Professor Draeseke did not like Strauss's music; but she just could not help herself, her heart was too full.

When he heard Elisabeth speaking of it, the Professor, with his usual charming smile, came up to her and the group of people she was with, only to condemn Strauss sharply: his music was unbridled, extreme, he was the one most responsible for the heresy of programme music.

But Elisabeth still went to the *Salome* rehearsals. She was convinced that it was wonderful music. Later she often said that

Richard Strauss had determined the way her life went once she had got to know him. But already in 1905 he was influencing her life indirectly, twelve years before they were to meet. As she experienced his opera music it became clear to her that, quite apart from her teacher, her circle of acquaintance in Dresden was not the kind she really needed; she suddenly recognized that the musical spirit of the Draeseke circle did not correspond with her artistic instinct. She began secretly to learn more Strauss songs.

So Dresden was now a closed chapter, as far as Elisabeth was concerned; but there was as yet no catalyst to induce her to make the break, and things went on much as before. She was by no means constantly depressed; mostly she remained her cheerful, fun-loving self. Her attitude was: "Somehow everything will sort itself out and I will achieve my aim."

Only for short periods did she ever experience feelings of despair and discouragement, as one afternoon in December when she was standing at her window looking down at the gloomy, twilit street. The lamplighter was already going from one streetlight to the next, conjuring up the greenish-white flames with his long pole. . . . A young gentleman came walking along, stood before the house as if searching for something and looked up to the windows. It was Walther, the student in Gotha!

A few minutes later they were sitting opposite each other in the lounge of the boarding house. Walther apparently had a few free days and wanted to make some architectural observations in the town. (Of course he had an additional reason for choosing Dresden.) Elisabeth was delighted: here was someone who was quite separate from her normal milieux; as she explained, he was neither from here nor Merseburg. She felt encouraged to pour out her problems to him.

When she had finished Walther concluded briskly that it was quite obvious that she should come to Berlin, not only for his sake! Berlin after all was the imperial city, centre of the German Reich. She could tell her teacher that she had been ill over the Christmas holidays and needed the good, dry air Berlin had to offer.

When Walther returned to his studies in Berlin after a few days Elisabeth felt quite abandoned, but was soon distracted by the première of *Salome* on December 9 1905. On this day she witnessed the most sensational operatic success at the Dresden Court Opera since Wagner. At the end of the performance the audience remained in place for ages calling back the soloists, the conductor Ernst von

Schuch and, above all, Richard Strauss. Elisabeth strained to get a glimpse of the great man: she had an impression of his being tall, rather lanky and with a high forehead.

Elisabeth's problem was not solved in the holidays. Her parents disagreed and thought she should persevere in Dresden and things would sort themselves out. But Elisabeth, with her unfailing instinct about singing, was convinced that Natalie Hänisch was no longer what she needed. She felt that there was a lot that she could do to improve her breathing, and that her voice was too small. But for the time being she had no choice other than to return to Dresden.

There she took courage into both hands and wrote a long letter to Pia von Sicherer, explaining all her worries and asking her advice.

As a result of this Elisabeth sang to her again at Easter, and Frau von Sicherer could hear at once that Elisabeth had got "stuck" in her technique, that her top notes and in fact her singing in general was less easy. She recommended a friend of hers as a teacher, a contralto in Berlin called Valerie Zitelmann, who had already agreed to take on Elisabeth if she would like to go.

Now there was the problem of overcoming the obduracy of her parents. The best thing would be if they thought the die had already been cast in Gotha. So she telegraphed to Merseburg: "Am going to Berlin."

This indeed had the desired effect. When she got home her parents' only worry was about the things that could happen to their daughter when she was all alone in Berlin – that Tower of Babel on the River Spree. One comforting thought was that Emma Schumann's old friend, Elisabeth Wintzer lived there, the friend who had noticed Elisabeth's musical ear as a tiny baby. Perhaps she could keep an eye on her. Emma had not seen her friend for many years, but as they had been brought up together, Emma having been orphaned, there was still a strong link.

By return of post there came a reply from Berlin: the young singer would be well looked after, and for the time being she was welcome to stay with the Wintzers.

Now the road to Berlin was clear.

CHAPTER 4

Berlin

T HE ELISABETH WHO NOW ARRIVED in Berlin was quite different from the schoolgirl who had jogged in a carriage through the streets of Dresden one and a half years earlier. At the Anhalter Bahnhof Walther met this young lady of almost eighteen years and escorted her to the landau which he had hired for this momentous occasion.

Elisabeth Wintzer saw the carriage roll up and greeted the pair informally in the entrance hall. She was an attractive woman in her forties with heavy blonde hair. There was something expansive in her gestures and in her whole manner, something free, unrestrained. As the three of them went upstairs Frau Wintzer called up: "Manfred, Manfred! Meet our new lodger!" Upstairs a door opened and a tenor voice called, almost singing: "I'm coming", and a moment later a small, agile man flew down the stairs towards them. He was wearing a cape which blew out as he ran, making him look bird-like. Having scrutinized Elisabeth he declared that her appearance inspired him to write a story about a gazelle. Frau Wintzer then explained that this was Manfred Kyber, writer of novels and stories about animals.

This was a liberal, free-thinking household which bore the stamp of Frau Wintzer's personality. She invited eminent people to the house, and lived in an atmosphere of art and intellectuality. She had written an excellent biography of Prince Louis Ferdinand of Prussia. She also composed with much skill. She lived a life which might be considered foot-loose and fancy-free; it was certainly not bourgeois. Yet she was the daughter of a clergyman. She had married an artist, the painter Gerlach, but this marriage had failed. Now she was living with Kyber, whom everyone called "Schwälbchen" ("little swallow") because of his flapping cape. Elisabeth's parents knew nothing about this, otherwise they would hardly have sent their daughter to Frau

Wintzer. For Alfred and Emma Schumann marriage was sacred and absolutely indissoluble.

The atmosphere was quite different from that in Dresden. Visitors to the Draeseke household were successful artists, often also received at Court and who lived in the upper-class or aristocratic style. Chez Frau Wintzer in Berlin there was a good smack of Bohemia. Even young artists who, like Elisabeth herself, were still struggling for recognition, visited here. Thus a stimulating and free and easy atmosphere was engendered, which suited Elisabeth's personality very well. Without mincing words they discussed performances, concerts, poems and paintings, sometimes with biting and witty criticism, sometimes with enthusiastic praise. She found some of the discussions too intellectual and dreary. "Clever" art was never to be her cup of tea. All her art and interpretation was concerned with communication of what she felt and what she saw depicted in music and text.

Elisabeth enjoyed her new life thoroughly, especially as her lessons with Fräulein Zitelmann seemed to be going well. She also saw a lot of Walther, and one day he declared that it was high time he introduced her to his old parents. She was invited to lunch.

These "old" parents were only a few years older than her own, in their fifties in fact. Hermann Puritz was a worthy actuary in the Royal Prussian Government. He, his wife Marie and Walther's two brothers and two sisters welcomed Elisabeth warmly and she at once felt at home.

This conventional household did not lack an artistic element – Walther's younger brother wanted to become an actor and Walther himself was, after all, studying architecture; but there was nothing Bohemian about it. Walther's older brother was an engineer; Lotte, the elder of the two sisters, was due to be married soon; Käthe was training to be a nurse. So it was a very middle-class household, the kind to which Elisabeth was accustomed.

Walther showed Elisabeth round his home town and took her to the picture galleries. In fact he introduced her to art; she had never before taken any great interest in it, but now she suddenly became so fascinated that she wanted to learn to draw. Walther started her off. Her favourite subjects tended to be old, historic buildings.

These new activities awakened in Elisabeth an interest in old things. In later years she was never able to pass an antiques shop – she had to stop and look at the treasures, and often she could not resist buying a silver teapot or a writing set or a small table, or maybe only a little old purse.

Elisabeth became more and more attracted to this budding architect, who was initiating her into the splendours of art. She had never had such deep conversations with a young man before. Walther seemed to be on a higher plane altogether, and this was something which Elisabeth always found very appealing in men. Refinement and a superior sensitivity – these were what she looked for in them all her life. If she felt that a man had a lot of soul she could fall deeply in love with him.

One evening in June, when Elisabeth had had a meal out with the Puritz family, Walther escorted her home. Frau Wintzer's house was in the Kleiststrasse. The two of them took the tram to the Nollendorfplatz. Then they walked very slowly along the Tauentzienstrasse towards the Kleiststrasse. However they did not turn into it, but walked straight on, and after a while they turned round and went back again, again passing the end of the the Kleiststrasse. On and on they went, walking backwards and forwards, not wanting the evening to end. They talked about all sorts of things, yet they were still addressing each other formally with "sie" and "Herr Puritz" and "Fräulein Schumann".

Finally, at three in the morning, they slowly approached Elisabeth's lodgings. Now the conversation became halting, and in the entrance to the house they stood silently before each for quite a while. At last Walther summoned up enough courage to say how nice it would be if they could remain together – for always. Elisabeth nodded slightly and suddenly flung her arms around his neck. They kissed each other for the first time.

From then on Elisabeth and Walther said "du" to each other and considered the little scene played out in the doorway as their secret engagement. In front of Walther's family they still called each other the formal "sie". But, as with any young couple in love, their hearts spoke through their eyes, and soon they had let out their secret; whereupon Walther's spry little mother said: "But I have known for a long time, my children!"

In next to no time the holidays had arrived again and Elisabeth went to her parents in Merseburg and shortly after that to Orlishausen. From there it was no distance to Pia von Sicherer in Gotha, and naturally Elisabeth visited her benefactress again. This time she was particularly lucky because it so happened that Fräulein

Zitelmann was staying with Pia for a few weeks, so Elisabeth was able to arrange a number of lessons with her. Sometimes the three of them made music together.

It was while they were doing this one day that something happened which Elisabeth found oddly reassuring. Frau von Sicherer suddenly said to her guest that she found her pupil's singing a little too dark. These were frank words from one friend to another. Valerie Zitelmann was not offended and the two of them discussed it for a while. When Frau von Sicherer then asked Elisabeth to colour the tone of the next song more lightly, she did so, and she had the marvellous feeling that she had made progress.

They were wonderful holidays. Walther managed to come to Orlishausen for a few days, and there was the Wagner festival at Bayreuth, about which Elisabeth read everything she could. How much, how very much she would have liked to have been there – just as a member of the audience, just to be able to sit in the famous Festspielhaus and to experience it all, in that place which was almost holy. She spoke to her father about it, but he shook his head and said: "Lies, it's not possible, it costs far too much money." But then he took her up to the attic room where the old piano of his student days still stood, and played to her excerpts from *Parsifal* (which at that time was still only allowed to be performed at Bayreuth) so that by the time she returned to Berlin in September she knew *Parsifal* almost by heart.

Although the holidays had been lovely she was looking forward to working again and having Walther near her. But the singing was not going as well as it should have been. It suddenly seemed to Elisabeth that she had gone back a step, that she could not recapture the brightness which she had put into her voice in Gotha. So again there were anxious hours, sometimes whole days. Walther tried to encourage her, but how could a person who did not sing himself understand the worries of a singer? Anyway Walther had just started his final year and was having to work hard for his diploma. It was a good thing that Elisabeth was such an optimist. Thinking about Bayreuth also distracted her, for she had heard that there were scholarships for talented music students to go and stay in Bayreuth during the festival. In some cases it was enough to submit a letter of recommendation from a well-known musician. Felix Draeseke kindly provided this for Elisabeth; he wrote of her "quite unusual talent" and that "if her health grows stronger with age one can expect exceptional achievements".

It seems strange that in letters of that time, when Elisabeth was eighteen, her health was often mentioned, for later she proved to be such a fit and vital person. But as a girl she was susceptible to infection. Now and then she had tonsillitis with a high temperature, and it also seemed then that she had inherited her father's asthma to some extent, for if there was a change in the weather, or if she had been running, she would occasionally suffer from breathlessness. This asthma remained a slight worry for the rest of her life. Often before a concert she had to take medicine so that she would have enough breath to sing.

But Elisabeth was not worrying about her health at the moment; she was concentrating on eliminating the darkness in her voice.

There was to be an All Souls' concert in the cathedral at Merseburg to which Elisabeth was looking forward with much excitement. She went home for rehearsals, making an effort to sing brightly and to concentrate on the soprano quality of her voice. Her father was well satisfied. And on the night she suddenly trusted her voice completely and was able to let the notes soar effortlessly upwards. On November 2 1906 there was written in the *Merseburger Lokalblatt*: "The soprano Fräulein Schumann has an exquisite voice. The sparkling notes pour from her lips in a delicious stream. Her singing is of a fresh and melting sweetness which is absolutely enchanting."

In the spring of 1907 Frau Wintzer had to give up her house, and Elisabeth and Manfred Kyber were forced to find other lodgings. Manfred Kyber, who was from the Baltic, found a room in the house of an aristocratic Baltic lady, Frau von Boltho; and it turned out that Elisabeth was also able to move into a room in her large house.

In later years Elisabeth often laughed about that move. The son of the famour sculptor Reinhold Begas was with them. He had arranged things with the removal men for Kyber, who hated moving and had gone away for a while; he helped with the packing and carried Elisabeth's suitcase down to the removal wagon for her. Then he suggested that they should ride on the wagon with their luggage.

Elisabeth thought this was a marvellous idea. So they sat in the back on a couple of cushions, one of the two doors was left open so that the passengers had some light, and off they went through Berlin. Of course there had to be some music. Elisabeth had brought her guitar with her and began to sing. People in the street turned and stared after the musical removal wagon. Begas joined in and even the men sitting on the box hummed along. Suddenly there was a loud bang, and Elisabeth stopped in fright: but Begas had only opened a bottle of champagne behind her back. That was the signal for one of Elisabeth's laughing fits. She laughed until tears poured down her cheeks. Between the spasms of mirth she took the odd swig, and the removal men, too, had their share passed through the hatch by Begas. They arrived at Frau von Boltho's house in the cheerfullest of moods.

In the Easter holidays Elisabeth travelled with Walther to her parents. The two of them were not able to hide their love for each other. One evening, when the women were washing up, Alfred said to Walther that he wanted to talk to him about a somewhat delicate matter. Walther knew at once what was meant, and with due formality he made it known that he would be happy to be able to call Elisabeth his wife.

Alfred had reservations about Elisabeth trying to combine her career with marriage. So much effort and money had been put into her training – would that all have been in vain? How could she be both a good wife and, that for which he had worked and lived, a great singer and an outstanding musician?

Walther was emphatic that he was absolutely determined to encourage Elisabeth's career. He himself was enough of an artist to appreciate her aims, and when they were married he would not be able, nor would he want, to put anything in her way.

When Alfred called for some wineglasses Elisabeth guessed what must have happened. Alfred did not say a word until the glasses had been filled, then he proposed a toast to the betrothed couple.

Elisabeth returned to Berlin with Walther in the highest of spirits. On Frau von Sicherer's advice she found an acting teacher and greatly enjoyed the lessons. By the end of May she had decided to leave her teacher and go to a singer at the Berlin Court Opera, Marie Dietrich. She parted from Fräulein Zitelmann on the best of terms; this good lady, who had after all developed Elisabeth's voice considerably, quite understood that her pupil now preferred to study operatic roles with someone at the opera. Frau von Sicherer gave her blessing too.

By the time the summer holidays found Elisabeth in Merseburg again she had already had some lessons with Marie Dietrich which had gone very well. She had also had a stroke of luck, for she had been given a scholarship to go to Bayreuth. Felix Draeseke had written to Cosima Wagner again, and now in August 1907 Elisabeth could go to the music festival.

It was a great experience for her. By now she had seen many first class performances in Dresden and Berlin, but Bayreuth had a very special magic. Wagner seemed so near. And the elegant audience had come from many countries for the sake of the music. Elisabeth could not help wondering whether such grand people might one day come so far to hear her. Why not? She was with the right teacher now, and had she not won the scholarship?

So, during her stay in Bayreuth, Elisabeth felt surer than ever of her future. She enjoyed *Parsifal* best of all, knowing it so well, and now hearing it in all its fullness. Edyth Walker, from Hamburg, sang Kundry wonderfully well. The young scholarship students were invited to the receptions at the Wagners' house, Wahnfried. There Elisabeth was able to meet, if only fleetingly, the Wagner family and the artists.

When Elisabeth returned to Berlin in the autumn of 1907 and resumed her studies with Fräulein Dietrich everything seemed to go well. She felt she was near her goal, and expressed her hopes to Felix Draeseke in a birthday letter. In his reply he wrote:

> It is so kind that you, who are not only so near to your artistic goal but also engaged, should still think of me . . . I am delighted that you will possess in your fiancé a masterful defender when you go on stage, which is a very dangerous place for a young lady . . . [little did Elisabeth know how masterful Walther would one day be when she least wanted it!] . . . But I hope that you will arrive there as an artist already so accomplished that due respect will automatically be yours, making all dangers flee before it. . . .

But what theatre was interested in engaging an absolute beginner? Surely only insignificant ones far from the centre of things and perhaps with low artistic standards. There one could stagnate, heard by no one of importance. Elisabeth thought she should perhaps give one or two concerts.

As usual she first consulted Frau von Sicherer, asking her in a letter whether she might not this winter be able to give a recital in Gotha. The reply was not encouraging: there was so much already on in Gotha and not enough money either; it would be better if she offered herself to music societies for which she would, of course, have to audition.

However, Elisabeth was to be distracted from her worries by

another development. At this time Walther was working as assistant to the famous architect Emil Schaudt. One evening when Elisabeth went to meet him after work, he told her excitedly that he was to go to Hamburg for Schaudt, to design and supervise the construction of the overhead municipal railway (the *Hochbahn*), first of all on probation for two months, then permanently.

In his joy at the thought of working independently for the first time he did not seem to have considered how significant this new step would be for Elisabeth. At first she was somewhat downcast, but soon she thought it would not be so bad, for if Walther went to Hamburg, then so would she!

With that decision Elisabeth Schumann herself destined that her career would begin in Hamburg.

Shortly before Walther had to leave, the news that he had passed his diploma arrived and there were great celebrations. Then, only a short time after he had left, sad news came: Elisabeth's grandparents in Orlishausen were very ill. Elisabeth's mother and sister Frieda went there to look after the two old people, but after a few days her grandfather died, and a few weeks after that her grandmother. Elisabeth was deeply affected by it. She had been their favourite, especially her musical grandmother's, and they had enjoyed a very warm relationship.

It was a subdued Christmas in Merseburg that winter. But a few days later Elisabeth's father showed her a letter, which he had just received from a colleague in the town of Dedeleben, and asked her whether she would like to sing a few songs there. They suddenly needed someone for their society's concert. It would take her mind off things.

There was no fee, but it was a good opportunity to get experience in front of an audience. And so, two weeks later, Elisabeth made the short journey to the little town of Dedeleben, where she shared the concert with a trio and got a write-up in the local paper:

> Sweetly and exquisitely, intimately and judiciously, with a voice wholly charming, Fräulein Schumann from Merseburg sang two soprano songs, "The First Violet" by Mendelssohn, and "The Siskin" by Wittich. It was a pleasure to listen to her. Let us hope that this is not the last time that this singer, so young and yet so excellently trained, so clearly destined for a great future, will rejoice us with her divine talent.

She returned to Berlin and continued her studies with Fräulein Dietrich. A few weeks later Walther moved permanently to

Hamburg, and the fact that she was now in a way on her own again made her throw herself into her work with renewed vigour and above all a determination to make a start at last.

A chance to do so seemed to come one day in that summer of 1908 when the famous Ibsen actor Emanuel Reicher heard Elisabeth singing informally at a party at the Klingenbergs in Grünau, where she was often invited to make music.* He was immediately enchanted and asked her afterwards whether she sang professionally.

He was incredulous when she replied in the negative. She asked whether he could give her a hint as to how she could make a start.

When she told him that she had already studied some roles he told her about the Lortzing Summer Opera: it was a fairly modest affair which put on operas in the summer months; he knew the director and would have a word with him.

Reicher kept his word, and what looked like the beginning of a career seemed to be happening. Elisabeth was summoned to the director of the Berlin Lortzing Opera and had to audition. One of the arias she sang was from the role of Aennchen in *Der Freischütz* which she had just learnt, so the director said that she could sing that role in the few performances of *Der Freischütz* which they were putting on.

It was just as well that her parents could not make it to the first performance because something quite unexpected happened. Elisabeth had only had two very brief rehearsals, and on the day of the performance she arrived at the theatre feeling very nervous. Almost creeping along the sides of the corridors, she went to her dressing room. On opening the door she saw a woman sitting at the make-up table who swung round and stared at her suspiciously saying: "Can't you knock? What do you want?"

Elisabeth, completely taken aback, stammered: "This room . . . but this is my dressing room. I'm singing Aennchen."

The woman snapped back: "*You*! You are very much mistaken! The person who is singing Aennchen is *me*! Now get out, if you please!"

How Elisabeth got home that evening she could never remember. She was filled with shame, disappointment and anger, and she wondered if life in the theatre would always be full of bitter rivalries.

---

*Alfred Klingenberg was an architect, married to the daughter of Reinhold Begas, the sculptor, whose son Elisabeth knew through Manfred Kyber.

But, as always, she soon got her courage back and was even able to laugh about the incident. After all, that was not a theatre with a great reputation. Now Elisabeth understood how things could be in the provinces.

In the end, though, Elisabeth did sing Aennchen at the Lortzing Summer Opera. The director wrote and apologized to her, saying it had all been a mistake, and he begged her to sing the last two performances of *Der Freischütz* after all. Elisabeth simply could not resist. So, in the summer of 1908, she appeared for the first time on stage. As with almost all her subsequent performances, her stage fright disappeared as she sang the first two bars: the music and the words afforded a firm path along which she could proceed. She proved herself to be an outstanding Aennchen. Everyone was enchanted, and her teacher Marie Dietrich praised her warmly.

Another person who deservedly shared her triumph was the *répétiteur* of the opera house in Berlin: Dr Walter Krone. With him Elisabeth was learning in all thirty-five roles. Marie Dietrich had introduced her to him. In fact Fräulein Dietrich was the teacher who had so far been of the most help to Elisabeth. It was only a pity that she lived so entirely in the world of opera and could not give Elisabeth any tuition in lieder singing. She admitted it freely herself and advised Elisabeth to go to the famous lieder singer Georg Vogel, which she did. She studied with him for three months, but without the least success. This fiasco strengthened her belief that a woman should not take singing lessons from a man. It seemed to her also that the ideal teacher was someone with the same voice type as her pupil.

On the whole Elisabeth considered her study with Fräulein Dietrich to be the end of her training. She was no longer looking for the right teacher but for a start to her career. But although her auditions were always successful and she was offered work wherever she sang, there seemed to be no real opening. Out of modesty she always auditioned in small towns where there was little financial stability in the theatre and where they could only offer small guest appearances.

With a little money which she had inherited from her grandfather, travelling to all these places was easier than it might have been, and sometimes she even visited Walther in Hamburg. She was enchanted by the beauty of the city and felt at home there immediately. She was also greatly impressed by the good productions at the Hamburg Opera. But it did not occur to her to try to audition there; and even if she had thought of it she would not have dared. She was far too awed by such an institution, which at that time enjoyed an excellent reputation in all Germany.

In the house where Elisabeth had met the actor Emanuel Reicher, at the Klingenbergs in Grünau, she met one of the most interesting people of that time: the famous surgeon Karl Ludwig Schleich, inventor of local anaesthetic and a brilliant doctor. He was also a widely educated man who had a feeling for poetry and loved art and philosophy. He loved music passionately (he even composed songs in his spare time), and when he heard of Elisabeth's talent he asked her when she would be singing again – he absolutely must come to hear her.

But when she went to sing at the Klingenbergs again he was nowhere to be seen. She sang more and more songs and arias, hoping that he might suddenly turn up. In the end she had to stop. Shortly afterwards the door opened and Professor Schleich entered the room. He apologized profusely – there had been an operation at the last minute – could Elisabeth not sing a little encore for him? But she said firmly that it was impossible, she had been singing for almost one and a half hours.

Schleich was not to be put off so easily. He took Elisabeth's hand and gazed at her with pleading eyes. Then suddenly he put on a very professional face and pointed at a mole on her arm warning her that it might lead to complications of a serious nature and should be removed as soon as possible. Elisabeth was rather alarmed, and, sure of his victory, Schleich suggested she come to him at the hospital the next morning and he would remove the mole, painlessly and gratis. For that he now begged one song of her. She agreed, but laughingly asked him to put it in writing.

Professor Schleich took a visiting card from the Klingenbergs and wrote on the back: "I herewith commit myself to operate on Fräulein E. Schumann gratis and painlessly. In case of breach of contract a penalty of 2000 marks. Service in return: singing lieder!" and signed it.

The operation was carried out as easily as promised, and while he performed it Professor Schleich could not stop talking about his patient's singing which had so delighted him.

The pressure of his work as a famous surgeon, which made huge demands on his time, prevented him from cultivating their friendship much more, but on the few occasions when he heard her sing at parties he became increasingly enchanted with her performing. It is very likely that he was inspired by her when he wrote in one of his "Aphorisms on music"[*]:

> Music has bestowed upon language a gleam of starlight and sunshine. Every singer has a feeling of spiritual exaltation. It is not the throat but the soul that sings.

By this time, the end of the year 1908, Elisabeth had, through Frau Wintzer, Manfred Kyber and the Klingenbergs, gained a large circle of friends. Should she not try to give a recital here in Berlin? She knew a pianist, Helene Praetorius, who also wanted to get launched. So they hired a medium-sized hall, had posters printed and advertised in the daily newspapers. Each invited all the friends they could think of, and, what was most important: through influential friends they succeeded in getting critics to come.

The great occasion took place in February 1909. Elisabeth's parents and a whole lot of relatives came from Merseburg. Even Walther's family were all there except for him; to Elisabeth's great disappointment he was prevented from coming by urgent work.

The recital was a success. Berlin critics tended to write very condescendingly about beginners' concerts, but the two who had been especially invited this time did no such thing. Erich Urban (the author of the polemical *Strauss contra Wagner*) wrote:

> Fräulein Schumann ... possesses a slender soprano voice and good technique. She has a charming personality and, what is more, sings with intelligence and temperament. She made a deep impression by her rendering of songs by Franz.

The other critic, Oskar Bie, was more analytical about Elisabeth's achievement:

> Her soprano voice is pleasant and well trained. The tone is very good in the upper and middle registers but dull in the lower. Her head-notes, although she exploits them too often, are successful. Her diction could sometimes be more distinct and her breathing is not faultless. Her interpretation was passionate and full of expression, which helped to hide her small weaknesses.

It was a joy to get such write-ups – because Elisabeth knew full well that she still had weaknesses she was in no way cast down when

---

[*]In *Die Weisheit der Freude*, Rowohlt Verlag, Berlin, 1921.

they were mentioned. The only disappointing thing was that nothing happened after the concert: no offer from an impresario!

Restlessness and ambition led to Elisabeth's being out of town more and more. She travelled around in the provinces doing auditions here, there and everywhere and was offered little oratorio engagements and even an engagement at the Stadttheater in Heidelberg. But in all modesty she could not bring herself to commit herself to a theatre where the standard did not satisfy her. Having experienced performances at Dresden, Berlin and Bayreuth her aims were high.

Now that Elisabeth only had lessons irregularly and was away from Berlin such a lot she moved in with Walther's parents.

In the spring of 1909 her career took a decisive turn. She travelled to Hamburg to visit Walther. Seeing him again, and the beautiful city on the River Elbe, put her into the jolliest of moods. She suddenly felt a tremendous urge to do something to prove herself. She found out which conductor put on the big oratorio concerts: it was Professor Julius Spengel, the director of the Cecilian Society.

Following more of a whim than any real purpose, she made her way to Professor Spengel's house and requested an audition. The professor heard her straight away.

She decided to sing "For love my Saviour now is dying". She felt so safe with this aria from the *Matthew Passion* that she was hardly nervous at all, and as she sang Professor Spengel often looked at her, nodding and smiling. At the end he asked her to sing soprano solo in a *Matthew Passion* he was giving in St Mary's Church, Lübeck in five weeks' time.

Elisabeth was overjoyed, but then admitted rather doubtfully that she had never sung with a big orchestra before. That made Professor Spengel laugh. He said she was far too musical for that to be a problem. (He was quite right: the concert turned out to be a great success, and Elisabeth had good notices.)

She was then asked to stay for coffee, and chatted with the professor and his wife for quite some time. This day was the start of a long friendship with the Spengels. The professor saw Elisabeth as his discovery and was proud of her, while she of course was grateful to him for giving her a start. Later, when she was already famous, she often sang in his concerts.

Elisabeth's success with Professor Spengel that afternoon gave her great impetus. She hurried back to Walther, related everything with great excitement and suddenly thought: why not try at the opera house? She was now in possession of a letter of introduction to the manager which the soprano Luise Reuss-Belce had written for her. Elisabeth had met her at one of the musical parties in Berlin, and Reuss-Belce had been very impressed by her singing. Elisabeth had brought the letter to Hamburg with her but had not really thought she would make use of it quite yet.

But the very next morning she entered the large building by the Dammtorwall to request an audition. All young beginners who wanted to be heard at the Hamburg Opera had at that time to sing first to the chorus master, Herr Harmans. If he thought the standard was good enough the singer was then heard by the theatre manager and the musical director.

So on that Sunday morning Elisabeth was first shown into Herr Harman's room. He was quite curt: "What do you want to sing?" was all he said by way of greeting. This time she chose an aria from Lortzing's *Undine*. She had barely sung half of it when Herr Harmans interrupted and rang for a theatre attendant. His mood had changed completely. He told the attendant to ask Herr Brecher, the musical director, to come to listen to an audition. Shortly after that the telephone rang. Elisabeth could not hear what was being said at the other end, but then Herr Harmans indicated that the director would be glad to hear her on stage.

Before she really knew what was happening she was standing on the poorly lit stage. The auditorium was so dark that she could hardly see who was sitting in the first rows.

Elisabeth began the aria from *Undine* again without feeling too nervous. After just a few bars she was interrupted by Brecher: "Thank you, that will be enough." Now he wanted to hear something which would show off the whole range of her voice, perhaps something from *Der Freischütz*? Then Elisabeth really was in her element. By now she was completely in control and concentrated on being expressive.

When she had finished no one clapped but a voice spoke out of the darkness: "Come into my office. I would like to engage you." It was the manager, Max Bachur. Elisabeth could hardly believe what she was hearing. This had only been a daring first attempt, made more out of curiosity than anything else; she had not seriously thought that she would be taken on straight away. And again, as when she was with Professor Spengel, she felt sudden dismay, and anxiously she cried: "But I have hardly any stage experience." A deep voice answered: "That doesn't matter, young lady, you'll learn that here with us." That was the producer, Siegfried Jelenko.

Filled with suppressed excitement, Elisabeth was shown to Bachur's office. The small, grey, bespectacled man read to her the draft of a contract which he always had ready, designed for people starting their first engagement. It was a three-year contract, and in the first year Elisabeth was to receive 150 marks per month, then 250 in the second and 400 in the third. She was thrilled when she heard these sums of money but felt she should show the contract to her parents before she signed.

Bachur was amused at this remark, since she was not yet of age and in any case would have to give the contract to her parents to sign.

A few minutes later Elisabeth was in the street. She ran to the nearest post office and telegraphed her parents: "Have been engaged. I tremble before the envy of the gods." Next she telephoned Walther, and that very evening they were celebrating the occasion in an oyster bar. The next day she travelled to Berlin to pack her things and go to Merseburg for a while, where she had so much to tell her proud parents and friends.*

But Elisabeth began to get cold feet. In that summer of 1909 she almost wished she was starting off in a smaller theatre. How would she cope next to all those divas of the Hamburg Opera, in-experienced as she was?

While she was in Merseburg she did as much performing as she could, at music clubs in surrounding towns, and in Merseburg itself under her father's direction.

She got quite a fright when a thick registered letter arrived from Hamburg. At first she thought it might be the cancellation of her contract. But as she tore it open the title *Tiefland* met her eyes. The theatre management had sent her her first role, that of Pepa in Eugen d'Albert's opera. In the accompanying letter she was kindly requested to learn the role thoroughly by the start of the season. That did not worry her in the least, she would race through it like the wind. But would her acting be up to scratch?

It was a good thing that despite everything the time passed quickly, and one day at the end of July, now of age, she travelled to Hamburg for the first rehearsals for the new season.

*Much of the detail about this audition comes from an unpublished biography of Elisabeth Schumann by Alfred Mathis.

CHAPTER 5

Hamburg, 1909–1913

HOW ELISABETH'S HEART was beating when she arrived at the theatre in Hamburg for her first rehearsals! But it was not only at this first visit that it beat fast. She later wrote in her biographical notes:

> When going to the theatre I always walked close to the wall. I felt terribly shy of prima donnas like Fleischer-Edel and Edyth Walker; they rehearsed in huge fashionable hats, although it was not allowed, and got such huge salaries.

Elisabeth experienced at once how unpredictable everything in theatre is: when she arrived she found out that *Tiefland* was not going to be put on for quite some time, and her role of Pepa would not be needed yet. Instead she was to learn two small roles: Shepherd Boy and First Page in *Tannhäuser*. Fourteen years before, when she had seen *Tannhäuser*, her first opera, she had not noticed the Shepherd Boy in her excitement, and now she was to begin her career by being a sensation in this role. Many people bought tickets for *Tannhäuser* solely in order to hear Fräulein Schumann sing the Shepherd Boy. Very rapidly she was given further roles, and not only small ones but ones such as Aennchen in *Der Freischütz* and Marie in Lortzing's *Zar und Zimmermann*.

On September 11 1909 Elisabeth wrote a long letter to her parents, the earliest letter written by her in existence:

> Many thanks for the parcel which has now arrived . . . The biscuits were delicious. And I have used the little corset a lot already. My second appearance as the shepherd went much better, and I was quite calm.
>
> My voice is creating quite a stir here. Just think – Thursday morning we had a rehearsal for *Zauberflöte*. After we had sung Frau Hindermann, the lead coloratura [Queen of the Night], and Fräulein

Alten [Papagena] came up to me to ask where I had studied etc., my voice sounded so enchanting. A short while later Jelenko comes and says: "Listen, have you studied Aennchen?" "Yes!" "So you would sing it?" "But of course!" "Well, fine, everyone is very pleased with you, keep it up." And off he went.

You can imagine how thrilled I was, for Aennchen is a first-class role – and if I progress this fast – that would be wonderful. I anyway have the feeling that I'm coming up in the world twice as fast here – there is no real soubrette here at all, and this is the voice type which I am adopting, since lively acting suits me better. Frau Strassmann-Witt, the lead actress at our theatre, watched one of the *Tiefland* rehearsals the other day, and because she particularly noticed me she asked about me, and she could not believe that I was on stage for only the fourth time. I hadn't thought I would get the hang of everything so quickly either, but I feel that I was made for the stage. One can see that talent always paves a way for itself.

Walther was enchanted by *Tiefland*, he said: "If only all our friends could see you." On Wednesday we're putting it on in Altona. I have also often heard people behind the scenes saying about me: "The little one is going to make it".

First Boy [Magic Flute] went well yesterday, but I have such a cold that I had to take aspirin beforehand and just now I had a rehearsal for *Rienzi*, but I was excused, as singing is impossible at the moment. I've got it right . . . on the chest, but the cough is still so hard, that's why it's so painful. I already had a poultice on in the night and today I've drunk hot milk and gluhwein, and I think that with this marvellous weather it will soon be better – and after all I haven't got to sing until Wednesday, because *Figaro* has been postponed, it should have been Tuesday.

So I wanted to ask you, dear Mother, to knit me a long shawl sometime which one can wrap round one's whole body, because it was on stage that I caught cold. The heating was on but there is such a frightful draught. I always have my jacket on, but then my legs are cold . . . .

Otherwise I feel very well – my body has got used to the work completely, at first I had backache from playing the piano so much. – Anyway we get 10 minute breaks in the rehearsals when we go and get some breakfast! That's always good fun, we usually go to the "Bräustübl" opposite where one can get a very cheap breakfast . . . .

Working with Brecher is really a joy, and what a nice person he is! He conducts wonderfully, you can read on his face every expression you are supposed to make, and at your cue you can read your words straight from his lips. And he is tremendously considerate. To the orchestra too. You never hear a loud word in a rehearsal – yet on Thursday he rehearsed from 9 o'clock till 3 – then from half past 4 till 7 and then at half past 7 he conducted Fidelio . . . But if you come to a Stransky rehearsal you can already hear the wild shouting out in the street. People are so different – but Brecher achieves decidedly more. But he [Stransky] doesn't just shout at beginners, but to people like Gura the other day, because she missed her entry. He screamed: "Are you mad – but you've sung it 1000 times." Whereupon she replied: "Herr Stransky, I know you lack restraint – but you have no right to shout at me like that, so I am leaving the rehearsal." Of course he quickly backed down and soon it was all right again. He's just so hot-headed.

Fräulein Metzger is tremendously kind; I am to visit her once work eases off a bit, everyone is so busy to start with. She possesses a motorcar, Edyth Walker and Brecher too [they were lovers], and then the Fleischer-Edel carriage with beautiful horses etc. After every rehearsal she is picked up – Fleischer her husband is at every rehearsal and performance . . . he is supposed to be very rich. In the spring she had a little boy; the second. She has been very friendly to me – otherwise people don't like her much, she gets away with too much, e.g. she hardly ever comes to a rehearsal.

Fräulein Alten has a maid who is always in the theatre in the evenings and takes her shawl off her on stage etc. That is always my dream, to have a maid.

. . . I haven't bought myself a wig yet – maybe I won't at all, for who knows how much longer I shall be singing pages – and then I may not need it any more. The costumes in the Magic Flute were marvellous again yesterday.

. . . Do come soon, for you must see me some time. I'll send the washing off on Monday, is that soon enough?

Write again soon, warm kisses from us both.
Your grateful Lies and Walther

Brecher had been a pupil of Mahler. He understood a great deal about singing. Everything he taught Elisabeth she positively soaked up. After a rehearsal with him her music would always be covered with marks. Sometimes these marks indicated an entirely novel way of phrasing something, or they changed the text, for Brecher tried to make translated libretti more singable.

In the year 1910 Lotte Lehmann was engaged by the Hamburg Stadttheater as an absolute beginner, and she and Elisabeth very soon became great friends. It was also in this year that Elisabeth met the man who was to have such a shattering effect on her life: Otto

Klemperer. He came to Hamburg in 1910 as a young conductor, at the same time as Lotte Lehmann. His parents were very musical and he had received, like Elisabeth, an all-round musical education. At the age of sixteen he began study at the Hoch-Konservatorium in Frankfurt am Main. Later he studied composition with Hans Pfitzner in Berlin. Gustav Mahler very soon recognized his outstanding talent and recommended the twenty-two-year-old to the Deutsches Landestheater in Prague. Mahler also recommended him to the Hamburg Stadttheater where he was appointed a junior conductor.

Already on the first day of his appointment his path crossed Elisabeth's. He was standing for a few minutes with the musical director, Brecher, and with Lotte Lehmann at the stage door. Elisabeth suddenly appeared at the door, quickly greeted Brecher – still a little shy – and went past into the street. Klemperer turned round after her and asked: "Who is that? Who is that? But she is charming!"

It is strange that these two people were so strongly attracted to one another, for they could not have been more different! Klemperer, tall, with jet-black hair, a penetrating, compelling look and angular, jerky body movements; Elisabeth small and gentle, with childlike charm. Klemperer was a loyal Mahler student, inspired by what had been achieved by Mahler, who had determined every – even the smallest – detail in the production of an opera in order to create the great whole: the fusion of drama and music. He followed Mahler's concept of the conductor-producer with an obstinacy bordering on fanaticism, encountering as a result much fierce resistance, so that only rarely could he realize his artistic ambitions. He also suffered from bouts of manic depression.

When they worked together Elisabeth was deeply impressed by his ideals and by his passion and determination. They grew personally closer. As it happened, it was under Klemperer's baton that Elisabeth made her first big mistake. It was the kind of blunder which for a moment puts the whole performance into confusion. By now she had participated successfully in five operas, in three of them she had even had quite large parts. Everything had always gone smoothly. In her fourth large role something happened which for several tormented hours Elisabeth thought must mean the end of her career. *Mignon* had been rehearsed with Elisabeth in the title role. As a child she had often sung the well-known aria "Do you know the land where the lemons blossom?", but singing only the main melody and leaving out the difficult middle section. This had become an ingrained habit. And now, in the excitement of her first performance as Mignon, she did the same thing and jumped straight to the words: "There, there I long to go with you, my love." Otto Klemperer was not in the least prepared for this. In seconds the orchestra and singer had come apart completely and there were terrible dissonances. Klemperer could do nothing except let things run their course. From the auditorium came giggling and excited whispering; then Elisabeth, at her wit's end, could only leave the stage. In the wings she burst into tears, and had the greatest difficulty in forcing herself to go on with the performance. She was convinced that she would be sacked immediately.

But at the end of the performance Klemperer did not say a word and Brecher was even comforting: to forget something occasionally – that was quite usual in the theatre . . . and no one was more surprised than Elisabeth when she was sent on as Mignon in the next performance. In all her worry she had not realized how much she had charmed the public and the critics, as the write-up of the theatre critic Ferdinand Pfohl of the *Hamburger Nachrichten* shows quite clearly:

> This time we had a more convincing Mignon, youthful, sweet and ardent; a figure of simplicity which had the charm of unspoilt naturalness still devoid of affectation. The young singer, who won our hearts with her delightful and convincing portrayal, was Elisabeth Schumann. The sweetness of her appearance matched the beauty of her musical interpretation. With her barely medium-sized, delightful voice, Fräulein Schumann enhanced the childlike quality, the charm of innocence, with which her Mignon was imbued. This fresh, melodious little voice would fit the role perfectly if Fräulein Schumann could concentrate more on her breathing technique and guard against certain doubtful and occasionally thin-sounding tones, which are caused by lack of breath . . . The blunder and terrible confusion which was caused by a memory lapse in the second verse of the song should not be dwelled upon excessively, painful though it was for the listener. Many a valiant man may have caught his breath when the good Mignon skipped the middle verses . . . when the orchestra produced a murky and indeterminate dissonance . . . and Kapellmeister Klemperer was, for perhaps a little longer than necessary, completely thrown by such an unexpected turn of events . . . [*]

So Elisabeth made up for her mistake, and to such an extent that *Mignon* became synonymous with "full house" in Hamburg. She had to sing the role almost too many times for her liking.

[*]Detail from Alfred Mathis's unpublished biography of Elisabeth Schumann.

What Pfohl said about a weakness in her breathing technique was justified. Elisabeth had always sensed this herself, but had not known what to do about it since none of her teachers had really been able to help in that field. Pfohl's words caused her some anguish. But in this very year, 1910, the solution to her problem turned up: Elisabeth found the greatest teacher of her life. Lotte Lehmnann was studying with a singing teacher in Hamburg and suggested that her friend should come along and listen one day. Here Elisabeth noticed that breathing was the first thing that was taught before any singing was begun. Instantly she recognized that this way of breathing, deep down in the abdomen and then supporting with the abdominal muscles was the right thing for her.

So Elisabeth began working intensively with Alma Schadow. And in later years, if ever she came for a guest appearance to Hamburg, she never missed the opportunity of having a few lessons to improve and consolidate her technique.

Alma Schadow's breathing technique was a revelation for Elisabeth. Her already beautiful high notes gained, through the depth of breath, that incomparable and unique floating quality. Her voice grew and really blossomed, so that she was given more and more roles and went from one success to the next.

Feeling well satisfied with her first season as an opera singer, Elisabeth travelled home to Merseburg for the summer holidays, where she was delighted to hear that her father had at last been appointed cathedral organist.

In August 1910 she went with Walther on a steamer trip round Denmark. As they were not married their parents made sure that everything was arranged as correctly as was possible.

Besides all that was new and exciting, Elisabeth made on this journey two important discoveries: that the food in Denmark was incomparably good, and that travelling and adapting to a foreign ambiance were things which she had no trouble with. Would she often have to travel abroad, often have to sing in foreign countries? Walther was in such high spirits that he promised always to come with her. He would simply abandon the drawing-board for as long as he had to. What was the point of having a freelance profession if one did not take advantage of it?

The two of them were very happy there in Denmark and they decided that they would at last get married the following summer, in June 1911.

1911 was altogether a very important year for Elisabeth. In it she was to achieve her first truly outstanding success. On the January 26 1911 the Dresden Court Opera gave the first performance of Richard Strauss's *Der Rosenkavalier*. Its success was great. In February the Hamburg Stadttheater was also to present the new opera. This naturally caused great excitement; for weeks almost nothing else was spoken of among the theatre company but who would sing what. The management had no problem casting the three main parts. Katharina Fleischer-Edel was to take on the Marschallin, Max Lohfing Ochs and Edyth Walker got the role of Octavian. Only about the casting of Sophie was there doubt for any length of time. The idiosyncracies of this character created difficulties. Hofmannsthal wrote to Strauss about Sophie on July 12 1910 that:

> within the framework of an intrinsically naïve personality and mode of expression [she is] constantly pouring out affectations, partly adopted from the convent, partly even from her father's jargon. She is a pretty, good, ordinary girl, like dozens of others, that is the joke: the real charm of expression, and also the greater charm of personality, is to be found in the Marschallin. It is just the fact that Quinquin [Octavian's nickname], in this tangled double adventure, falls for the *very first girl* to turn up, that is the joke, which makes the whole, which holds together both plots. Yet the Marschallin remains the dominating female figure, between Ochs and Quinquin – Sophie is always one step below these main characters.

The role therefore demanded a singer of convincing youthfulness, with girlish innocence. The Hamburg Stadttheater already had two possible ladies: Lotte Lehmann and Elisabeth. Lotte had just had a great success with the role of Anna in *The Merry Wives of Windsor*, and was virtually promised the role of Sophie by Gustav Brecher. So she began to learn the role. But the management also instructed Elisabeth to get to know the part; that way there would be an understudy in case of illness. As there was a shortage of music the two young ladies had to share one score. As the première drew nearer the management suddenly decided that Sophie should first be sung by Elisabeth. Lotte Lehmann was beside herself. In her autobiography[*] she wrote:

> I studied it [the role] with fanatical zeal, and it was a bitter disappointment to me when I didn't sing it on the first night. Elisabeth

[*] *Wings of Song*, Kegan Paul, Trench, Trubner, London, 1938.

Schumann, already one year in the theatre and a great favourite in Hamburg, with considerable and honourable successes to her credit, sang at the first performance by special request of Edyth Walker, the Octavian. Brecher, too, was speedily won over to Schumann, who, as well as singing enchantingly, was also a clever and graceful actress already, and didn't give Jelenko, the producer, as much trouble as I, suffering as I did from terrible inhibitions and being hopelessly self-conscious on stage. At the time, of course, I thought it an atrocious injustice that I hadn't been allowed to do the first performance. I regarded Elisabeth as the world's greatest intriguer – a role which, heaven knows, was quite foreign to her nature – and felt myself misunderstood and ousted from my rightful place . . . Elisabeth, always a good colleague, was well aware of my unjustified mistrust. She took great pains to be specially nice to me, but all the precepts of all my friends and relations that I had once laughed at and now mistakenly found true recurred to me: All colleagues are bad. They're all your enemies . . . .

The Hamburg première, on February 21 1911, was a sensation. The score had been studied particularly carefully. Gustav Brecher and Edyth Walker had even been to Dresden to see the world première and to discover from discussions what the writer and composer wanted done in their work. In Hamburg they then went through the opera bit by bit with the whole ensemble.

Elisabeth took the public by storm. With her Sophie she simply portrayed herself: a young, innocent girl; musically and vocally it was as if the part had been written for her. So it was, that during the presentation of the rose in Act 2 she evoked an almost celestial atmosphere. The phrase "wie himmlische, nicht irdische, wie Rosen aus dem hochheiligen Paradies" ("like heavenly, not earthly roses from the most holy paradise") seemed to come from other spheres.

Shortly after the performance a critic actually wrote to her personally:

Hamburg, Tesdorpfstrasse 6, 21.2.11

Dear Fräulein Schumann,

Certain things in life are surrounded by an everlasting light. Only everlasting, however, in the sphere of personal feeling.

You will I'm sure take it kindly if I – still quite spellbound by the performance – impulsively express my personal feeling.

. . . I congratulate you . . . on your achievement in *Der Rosenkavalier*. Among all the great achievements [of the artists] yours stood out like a flower among all kinds of rare plants. Not as strongly, not as self-assuredly as these, but in a light of indescribable loveliness, and shining more brightly! Everything, your acting, your appearance, your voice seemed enveloped in a fragrance, a wonderfully tender, girlishly chaste fragrance. Thus you seemed to be the symbol of the motif of the silver rose, which reflects so much the deep sweetnesses of life.

If one imagines the performance without you the silver light disappears from the stage. Your achievement was therefore a great and sincere joy for me – and for many with whom I have spoken. Bravo!

. . . Again many congratulations. May destiny always give you silver roses.

Edgar von Schmidt-Pauli jr.

The Hamburg production showed what a "silvery light" Sophie could impart to the opera. The librettist himself, Hugo von Hofmannsthal, when he one day heard Elisabeth as Sophie, declared afterwards: "I thought I had created a minor role in Sophie, but she dominates the whole of the second act!"

There was another aspect to this her first really outstanding success: Elisabeth's love and understanding of the music of Richard Strauss. With Sophie, Elisabeth for the first time entered actively into the realm of Strauss; and she took on this role as if it were her great task in life; and indeed it became her greatest role: to many music-lovers the names Elisabeth Schumann and Sophie became one and the same.

Richard Strauss had not been able to attend in Hamburg, but he received a rapturous report about Elisabeth from a friend of his. It was to be another six years before Strauss saw Elisabeth and heard her sing, but he was already influencing her life. Through him she received an offer from Berlin. Nothing came of it because, although she was obviously delighted, she did not want to leave Hamburg. Firstly Hamburg was so lovely. Secondly it would mean separation from Walther again; and lastly she was still studying: she could not leave Frau Schadow now, when she still had so much she could learn from her.

At last it was time for the wedding. So often she had said to Lotte how she could not wait to be married. It was such a relief that this everlasting state of being engaged would be over. Yet sometimes she had feelings of doubt. Did Walther really suit her? They had totally different tasks in life, and neither could follow the other's task undividedly. She could not discuss with him any of the finer points of music, in which she had a burning interest. This she had to do with her colleagues – with Lotte or Edyth Walker, with Brecher or Klemperer.

When one day she very gently hinted at her feelings, she recognized that he had never had such doubts and would never be able to understand hers. He claimed that they would always be happy because they both served art – he always shared in her singing, her music!

Yes – he often whistled when she was singing.

On June 2 1911, Walther and Elisabeth were married in the cathedral in Merseburg. The reception was held in the Schlossgartensalon, where Elisabeth had "performed" for the first time at the age of four. That same evening they set off on their honeymoon to the Thuringian Forest, which Elisabeth so loved.

The young couple also visited Gotha, and Elisabeth took the opportunity to look up her old benefactress Frau von Sicherer again and to introduce Walther to her. On July 29 she wrote to Elisabeth: ". . . I was very glad to meet your dear husband . . . I wish you great joy together in your beautiful home and I hope that no shadow from your theatrical career is cast on your marital happiness, that everything will happen as you could wish it . . . ."

Elisabeth and Walther certainly had need of such good wishes for soon they were facing problems. Elisabeth was not very well. The doctor detected an inflammation of the kidney, or at least an irritation, and urgently advised rest; and on no account was she to have a baby while in this state. That was a terrible blow, for she loved children and had quite decided to have them, despite her profession.

Also in her relationship with Walther things were not quite as they should have been. What she had feared was, indeed, happening: soon both of them were living their professional lives quite separately. As Walther advanced in his career his dedication to architecture became increasingly intense and all-absorbing. He was particularly interested in urban development, so he travelled once or twice a week to Berlin to hear lectures on it. Often he stayed there overnight or returned home very late in the evening. So Elisabeth was alone a lot of the time in her big new flat in the Curiohaus (named after the educationalist Carl Daniel Curio). It was lovely and exactly to her taste. Walther, with Emil Schaudt, had designed the whole apartment block, and every piece of furniture in the flat was made according to Walther's specifications. Everything had a quality of tasteful simplicity. But what was the use of a beautiful home when you were in it all alone all day? For Elisabeth was having to rest instead of going to work. And when Walther came home he was worn out. Somehow he could always talk about his day's work, but he was no longer capable of participating in a discussion about theatre and music.

Elisabeth was a person who deeply appreciated "the home". Many years later she wrote to a friend: "I am back at home, among my beloved furniture. I call that living!" But in Hamburg her life's centre remained in the Stadttheater, to an extent which could not be good for a marriage.

In addition to this the young conductor Otto Klemperer was beginning to exercise an ever greater influence over her. In him she found the musical understanding which Walther could not provide. The two colleagues grew closer and closer. It happened so gradually that they did not perceive the danger in it.

The new season of 1911–12 brought much excitement: the musical director Brecher was coaching Busoni's opera *Die Brautwahl* for a world première (which took place at the Hamburg Stadttheater on April 13 1912). Elisabeth got the only female role, Albertine. Ferruccio Busoni came to Hamburg himself towards the end of the rehearsal period. To see and speak to him and to hear the work discussed was for Elisabeth very important. Busoni was at that time *the* great pianist, and his compositions showed him to be a champion of a new post-Romantic movement. During the rehearsals he sat in the stalls and keenly watched as his work took shape. One day they were rehearsing the scene in which Albertine accompanies herself on the spinet. Busoni turned to the producer and asked where the spinet was. When told that it was on stage and that Frau Schumann would accompany herself he exclaimed that this was out of the question since the piece had to be played with the utmost accuracy, by a proper keyboard player – from a singer one could only demand an approximation, and that would not do!

But when Busoni noticed with what fluency Elisabeth played the spinet during the scene, he was totally won over.*

---

*From Alfred Mathis's unpublished biography of Elisabeth Schumann.

The performance was first class. Only the best singers of the ensemble took part, and in the musical interpretation Gustav Brecher brought the whole weight of his imagination and intellect to bear. But the opera was not a success with the public who did not seem to understand the work fully, and so it soon had to be withdrawn.

Busoni's *Brautwahl* was only one of the exciting happenings of that eventful season of 1911–12. There was a new manager for the Stadttheater: Dr Hans Loewenfeld from Leipzig. He had *Aida* put on in August as the opening performance of the season; the second was *Fidelio*. Florestan was sung by the later very popular Karl Guenther, formerly a coppersmith in a Hamburg shipyard. Elisabeth sang Marzelline, and Otto Klemperer conducted. Annie Pollak, the wife of the conductor Egon Pollak, who was later for many years general musical director in Hamburg, was at that *Fidelio* performance. Afterwards Frau Pollak spoke to Klemperer and asked him: "Wasn't Schumann fantastic?", whereupon Klemperer said: "*The* singer."

And for Elisabeth, Klemperer was *the* conductor. To be on stage and to watch him across the orchestra, to understand and follow in an instant the fine indications of his baton and hand, knowing by them exactly what she was to strive after, and achieving it by putting everything into it, finally to read the thanks and joy in his eyes – that brought a blissful happiness she had never known before.

Two years before her death Elisabeth Schumann looked back on her life and dictated some thoughts about love to a friend:

> It seems to me personally that the intense, electrifying sensation of love has never been felt by anybody as much as artists whose performance is dependent on another's ... the sensation of expressing oneself in supreme harmony with another who controls with his baton the tempo, the spacing, the very colour of that expression ... To face the world together, to be engaged in a common task is the poetry of love almost anywhere. But let this joint dedication happen in music, in that sweet flow of human self-expression, let it become a firework of reciprocity, and love seems to outdo itself and fuse every trembling move of one's soul with art, permanence and the mirage of eternity ... there can be no more sacred, passionate and pure communion between love, art and two human beings than the electric understanding between a performer and the conductor of the orchestra ... when it occurs ... the audience will cherish the feeling that they are witnessing a secret of the gods.

What Elisabeth Schumann described in front of her cosy open fire in her flat in New York in February 1950 was exactly what happened in the years 1911–12 between her and Klemperer when she sang in rehearsals and performances which he conducted. Naturally she had been brought up to consider wedlock a holy thing and to regard it as a sin even to think of another man when one was married. She still tried to keep to these principles. But the heights of this sublimated love which Elisabeth experienced during a successful performance seemed almost heaven-sent and not sinful at all.

Then there were the rehearsals too. Not those in the theatre, but those out in Gross Flottbek. Klemperer was never satisfied, the rehearsal time at the theatre was never enough for him, so he would often invite the singers to his apartment in a villa in Flottbek, which lay on the high north shore of the Elbe and commanded from its terrace a view of the wide river and the whole of the broad, flat Elbe valley. Except for the grand piano the music room was cleared completely – and this was the stage on which Klemperer sought with passionate dedication to realize his ideas. The acting and the music had to correspond; even the slightest gesture would be decided on, so that it fitted the music.

One role which Elisabeth rehearsed in Flottbek was Cherubino in *The Marriage of Figaro*. She had great success with it. One critic mentioned how natural and unforced her comical acting was and that she sang the aria "Voi che sapete" charmingly, instead of ruining it with the sentimentality with which many singers imbued it.

Klemperer was absolutely delighted with Elisabeth's Cherubino, and one evening after a performance he said to her that he thought she should sing Octavian rather than Sophie; her boyishness would come out beautifully.

Elisabeth again had to go out to Flottbek to rehearse particularly the scene between the Marschallin and Quinquin in the first act, which meant a lot to Klemperer. From the piano he directed Elisabeth's singing and acting, often jumping up to demonstrate details of step, movement and gesture. He was anything but an actor himself, and his tall, thin figure was in stark contrast to that of the graceful little rococo nobleman. Whether it was this discrepancy, or whether Elisabeth was distracted by her feelings for Klemperer, she could not quite portray what he was striving at. He particularly wanted to bring out the contrast between the Marschallin's sadness and resignation, and Octavian's stormy protests. Suddenly he cried for her to stop. *She* should be the Marschallin now, while he acted

Quinquin. With that he rushed up and knelt down next to her. He grasped her fingers with his powerful hand and sang:

> *When you have me here,*
> *When I entwine my fingers in your fingers,*
> *When I search with my eyes for your eyes,*
> *Even then you really feel like that?*

Within seconds Elisabeth and Klemperer were in each other's arms – and they were not acting when they kissed and declared their love.

After the first blissful minutes a great disquiet took possession of Elisabeth. The room seemed to shut her in. It was the sure knowledge that this was the one true, the great, the only love; and at the same time there was the tormenting thought that she was not free, that she was Walther's wife, and he loved her . . . .

But how could such thoughts succeed against the overpowering, all-enveloping conviction that Walther was not the right man for her? Now it was clear to her how much a man and a woman could have in common. She could see it in Klemperer: how he understood, better than she, every finer point in song, in music; and above all – how he understood *her*, how he helped her. Only with him could she spend her entire life, only with him!

Medically speaking Klemperer must have been in a manic phase at this time, a phase of euphoria, optimism and confidence (which almost lost him his career).

The following months passed in a mad whirl. Every possible opportunity to meet was exploited, every moment which offered itself was grasped. Elisabeth dashed backwards and forwards: from rehearsal to home; from there to a rendezvous somewhere on the bank of the River Alster or far out of town, where there was less chance of being seen by people who knew them; from there to visit friends; and before Elisabeth went home again, to be there when Walther returned, she might race off in a taxicab to the man around whom her whole life now revolved.

Miserable were the days when Elisabeth could not meet Otto Klemperer. But thank God for the telephone! She often wondered: how on earth did Goethe cope without one?

Soon things came to a head. On November 28 1912 Elisabeth sang her only performance of Octavian, conducted by Klemperer (who never conducted it in Hamburg again). While Lotte Lehmann's Sophie was praised, Elisabeth's performance was not a success with the critics who thought that she was miscast, being too girlish for the part: the role clearly demanded a heavier quality of voice.

The following evening Elisabeth heard Lotte Lehmann's debut as Elsa in *Lohengrin*. Walther was not in the box with her as he was at a meeting with his old student corps, but he was due to have supper with Elisabeth and some mutual friends, Hans and Lisl Bontemps, in the restaurant of the Curiohaus afterwards. The Bontemps waited and waited for the couple to arrive, and after an hour walked up to their flat to find out where they had got to. There sat Agnes, the maid, saying tearfully that no one was at home and that she was not allowed to say anything. She had in fact already told the truth to Walther: Elisabeth had gone off with Klemperer. The outraged husband was informing the police.

They had gone to the conductor, Egon Pollak, who found them somewhere to stay in the Spessart, the hills southeast of Frankfurt. They only stayed away a few days. Threats were coming from Loewenfeld, saying that if Elisabeth broke her contract in Hamburg she would not be able to find work elsewhere. At any rate she was back singing Humperdinck's *Königskinder* by December 5.

But she had not gone back home. She and Klemperer moved into the Hotel Vier Jahreszeiten. Of course they were now within Walther's reach again and he managed to play rather a nasty trick on his wife. One evening he asked Hans Bontemps to fetch her from the theatre. Bontemps got into a carriage with her and they set off, but not, as Elisabeth had expected, in the direction of her hotel. When, to her horror, he explained where they were going, she said "Hans, I would never have believed that you could do such a thing!" They were bound for a psychiatric clinic, whose head doctor Walther knew personally. Walther's logic was: someone who behaves as my wife has done must be mad. He still loved her deeply and found her infidelity unbelievable. Elisabeth, suddenly finding herself imprisoned, knew she had to stay happy and calm to prove that she was in no need of treatment. Her naturally happy disposition came to her aid. She read poetry by Goethe. The chief psychiatrist had quite the wrong impression of her, thinking her to be a flighty frivolous theatre girl. In despair Elisabeth bribed a night nurse to contact her solicitor who succeeded in getting her released from the clinic three days later.

Elisabeth moved to furnished rooms on the opposite side of town from the Curiohaus. She missed the far greater comfort of her home, but staying with Walther was now quite out of the question.

Walther Puritz, very much the man of honour, challenged Otto Klemperer to a duel with pistols. Klemperer declined, saying that he would point no weapon at a human being – if anyone felt like shooting, they could go and shoot ducks. Walther then issued a threat that "other measures" would be taken. Klemperer must have taken this seriously, for he began to keep a very low profile, did no conducting for almost two weeks, and always travelled around town in taxicabs or carriages with the blinds drawn.

On Boxing Day 1912 came the crisis which made the affair really public. Klemperer was conducting *Lohengrin* with Lotte Lehmann singing her second Elsa. Again Elisabeth was giving her moral support, watching from a box. She noticed that the seats in the middle of the front row of the stalls were empty. During the second interval she remained in the box, not wishing to meet anyone. Hidden in the half darkness she looked down at the colourful throng in the stalls. With a shock she suddenly saw Walther. Wearing a frock coat, he was walking along the front row with a group of friends and then sat down directly behind the conductor's stand.

Elisabeth knew that those "other measures" were now going to be taken, whatever they might be. She ran down to the dressing-rooms to find Klemperer and warn him. When she did not find him she hastily scribbled a note: "My husband is sitting behind you" and gave it to an attendant to give to him.

Klemperer did not seem noticeably disturbed when he returned to conduct the third act, he did not even look up, let alone at the seat behind his stand.

Except that Elisabeth was in a state of suspense, the performance proceeded quite normally – until the last few bars of music, when the singing had stopped. At this point Walther Puritz jumped up and shouted: "Klemperer, turn round!" and drew a riding whip from under his voluminous coat. As the conductor turned to him he slashed his face with it twice so that Klemperer fell back into the pit. During the pandemonium which followed, Walther was hurried out of the theatre by his friends while Klemperer clambered out of the pit. Back on his podium he hushed the audience with a gesture. Into the expectant stillness he then stated loudly and clearly: "Ladies and gentlemen, Herr Puritz has struck me because I love his wife. Good evening."

Elisabeth knew that this meant the end for her here at the

Hamburg Stadttheater. She could not possibly stay now. Tomorrow the papers would be full of this appalling scandal. Klemperer would have to leave too, no doubt about that. It was dreadful ... but at least there had been no shooting.

Klemperer certainly did leave – with Elisabeth: for the second time in a month the two of them eloped.

That night there was a terrible gale in Hamburg which tore up paving stones and damaged many roofs. The fleeing couple managed to get a room in a hotel with the help of the conductor Fritz Stiedry who was staying there. The next morning the press had a ball, and there were statements from each of the parties: Walther maintained that he was forced to give Klemperer a thrashing since the challenge to a duel had been declined, and that he had chosen the theatre as an appropriate scenario since this place had made the misconduct possible; Klemperer's lawyer denied that Schumann had been pressurized into a love affair and further claimed that no damage had occurred to Walther Puritz's marital rights. This was true, but it was soon to change.

Elisabeth and Klemperer contacted Direktor Loewenfeld that day too. He was a man who had great understanding for such situations; in this case, however, he saw no alternative but to suspend the two of them. The newspapers had reported, in their big spreads about the incident, that here and there people had sharply criticized Klemperer's and Elisabeth's relationship. It would therefore doubtless be better to let time draw a veil over the matter. He promised that he would renew Elisabeth's contract whenever this became possible. In the case of the conductor he could not make such an assurance: it would probably be better if he never came back to the Stadttheater. He was dismissed.

Now began a difficult time for the couple. They found very little work. For one thing the news of the scandal caused by the public thrashing had found its way around all the theatres; everywhere they went they were met with regretful shrugging of shoulders, indicating that a guest appearance was not possible. On top of this Walther had publicly declared that at any concert in which the two of them performed together he would repeat the scene which had taken place on Boxing Day. Not only that: if he heard that Elisabeth was planning a concert with Klemperer anywhere in Germany he sent a warning to the organizers. It is likely that he got reports of concert advertisements from his network of student corps members, who were after all very keen on matters of honour. Very often, therefore, when the two artists had a concert in the offing and all was settled, a letter would suddenly arrive stating with great regret that "under the circumstances" a concert would no longer be possible, the management could not risk a scandal.

From Frankfurt Elisabeth tried to start divorce proceedings, but every legal impediment which Walther could find was found, and it seemed hopeless. He also had Elisabeth's bank account closed. Klemperer never seemed to have any money, so now they had a financial crisis. They travelled to Vienna to stay with the widow of Gustav Mahler, Alma Mahler, who not only gave them money but also found them a place to stay with friends on a country estate in Czechoslovakia. Here, at Klemperer's persuasion, Elisabeth studied the role of Madam Butterfly. She did it reluctantly as she knew it was too dramatic for her, and exhausting to perform: Butterfly is on stage for almost all of the opera. (She never did perform it but made a recording of the aria "Un bel dì vedremo" in German some months later.)

Klemperer's euphoric manic phase gave way to severe depression and he decided to seek treatment in a sanatorium in the Taunus Mountains west of Frankfurt. He had been there before, and the director, an eminent psychiatrist called Oskar Kohnstamm, had become his friend. When they arrived there Elisabeth found that she was not permitted to stay in the sanatorium too. She found a boarding house in the village but ate her meals at the clinic.

One day the two of them went for a walk in a wood and discussed their predicament. Suddenly the path they were on stopped at a stream: they could go no further. This seemed symbolic to Klemperer who said: "This is our life. You jump across." With this he was suggesting that they should part.

Back at the clinic the doctors told her some hard truths: Klemperer's condition was worsening. He needed to conduct again, yet he was still suffering inner conflict about his feelings for Elisabeth. The lovers really should part. She responded that if she was ruining him she would give him up. But she was told that things were not so simple: Klemperer would not believe it unless she actually went back to her husband.

She could not make up her mind to this last proposal. Her predominant feeling was: all in vain, rejected, endless poverty. But she acted. That same evening she caught the night train to Halle and went to her parents. What had been decided should be carried out.

Her parents knew all about what had happened. Elisabeth had already written to them about it, and Walther had also let them know. They were on his side but, now that she had left Klemperer, they forgave her.

Direktor Loewenfeld wrote saying that Elisabeth was proving to be an irreplaceable loss to Hamburg; everyone wanted her back and there was really nothing stopping her taking up her post again, the sooner the better.

For days Elisabeth could not make up her mind. She was still overwhelmed by the huge disappointment which had met her on that forest path. Everything seemed pointless. She hardly went out of the house; she neither sang nor played the piano. Her parents advised her to go back to Hamburg: work was the best way of coping with unhappiness. She just shook her head. But her naturally positive attitude to life did not leave her paralysed for long. One morning her parents heard her quietly warbling to herself as she came downstairs. Hardly had she sat down to breakfast when she declared that she *would* like to tread the boards again – to hear the music of the orchestra wafting up from below for her to mingle her voice with it . . . .

Yes, Elisabeth loved her profession far too much to last long without the exciting atmosphere of the theatre. Nor could she for ever be a burden on her parents' purse. The 1912 – 13 season was not yet over, there was still time to start again.

She telegraphed Direktor Loewenfeld to say that she was prepared to work again and when should she come? He telegraphed back: he needed her the very next day. So Elisabeth rushed headlong back to Hamburg.

But she did not go near Walther. She again took the furnished rooms on the left bank of the River Alster, where she lived very frugally. No taxicabs to the opera any more: now she went by tram. She was greeted by the loyal Hamburg public with a storm of jubilation. No one seemed to hold it against her that she had been caught up in a theatre scandal. It seemed that no such thing had ever happened. And yet – how often was she painfully reminded of Klemperer when she was working. And how she missed him when studying lieder. He had often worked on them with her, especially Beethoven lieder.

Shortly after her first performance back in Hamburg Elisabeth found in her dressing room a huge bunch of flowers with a letter – both from Walther. He asked if he could see her again. The next day they met. He said he wanted to forgive her, she could come back to him. When she asked him if he thought they could ever live together again he was amazed. There seemed to him to be no problem: he was prepared to forgive and she must show goodwill. She avoided the issue. "Perhaps", she said.

After that he did not leave her in peace. He sent flowers; he came to performances in which she sang; he wrote her letters in which he begged and beseeched her to come back to him. When none of this helped he would wait loyally, like a besotted schoolboy, at the stage door and accompany her home. He was able to joke and talk light-heartedly with her as in the old days, and he assured her that he would not touch her, if only she would come back to him.

Walther's efforts and tenacity were not without effect. Elisabeth was living to some degree in social isolation. Adulteresses tended to be avoided, after all; and it was not easy for her acquaintances to socialize and remain friends with her and Walther at the same time. This could lead to embarrassing situations.

The end of the 1912–13 season came without a decision having been made. Elisabeth left Hamburg. She told no one where she was going. She had accepted an engagement at the Kroll Opera in Berlin where opera was performed through the summer. It was only for about six weeks, but that suited her very well: firstly she needed the earnings and secondly she wanted to get out of the Hamburg atmosphere and sort herself out without the influence of Walther. Her debut there was in the role of Aennchen. The applause for her was so rapturous that, suddenly noticing friends in the audience, Elisabeth could not resist waving at them. Afterwards she was officially reprimanded for such unprofessional behaviour.

Walther thought at first that she was in Merseburg, but Emma Schumann wrote him that she was not there. For a few days everyone was worried, they even suspected that she might be back with Klemperer again. Then came news from Walther's family that she was singing at the Kroll Opera. So he was soon confronting her at the stage door in Berlin with a huge bunch of sweetpeas – her favourite flowers. She had to laugh at his obstinacy and was quite pleased as well. Now he besieged her constantly.

In Berlin Elisabeth found a letter from Walther's mother. It was a friendly invitation to come for coffee or for supper some time.

So Walther's parents forgave her as well. Should she accept? Looking through the rest of her post she found a card from Norbert Salter, the agent. "Please come tomorrow morning at 10 o'clock," he wrote, "to sing to Gatti-Casazza."

Elisabeth had no idea who Gatti-Casazza was; probably some impresario who wanted to catch her in his net and make money out of her. Anyway she had not got time, what with the Kroll Opera and then Hamburg again. That sort of audition was no fun anyway, usually in front of a whole lot of other victims. She would not go.

This decision suddenly made her decide what to do about Walther's parents. She took pen and paper, thanked them warmly for the invitation but wrote that it was perhaps too early to take it up. She took no more notice of the card from Salter. She did not ask who Gatti-Casazza was, otherwise she would have found out that no less than the general manager of the Metropolitan Opera in New York had shown an interest in her and had wanted to hear her the following morning.

In this way Elisabeth missed the opportunity of singing Sophie in the *Der Rosenkavalier* in the next New York season of 1913 – 14. It was not by chance that the great man was interested in Elisabeth. Richard Strauss had recommended her for the next New York season, and as his close friend Willy Levin had reported so enthusiastically about her, had suggested her as Sophie. Giulio Gatti-Casazza left for America without having heard her, but he instructed Alfred Hertz, a conductor at the Metropolitan Opera, to listen to her as soon as he could.

Elisabeth had no notion about all this, and when the Kroll Opera closed, travelled to her parents in Merseburg. She had decided to try to make a go of her marriage again. "But now I want to have a child!"

CHAPTER 6

Hamburg, 1913–1917

WALTHER GOT A LETTER from the Schumanns saying that he had his Elisabeth back. He telegraphed and asked to be allowed to come at once.

With a beating heart Elisabeth met him off his train. He kissed only her hand, was quite the cavalier, not the husband. He suggested that he should stay only two days and discuss and plan with her a journey, preferably one abroad, in a completely different environment where they could "find one another again." Relieved that things did not immediately have to revert to what they had been, Elisabeth agreed.

About a fortnight later Elisabeth left Merseburg to meet Walther on the Frisian North Sea coast. They intended to stay ten days, from August 4 to 14, on the island of Borkum, and then go to Holland.

The days on Borkum and in Groningen largely fulfilled their purpose. The novelty of being together again had the effect of pushing everything that had happened into the background. Soon the two of them were able to talk freely again.

Not many weeks after their return to the Curiohaus she was expecting her only child. She did not spare herself, singing and working as normal, and, six months pregnant, she was still jumping out of the window as Cherubino in *The Marriage of Figaro*. Perhaps that was why the birth was premature, or perhaps it was the inflammation of the kidney, which Elisabeth still occasionally suffered from.

Premature birth did not, however, mean an easy birth. Elisabeth suffered for thirty-six hours. At last, in the afternoon of July 7 1914, in very hot weather and a mighty thunderstorm, she brought a boy into the world. During the labour she had not dared to cry out as she was afraid of hurting her voice. Now she lay totally exhausted in her bedroom, too feeble to notice that everyone was very anxious about the child, for he was extremely weak and did not even weigh three pounds. Not until the next day did her anxiety begin and for a week she was in fear for his life. But then things started looking up for Gerd, or "Schnuck", as she called him, and he became everything to her.

A little over three weeks after Schnuck's birth the First World War broke out. Elisabeth could not comprehend it. She was an apolitical person and simply could not understand how in the twentieth century there could still be issues over which people had to shoot each other. Already then, as a twenty-six-year-old, she had hardly any nationalistic feelings; and later, as a mature woman, they were completely strange to her. Often she would say: "What does it matter whether one is German, French or English – whether Jew or Christian?"

Nevertheless she soon got used to the idea that a war was raging. She was far too happy a person to be depressed by it for too long. Work went on and so did life. Unlike many other women, she was not immediately separated from her husband. Walther did not need to go to the front yet: having studied for so long he had not yet done military service. She hardly dared admit it to herself, but she would almost rather have been separated from him. In that one year since the trip to Borkum her relationship with Walther had not improved significantly. In fact it had imperceptibly slipped back to the old state of affairs. He loved her, there was no doubt about that. But this love seemed to come through a kind of wall so that it was deadened and cool like light shining through thick glass.

The child compensated Elisabeth for this, and so did someone else: Helene Jung. Fräulein Jung came to the Hamburg Stadttheater in 1914. She possessed a beautiful, warm contralto voice, she was Elisabeth's age and came from Weimar, almost the same homeland as Elisabeth's. Lene was a very natural person who, with her dry humour, said exactly what she thought. They understood each other immediately. They had to work together a lot (as Hänsel and Gretel, for example) and became the closest of friends for life. And although they were later separated, they always shared their joys and sadnesses in letters, visited one another whenever they could or met at a railway station when travelling through. At the Hamburg Stadttheater they were soon known as the inseparables. Their friendship did not, however, stop them from playing practical jokes on each other during performances. Sometimes this led to their being unable to sing for laughing. In the end it became impossible to let them perform together, for just the appearance of Lene strenuously keeping a straight face would make Elisabeth explode with laughter. Direktor Loewenfeld had quite a headache with the two ladies. He could not really punish them: Elisabeth now had such standing at the Stadttheater. She had other offers from theatres and was not obliged to stay in Hamburg. How strong her position was is illustrated by the fact that in October 1914 she went to the Metropolitan Opera in New York for five months. They had to let her go.

Alfred Hertz, the conductor from the Metropolitan, had done what the general manager Gatti-Casazza had asked him. While Elisabeth was still singing at the Kroll Opera in Berlin in July 1913 he had heard her as Eva in *Die Meistersinger*. Elisabeth had never sung "Evchen" before. A critic wrote rather unenthusiastically: "She was an Evchen but not the mature Eva which Wagner intended . . . her costume was not in the right style and was too simple. . . ."

Nothing about how Elisabeth sang. But Alfred Hertz was thrilled. During the interval he was taken to her dressing room where he asked her outright whether in principle she was prepared to come to New York one day, to the Met.

In the spring of 1914 the negotiations began and the management of the Stadttheater finally agreed. When the war broke out it almost seemed as if the guest appearance would fall through, but Elisabeth obstinately pursued her goal: to sing at the Met. Although her child was still so small she believed that she must cross the Atlantic. Now that there was war, when would she have another opportunity to go to America? It was already bad enough: she was able to cross only on an Italian boat from Naples.

On October 14 1914 Elisabeth left for Naples. The *Hamburger Fremdenblatt*, which called her "one of the most popular and most talented artists of the Hamburg Stadttheater", announced her departure in a small notice.

She was a little heavy-hearted, mainly because of her child, but she had Walther's sister Käthe with her as a travelling companion. They got on extremely well and Elisabeth was glad not to be alone.

The crossing from Naples in the *Canopic* was great fun. Elisabeth found herself in prestigious company, all heading for the Met: apart from the great Caruso there were Emmy Destinn (who, poor lady, suffered from sea-sickness the whole way), Geraldine Farrar and

65

Arturo Toscanini (who were just beginning a great love affair – Elisabeth almost tripped over them in their deck chairs on an evening walk on the promenade deck), Frieda Hempel (who assured Elisabeth kindly that she would *not* have to study the role of Oscar – although Gatti-Casazzi had asked her to – since that was *her* role!) and Antonio Scotti. Emmy Destinn did not show her face during the entire crossing, and on the evening before their arrival in New York Caruso, Scotti and Elisabeth sang a serenade at her cabin window. Suddenly Caruso's voice was no longer to be heard and presently he appeared at the porthole dressed as a prima donna and bowing his thanks.

Early next morning on the quay the singers were surrounded by photographers, and by midday the newspapers were already celebrating the opening of the new season at the Met with pictures of the artists arriving.

What a wonderful country this America was, where so much attention was paid to artists! And what a lifestyle! Everything went at such a pace; there was so much technology to make things comfortable for people in every way; and the people were so industrious: at midnight one could still go shopping, or even at one or two in the morning.

The hustling, bustling life, in fact the large scale of it all – this was absolutely to Elisabeth's taste. Although she liked to be able to withdraw peacefully into her quiet home surrounded by antique furniture, yet she always needed to be near the stream of life so that she could jump in and swim in it if she felt like it.

The work at the theatre was fascinating. Like so many Europeans Elisabeth had suspected that the performances at the Metropolitan Opera would not achieve true artistic polish, that they would rely wholly on the effect of collecting so many stars together. Now she was personally experiencing the Met's team spirit and hard rehearsal work. *Fidelio*, which was in the regular repertoire, was to have sixteen orchestral rehearsals!

Elisabeth's debut in New York was Sophie in *Der Rosenkavalier* on November 20. After much rehearsing came the evening which she had anticipated with such nervousness. The second act had already begun, the curtain had not yet gone up. Half turning her back to it Elisabeth stood, small and dainty in her white crinoline dress, on the wide, high stage where the air was gently on the move, as if one were standing in the open air on a still day. Through the golden curtain

66

the sounds of the prelude penetrated – sounds of the great master whom she had to thank for being here at all and whom she had not yet met. And behind those sounds the unknown public of the New World and her critics lay in wait.

Curtain! It was like a silent flutter of wings brushing one's face, startling one and making one tremble. The orchestra, to which Elisabeth still had her back half turned, swelled, and behind it, now perceptible to her tensed nerves, the enormous semicircle of thousands of eyes and ears. Elisabeth trembled as she followed the chatting of the duenna. And then came her entry: "In this solemn hour of trial. . . ." She had time to register: "Truly a trial." And with that all trepidation vanished.

Elisabeth suddenly knew again: this was her role, her very own, which had always brought her happiness, in which she felt as at home as a fish in water.

Storms of applause broke out at the end of the second act; again and again the artists had to come out in front of the curtain. Her colleagues let Elisabeth have one ovation all to herself; but she still did not realize that she had created a sensation. Only next morning was this clear to her, as she leafed through the newspapers and read heavily printed headlines: MADAME SCHUMANN WINS TRIUMPH; METROPOLITAN PERFORMANCE OF STRAUSS'S OPERA GAINS THROUGH AID OF MADAME SCHUMANN; NEW SINGER WINS IN "DER ROSENKAVALIER"; SCHUMANN SCORES AT DEBUT.

The critics did not merely praise her strongly, they wrote columns and columns about her. Elisabeth translated feverishly with the help of a pocket dictionary (her English was not good) or by asking a friend what this or that meant. The critic Max Smith had given her the most print space. He wrote:

Giulio Gatti-Casazza sprang a surprise on those of his subscribers who attended the season's first performance of "Der Rosenkavalier" last night . . . by introducing to them, in the role of Sophie . . . one of the most delightful artists he has drawn into his fold in recent years . . . the role of Sophie is vocally exceedingly exacting. For Mme Schumann, however, the difficulties had apparently no terrors. With remarkable ease she coped with Strauss's long-sustained phrases, spinning out her sweetly appealing and expressive tones, even in the loftiest altitudes, in a way that could well have served as an object lesson for students of singing.

Mme Schumann's lyric soprano is not large. But it is admirably placed, finely concentrated and supported by an excellent control of breath. At no time last night did the singer force her voice and not once did she wander from the correct pitch. . . .

It was not only in her singing, however, that the new soprano revealed herself as a true artist. Histrionically, her study of Sophie was quite as impressive as vocally.

The next evening Elisabeth stood again on the great stage of the Met, this time as Musetta in *La Bohème*. Mimi was sung by Lucrezia Bori, Rodolfo by Luca Botta, and Antonio Scotti sang Marcello. The conductor was Giorgio Polacco.

With Sophie and Musetta Elisabeth sang herself to stardom in the eyes and ears of the New Yorkers, the management of the Met was therefore able to include her in an "all-star performance" of *The Magic Flute*, in which she sang Papagena. A critic of that performance referred to her as "the new star Fräulein Schumann" and said that "her voice is full and strong, her diction very careful and her acting alive and vivacious."

Elisabeth appeared in two further main roles in that New York season of 1914–15. One was Marzelline and the other Gretel. She also sang a Rhinedaughter in *Götterdämmerung* and a Flower Maiden in *Parsifal*. She was, incidentally, only the second Gretel the Met had ever had, Bella Alten having been the first.

Her successes at the Met brought a number of concert engagements her way as well, and the five months should have passed very quickly for her. But soon she was counting the days, once the novelty had worn off. She was working out when she would be with her Schnuck again. She was worried about him. In Europe there was still a war on. Would he have enough to eat? Letters took so long because everything had to travel in a round-about way. Elisabeth regularly sent telegrams to Hamburg. The replies were always reassuring: the nurse, Luise, who was caring for Schnuck, was apparently a gem and could be relied upon.

Elisabeth's colleagues tried to persuade her to accept further engagements and stay in America where opportunities were much better than in Germany; above all the passage would be so dangerous now, with all those mines and destroyers. None of this could induce Elisabeth to remain one day longer than her contract demanded. She reserved a cabin on a steamer to Sweden.

The crossing was certainly anything but comfortable. Sometimes there was an unbearable tension among the passengers. Conversation mainly revolved around the lurking dangers of foreign ships or submarines who could hold them up for inspection. At meals they found out from the ship's officers what precautions the captain was taking: they were travelling a zigzag route and a very northerly one.

In fact Elisabeth was only really afraid at odd moments. On the whole she was convinced that her usual luck would be true to her. And she kept saying to Käthe: "Eta, we'll get there all right, I know it." She was gay, in good cheer and full of joyful anticipation of seeing her Schnuck again. And at the beginning of May 1915 she arrived back in Hamburg safe and sound.

It was so blissful to be back with her child, in the safety and comfort of her own home surrounded by her familiar things, that for a while she felt more drawn to Walther. He had in the meantime become a soldier and was serving as a volunteer with the air corps in Hanover, so they were apart for much of the time. Elisabeth was able to visit him there from time to time.

In July there were some lovely days for Elisabeth and Schnuck on the Baltic coast at Timmendorf. Elisabeth's cousin and closest childhood girlfriend, Loksch, was able to join them for some of the time, and even Walther was with them for a few days. Holiday snapshots show carefree bathing, Elisabeth and Walther with their arms around each other in shallow water on the beach. But in fact there was something missing: they were having problems communicating again, and in the months that followed they found that they could not talk to each other about work – it was hardly ever mentioned in letters. For example, in August 1916 after a very successful concert tour in Denmark (only her second engagement abroad in her life), Elisabeth added laconically at the end of a letter to Walther: "Copenhagen charming and had much success." She brushed over it in a few words, knowing that Walther was not really interested. Later in the same year she wrote him another typical sentence: " . . . from the Charlottenburg Opera to the Munich Court Opera all doors were open to me; you see, you still don't really know who your wife is."

Walther was similarly laconic about his work: when he was taking part in an architectural competition he wrote only that the draught must be finished by such and such a date. No mention of what the competition involved. In fact it was for designing a war memorial for the Ohlsdorf cemetery in Hamburg, and Walther won first prize.

Although it was wartime Walther was able to participate as he was not at the front: since August 1916 he had been made an engineering supervisor of the air corps in Halberstadt. During the months before this post he had hardly been earning at all and their letters often mentioned shortage of money. Elisabeth had to cover the household expenses of their large flat and the nurse almost single-handed. Fortunately she did not let it get her down too much, but she did seem to want to keep Walther rather at arm's length: her letters often mentioned how much work she had to do and that she could not visit him. Even in July 1916, which was holiday time, she said she had new roles to study for the autumn, and was also preparing a lieder recital for November 5. Now she did not even have her son to comfort her: because of the shortage of good food in the city, he and nurse Luise were staying with Elisabeth's sister in the country in Löbejün. There she was, alone in the flat, with very little social life: the war was getting hold of people's lives and preventing normal activities. On July 10 1916 she wrote to Walther: "This loneliness is positively stifling, on top of not feeling so well. I shall go on working hard this week."

She had just spent two days in bed with her kidney trouble, which had made the loneliness much worse. But still she would not go and visit Walther in Schneidemühl, telling him that she would come in August as she first had to visit Gerd, and then she was off for a stay in Weimar for a week, Lene Jung would be there too. Walther was quite understandably hurt and did not write for some time.

On July 25 Elisabeth wrote to her parents from Weimar:

> ... Every evening we are invited out to friends of Lene's, yesterday there were guests here, and now in three hours' time I am going with Lene to Scheidemantel. Of course everywhere we go the cry is: sing! I now have a letter too from the agent in Denmark – 6 concerts at 500 marks it's to be. Really marvellous! But the difficulties with the passport are awful. Lene has just got hers here this morning, but I have to go back to Hamburg for it – otherwise we would have travelled direct via Berlin ... It is charming here – you really can live it up in Weimar....

The visit to Scheidemantel, Lene's teacher, turned out to be an unforgettable afternoon for Elisabeth. The famous Dresden singer was staggered by her artistry and said that all Weimar was already talking about her (people had even come to where she was staying to hear her). When Elisabeth told him that her father had once written to him asking for help and advice in promoting her singing studies (to which he had not replied), he went very quiet and looked at her with great regret.

In Hamburg Elisabeth managed to overcome the "awful passport difficulties". Until then no one had needed a passport; anyone could go abroad as often as they wanted; anyone could also work and earn money abroad without trouble. The First World War radically changed all that; no nation trusted another, even the neutral countries were becoming suspicious. All her life Elisabeth had to put up with repeated border controls. She often felt a little nervous about them – everyone was so strictly scrutinized – and every now and then she would mention in a letter whether she had had a "good border" or not.

The short tour of orchestral concerts in Denmark and Sweden was great fun and Elisabeth was very successful. Back in Hamburg on August 8 she wrote to her parents:

> I must say that almost the nicest thing about the trip was being able to bring back ham, bacon and butter. If I go back in the winter I shall definitely bring back 12lbs of butter; you are allowed to if you have a certificate ... at the customs ... the controls were *very* strict, one had to strip naked and every little piece of paper (including my good notices) was confiscated and destroyed. Even my music on the journey there – I had to buy it all over again in Copenhagen. I sang three times for 1500 marks – it was quickly and easily earned money ... I had great success – again I noticed no anti-German feelings. – We had wonderful weather, the best bit was a beautiful motoring trip through the woods and along the sea to all those castles ... In Copenhagen I bought myself a lovely handbag, a pair of shoes and a platinum brooch with a sapphire and a couple of little diamonds – it only cost 165 crowns and is charming. Everything is much cheaper than at home. I have put on 3lbs in that short time – it seems to have been the rich food ... I haven't heard from Walther for ages ... nurse Luise yesterday sent me on a letter which had gone to Löbejün and was dated 26th July. I have no idea where he is now ... his letter was full of reproach for not having visited him ...

Finally Elisabeth did manage to visit him in mid-August. Being together for a time improved their relationship. Walther was lucky enough to be living privately so they were able to talk things over in peace.

The start of the new season brought certain problems to the artists of the Stadttheater. Direktor Loewenfeld, now that it was wartime, no longer had enough money to run the theatre in the same style as before. The Hamburg Senate could not give as high a subsidy as hitherto, also the audiences had slackened off noticeably. So he expected his artists to perform for half their salaries. For Elisabeth this was a great blow as she was always short of money. Walther still had very little pay, and household, food and clothing expenses had risen. So when Loewenfeld called a meeting to announce his decision Elisabeth acted; it was one of the rare occasions when she took her fate in her own hands. On August 27 1916 she wrote about it to Walther in Halberstaft, where he had just started as an engineer:

Dear Hasie [little hare],

I have just left the meeting which Loewenfeld called in order to tell the members that they must again perform for half their salaries. Well, I am the only one who refused. Mind you, I didn't speak up in front of all those people but went to see Meyer afterwards (the Doktor was taking a rehearsal) and told him the following: "the pay for which I work here is rubbish and I absolutely do not want to hold a pistol to the Doktor's head. He has explained that he *cannot* pay, consequently I do not want to demand any more of him but wish instead to tell him that I shall go somewhere else." . . . I can't imagine that they will let me go – nevertheless I telegraphed Drenker and Harder (I don't work through Salter any more) to see what vacancies would be open to me straight away. . . .

Walther was afraid that Elisabeth might have gone a bit far, besides which he did not want her on any account to go to another theatre, which would mean separation; so he wrote a placatory letter to Direktor Loewenfeld. On August 30 his wife wrote to him:

. . . your writing to Loewenfeld did not please me at all, not being in the picture you might have ruined things for me. But now we are in agreement and I have everything in writing too. I have knocked a salary of 9,500 marks out of them for this season. But now I'd just like to make it clear that caution had absolutely no place here, on the contrary it was only due to my energetic action that I achieved it. You have no idea how charming Loewenfeld was to me, and how he trembled at the thought of my going. . . .

Things went better between Elisabeth and Walther that autumn of 1916. Their letters were far more detailed and informative. On October 13 Elisabeth wrote:

. . . I have been ill all this time, had terrible tracheitis and am still seeing [Dr] Thost. *Schneider von Schönau* – it all had to be postponed – well, *that* was a to do – the day before yesterday I sang Veronika [in *Schneider von Schönau*] for the first time but it wasn't quite right yet – today it's *Mignon*, and in a minute I am off to the dress rehearsal for *Robert u. Bertram*, in which, as a concert interlude, I am singing a trio with Ader and Kreuder from Mozart's *Der Schauspieldirektor*. The performance is on Saturday. . . .

And on October 20:

. . . I haven't yet noticed any ill effects from the wartime food in him [Gerd]. He still has his milk mixed with cocoa – I now have a fantastic admirer – a shopkeeper diagonally opposite us – he sends round cocoa, tea, rice, sugar, cheese, coffee and the other day even a goose leg. Oh yes, enthusiasm for the arts shows itself in various ways, but just now it is very handy . . . Sunday I'm doing Pamina again – I'm as excited as a child. . . .

On October 27 she reported to Walther:

. . . I'm just about to go to Warnemünde for 3 days to cure my catarrh as it can't go on like this. On Monday I have to sing Sophie again – I hope I shall be in perfect voice by then. I had great success with Pamina on Sunday – had to go in front of the safety curtain 4 times, and the audience was cheering. . . .

Three days in Warnemünde, a resort on the Baltic coast. Walther found that rather strange. But he did nothing about it. Many years later he wrote in the margin of Elisabeth's letter "with whom?". On November 2 she sent him a happy report about her stay:

. . . I had heavenly weather, and even if the 3 days didn't make me *quite* well they certainly did me some good . . . Now I have masses to do again because on the 15th is the first performance of *Ferdinand u. Luise* in which I am singing Luise. This morning I was at the dress rehearsal of [*Tales of*] *Hoffmann* – Loewenfeld has got up a new production – a lot of it magnificent. Ader is singing Antonia – I found her very affected. And the room in the last act was quite palatial – I didn't like that at all, and I don't really understand why Loewenfeld had it made like that – after all, Antonia's father is a simple musician. The doll act is charming, one sees her at the beginning sitting in a glass cabinet.

Elisabeth was able to work again normally and she had a lot to do. In her letters she mentioned charity concerts which were put on during the war in aid of orphans and widows; there was also a church concert under the well-known Hamburg organist Alfred Sittard. Loewenfeld was none too pleased with all her little absences (asking her sarcastically whether he should announce her as a guest artist), and probably due to this and pressure of work her own recital planned for November 5 had to be postponed. On December 8 1916 she wrote to Walther:

> ... and now I must start working on him carefully so that I can get leave for the guest appearances in Switzerland (*Rosenkavalier*, *Figaro* and *Don Giovanni*) – they are to be in February. He has offered me a salary of 18,000 marks for the year 1918–19, whether war or peace – I told him I would have to think about it. It is the highest salary ever offered here for my voice category, Alten only got 16,000 marks. . . .

The prospect of this tour of Switzerland was very exciting for Elisabeth, it not being an ordinary tour but Mozart festival productions to be put on in Zürich, Basle, Berne and St Gallen. Richard Strauss was to be musical director and had chosen for his singers the tenor Robert Hutt from Frankfurt am Main and the bass Josef Geiss from Munich. From the Berlin Court Opera he picked Barbara Kemp, Lilian von Granfeldt and the famous bass Paul Knüpfer. Then there was the Czech bass-baritone Pavel Ludikar (with whom Elisabeth was to experience an amusing incident on stage). And finally, Elisabeth Schumann.

Wartime Christmas came. It was to be the last Christmas which Elisabeth would spend with Walther. The latter, who since the beginning of December had been given, in his capacity as engineer, the rank of captain and better pay, came to Hamburg, where they celebrated with Schnuck in the big flat in the Curiohaus.

Elisabeth's best Christmas present was the news that the Mozart festivals in Switzerland had been postponed until May. Now she would be able to get leave more easily, since in the closing weeks of the season one could always manage with fewer people.

But before she went to Switzerland Elisabeth managed at last to give her own recital, on April 24 1917. Her accompanist on this occasion was Kapellmeister Gotthardt who by now had been conducting and coaching at the Hamburg Stadttheater for about two years. Elisabeth had for some time been attracted by his talent and intellect. His career had been remarkable: he had started as a hairdresser's assistant but had always been fascinated by music, had taught himself the piano and had then earned the money for a proper musical training by playing in cafés. His outward appearance was not attractive: he was less than average height; thin, blond hair sparsely covered his large head; his face was as round as a full moon, and his mouth with its fleshy lips gave him a somewhat fish-like appearance. But Carl Gotthardt was an outstanding musician; and not only that: he had a particular feel for the poetry of music and knew how to bring it out. This was absolutely after Elisabeth's heart. Gotthardt was supremely good at the piano, and as he admired and loved the lyrical, he had a particularly soft spot for song, and this was an incentive for Elisabeth to work on lieder again – since Klemperer had left she had almost neglected them. Elisabeth and Gotthardt first discovered that they shared the same empathy for lieder one day at the end of a piano rehearsal. The singers were still standing around chatting, almost out of the door. Gotthardt had remained at the piano. Absent-mindedly his hands were still running over the keys and suddenly the room was ringing with a melody: "On wings of song". Elisabeth playfully joined in. As she sang Gotthardt frequently turned round, his face radiant with joy. Her colleagues had stopped talking and had moved closer. When the last note had died away they cried: "Bravo, Elisabethchen. Da capo Schumännchen!" Gotthardt leapt to his feet and made as though to grasp her by the hands; he did not, but burst out: "You are *the* lieder singer!"

Their subsequent work on songs together was a great joy to Elisabeth. Through the intensive sharing of musical experience they became good friends. As far as Elisabeth was concerned it probably would have remained at that had Gotthardt not fallen under the spell of her voice and her personality. Soon this manifested itself in the form of warm compliments and bunches of flowers. She pretended to be charmed, for she was far too kind-hearted to show that she was amused. But then came a day when this changed, when amusement gave way to the gratification of being loved.

It was strange, this relationship which Elisabeth had with Carl Gotthardt, with a man of character inferior to her, a man who borrowed money from her and did not give it back. They simply were not compatible. And she realized this when it was too late. Gotthardt's love and talent for music had concealed weaknesses, and Elisabeth had only seen what she was always looking for in men: soul, tenderness, intellect. In addition she had a trait which she admitted in later life: "I was really more in love with being in love than with men."

She had her first bad quarrel with Gotthardt just before Easter 1916 and left for the holiday without saying goodbye. She had hardly returned when he rang her up begging forgiveness and protesting his love – and he was forgiven. Elisabeth was only too glad to have someone who was always there, always caring for her; it helped with the loneliness, particularly at this time when Schnuck was staying in the country.

The recital which Elisabeth gave in Hamburg in April 1917, accompanied by Gotthardt, confirmed her reputation as a lieder singer. The critics praised her enthusiastically and emphasized how rare it was for an opera singer to master the art of song so completely. Heinrich Chevalier wrote:

> ... all cheerful lieder gain from the sparkling, sharply defined and stimulating *parlando*, from the grace and beauty of her perfectly placed stresses; from the depth and immediate warmth of her soprano those songs profit which are based on quiet suffering and little griefs. But everything which she sings is enhanced by the glowing beauty and youthful sound of her voice which seems to bud and sprout as in the spring. . . .

The *Hamburger Neueste Nachrichten* commented: "All our opera singers have the ambition to win their laurels through the lied as well. This is granted to very few. In the case of Frau Puritz-Schumann it is a different matter."

In May came the long awaited meeting with Richard Strauss, on the stage in Zurich, at a rehearsal. Elisabeth described it:

> I had to sing Zerlina, and as Zerlina does not have to sing near the beginning of the opera I did not turn up until all the others were already gathered – of course I was trembling with excitement. As soon as I arrived Strauss stood up and greeted me most warmly. I was absolutely stunned by his expressive eyes. We started to rehearse again and as I sang I noticed that he often looked up to observe my facial expression or to see how I took a note. I have to admit that I sang with full voice; I did not treat it like a rehearsal.

Three years later, in a music magazine, Elisabeth wrote in more detail about her first impressions of working with Strauss:

> His intellectual face, his open features, his clearly defined yet polished gestures conveyed to me the whole nature of the man, and at the same

time gave me the sense of his greatness as a person and artist. His impulsive kindness, which was not of that smarmy, often unpleasant kind, delighted me. The guest appearances with Strauss were for me a period of the most fruitful work. In Zurich we also gave a concert together for the internees. I sang some of his songs. He is a wonderful accompanist. I have never before heard the sound of a whole orchestra coming from a piano.

With him music acquired something wonderfully free and wide-reaching. He did not seem to work at rhythmical detail much. But every phrase was shaped to the meaning, and the singing of the melody as a whole was such joy. He was very considerate to singers: they were never drowned by the orchestra. But his way of working at precise phrasing demanded a high degree of musicality.

After their first meeting at the *Don Giovanni* rehearsal Elisabeth and Strauss became good friends. He was staying in the house of the well-known Zürich family, the Reiffs, in the so-called "Genie-Hospiz" ("hostelry for geniuses"), for the Reiffs were exceptionally hospitable to artists. Strauss invited Elisabeth there, where he asked her to sing a couple of his songs. He suggested "Blauer Sommer". When she had sung it he cried: "Ah, a singer who can even sing triplets!"

One or two days later Strauss suddenly said that he thought she should sing Salome. When Elisabeth protested that she was a lyric soprano and could not sing such a dramatic role Strauss replied that the youthfulness of her voice, the silvery quality, was exactly what he wanted in the character of Salome. He would go through the role with her and alter bits here and there; anything which was too low he would transpose. He would conduct it himself and keep the orchestra's volume down so that she could last through without any strain.

Elisabeth wavered for a few moments, but then her common sense won and she said that one performance of *Salome* would ruin her voice. Richard Strauss recognized it in the end, so his idea was never realized. This sudden idea that Elisabeth should sing Salome gives an insight into Strauss's artistic persuasion at this time. He was now far removed from the beginning of its development; under Hofmannsthal's influence he had laid aside the "Wagnerian armour" and aimed at bright, transparently "woven", chamber-type music, as achieved in *Ariadne auf Naxos* with its small orchestra, and as was later to be seen in the orchestration of *Die Frau ohne Schatten*. This development shows itself in something he once said to the singers on the Swiss tour: "Don't yell, sing! If you don't sing so loudly the orchestra won't play so loudly either."*

The standard of the performances – only *Don Giovanni* and *The Magic Flute* were performed in the end – was particularly high, and the critics in Zurich and Basle were full of praise in their scrutiny of every detail of music and production. The *Zürcher Zeitung* particularly praised Ludikar and Elisabeth, writing:

> In Frau Elisabeth Schumann-Puritz we had an absolutely charming Zerlina and a wonderful singer. Her singing of "Là ci darem la mano" with Ludikar and the comforting of Masetto, "Vedrai carino" in the second act, belonged to the most unforgettable moments of the evening.

The famous duet was indeed delivered in a very moving way by Ludikar and Elisabeth. The seducer and his victim sang with a minimum of voice, it was almost as if they were whispering the phrases to each other. The effect was electrifying.

By arrangement the two of them had already done it that way at rehearsal. When it had finished Richard Strauss had said to Ludikar that he assumed he had only been marking. How would they sing it at the performance?

At first Ludikar was alarmed at what seemed like criticism on Strauss's part, but he defended his and Elisabeth's conception saying that that was how they intended to perform the duet.

Then Strauss said with a twinkle in his eye: "Good, do it exactly like that."†

During the performance in Berne something odd happened with Ludikar, which at first perplexed Elisabeth completely. She described it in her biographical notes:

> I was singing, standing at a massive, stone bench, which was close to the wings. As Ludikar made his entrance he darted behind it and called to me: "Don't move from this bench!" I had no idea why. Ludikar sang, all the while protected by the bench, until we both tripped off into the wings, and I learnt that he had not managed to

---

*The information in the above two paragraphs comes from Alfred Mathis's unpublished biography of Elisabeth Schumann.

†This anecdote also comes from Alfred Mathis's unpublished biography.

finish changing for the champagne aria and had slung a toga over only his underpants; so the bench had to cover his nakedness.

On the train journeys during the tour Strauss whiled away the time with his beloved card game, skat. Elisabeth soon learnt that this playing of skat did not signify his unwillingness to enter intellectual discussion, but was Strauss's way of resting and relaxing. Elisabeth, who was always fascinated by the work of a conductor, held Richard Strauss's conducting art in high esteem. For her biography she dictated:

> Many people think that Strauss was a boring conductor. But that is because he did not do any antics which one could see well from behind. Everything that went on in his face, the inspiration which he thereby imparted to the singers, was superb. Only sometimes when he was bored he would beat in a strange way, in sort of figure of eight movements. Also he would often beat on mechanically while he turned back the pages of the score to look at something which particularly interested him.

During that first encounter with Elisabeth in Switzerland Richard Strauss also began to admire more and more the young singer from the Hamburg Stadttheater. Once or twice he said to her half joking: "Why not come to us in Berlin?" But she replied that her contract went until 1919 and Loewenfeld would not let her go. The longer period of collaboration with the great master was yet to come. Before that a lot was to happen in Elisabeth's life.

CHAPTER 7

Hamburg, 1917–1919

THE BREAKDOWN OF Elisabeth's and Walther's marriage was virtually complete. Already in November 1916, when Walther was on leave in Hamburg, Elisabeth had come to the conclusion that she could no longer live with her husband. She explained to him calmly and frankly that she thought they simply were not compatible, either physically or temperamentally. Amazingly – perhaps due to hurt pride – Walther agreed immediately to a separation.

In the spring of 1917 he tried belatedly to win her back. But he used the wrong tactics: he put pressure on her by demanding the child, saying he should live with him in Halberstadt. In reply to this demand she replied, on March 2 1917:

> ... I still can't believe that your decision is a serious one. Above all we must consider the well-being of the child ... you know how delicate he was and basically still is, and then you want to give him into the care of strangers and occasionally – when your time allows – see him a little! ... you want to tear him away from here, where everything in the household revolves around him, where he is so well cared for – because of egoistic feelings! ...
>
> I can well understand that you would like to have him with you; of course I will gladly let him visit you with Fräulein for 2 weeks in May or June ... but only if you give your word that you will send him back to me.
>
> Please answer this letter soon, and many thanks for the parcel which we were very glad of....

By continuing to put her strong arguments in this calm and friendly way, Elisabeth won her point and Walther allowed Gerd to stay in Hamburg. However, he did reproach her for having caused the separation, blaming it on the bad influence of her theatre life and exhorting her to give it up for a while so that she would come to her senses. . . . How little he understood his wife! He was unable to acknowledge that her vocation for music was as strong as, or even stronger than, his for architecture.

For some time the total break up of the marriage was postponed. Elisabeth had breathing space during which she gave her successful recital with Gotthardt and then worked with Richard Strauss in Switzerland. When she travelled to Zürich in the middle of May she allowed Gerd to go to Walther in Halberstadt with his nurse. After Switzerland she too visited Halberstadt – for the first time since Walther had been made a fully authorized engineer at the aircraft works there. He lived in an inn, the Forsthaus, not far from the airfield, on the edge of a wood. He had enough room to accommodate Elisabeth, Schnuck and his nurse, Fräulein Otto. In this tranquil spot she and Walther had one of the worst disagreements of all. Walther attempted to steer his marriage back onto a normal course, at first with gentle reproaches, then with accusations. Elisabeth remained unshakeable. Then Walther began to suspect, as he had often done before, that there was another man. Elisabeth was not the sort of person who could save herself with excuses and lies: keep something secret, yes, but lie to someone's face, no. So she admitted that she was having an affair with Kapellmeister Gotthardt.

The very next moment she regretted her words: Walther pointed out that there was now no question of Gerd living with his mother.

Elisabeth summoned up every argument she could, particularly those relating to the welfare of the child. She tried to placate him, she begged – it was hopeless.

She accepted her fate – for the time being. She went back to the inn and packed her suitcase. She played with Schnuck for a bit. Then, as she sang him the Brahms lullaby, "Guten Abend, gut' Nacht", gently stroking his head to make him fall asleep, he noticed that there were tears in her eyes. Walther had gone to his office at the airfield, she did not need to say goodbye to him.

Many years later she wrote in her biographical notes:

> The most wonderful thing that a woman can have in life is a child – especially if it is a son. Even if my first years with him were difficult times . . . I would never wish to have been spared this pain, because it meant that I could call a child my very own.

For years Elisabeth was to suffer because of her child. The hardest time in her life had begun. Even on her deathbed she did not suffer as much as in the last two years of the First World War. It was an appalling time full of fear for Schnuck, full of yearning and the agonizing realization that the child was becoming estranged from her. Hardly back in Hamburg, she heard something dreadful about Fräulein Otto which had apparently been going on since before Gerd had gone to stay with his father. Lina, the serving girl, and two cleaning ladies told her indignantly that the nurse had beaten the child cruelly. Elisabeth had often wondered why Schnuck had been so subdued and quiet recently, and now the penny dropped. She got the three witnesses to dictate their statements and sign them. When Walther returned from the front he found the statements in his post.

Walther dismissed Fräulein Otto within minutes of reading the statements. When Elisabeth rang him he was able to reassure her. She asked to see Gerd, longed to visit him, but Walther flatly refused: she could see her child only if she renounced her former way of life and came back to him.

Now began a tough, determined tug of war for the child. Elisabeth was not going to give in. She no longer helped Walther financially; she had in any case had a separate bank account for the last year. This was a blow for Walther, who was having to cope on his meagre officer's pay. It was not going to be easy to keep the boy and pay for someone to look after him. At first his sister Käthe did this, then he found a friendly family who took the boy in as a "guest", and he told Elisabeth that she could not see Gerd if she did not help finance his upkeep.

Walther had a separation agreement drawn up according to which Elisabeth was to devote two-thirds of her income to Gerd's maintenance. But Elisabeth would not be pinned down and refused to sign.

Her last letter from her parents for a long time was from her father, dated August 19 1917. It was a well-meaning letter, but it was reproachful and showed that her parents failed to understand what the problems really were. They were completely on Walther's side and considered her no longer as their daughter. Correspondence ceased. Very embittered, they asked her, through Walther, to give them one-sixth of her income as compensation for all the sacrifices they had made for the sake of her artistic training. They even referred to her as a whore, so convinced were they of her guilt.

Frequently during this nightmare Elisabeth applied to the guardianship authority for permission to see her child, but Walther always queered her pitch by intervening against her.

Elisabeth then threatened to leave the flat in the Curiohaus, which would mean Walther would have to pay the rent, which he could not afford. Again he played a trump card: he decided to let the flat, forcing Elisabeth out.

For months she did not see Gerd. Walther would not even let her send him presents. It was not until the end of September 1917, when the child became severely ill with dysentery, that both parents were forced by their anxiety to reach an agreement. Elisabeth was now free to come to Halberstadt, but alas, the opera house could not spare her until mid-November, when she finally managed to get away for one and a half days.

Although she had signed Walther's form of agreement and was paying him quite heavily, he was clearly not going to let her see Gerd whenever she wanted to: he was evasive when asked when she could come again, saying that that depended on the child's health; excitement was not good for him. Well, if that was the way Walther was going to honour the agreement, she certainly was not going to honour her side of it either. She did not send another penny to Walther.

Soon Elisabeth was wanting a divorce. She knew that this would mean seeing less of Gerd than ever, but at least her quota of visits would be laid down officially.

Walther, too, recognized that divorce was the only sensible course of action now. Something unexpected had contributed to this change of heart: he had fallen in love with Hertha Wruck, the youngest daughter of the family where Gerd was being looked after.

At last, on November 13 1918, Elisabeth was free. The terms of the divorce laid down that she could have Gerd to stay for a few weeks each summer; if she wished to visit him at other times, she could do so only with Walther's permission. And this continued to be so until Gerd was in his teens, old enough to claim increasing freedom to come and go as he pleased.

What brought Elisabeth through those terrible two years was her natural optimism and being forced constantly to cope with new artistic tasks. It was a time decisive not only for her private life but also for her professional life.

At the beginning of the season, in September 1917, she first had to sing Susanna in *The Marriage of Figaro*, in which she was such a success that the Hamburg critics all agreed about her capabilities as a Mozart singer:

Frau Schumann-Puritz is just as a Mozart singer should be. With absolute musical accuracy she steers a perfect artistic course. Voice and performance express grace, depth and beauty . . . .

And another critic:

Here – in the singing of Mozart – I suspect will lie Frau Schumann's greatest talent and her most rewarding sphere.

In the same month she had to sing Marguérite in Gounod's *Faust*. Here she did not meet with such success; her critics, while praising her effortless technique and musical competence, commented that her portrayal was too much like Goethe's Gretchen and not enough the charming petit bourgeois French girl intended by Gounod and his librettists, Carré and Barbier. One critic, Elisabeth's sworn enemy W. Zinne, went into great detail about her failings: how she could not put enough passion into the scenes which needed it; how she was really only effective in scenes where virtuosity was not required; how she could not produce a big enough range of expression in the dark ballad of the King of Thule; and how she lacked poetic charm. Elisabeth, who knew that Zinne had a personal antipathy towards her, did not let such articles worry her; instead she would write comments such as "what a hoot!" in the margin.

At the beginning of the new season of 1917 – 18 a young conductor arrived at the Hamburg Stadttheater: Carl Alwin.* He was tall, slim and dark; the brown eyes in his narrow face positively sparkled with liveliness and unspoken thoughts, and his rimless spectacles seemed to make them sparkle the more. Elisabeth had rarely met anyone as singular as Alwin. He got straight down to brass tacks with astonishing directness, he had no inhibitions and took life as it came. One might have expected to find in him, as in any musician, a certain unworldliness or perhaps every now and then a slight pensiveness. Not so with Carl Alwin. And yet he was body and soul a musician. For hours he would sit at the piano playing opera scores and lieder, his amazingly supple fingers held absolutely horizontally, singing the vocal parts enthusiastically in a hoarse, croaking voice. Elisabeth, although she thought very highly of his musicianship, sometimes could not help laughing when she heard him, and his pranks and intelligent talk often made her forget the difficulties she was going through at the time.

*His first name is spelled "Karl" in reference books and on record labels, perhaps because that, at one time, was officially the preferred spelling in Germany. K was considered more "Germanic" than C.

Professional developments helped her to forget too. At this time she received an enquiry from the director, Count Seebach, whom she had met through the Draesekes in Dresden, as to whether she might be prepared to be engaged by the Dresden Court Opera and whether she would give two trial guest performances. How she had longed to be given an audition by Count Seebach all those years ago!

Her contract with the Hamburg Stadttheater ran out in the summer of 1919. So she agreed to Count Seebach's proposal and in October 1917 she sang Eva for him. The house was packed and she was a great success. A few days later she sang Sophie and was offered a five-year contract. This fact, and her successes in Dresden were reported in the Hamburg press.

On her return to Hamburg Direktor Loewenfeld tried to persuade her not to sign the new contract. But she remained firm. Nothing in her personal life tied her to Hamburg now, besides which Dresden was a far more prestigious place to sing, and her position there would be important: she was to replace the famous Minnie Nast.

But things turned out differently. It began in a tram where Carl Alwin asked her in his direct way: "Why don't you marry me?" (She had just told him that she wanted to get a divorce from her husband.)

Elisabeth responded: "Why you, of all people?"

"Because we're perfect for each other."

And there in the tram he kept on and on, in a low voice, but with his usual intensity and great liveliness. And as always he hit the nail on the head: she needed a musician like him for a husband, someone who could accompany her. They both admired Richard Strauss very much, that was very fitting. Besides, he had noticed that she was not ambitious enough. She needed someone who could do some elbowing for her.

It had never happened to Elisabeth before that a man proposed marriage without any mention of love. Actually it was slightly insulting, but at the same time there was something rather attractive about him.

From now on she was with him a great deal, and it did her good. In those months of 1918 which were so difficult for Elisabeth it became quite clear that Alwin did love her, in so far as someone who concentrated wholly on the intellectual was able to do so. Later she often said of him that he had kissed as butterflies did the flowers.

Elisabeth grew to love him too; perhaps she saw a little of Klemperer in him: the obsession with music, the absent-mindedness, but without the genius. Early in 1919 a short notice appeared in the Hamburg evening papers: "Carl Alwin and Frau Elisabeth, née Schumann, were married on 11 March 1919 in Hamburg."

This time Elisabeth married only in a registry office. On the evening of the wedding day she had to sing and Alwin was conducting; it was a memorable performance. The audience rose to the occasion. In the *Hamburger Fremdenblatt* a short article had appeared announcing that Kapellmeister Alwin was to be married to the "much admired and much loved Elisabeth Schumann", and was to conduct *The Marriage of Figaro* – all on the same day.

Events were coming thick and fast. It was as if the great political upheavals at the end of the First World War were setting the ball rolling in her life too. A few days after the German Revolution of November 1918 her first marriage had come to an end. She accepted Alwin's proposal. But what was now to happen about Dresden? In Saxony there was a revolution too, the King had abdicated. Now the Workers' Councils were in power, even at the opera: Count Seebach had gone, and so had the splendour of the Court. Was it still worth going there to work? And in addition it would separate her from C, which was what she called Carl Alwin.

She wrote to Richard Strauss, asking him if he might consider being her accompanist on a concert tour in Scandinavia, where she was intending to sing a lot of his songs. In the same letter she mentioned in passing her contract with Dresden. (Secretly she wanted his advice.) Strauss replied on December 17 1918:

> Dear Madam,
> Thank you so much for your kind invitation, but I am unfortunately unable to follow it up. I have cancelled all concert tours this winter: even you, dear little Zerlina, do not seem to be aware what a journey to Kristiania would involve. At any rate I have given up for the winter, my necessary journeys to Berlin and Vienna are quite enough! I would not take a step in any other direction, not even with you!
> Are you really going to Dresden? If you want a "change" please do not make one without letting me know beforehand.
> With the warmest greetings I am sincerely yours,
> Dr Richard Strauss

The last sentence of the letter seems to have been a reminder that he rather wanted Elisabeth to come and work under him. But this would no longer mean Berlin: he was shortly to be appointed co-director with Franz Schalk at the Vienna State Opera (as the new republic now called it). The writer Hugo von Hofmannsthal, with whom the composer had collaborated so fruitfully for many years, had strongly recommended him as a suitable addition to the opera house: a world-famous composer with considerable organizational and managerial powers.

But Elisabeth's thoughts were not directed towards Vienna at this stage: her main concern was how to wriggle out of the Dresden contract, for now she felt she must. She racked her brains for some person in Dresden who might help her. Felix Draeseke had died in 1913, and his wife was far too old to burden with it. She then remembered the name of the prompter, Steinmann, who had worked at the theatre and had been a cultured, sympathetic man. He wrote back within a few days. It so happened that he sat on the committee which ran the opera house. He promised to bring her problem up at the next meeting. Barely a week later Elisabeth received from the committee a letter, signed by Steinmann and others, stating that due to such very altered circumstances Frau Schumann's wish to break her contract was being granted.

Elisabeth was speechless. How on earth had Steinmann managed it so quickly? She hastily opened his accompanying letter and was tickled pink by its contents: he had persuaded the committee that it would be only too fortunate if Elisabeth Schumann did not join their ensemble, for she, who had in the past looked quite well on stage, had in recent months become so dreadfully fat that she would be a disgrace to the Dresden State Opera; fat singers were fortunately a thing of the past, best quickly forgotten and not to be encouraged. The committee had agreed unanimously.

Elisabeth was blissfully happy (and so was Direktor Loewenfeld), but things did not end there. Word had got round in the theatre world that she had cancelled her contract with Dresden, and one day, as she walked into the theatre she was handed a telegram from Berlin. She read: "Have just heard that you are free. Offer you contract with the Vienna State Opera. Dr Richard Strauss."

Carl Alwin was adamant that she should not turn such an offer down even if it meant being separated from him. That would be utter madness. He would just have to find a job conducting a Viennese waltz band if necessary!

Elisabeth had an idea that she might be able to persuade Loewenfeld to let her sing for half the season in Vienna and the other half in Hamburg.

Loewenfeld absolutely refused: he knew that as soon as Elisabeth sang in Vienna he would lose her for ever. He even went so far as to make it impossible for her to give the obligatory guest performances there: he would grant her no leave for them.

Elisabeth's letter explaining this could hardly have reached the maestro before a second telegram came from him: "Will engage you without guest performances."

This was unprecedented. Singers who wanted to be engaged by the Vienna Opera always had to pass the test of a major performance: they had to prove their worth to the critical, cultured Viennese public. But Strauss was determined not to let Elisabeth slip from his grasp, and he was such a personality, such a celebrity in international musical life, that he could assert himself and break the sacred tradition.

This action by Strauss caused an emotional dichotomy in Elisabeth. Now she was going to have to make a decision quickly, and she could not make up her mind: she lacked ambition enough for it to weigh equally against her love of domestic happiness and peace. In addition Loewenfeld was leaning hard on her to stay, offering tempting terms for a new contract; also times were so uncertain: no one knew what was really going to happen to the old royal opera houses in the new regime, especially in Austria, which was losing so much of its territory.

By the time Strauss received Elisabeth's indecisive letter the contract was already in the post to her. He had been so certain she would accept. He addressed his reply not to Elisabeth but to her husband. He felt sure that such an ardent admirer of his as Alwin would do all he could to sort things out. He wrote on April 13 1919:

Dear friend and colleague!
Please say to your dear, charming but, as it seems, rather indecisive wife that I cannot and will not accept her refusal of the Vienna contract, for I have looked forward to having your wife far too much for me to release her just like that, simply because Dr Loewenfeld is putting all sorts of ideas into her head. The situation in Vienna is as safe as anywhere, and for an artist like your wife *prospects couldn't be more brilliant* – whoever the government might be and whatever might happen . . . I do not understand the dear little lady. Hamburg compared to glorious Vienna!! Please talk to her and don't let her think of being unfaithful to me.
I am firmly relying on your authority as husband and on the pull

of Vienna. I know what a magnificent position your wife would win for herself in Vienna, and she would languish under Hamburg's rain-drenched skies! Be a kind, wise fellow and keep your word with me.

With warm regards to you both

Dr Richard Strauss

I am unfortunately not very well otherwise I would write more insistently!

This letter dispelled Elisabeth's doubts for the most part and any remaining reservations were eliminated by Alwin's "authority as husband", so Elisabeth put her signature to the contract sent to her by the Austrian Federal Theatres.

Now only six weeks remained for her at the Hamburg Stadttheater, where she had been for almost ten years. Direktor Loewenfeld made her remaining time at the opera anything but easy. He was offended that she had preferred the Vienna contract to his terms.

But Loewenfeld could not prevent Elisabeth's farewell performance from being a demonstration of her greatness and popularity. For the last time she sang the role of Mimi before the loyal Hamburg public. Carl Alwin conducted and lovingly nursed every step and every note of his Mimi, as a critic remarked. It was a memorable evening, and Elisabeth carefully stuck all the press notices about her farewell performance of May 31 1919 into her big green album. One of them she marked in red, intending to include it in her biography. It is more a song of farewell than a notice:

Away with those handkerchiefs, away with those regrets that we are losing something here which may not come back in a hurry. The good man thinks of himself last. We should be happy that once again a strong talent, an outstanding singer, who is striving to the giddy heights of her art, is being admitted to a sphere of activity which will allow her gifts the richest opportunities. If she should come back to us, if only for a short time, we shall also be happy . . . A sign of happiness is . . . flowers. . . . We saw a whole shopful of them on stage on Saturday, they flew from the underworld of the stalls, from the Olympus of the gallery and from the middle spheres, where the ordinary bourgeois person has his quarters. There were wild scenes, laughing and crying. Frau Schumann spoke, one could even hear something like "Wiedersehen", in a word: the "last evening"-atmosphere dominated the situation. It crowned ten years of activity at the Hamburg Stadttheater, which could be compared to a crescendo from pianissimo to fortissimo. What now lies ahead will surpass all that went before: the favour of a great master, a huge salary, idolization by the public ... Who would weep at that? Only in the success of his neighbour does the good person find happiness.

Elisabeth took her farewell of the people of Hamburg for a second time, three days later, on June 2 1919, with a recital. Her C-chen accompanied, of course, and she even sang two of his songs. The large hall in the Musikhalle was almost sold out. At the end, encore after encore was called for in the endless storms of applause, and every time Elisabeth returned to the piano with Alwin, the audience, pressing against the platform, broke into cheers.

Elisabeth had not been so happy for a long time. The unhappiness of the war, of her first marriage, were forgotten, over. Now she had her C who accompanied so beautifully; it was as if with him she could conquer the world.

But in the autumn she would be alone, standing up to a critical audience in a strange city – she had to admit she dreaded the separation. Richard Strauss had hinted that in the course of time it might be possible to bring Alwin to Vienna too, so there was some hope. When she thought of Strauss she felt a little comforted. As long as he was there everything would be all right – but she would reach Vienna before he did; he still had things to finish off in Berlin. So she would have to go through her baptism of fire quite alone.

Something else cast a shadow over her farewell from Hamburg: the discord with Direktor Loewenfeld. He could not forgive her leaving and would not speak another word to her. He also declared that while he was still director of the Hamburg Stadttheater she would not be allowed to sing there again. (And indeed it was not until after he was succeeded at his death in 1922 by Leopold Sachse that she was able to return.) Luckily Elisabeth and Alwin no longer had to go to the theatre: the holidays had begun.

And now something very important had to be done: she must be reconciled with her parents. For a long time they had suffered the pain of their disagreement with their daughter. Through a third party they had heard about the divorce and the marriage to Alwin. When in March 1919 the news of Elisabeth's engagement in Vienna got through to the old Schumanns, pride in their famous daughter did the trick: Alfred and Emma could no longer keep silent – they sent Elisabeth a telegram congratulating her with all their hearts. The ice was broken and letters started to go backwards and forwards. It was arranged that the young couple should go to

Merseburg in June so that her parents could get to know their new son-in-law.

Thus it came to a moving family reunion. Alfred, despite his asthma, could not be dissuaded from meeting the train, with Emma of course. Alwin, quite at ease as always, leaned far out of a window of the arriving train, and when he saw the unmistakeable dazzle of Alfred's white waistcoat, he waved his hat to attract the attention of the old couple, stepped back quick as a flash from the window and pushed Elisabeth forward so that she was suddenly face to face with her parents.

Alfred and Emma were at first somewhat taken aback by this high-spirited behaviour, but after a short time Alwin had won their hearts completely. Emma was fascinated by his fiery idealism and his almost youthfully romantic appearance. And Alfred was soon completely captivated by the musicality of his new son-in-law, by his enormous musical knowledge, by his phenomenal memory which made it possible for him to play something off by heart after going through it once. For whole mornings and afternoons they sat together, playing and discussing. Alwin introduced his father-in-law to a lot of the new works which had come out over the last few years. The scores had been virtually unobtainable during the war and Alfred wanted to hear the new operas which Elisabeth had sung in.

This happy summer was made yet happier because Schnuck was able to come from Halberstadt and stay for the whole of June. On her birthday, June 13, Elisabeth wrote to a young friend and admirer in Hamburg, Lieselotte Laudan:

> You wouldn't believe how popular he is – his joy at our reunion was so "loud" that the whole house heard it. He is tremendously affectionate to me . . . the other day he said: "I am quite in love with you, but most of all in your teeth." – Every morning we go for a cold swim – of course he entertains all the other swimmers. And then we row almost every day on the lake. . . .

Then came the real holidays, the weeks in which Elisabeth could be alone with Alwin – their honeymoon in fact. They went to Sylt, an island in the North Sea. They had booked a room in Kampen, at the Kurhaus. With Alwin there was never a dull moment. He always had something to discuss, or he sat at the piano in the ballroom and played and played, sometimes in his enthusiasm singing a few bars in his croaking voice, making Elisabeth break into peals of laughter.

He was not at all put out. He was also able to imitate colleagues in the funniest way: he could make up satirical verses in a flash. Sometimes, in the street, he would suddenly start limping simply to attract the attention of passers-by, or he would take off his hat to someone whom he did not know in the slightest.

At the end of their stay she and Alwin gave a recital in Westerland. It was one of several concerts they gave together that summer, including one in Berlin, in which Elisabeth again sang some of Alwin's compositions. Since Alwin had entered Elisabeth's life, giving recitals was becoming an integral part of her work. The reason for this was, in the first place, that she was now mature enough for the fine art of lied. But Alwin played a huge part too. He was ambitious for his young wife; he had soon realized that Elisabeth was as talented in the interpretation of song as in creating operatic roles. Of course, he was also ambitious himself: as the accompanist of such a famous singer he could make a name for himself, and in the end he felt sure that he had done a great deal for Elisabeth as a lieder singer. In 1937 he said to a friend: "Before you had even heard of Elisabeth Schumann I had already laid the foundation of her becoming on the of greatest lieder singers of our time."

After a two-week stay in Jena with Lene Jung the start of a new phase in Elisabeth's life began: with feelings of foreboding she set off by train to Vienna. She did not know that her time there was to be the happiest and most successful of her whole life.

CHAPTER 8

Vienna, 1919–1921

SLUGGISHLY, reluctantly the night train from Munich pulled into Vienna Westbahnhof two hours late. Elisabeth searched for anything that might cheer her up. In vain: everywhere and on everything lay the bleak, shabby greyness of the early morning. So this was the celebrated city on the blue Danube! How dreary, dead and desolate it all seemed. And how foreign everything was; what a contrast to North Germany, to Hamburg with its wide stretches of water. As Elisabeth was jolted through the empty streets in a hackney cab, weary from lack of sleep, it seemed as if she had been driven off course into the vast unknown interior of a new continent, unfamiliar and hostile.

She noticed during the days after her arrival that Vienna had undergone a huge change which made it seem strange even to people who knew it well. War had brought about this change, had brought hunger, disease and all kinds of shortages – shortages of the most basic necessities of life, with the endless toil and drudgery needed to counteract them. The toil was often futile, even now, a year after the end of the war. The inhabitants of the once glorious international centre were spiritually and physically emaciated. The city itself had sunk from the status of the metropolis of the mighty Austro-Hungarian Empire to that of capital of a small state. So much of that which had given Vienna its glamour had been swept away by history.

So the glamour, which Elisabeth subconsciously thought she saw, was only vestigial and was grotesquely tainted with the very evident misery which confronted her: the ragged hollow-eyed children who begged on the streets; the old and sick who wasted away on the park benches; the war cripples, dressed in filthy, tattered bits of uniform, struggling about on crutches and peg-legs; the great housing shortage: in the rooms of neglected buildings from which emanated a sour stench, people lived crowded together, the people who had always lived there and, in addition, many refugees driven by the war from the east of the empire.

In Germany there were terrible shortages too, Elisabeth knew that; but there at least it was not so obvious. In Vienna it was on show in broad daylight: the needy were there to be seen. In this respect Vienna had a touch of the Orient, where people were less inhibited ... Elisabeth felt oppressed by it. All the time she had the feeling she should be helping, but that she did not remotely have the strength to make any real difference.

Her great comfort was the humour of the Viennese which won through in the hardest of times, and their expertise in the art of living. But her separation from Alwin was proving very hard to bear. On September 19 she poured her heart out to Lene Jung in a letter:

> ... this separation! We are robbing ourselves of the best years – it is so cruel to be torn apart in the spring of one's love. And poor old soul – he is so sensitive, his heart must bleed so, and what's it all for? I really admire his courage and strength – he is immensely kind, really touching, and he is fanatically convinced that Vienna is the right thing for me. . . .

Elisabeth herself already knew that she was at a theatre which had no equal, for she wrote in the same letter:

> It's all *Frau ohne Schatten* here at the theatre. The other day I heard a bit of the orchestra – it sounded so beautiful that I felt a shiver down my back. This orchestra and this opera house! I often think I'm at the Metropolitan. The artistic side of it is of course wonderful, and I believe that settling down in any other theatre would be very difficult. Yet I still often think of giving in my notice. . . .

It was the artistic side of things which made Elisabeth stay at the Vienna State Opera. Already at the first rehearsals of *Der Rosenkavalier*, in which she was to make her debut in September, she was deeply impressed by the high artistic level at which work was done here. Franz Schalk sat at the conductor's stand and led the rehearsals. In the light reflected from the score his lean frame topped by the very narrow head, its length exaggerated by the pointed beard, took on a faunlike quality. He had a sharp wit, with which he hit out when things went wrong.

Elisabeth looked on Franz Schalk with awe; he almost seemed to her like Gustav Brecher ten years ago in Hamburg, before whom she had stood on stage as an absolute beginner. She felt almost as anxious as then, even though she was now a great artist. Now, just as then, she had to prove herself. Franz Schalk belonged to a great tradition: he was old enough to have experienced the great days of Mahler here at the opera house. She did not feel immediately at home with him, she did not feel at once that he was satisfied with her; he was much less approachable than Strauss.

One comfort was that there was an old friend in the ensemble: dear, kind Emmerich Schreiner, who had come from the opera in Graz to perform Faninal as a guest performer. Naturally they spoke of Merseburg where the twelve-year-old Elisabeth had admired him and his wife in the opera company from Düsseldorf under Direktor Dörner. That had been almost twenty years ago – it seemed unbelievable. And then, in 1911, the first performance of *Der Rosenkavalier* in Hamburg (in which Schreiner had also taken part). How wonderful that had been, how different from now in Vienna. Here Elisabeth felt she was an outsider, not united in spirit with the others, even though Lotte Lehmann was her Octavian – Lotte, with whom she had spent so many happy times in Hamburg. Lotte had already been here for three years and was completely at home.

Elisabeth's debut drew near. It was the start of the new season and the production had been spruced up, musically and scenically. Thus it was expected that there would be plenty of critics, if not only for the reason that Elisabeth had been engaged without doing a guest performance and they were on tenterhooks to hear her. But Elisabeth feared the public more than the critics. Despite all the destitution in the city, the Viennese were still avidly interested in art and their opera. They hungered after cultural pleasures, and they were more critical than ever because they feared that things might go downhill with their old Court Opera, that they might lose their supremacy in Europe. In the cafés, where chicory was more often drunk than coffee these days, there was much lively discussion about the fate of the Opera and the Burgtheater. The Austrian government, in which the majority were Socialists, had decided that the two theatres should now be run as state concerns. At the Opera Hans Gregor, who had run it for seven years under the monarchy, gave way to Franz Schalk, who had already been principal conductor there for a long time. And now Richard Strauss had joined him as co-director, something which was unprecedented.

Elisabeth noticed that all sorts of everyday people whom she ran into during the days before the performance – the hotel porter, the paper boy, the bank clerk – were interested in the concerns of "their Opera" in a way that she had never noticed in Hamburg. They would probably be unable to afford a ticket to the performance, but the Opera would still be the talk of the town.

By the time the evening of September 4 arrived Elisabeth's nerves were almost unbearable. The thought of waiting for the first act to be over before it was her turn was so awful that at first she thought she might spend that time in her hotel. But in the end the fear of missing her cue made her wait in her dressing room. But she could not sit still; she was on her feet more often than not, walking up and down, singing exercises and passages from her role. Every few minutes she opened the door to hear how far the opera had progressed. At last the interval came, but even that seemed to last for ever. Apparently the house was full.

At last the characteristic draught of air as the curtain went up, behind it the cavernous space of the fifty-year-old opera house. Very quickly Elisabeth's eyes grew accustomed to the half dark out there and she could see the huge semicircle of the auditorium. In great agitation she followed the music to her cue, but she still had time to think: "Metropolitan!" and then she thought: "By the presentation of the rose I must have got over my nerves!"

She managed it, the paralysing fear went, but not as quickly as usual – there was too much at stake. So this time the beloved and so familiar music only gradually became a firm path along which Elisabeth could surely stride. The experienced ears of the Viennese sensed this and a critic wrote:

> Sophie was performed by Frau Elisabeth Schumann . . . a dainty, unpretentious little person with intelligent, roguishly sparkling eyes and a strong personality which, with its charm and unfailing theatrical instinct, might remind one of [Pauline] Lucca. Add to that a talented singer, a singer of great art. From an understandably nervous start Frau Schumann achieved a vocal production of uncommon finesse and nobility. The well-projected piano and sweet head tones of the artist were remarkable . . . She in no way failed the composer in the amount of tender animation of expression and overflowing feeling, and we have not enjoyed such a perfect rendering of the ladies' trio and the final G major duet here . . . since the days of Gertrude Förstel . . . With growing interest, one could say: with growing enchantment we followed the achievement of the newcomer in whom the Operntheater has at last gained another valuable employee, an artist of compelling

individuality. After Frau Schumann's Sophie we would like to hear her Susanna too.

Richard Specht, then a music critic and later Richard Strauss's biographer, wrote of Elisabeth's performance:

Frau Schumann . . . is a joy, a real joy. Here is a musician capable of carrying out exactly the composer's intentions by the finest dynamic variations and slightest changes in rhythm . . . she must be an exceptional Mozart singer (otherwise she would not be able to sing Sophie so "Straussishly"); . . . we have never seen Sophie better acted (this does not say much and it should be mentioned that no singer, not even Frau Schumann, has ever managed to pull off the first scene perfectly . . .). But never before have we heard the role so well sung. The trio at the end was a sheer delight: to this Lotte Lehmann's voice contributed – an adorable Octavian, young, warm-hearted, boisterous and gay . . . Everywhere there were happy faces; nevertheless the applause was weak. . . .

Elisabeth could only attribute the weak applause to the fact that she had not sung well enough or that her style of singing did not suit the Viennese theatre audiences. She still did not realize that the public these first days after the war was no longer largely made up of discerning opera-lovers, but of many people who had been washed up by the tide of the war. The good press notices comforted her somewhat, although in one of them she read with horror that "her organ will gradually have to get used to the colossal dimensions of our opera house" and that there was a certain "coldness" about her voice and acting, perhaps attributable to the northern climes whence she hailed.

Elisabeth wondered whether she would ever be able to sing with the warmth demanded by the Viennese. Her problem was that she did not yet feel the enchantment of the city, and probably never would, since she felt so unhappy here, living as she did in a little hotel with her suitcases not even properly unpacked. She would walk the few minutes to the opera house for rehearsals and performances, and then back again. She hardly went out and about but rested a lot in order to be fit for the evenings. On September 6, two days after *Der Rosenkavalier*, she had to sing again: Micaela in *Carmen*. Carmen was sung by Marie Gutheil-Schoder and Don José by Carl Aagaard-Oestvig.

This time the critics gave an explanation for the lameness of the audience. Elisabeth heaved a sigh of relief as she read:

Elisabeth Schumann is the finest of artists, exactly to the taste of the cultured Viennese public. However, the latter is not to be seen at present in the opera house, which has been taken over by a quite differently orientated audience showing no understanding of the true art of singing . . . Micaela's aria in the third act was rendered absolutely perfectly by Frau Schumann . . . Yet the aria awakened no response. Let us hope that soon there will be true Viennese going to the opera house again, and then the time will come for Elisabeth Schumann, one of the most original and charming artists we have ever had.

On September 10 she had to sing yet another role: Blonde in *Die Entführung aus dem Serail*. The critics described her as a "hit" for the State Opera. Shortly after that, outward circumstances improved for Elisabeth: she at last found pleasant furnished rooms and wrote in her letter of September 19 to Lene Jung.

Thank God I have found two delightful rooms on the Brahmsplatz, kept by a charming old lady; I am moving there tomorrow. It is . . . absolutely quiet and peaceful . . . I am sure I shall feel better there – where one lives makes such a difference to one's well-being, and when Alwin comes it will feel like home.

Yes, Alwin was coming to Vienna, about two weeks later, but not yet for good. Nevertheless it was a step in that direction. Elisabeth had not been idle in her first weeks. She wrote in the same letter to Lene Jung:

I am wild with joy when I think of 7th October – and for ten full days Alwin will be with me, I really can't complain. What's more we are giving an orchestral concert together – my first concert [here] – which I have wangled for him. He's doing a Mozart overture, *Tod und Verklärung* [Strauss], I'm singing Mozart arias, Strauss lieder, his [Alwin's] songs (all with orchestra) and then 4 Wolf lieder with piano as well. Oh, there is a ray of hope, Lene. But on the whole I still feel miserable here.

Alwin duly arrived, and rehearsing for the concert began. They were happy days, full of love, satisfying work and making plans for their possible future together at the Vienna Opera. Until everything was sorted out there were plenty of dramas, especially with the members of the orchestra. Influenza was rampant in Europe and a lot of people suddenly went down with it. The ticket sales were the only thing which seemed to proceed without a hitch: it was obvious that Vienna was eagerly anticipating this concert.

After all their preparations the success of the performance was qualified. One critic complained that the programme had not allowed either of the artists to shine. Nevertheless a critic commented that "Frau Schumann proved herself a Mozart singer of the first water." Yet Elisabeth could not get over her disappointment that her beloved C had not been similarly praised. Not much was thought of his songs. More positive comments were made about his conducting, but one critic hit the nail on the head: "What he lacks is disciplined energy." Energy was something he had plenty of, but it was not controlled: it was constantly being applied to more than one thing at a time and thus dissipated.

On the whole the concert was a disappointment, especially as it had been intended to justify Alwin's possible appointment by Strauss to the Vienna Opera.

On November 10 Elisabeth was due to give a concert in Berlin with orchestra under Arthur Nikisch. This meant the possibility of seeing Richard Strauss. She wanted to ask him about Alwin's situation. By a remarkable chance this was made easier than she expected.

On the day of her arrival in Berlin a messenger brought a letter from the concert management saying that because the railway system was still not working properly Herr Nikisch was unfortunately not going to be able to make the concert in time; Herr Strauss had agreed to take over and she was to contact him immediately. This she did joyfully. In discussing the programme they both agreed that it would be a shame not to take the opportunity of singing some of Strauss's own songs. They decided on " Morgen", "Die heiligen drei Könige" and "Meinem Kinde". They also added Mozart's *Exsultate Jubilate*, which showed off Elisabeth's coloratura so well. Strauss wrote her a cadenza for the first aria. He scribbled it in pencil on the back of a hand-written orchestral part which was not going to be used, and when he gave it to her he said with a twinkle in his eye: "It's not so easy composing Mozart."

This concert in Berlin with Strauss, and also a recital with him on November 19, were in a way a starting point from which Elisabeth rapidly became world famous. It was as if the peace which now reigned was relaxing an iron grip on her existence. Suddenly she could radiate far and wide – the restrictions of war had been blown away. People were still hungry, but they were not hungry only for food: they flocked to the many concerts which were put on every evening. Inside eighteen days Elisabeth herself gave three concerts: the two with Strauss and, on the 28th, one with Alwin, after which a critic wrote: "Schumann has become famous overnight." With those three concerts she truly conquered Berlin. When commenting on her performance of *Exsultate Jubilate* the critics said that she had the purest Mozart style since Lilli Lehmann (who in fact had rediscovered the motet); that "her singing rises out of the subconscious. She does not sing, the singing is in her, flows out of her. In a sense she just stands there, and the miracle happens"; that she and Strauss made a rare duet of conductor and singer in the spirit of Mozart; that Frau Schumann had the Berliners in her pocket.

In between her concerts in Berlin she also sang several opera performances in Hamburg – but at the Volksoper, not at the Stadttheater from which she had been "banished". She sang Adele in *Die Fledermaus*, Eva in *Die Meistersinger*, Marguerite in *Faust* and Elvira in *Fra Diavolo*: her first guest appearances in Hamburg. Even her arch-enemy among critics, Zinne, deigned to compliment her singing, saying that it had gained in warmth and femininity.

Apart from Elisabeth's professional successes and her happiness at being with Alwin in Berlin and Hamburg, there was also another great joy: Richard Strauss discussed with Alwin how he could get him to come to Vienna, making concrete offers and suggestions. The management of the Vienna State Opera began to make arrangements, and without Elisabeth or Alwin knowing anything about it, since they were not there at the time, a big argument began in the Viennese press. In the *Musikalische Kurier*, in an article entitled "Freunderlwirtschaft" which was then also printed in the *Neues Wiener Journal*, Strauss was accused by Max Graf of being a true happy-go-lucky South German who would exercise nepotism for a friend ("Freunderlwirtschaft"), a friend who was a mediocre conductor compared to many other young Austrian talents. It was understandable, Graf wrote, that he would like to engage someone with whom he could play skat after the show, while his wife, Pauline, could have a gossip with Elisabeth. But the reputation of the great Vienna Opera should not thus be jeopardized.

So incensed was Pauline Strauss, that she defended her husband in his absence by having a reply published in the *Neues Wiener Journal*:

> . . . Firstly I have far too much to do to be associating with gossips.
> On the subject of gossip, I would like to suggest that the gentleman

so concerned for the Opera seems to have succumbed to it himself. From a journalist, even if only a music editor, I expect a greater "sense of responsibility". *I declare quite categorically that I have spoken to Frau Schumann precisely once in my whole life*, and that was on the occasion of her concert in the big Konzerthaussaal. She has never been to my house, which indeed I regret, for I think she is a charming person, and I believe that the choice of one's personal friends is nobody else's business. As regards Herr Alwin, I can truthfully maintain that his personal relations with my husband are of a most tenuous nature. The two gentlemen can have as yet spoken very little with one another. Thus it follows that Herr Richard Strauss has never played skat with Herr Alwin and has no intention of doing so in the future. I am not in a position to assess the capabilities of Herr Alwin, but I believe that my husband is at least as able as the writer of the article to judge the qualities of a conductor. The article failed to mention where all these Austrian talents are. My husband will undoubtedly seek them out and secure them for the Opera. The fears of this concerned gentleman, that my husband's "Freunderlwirtschaft" will lower the Opera's reputation, are unfounded; on the other hand it could easily happen that if my husband is annoyed by inaccurate press reports before he has even arrived, *he may well leave Vienna in disgust*. That would be the consequence of "Freunderlwirtschaft", which certainly is not something you will find with us but in the partiality of gossip-columnists.

I thank you in anticipation for your understanding and am

Yours faithfully,
Frau Dr Richard Strauss
née de Ahna

In Hamburg neither Elisabeth nor Alwin had the faintest knowledge of the feud which was being fought about them in far-off Vienna. But their blissful ignorance did not last more than a few days. At breakfast one morning, when C was rustling his way hastily and impatiently through the usual great stack of morning papers in order to read his wife's notices, Elisabeth opened an envelope from Vienna and was horrified as she read a newspaper cutting headlined "Freunderlwirtschaft".

Alwin's first reaction on reading it was: "But I can't even play skat!"

They laughed a lot about the "Freunderlwirtschaft" while Elisabeth was still in Hamburg, but when she was back in her two little rooms at 4, Brahmsplatz, Vienna, she felt for the first time in her life that certain musical circles were hostile to her. She had never before been the victim of such an open attack as in this argument about the appoinment of a conductor. And if she was honest with herself she had to admit that, talented though Alwin was, he naturally did not have the experience or the standing normally needed by a conductor of the opera orchestra, the Vienna Philharmonic.

But Strauss told Elisabeth that he was determined to have him. In the meantime she was forced to remain alone in "this miserable Vienna" until the summer of 1920 when Alwin's contract with Hamburg ran out. They were not even able to spend Christmas together.

It was a gloomy Christmas. What upset Elisabeth perhaps more than anything was that her relationship with Walther had got worse. He had married Hertha Wruck. It seemed that this new union had made him harder towards Elisabeth instead of the opposite. Despite much legal wrangling the situation had not improved by the spring, and by the summer it was a year since Elisabeth had seen her son. The only person close to Elisabeth who occasionally had access to him was her mother. One day she said to C that she would like to have another child to help her to bear the separation from Gerd. In his typically extreme way he declared that to bring children into the world was plain madness. It only caused worry and suffering.

It was Elisabeth's first disappointment in the early part of her marriage with Carl Alwin. She was never able to make him change his mind.

Life brightened up considerably when Alwin arrived in Vienna as early as the beginning of April 1920: he had been released from Hamburg earlier than expected. Until the start of the 1920–21 season he had time to devote himself entirely to Elisabeth and helped her a great deal in her fight for Schnuck. With his great energy and industry he succeeded in making Elisabeth stand firm against all of Walther's obstinate refusals and constantly make new claims. "Perseverance, Elisabethchen, perseverance!" he always cried. And perseverance triumphed, for the authorities decided that Schnuck should be allowed four weeks' summer holiday with Elisabeth in Merseburg.

Before Alwin started to work at the opera house he attended many rehearsals and performances. He had been in quite a number of opera houses before, but such a huge ensemble of so many first class forces such as Bahr-Mildenburg, Gutheil-Schoder, Ivogün, Jeritza, Kurz and Lehmann was as yet outside his experience. These were only some of the sopranos; among the contraltos were Anday, Kittel and Olszewska, and the tenors Maikl, Piccaver and Schmedes. Duhan, Jerger and Weidemann were celebrated baritones; and Manowarda, Mayr and Weidemann dominated the bass or bass-baritone roles. Some of these stars had sung under Mahler. As Mahler had always wanted, even the smallest parts were sung by outstanding artists. It was hardly surprising that Alwin had cold feet at the thought of conducting such a prestigious team. Now it was Elisabeth's turn to do the encouraging.

Elisabeth, Alwin and Schnuck spent their summer holiday in Merseburg, as planned. Schnuck was everything to her in these weeks; life revolved around him. She anticipated his every wish, she wanted him to have the feeling that she, and no one else, was his mother. She tried to squeeze all the love he had missed from her into these few weeks.

At the beginning of August Elisabeth and Alwin were invited to stay with wealthy admirers in Holland and they gave some concerts. The Munich opera festival, at which Elisabeth was due to sing in only one performance, was the next port of call, but when she got there she had to give up any idea of performing as she was completely hoarse.

Back in Vienna Elisabeth still did not feel at home, even though she now had Alwin. He was rapidly finding his feet at the opera house; naturally the protection and support of Richard Strauss was a great help, and his energy carried him along quite successfully.

It was not all that easy having two musical directors at one opera house. Richard Strauss was to add to the prestige of the house by conducting frequently while Franz Schalk, although also conducting a great deal, was more responsible for the organization and running of things. At first Schalk got on well with his co-director, he even conducted the successful première of Strauss's *Die Frau ohne Schatten*. It was not until later that the relationship between the two men deteriorated. Strauss quite often allowed singers to perform at other theatres in order to sing in his works. This led to tension, for Schalk was struggling to cope with a deficit in the opera house's finances, and fewer stars meant smaller audiences.

Elisabeth had already scored huge successes in her first season under Strauss's baton. On December 11 1919 she appeared as

Pamina in a new production of *The Magic Flute*. With that she finally won the hearts of the Vienna public. A critic wrote: "In this difficult role one could for the first time truly admire the good qualities of her noble, cultivated voice and her delightful acting. It was a quite outstanding achievement." Richard Mayr's Sarastro, Hans Duhan's Papageno and Lotte Schöne's Papagena were also praised. Elisabeth was also extremely successful in Korngold's comic opera *Der Ring des Polykrates* which was performed a great number of times.

The first première in which Elisabeth took part in Vienna was Felix von Weingartner's *Meister Andrea* in which she sang Malgherita, the singing niece of the music master, gaining special applause for her coloratura aria. But this opera only had a short run.

Probably her most important role that season was as Despina in a new production of *Così fan tutte* conducted by Richard Strauss. An attempt at achieving the greater intimacy of a chamber opera was made by building the stage out over the orchestra pit, where most of the action then took place. The lights in the auditorium were not dimmed throughout the opera, thus bringing the audience much nearer to the action. A critic maintained that this role was so far Elisabeth Schumann's best and that they had not had such a talented soubrette in Vienna for many a year. She had made it: she was already a star in Vienna in her very first season there. In at least one press notice of the time it was even said that had she been born a man she might well have become a conductor.

But now it was March 1921 and it was Carl Alwin's first night. Elisabeth was not singing (it was a performance of *Aida*), so she sat inconspicuously in a box, suffering the most appalling "stage fright". And unlike when she was performing, once the music started the nerves did not vanish; and she was in such a state throughout, that she was utterly unable to judge the quality of the performance. She had promised to see C in his dressing room at the end. Having no idea whether the performance was good or bad, she had to put on an act of admiration, saying: "C-chen, how beautifully, how wonderfully you do it!" But he was hardly noticing her; he was pacing up and down, repeatedly exclaiming: "What an orchestra, what first-class people – first-class artists!" The press notices the next morning were very good, to Elisabeth's surprise, and at last she felt reassured about Alwin's future.

Perhaps Elisabeth would begin to feel comfortable in Vienna after all, but what she still missed was a proper home. Alwin felt at home between any four walls and there was still a housing shortage, so for a whole year they lived in furnished accommodation: usually flats belonging to other musicians who were away on tour. This unsettled existence began to get on Elisabeth's nerves so much that the management of the opera house looked around for her. They came up with a grand suite of rooms which, as Elisabeth's home, was later to be admired by visitors from all over the world. It lay in the Stallburg in the Reitschulgasse, above the famous Spanish Riding School, in what had been the stable quarters of the Hofburg. The rooms of the apartment were huge and high-ceilinged, with lovely old tiled stoves – the perfect setting for antique furniture, which Elisabeth loved so much and with which she soon filled them.

Every day Elisabeth could watch the snow-white Lippizaner horses being ridden across the cobbled courtyard into the large, baroque riding chamber. She would often follow them in to watch the detailed training of the dressage. She always brought with her some sugar for the horses. One stallion was her particular friend; as soon as he saw her he would go down on his knees and wait for her to give him a sugar lump. One night Elisabeth could not sleep: the wind was howling outside, and she kept thinking of the horses – there was influenza in the stables. Suddenly from below there came the sound of a gunshot. Elisabeth immediately imagined her favourite stallion lying dead in the straw. Next morning she stood at her window watching the horses being led out for training. And then she saw her favourite. Joyfully she sang out his name and hurried down with a handful of sugar. But she had been right: in the night a very sick horse had had to be put down.

When she and C had moved into their new home a wonderful time of domesticity began for Elisabeth. Yet there was one great sadness behind it all: her father would never see this lovely home. . . .

It had been such a happy summer: holidays with C on the Frisian island of Norderney, and her son was with them for all the four weeks. Elisabeth had visited her father for a few days on her way to the sea, and he had seemed in particularly good health. His tiresome asthma seemed to have gone for good. He was enjoying retirement and was very happy to have had the title of Conductor Emeritus of the Merseburg Liedertafel conferred upon him.

During the blissful days on Norderney Elisabeth suddenly received a telegram: "Father very ill. Please come." Elisabeth wanted to set off at once, but the ferry to the mainland had already gone and she had to wait until the next day. Once she was on her way, a second telegram arrived saying that her father had died. So C and Schnuck already knew what had happened, while Elisabeth was rattling across Germany by train. Late in the afternoon she arrived at her parents' home. By this time she knew: a cousin of hers had waited for every train, to meet and warn her. Her father had died of food poisoning. He was laid out in the large drawing room, and Elisabeth thought that she had never seen him look so peaceful. But how sad it was that now he would never see her perform in the splendid opera house in Vienna. That would have been the crowning glory of his life.

And now she was in her beautiful apartment, and he had not lived to see that either. Elisabeth suddenly felt how transient life was: how long would it be before she had to leave this lovely home – perhaps alive, perhaps dead? And the glamour of opera seemed somewhat superficial now; Elisabeth felt an urge to immerse herself more in lieder again: the lied was more soulful, the marriage between poetry and music so poignant.

At the opera house there was someone who could always show Elisabeth where words and music were joined in a unique beauty. He was the répétiteur Ferdinand Foll, an elderly gentleman who had been close friends with Hugo Wolf. His modesty and quiet way made him look like a scholar, but at the piano he proved himself to be technically accomplished and an artist, through and through. He had a way of quietly leading the proceedings while appearing to be subordinate to the singer's wishes. Elisabeth thought it would be sensible to work with someone who could coach her more objectively than Alwin, who admired her too much to be constructively critical. So she worked on song with Foll, usually at the opera house on the evenings when she was not performing. Through him she acquired a greater insight, especially into the songs of Wolf. In her book *German Song*, published many years later, she wrote of Wolf: "More than any of his predecessors, he had imparted a full significance to the poetic element, that is the words, and was thus the true creator of the so-called 'Word-Tone-Song'.* In a radio broadcast in America, shortly after the Second World War, she said: "In Wolf's lied the words assume a new importance. Melody and words are united as one, and he only could set great poetry."

*Max Parrish, London, 1948.

Now Elisabeth really was content. The Vienna Opera was, after all, the greatest opera house in Europe, and she was living in an apartment where princes had once resided – she even had, at last, the longed-for lady's maid. What more could she ask for? But Carl was always on the alert for new opportunities for his wife. He refused to let her get into a comfortable rut. One day he rushed home from rehearsal and told her excitedly that a telegram had arrived from New York which said that a woman was required to sing with Strauss on his tour, instead of the baritone Franz Steiner.

Why could not *she* go! He rang up Strauss, full of enthusiasm. And the maestro agreed at once.

So, in the early summer of 1921, the Viennese read in their newspapers:

Director Dr Richard Strauss and Elisabeth Schumann of the State Opera have been engaged for a concert tour throughout North America. Frau Schumann will leave for New York on 20th October and stay until 10th January in America, where she will sing Strauss works in sixteen concerts.

CHAPTER 9

With Strauss in America, 1921

ELISABETH'S TRAIN rattled its way through the night towards Munich. She took out of her handbag a little blue book, which was to serve as her diary for the tour, and wrote:

> 14 Oct. '21 at 10 o'clock in the evening in a sleeper. Exactly seven years ago today, shortly after the outbreak of the World War, I set out on my first trip to America – at that time from Hamburg. A strange coincidence.

Elisabeth often thought she saw the hand of fate working in a supernatural way. This time it was the magic number seven at play again.

The next day was a dreary one spent in Munich waiting in her hotel for Strauss to join her from his villa in Garmisch. Franz, or "Bubi", Strauss's son, was coming to America with them, but was not joining them until Karlsruhe. Both Elisabeth and Strauss were unhappy at leaving Europe: Elisabeth because of the length of time away from Alwin, and Strauss because he feared the tour would be boring. With that comment he raised his eyes heavenwards in a typical gesture. "Oh well, at least I've brought plenty of manuscript paper with me," he then said cheerfully.

On the platform Clemens von Franckenstein, General Manager of the Munich State Theatres, was there to wave them off. He was to be a lifelong admirer of Elisabeth's and invited her to the Munich opera festival almost every year.

Elisabeth and Strauss travelled through the night in adjacent sleepers, Franz Strauss joining the train at midnight. By the time they reached Paris Strauss had persuaded Elisabeth to come and stay in the Grand Hotel with him instead of the Majestic. "We want to see Paris," he said, "so we must stay together." Strauss loved Paris; everything there was to his taste. For their first lunch he chose

Prunier, where they enjoyed oysters and Elisabeth's favourite: lobster. She praised his choice of restaurant, whereupon he said: "Yes, I'm a good courier, a middling composer and a dreadful theatre director." He was not, however, always so modest: later, in America, he said one evening to Elisabeth: "It is difficult writing endings. Beethoven and Wagner were able to do it. Only the great can do it. I can do it too."

On the evening of their first day Elisabeth summed up its events excitedly:

> After lunch we went at once to the Louvre – wonderful impressions – stood for ages in front of the Mona Lisa too – then by car to the Château de Madrid in the Bois – beautiful drive, coffee – elegant people – discreet music with modern dances – we sat outside "au soleil" – back by car as far as the Place de [la] Concorde from where we walked down to the Seine and enjoyed the view. Strauss spoke about architecture – I admire his many interests – we returned to the hotel – I announced that I had to go to bed or else I would keel over with tiredness ... the Dr ... has just shown me the separate entrance to his bathroom which he says I should use as well. He is so sweet.

The next day they went up the Eiffel Tower:

> Wonderful view – had coffee, Strauss talked about his new ballet, which he wrote in the summer. It is called "Schlagobers" [whipped cream] and he said jokingly: "Oh yes, when one gets old one has ideas like that."

So far the journey was not proving quite so bad after all; there was always something interesting happening. Having embarked on October 19 at Cherbourg, Elisabeth was lying in her rather cramped cabin writing when Richard Strauss knocked at the door. He was wanting her plan of the ship because he had met the great Russian bass Feodor Chaliapin on board; the latter was going to try to find them better cabins. "What fun this is going to be!" Elisabeth immediately noted in her diary. "What interesting company!" But Chaliapin was not often around: "he sits in the Turkish bath all morning," she wrote two days later. But every now and then Elisabeth would play an amusing game of poker, with Strauss, Franz, Chaliapin and the singer Lucrezia Bori. Chaliapin kept calling Elisabeth "Madonna" because she reminded him of a Madonna he had seen in a Russian church.

One day at table the captain asked Elisabeth if she would be willing to take part in a charity concert on board in aid of seamen's widows and orphans; Chaliapin had already agreed to take part. Elisabeth was glad to oblige, and Strauss willingly accompanied.

25 Oct.'21 . . . had great success with three Strauss songs. Chaliapin sang too – wonderful artist – unfortunately not *quite* on top form any more. Then a lady played a violin sonata by Strauss too. Strauss is so delightful and always intent on my success. Before the concert he said: "Why not hold your top notes a little longer, don't always sing so precisely." Afterwards I asked him: "Well, did I sing the top notes long enough?" – "Yes," he said gaily, "but always with a bit of a guilty conscience." . . . He beamed at my success.

Forty hours later, on October 27, the New World was near at hand. It lay somewhere on the edge of the western horizon, the last shimmer of which was fading; at one point, however, it seemed to grow again, like a distant fire: New York, aflame with light!
Elisabeth wrote in her little blue book:

Arrival with all the brightly lit skyscrapers absolutely fantastic – overwhelming impression. I am beginning to feel well and to enjoy the journey. New York is the grandest thing in the world – if only C could experience all of this with me!

They groped their way down the gangway, Strauss with Elisabeth and Franz, accompanied by Diamond, the tour manager who had come aboard to meet them. There were bright lights, and shouts: "Move on! Fine!" Drawling voices. Then there was a whirring sound. People were filming. "You'll be in the movies tomorrow," said Diamond. What, tomorrow already? Jostling reporters, all trying to get near, and asking questions, questions, questions – which the travellers could not understand. To be on the safe side they answered "yes" to everything. "Like wild animals" noted Elisabeth two hours later in Hotel St Regis.

She was already lying in bed as she wrote, enjoying the stability of her bedroom, although it was on the sixteenth floor. The door to the drawing room was slightly ajar so that Elisabeth could see the masses of roses – in "American quantities" – on every small table. Strauss had so many friends here. And there was even a grand piano in the drawing room! In fact they were in the lap of luxury. How poor Europe seemed compared to this. "I feel as if I'm in the land of milk and honey."

The very next day Elisabeth had to start working with Richard Strauss; their first concert was on the following Tuesday, in Philadelphia. It could be quite strange working with the Doctor sometimes: rather grumpily he would sit down at the piano – it made Elisabeth a bit nervous. But in the first song his face would clear. He would nod encouragingly and not interrupt until they had gone right to the end. Only then would he pick out the odd place for rehearsal. He would grow warmer by the minute. At the end he would beam, stand up, kiss Elisabeth's hand and say: "You sing like an angel, like a violin."

But there was not much time to rehearse. Invitation upon invitation flooded in: there were receptions galore. First Diamond's great dinner to which mostly German artists were invited, including the singer Claire Dux and the pianist Elly Ney who were both engaged to perform in orchestral concerts with Strauss. And then, at noon on Sunday October 30, it was out to the Untermyers' beautiful estate by car. It lay in a charming location, high above the River Hudson. There was a garden with little Greek temples, an open-air theatre and wonderful Greek archaeological finds. All this grandeur was hardly surprising, since Samuel Untermyer was the best-known advocate in the land: he had once allegedly been paid £300,000 not to take part in a court case. Strauss's reaction to the marvellous setting was: "Reinhardt must stage 'Midsummernight's Dream' when he comes here next summer." And all those important people! Twenty sat down to luncheon, among them Elena Gerhardt and Artur Bodanzky, the conductor from the Met. In her diary Elisabeth wrote that evening:

> In the afternoon I sang Strauss songs, the new ones ["Schlechtes Wetter", "Einerlei", "Der Pokal", "Waldesfahrt", "Der Stern"] – everyone cheered enthusiastically. Tomorrow Mrs Untermyer is moving to her town apartment which is also in 5th Avenue, very near to our hotel – and we are invited to lunch with her again the day after tomorrow. If it goes on like this we can save a lot of money; so far I haven't paid for a single lunch!

Just a day later there was another big do: a huge reception given by the Mayor of New York. Elisabeth, Strauss, Franz and Claire Dux were driven there, with a police escort, in cars bearing the municipal arms. "Strauss travelled through New York 'like a king'." The front of the Town Hall was teeming with photographers, clicking and whirring.

The guests were crowded into the great hall. Speeches were made including one by the nephew of the composer Karl Goldmark and, of course, one by the Mayor personally.

> Strauss stood up and replied – at first very haltingly – then fluently and full of esprit. He apologized that he was doing it in his mother tongue. But his short speech was translated into English and immediately afterwards read out, whereupon there was tremendous applause.
>
> Strauss was moved by the great honour – he looked quite pale . . . In the evening was the big occasion of Strauss's concert in the Carnegie Hall, which was like a victor's triumph – afterwards we sat up in our hotel room and had a midnight snack.

The next day Strauss was tired and on edge. But the train was very comfortable and the journey to Philadelphia not long. Elisabeth hoped Strauss's mood would have improved by the time of their recital. And sure enough, when the moment came for them to go on stage, he was as calm as he always was before performing. Elisabeth was dreadfully nervous.

> Now I have survived the first concert – it was, thank God, a great and wonderful success. Of the new songs "Schlechtes Wetter" won hands down – we even had to do it again. I was in good voice, but I didn't enjoy myself one bit – I was unbelievably nervous and agitated – oh, this profession! My nerves aren't on top form at the moment. If only it were all over and I were at home! After the concert I ate quite alone with "Richardl" – he congratulated me so sweetly on my success and was delighted. By tomorrow midday we will be back in New York, thank God . . . Now I shall sink dead tired into bed.

Elisabeth's happiness at being able to work with Strauss is conveyed in a letter written to her friend Lene Jung on November 7:

> Warmest greetings from our chase around America. Have already celebrated many triumphs and am happy at my success . . . Everywhere mayors hold receptions for Strauss – this is an important time for me and it is a great joy to be able to tour the New World with this man! And of course we are together all day, we usually share a little apartment in a hotel, and on a personal level it is a particular pleasure to live so close to him. . . .

Strauss made music-making a pleasure. He would radiate calm, and Elisabeth could interpret in the confidence of knowing that the authority of the great man was right behind her. The audience could sense this and were all the more enthusiastic. The concert in Chicago was a good example of this:

Evening of 6.XI.21. Wonderful concert – huge success – the hall had about 4,800 people in it – but a heavenly acoustic. Didn't get at all tired. Countless repeats and encores. [The singer] Mary Garden applauded like mad. Also saw [the conductor] Giorgio Polacco again. After the concert, supper at the German Club. Will sleep well tonight, am pleased with myself today.

Everything with the concerts seemed to go well even when there were problems:

9.XI.21. [In] Pittsburgh terrible rain – impossible to put a foot outside . . . Concert great success – [audience] not as warm as in Chicago. Strauss said: "You sing much too beautifully for these people" . . . The music was missing for the last number, "All mein Gedanken". Strauss said: "I know it off by heart". But he played such a hotchpotch of notes that I can't think how I managed to keep in the right key. Otherwise I was very calm, I wasn't even tired afterwards – I've learnt the trick of pacing myself.

She had discovered that one could sing with less volume, yet focus and project in such a way that the voice carried just as far. It was a good way of saving strength over a long tour. Strauss must have been beginning to feel the strain, as his grumpiness on their arrival in Baltimore on November 10 indicated. One could see it in his angular movements as he stepped off the train. Nothing pleased him. The porter seemed to be mishandling the cases: the bottle of Château Margaux was going to get smashed! Bubi, the idiot, was standing around doing nothing; instead of seeing after the luggage. What did he come on this barbaric journey for in the first place? What a trial and a sacrifice this tour was!

Once in the car Elisabeth asked Strauss how he could think of the tour as a sacrifice considering how many marks they got to the dollar – 180! "Yes, yes," he replied, "I'm only doing it so that I can one day afford to live in Italy again." Elisabeth wondered how he could not afford to anyway, and remembered how he had made Franz clean his own and his father's shoes in the hotel in New York in order to save 50 cents.

Not until the next morning did Elisabeth's cheerfulness get the better of the situation:

113

We were sitting at breakfast – his elbows were working – bad sign – at last I broke the spell and made such fun of everything – especially his scolding of Franz, that we started laughing like mad. Otherwise I couldn't stand it if he moaned all the time. But mornings are a bad time – that I have learnt. At midday his mood clears – then he is sorry about his gruffness – and in the evening he is charming . . .

Somehow Baltimore made Elisabeth's spirits rise. There was a sparkle in the air, a brightness, a cheerfulness. It gave her confidence for the recital, despite the night spent in a sleeping car.

Baltimore is a charming town, and the people are very enthusiastic – it was a colossal success with countless repeats and encores. I was a tiny bit tired . . . but paced myself well. I now know the trick. After the concert there were masses of people in the artists' room – everyone was thrilled. "Yes, that is how we sing in Germany," said Strauss . . . Two daughters of a musical director in Baltimore came to me quite beside themselves. I was sitting on a chair in the artists' room, they knelt on either side of me and kissed my hands. They were lovely young creatures, pretty as pictures.

Elisabeth did not mind sleeping on trains. But the clockwork precision with which the schedule had been planned, and with which it had to be kept, was somewhat trying. It had been planned in order that concerts could be performed in the maximum number of places in the most logical and economical order. Everything was mapped out to the last detail: travel tickets had been bought, sleeping cars and hotels booked, and everywhere there were cars to pick them up and drive them around. Better though this situation undoubtedly was than chaos, Elisabeth nevertheless confessed later in a newspaper interview in Vienna:

In the end I felt more than anything else like a piece of luggage which is transported from train to ship, from ship to car, from car to hotel, from hotel to concert hall.

She thought this efficiency typically American. But there was an unpleasant side-effect to all this precision and punctuality: it ran so smoothly that she did not have to think, and sometimes forgot where she was. In her interview she further related:

Once, to my great regret, I hurt the feelings of a very nice lady. She asked me where I was going to sing the following day, and I said, after careful deliberation, "I think in Baltimore!" "Excuse me," the lady retorted, somewhat piqued, "you're in Baltimore now!"

And this might have gone on into the new year had Elisabeth agreed to a proposal made by the manager, Diamond, that the tour should be extended to Mexico. Strauss said he would not go without Elisabeth, but she absolutely refused, saying that she had arranged to spend a few days in Paris with her husband, besides which she could not bear to stay away from home any longer than planned.

No, she did not want it to go on a minute longer than necessary, even if she had such successes as the one reaped in Boston:

It was a beautiful hall with 3000 people who cheered us on with feeling. And just this town is supposed to have been the most anti-German. It was wonderful, and I enjoyed performing hugely. "You are the greatest German singer we have ever heard" and 1000 other such compliments were paid to me in the artists' room, where we had to sign at least 50 autographs.

I have rarely before seen Strauss so radiantly happy about a victory as the one we won here, for we were both aware beforehand that it was not easy to conquer this city of music.

And the things he said to me: "It could not be sung more perfectly or more beautifully". He almost reminded me of C!

They had time to have a quick evening meal in Boston. "Strauss christened me 'Elobsterbeth' . . . (because I once again had a lobster on my plate) . . ."

They travelled overnight to Philadelphia where they had a rehearsal with the Philadelphia Philharmonic Orchestra for the concert in New York the following day.

15 November '21. The great day is over. I was received with great warmth right from the start – everyone still remembers my "Sophie" 1914–15. The audience vociferously demanded a repeat of "Morgen" – incidentally the first time I have ever done an encore in an orchestral concert. At the end I had to come back on countless times – I can be proud of my success. Was *not* in good voice, I was almost unbearably nervous – did not enjoy singing *at all*.

Afterwards a huge supper at Mrs Untermyer's – was *so* tired – I'm feeling the strain of the last few days very much. Now it's 2 o'clock – quickly to bed.

The next day they were invited to lunch at the Goldmans, friends of the singer Elena Gerhardt, and Elisabeth was very amused to note that Gerhardt, perhaps out of envy, could not bring herself to say a word about the previous day's concert until they were leaving, when she mumbled something hurriedly. A note in the diary reads: "Yes, one's dear colleagues. But I am pleased, I think it is the best kind of compliment."

After a few days of rest, when tiredness really hit Elisabeth worse than ever, they were off on a twenty-five-hour train journey to St Louis. Despite this, Elisabeth was in good voice, and the concert on November 21 was a great success. (Upon their arrival, the local paper had been full of the fact that "The Waltz King is here", with a picture of the statue of Johann Strauss in the Vienna Volksgarten.) That night Strauss and Franz travelled on to Kansas City, where Strauss was to conduct a concert with Claire Dux singing. They tried to persuade Elisabeth to come too, but she was too tired.

Elisabeth felt dreadfully lonely when they had gone; she had to put up with it for four days, and she did not find there was much to write home about in St Louis. At last, at 8 a.m. on November 26, she met up with her companions again at the station. The first thing Strauss said to her was: "Dear Dux has unfortunately become very mannered, I much prefer my Schumännchen."

On the train to Indianapolis they had great fun playing a game of poker: "Took $2.60 off them. Ha, ha!"

Elisabeth liked Indianapolis much better than St Louis: "Quite a pretty town." But on the day of the concert the weather was awful:

27.XI.21. Dreadfully foggy day – you couldn't see a thing. I started the first song full of catarrh – felt that Strauss was laughing at me, turned my head slightly and saw the corners of his mouth near to his ears. I wasn't bothered by the frogs – in fact we were both in such a silly mood. Few people in the hall – virtually performed to ourselves – got through it fantastically so that Strauss said at the end: "One cannot sing more beautifully than that, no, one cannot sing more beautifully than that." Just now we played poker in the train and he told me that I look particularly pretty from the side when singing ... He often says nice things to me, strokes me a lot – he likes me very much.

Now in my sleeper. Tomorrow midday in New York, where I hope there will be lots of post.

Elisabeth was not disappointed: there was a mountain of post which she read and re-read. But at the same time she started to have a sore throat. She *had* to be all right for the concert in Washington two days later, on December 1.

There was nothing for it but to go to bed. Strauss wanted to call a doctor, but Elisabeth knew how to deal with throats: gargling and

116

poultices, and above all, rest. But how could she miss Strauss's concert with Claire Dux! She would have to get up for that. But Strauss would not hear of it: with charm but great firmness he forbade Elisabeth to leave her bed.

The treatment paid off, for Elisabeth's tonsils calmed down enough for Washington, where she went with Franz alone, as Strauss had to conduct in Philadelphia. Fortunately it was not a very taxing performance for Elisabeth as there were other soloists taking part (in her diary the Polish violinist Bronislaw Huberman is mentioned).

The next evening, in Cleveland, the public went mad with enthusiasm, making Elisabeth sing almost another whole concert, what with all the encores they demanded. Strauss was, as always, lavish with his praise. In fact, he often made it sound as if their successes were largely due to Elisabeth's performance, but she knew perfectly well that his reputation and genius played a large part. Later, in Vienna, Elisabeth said in her interview:

> Everywhere one could feel the terrific anticipation with which people regarded Richard Strauss, and nowhere did we feel that these people had come out of snobbery or plain curiosity. Their enthusiasm was clearly genuine, and for the first time in my life I saw, twenty times in succession, concert halls completely packed with people ... I experienced the most wonderful thing in one town where, when Strauss entered the hall, the whole audience, from the front row to the back, stood up. Quite spontaneously and silently.

After the great success in Cleveland Elisabeth could at last have a break in the travel programme. While Strauss had to return to New York for rehearsals, she and Franz made a rushed trip by train and car to the Niagara Falls.

Back in New York there was time to look at some antiques. The art dealers Duveen were at the top of Elisabeth's list: they had just bought Gainsborough's "The Blue Boy" and Reynolds's picture "Mrs Siddons as the Tragic Muse" from the Duke of Westminster for £200,000. "Wonderful paintings, tapestries, carpets ... Strauss said about one carpet: 'If I had that one I would make myself compose lying on the floor' – and he threw himself full length onto the carpet and pretended to scribble away." Unfortunately it did not occur to anyone to present him with the carpet with the compliments of the management.

This carefree day was to be crowned, in this land of prohibition, with a special pleasure. Strauss, Elisabeth and Franz wanted at last to open the bottle of Château Margaux 1888, which had travelled in their luggage for so long, surviving all the perils of a long journey. Laconically Elisabeth noted later: "Strauss gave the bottle to the waiter who brought the wine, the wonderful old Château, in a bowl with pieces of fruit and oranges in it. Strauss said something rude about American waiters."

> Detroit 7.12.21. Arrived 9 a.m. Unlucky day – trunk did not arrive. Had to buy dress, shoes, stockings, while the manager rushed around trying to find music. He only got hold of some of it....

Here was a real panic situation: a concert that evening and only half the music there! In her newspaper interview in Vienna Elisabeth described how they coped:

> I suggested putting one or two Schubert songs into the programme, and Strauss rehearsed them with me in the hotel. He played, then he took his hands from the keys, looked at me and said: "You know, I'll spoil my chances if you sing these wonderful pieces after my songs!" The joke was that the American public, who had come to hear compositions by Richard Strauss, only accorded Franz Schubert a *succès d'estime*.

Elisabeth wondered whether she was singing the Schubert songs to Strauss's liking. But when she asked him rather doubtfully whether he liked her interpretation, he answered: "I'm really not that musical. My ear isn't that precise either."

Not surprisingly the concert proceeded quite differently from normal; one particularly remarkable thing happened:

> Strauss as always completely calm. Thank goodness, because I was rather nervous. But in the evening I was in good voice – great success. I announced each song individually, which the audience particularly liked. Schubert songs "Musensohn", "Frühlingstraum", "Forelle", "Geheimnis" and "Lied im Grünen". We had managed to get various Strauss songs, and some of them Strauss played from memory. He is not a good by-heart-player, and something extraordinary happened in "All mein Gedanken". Already after the third bar he didn't know what he was doing any more and composed an entirely new song. I leapt along with him, the words fitting perfectly, no one in the audience suspected a thing, and when we got to the end I turned my eyes to the right to see what his reaction was. All I saw was him grinning from ear to ear – I really found it hard to find the calm and seriousness required for the next song. After the group we couldn't stop laughing

in the artists' room, and I asked him to write down the new "All mein Gedanken" straight away afterwards, but he replied: "Oh, I've already completely forgotten it. " What a pity! I liked it much more than the original.

On the way to the station afterwards Elisabeth asked Strauss again if he could not write it down. He replied: "It just leapt down the stairs – and no one saw it."

It began to be so routine that the concerts were a success, that Elisabeth began to write in her diary things like: "Successful concert as always". What she began to write about with more emphasis was, for example, the fact that she had arrived dead tired in Milwaukee because she had been tormented by bed bugs in Madison! Even the success in Madison was not of particular note, although the music was still missing and the programme had to be changed again. (This time Strauss practised "All mein Gedanken" beforehand to make sure he got it right!) But one thing never seemed routine: the way Strauss played. "Milwaukee 9.12.21 . . . had to repeat 'Schlechtes Wetter' *three times* – Strauss really does play it like a dream."

But this endless performing began to blunt even Strauss's enthusiasm. Two days later the two of them were giving a concert in Cincinnati at three o'clock in the afternoon. Suddenly Strauss stood up from the piano and walked out, right in the middle of a group of songs. He had mumbled something which Elisabeth had not understood. Should she follow him out? Undecided she remained at the piano. The audience sat quiet as mice waiting for something to happen. The passing seconds seemed like eternity. What was the matter? Had Richard become ill? After a few minutes he was back, seating himself at the piano as if nothing had happened. He explained afterwards, grinning: "My digestion seemed more important to me than the concert."

The next day they were all in New York again for a break of two and a half days. This was much needed, as the second big New York concert was soon upon them.

15.12.21. Huge success in the Town Hall – in wonderful voice – no catarrh, not at all nervous. Am blissfully happy – have telegraphed C. Strauss was beaming . . . Strauss wanted me to do as an encore Otto H. Kahn's [the banker's] favourite song "Mit deinen blauen Augen" – but I was afraid of the low notes and didn't sing it. He was a bit peeved.

119

After an even longer break of six days Elisabeth was again caught up in the excitement of New York musical life, but this time in quite a novel way. She agreed to take part in a trial of that new technological achievement which was so strongly to influence the civilized world and which was to become so important for musicians. The big New York piano dealers, Knabe Pianos, were putting on a musical afternoon, in front of an invited audience, for those new "wireless" machines about which the whole world was talking. In addition, a new kind of player-piano was to be introduced, the Ampico.

So on December 22 1921, Elisabeth Schumann became one of the first great singers ever to sing in a radio broadcast − and it was live, of course. First she performed three songs with Strauss at the piano. Then she sang to some other, played back, accompaniments, which Strauss had just before recorded with the Ampico.

> 3500 wireless sets were tuned in, and I could be heard all over America and at sea. The audience, about 300 strong, were very enthusiastic − a very interesting audience, the cream of society, and all the artists staying here, including [Artur] Schnabel . . . when I sang with his [Strauss's] accompaniment while he was sitting in the audience, he beamed like a child at Christmas.

Christmas had arrived, Elisabeth's second in America. She felt quite lonely. Strauss was conducting in Philadelphia, Franz was out with friends, but in the end Elisabeth spent quite a tolerable evening in a restaurant with Elly Ney, Artur Schnabel and others. The evening ended with them all having a lively chat in Schnabel's hotel room.

On December 26 Strauss and Elisabeth experienced something which had not happened on the whole tour up to then: "In the evening, concert in Brooklyn to empty seats". Not even a Richard Strauss could lure New Yorkers away from their homely hearths on Boxing Day!

For their last concert they set off for the pretty town of Reading in Pennsylvania, where many people of German origin lived. "28.12.21 . . . very lovely concert. Was . . . in good voice. Pretty theatre with good acoustics and very warm audience. Lovely way to finish."

The last few hours before embarking for Europe turned into a mad rush. Not until she was out at sea could Elisabeth breathe easily again and draw a line underneath the tour.

Elisabeth in December, 1907.

Above: Emma and Alfred Schumann.

Below: Elisabeth when she was four, with her elder sister Frieda; and when she was fifte

Elisabeth and her fiancé, Walther Puritz, in 1907.

Above: Her first role, the Shepherd Boy in *Tannhäuser*, in 1909; and as Mignon in 1911. *Below*: As the Goosegirl with Otto Marak in *Die Königskinder* in 1912; and as Aennchen in *Der Freischütz*, in 1911.

As Sophie in *Der Rosenkavalier*, in 1911. ". . . without you the
silver light disappears from the stage".

als Zerline i. „Don Juan"

Above: As Susanna in *The Marriage of Figaro*; and as Zerlina in *Don Giovanni*. *Below:* As Musetta in *La Bohème* – part of her spectacular New York triumph in 1914; and with her best friend, Lene Jung.

Walther Puritz, his duelling scars not yet quite healed.

Below: two views of the Curiohaus in Hamburg, of which Walther Puritz (with Emil Schaudt) was the architect, and where the author of this book was born.

Otto Klemperer in 1915.
(He did not have a beard when he and Elisabeth met.)

31.12.21. Evening, on board the *Olympic*. So Strauss did manage it after all that I should make records with him. He gets so much done on my behalf, and with what tenacity!

In Reading someone asked him when records of him and me would be coming out, and he replied dryly: "Whenever Frau Dux permits it." He told this to the "International" – and this did the trick. For eight weeks we were in America, and on the last morning, two hours before my departure, I had to sing records. At a quarter to 12 I raced on board, at 12 the *Olympic* set sail. It was a frightful rush, I just hope the recordings turn out well [they were in fact never issued]. No one was happier over his triumph than "Richardl", and at our parting [he still had some orchestral concerts to do] he folded me in his arms and kissed me on both cheeks. . . .

Here I shall end this little diary . . . and of you, great man, of you *RICHARD STRAUSS*, I think with a grateful heart and thank you with all the sincerity I can command. You were a wonderful friend – at your side I was protected from all intrigues and manager's tricks.

You were always intent on *my* success, cared for my wellbeing and brought me medicine, like a father to his beloved child. I have got to know you as one of the noblest of people, who supports, with the whole of his personality, the cause of truth and honesty. It was a wonderful time, these two and a half months, being daily, even hourly at your side. You *always* have something to give, even when you are silent.

I am indebted to you for the rest of my life – one day you will see how grateful I am and that I will *never* forget you!

CHAPTER 10

Spain and Vienna, 1922–1924

E LISABETH DID NOT RETURN TO Vienna at once. First there was the
longed-for stay in Paris with Alwin. Despite the cold, it was a
blissful week. On January 16 they travelled together to the early
spring of the Mediterranean, to Spain. Elisabeth was to sing in
Barcelona, but the mild air, deep blue sea, the fascination of this
foreign country, and having C with her made her feel as carefree as
if she were on holiday.

It was not as if the singing posed any problems: she had to perform
Sophie a few times in the Teatro Liceo, and the Spaniards made such
a grateful, music-loving audience. Even though they would whistle
and hiss if they felt a singer was not up to scratch, if anyone gave a
really splendid performance there would be the wildest applause.
Elisabeth had already brought them to this pitch of enthusiasm in
April 1921, when she had first made guest appearances there,
together with Delia Reinhardt as the Marschallin and as Agathe.

Performances in Spain did not begin until half past nine in the
evening, and when the curtain went up the auditorium was almost
empty. Only gradually did the stalls and boxes fill up with the
elegant audience – throughout the whole of the first act. This was
considered to be the done thing, and once they were in their seats
they could not have been more attentive.

Elisabeth was so popular that she was invited back in December
1922. She was again in an ensemble of German singers, among
whom were the baritones Joseph Groenen and Gustav Schützendorf,
and the tenor Rudolf Laubenthal. This time she sang Susanna in *The
Marriage of Figaro* and Eva in *Die Meistersinger*. Later she also sang
in Beethoven's Ninth Symphony, and her beautifully held top B was
so unforgettable that in the following few years she was obliged to
return to Barcelona three more times simply in order to sing in the

symphony. Unfortunately these visits always involved many hours of torment in the slow Spanish trains, which in summer were like ovens and in winter like iceboxes.

It was not long before Madrid wanted her for guest performances too. King Alfonso XIII heard her and invited her for an audience with him. After a stimulating conversation in German (his mother was Viennese), largely about Wagner, he asked Elisabeth if there were a favour he could grant her. Without the slightest inhibition or hesitation she begged with clasped hands: "Oh yes, your Majesty, please get better trains for your country!" Unfortunately not even the King had any influence over the Spanish railways, so Alfonso XIII could only promise laughingly to do what he could.

The years of Elisabeth's guest appearances in Barcelona, 1921, 1922 and 1923, were the beginning of an important new time in her career. Now she was performing abroad at least once a year. In 1923 she was already thirty-five and yet still largely unknown abroad. It had chiefly been the fault of the war, of course. It took a long time before German artists could perform again in former "enemy territory". In the USA, where the war had not been brought home to the people so much, there was relatively little difficulty, but at the Royal Opera House, Covent Garden, for instance, German artists did not perform until 1924, and Elisabeth did not sing in France until she was thirty-eight, in 1926. But a good part of the reason for her lack of foreign engagements was her apathy towards them. She was now so happy in Vienna, why should anyone want to go anywhere else? Vienna seemed to be the centre of the musical world. Every evening there were several concerts to choose from: the subscription concerts given by the Vienna Philharmonic under Weingartner and later Furtwängler, those given by the Vienna Philharmonic Choir under Franz Schreker (who had founded the choir in 1908, and conducted it singing many first performances of modern works, such as Schönberg's *Gurrelieder*), and those given by the Vienna *Singakademie* under Bruno Walter. People came from far and wide to witness the musical sensations occurring in Vienna. Elisabeth was, of course, one of the magnets which drew them to the capital, and not only as Susanna, Sophie, Zerlina, Blonde, Micaela, Mimi and Eva. She, too, was involved in concert activities. In addition to her recitals with Richard Strauss, Franz Schalk engaged her for his big oratorio performances, such as Bach's *St John Passion* and the *German Requiem* by Brahms. Yet Schalk might have been expected to ignore Elisabeth: he was getting more and more into conflict with his co-director, Richard Strauss, with whom she was linked as a friend as well as artistically, and who had said about her to her friend Lisa Reitler:[*] "I would give the whole opera for one note from Schumann." (Naturally Carl Alwin was also uncompromisingly in the Strauss camp if there was ever any difference of opinion.)

As far as her profession went Elisabeth had a very full life in the city on the Danube, and her private life was almost fuller. So many important people lived in Vienna or visited it, and Elisabeth was constantly meeting new admirers and old friends. Apart from the many musicians in Vienna, she came to know writers, such as Hugo von Hofmannsthal and Stefan Zweig, and politicians, ministers and diplomats – even princes and kings, such as Ferdinand of Bulgaria. She often invited people to her home in the Hofburg: in fact she was seldom without guests when she was at home and not performing. Some evenings were hilarious, as, for instance, when she, C and one or two colleagues from the Opera were invited to the Becherts, a manufacturing family. Alfred Jerger was there – the baritone so wonderful in the roles of villains such as Scarpia – and so was the contralto Rosette Anday. Suddenly Elisabeth started to mimic the progress of a singing lesson: the teacher puffed up with importance at the piano, demonstrating with scratchy voice; the humble pupil, trying to imitate faithfully with a constricted little sound. Everyone then laughed, then someone else started to sing, not an aria or song, but the conversation going on during the "lesson", as it were in recitative. The others joined in in similar vein, and the "conversation" continued, in improvisations and known melodies. C rushed to the piano and made up an accompaniment; someone tapped a glass rhythmically; another ran to the kitchen and fetched pot and frying-pan – excellent musical instruments in the right hands. After several minutes of heavenly cacophony the musicians suddenly got quite out of tune and rhythm with each other and gradually faded into silence – the last sound echoing round the room being the "bong, bong" of the frying-pan. Gales of laughter followed.

So what was there to attract Elisabeth away from Vienna? She was a star of the Opera, well-known interpreter of Strauss songs, had a princely home, dear friends and a loving husband, who protected and idolized her. While he would prevent her from overtaxing herself

---

[*]The wife of Milan Reitler, Elisabeth's banker in Vienna.

at concerts – giving too many encores, for instance – Alwin was nevertheless ambitious for Elisabeth. Once she was back from America and Spain he made sure that she bestirred herself again. A Strauss recital for Berlin was arranged, C was to accompany and it was to be at their own expense.

A Berlin critic wrote:

> The warm appreciation with which Frau Schumann was received and the thunderous applause which followed the performance of every song proved she is valued here as a lieder singer and in particular as a competent Strauss interpreter in the fullest sense of the word.

In fact, Elisabeth sang one or two passages differently from the way they were written, as for example in "Freundliche Vision". Small changes had naturally developed on the American tour: as he worked with Elisabeth, Strauss had sometimes changed his mind about phrasing.

The critics noticed nothing. But one day, at a social gathering in Vienna, Elisabeth met the Dutch lieder-singer, Julia Culp; C was there too and the song "Freundliche Vision" came up in conversation. Elisabeth demonstrated the passage which she sang differently: "*Hell am Tage sah ich's schön* (breath) *vor mir: eine Wiese* (breath) *voller Margeriten*." [In the brightness of day I saw it beautiful (breath) before me: a meadow (breath) full of marguerites]."

Frau Culp was amazed, even indignant that she did not sing the correct phrases: "*sah ich's schön vor mir*: (breath) *eine Wiese voller Margeriten*."

When Elisabeth explained that Strauss had said she should sing it her way, Julia Culp replied, short and to the point: "If I sang it like that people would start throwing rotten eggs!"

That stung, and in a moment Elisabeth and Frau Culp were locked in verbal combat. It became so heated that C leapt to the piano and played the *Ride of the Valkyries* as loud as he could. He did it so amusingly, and drowned the battle cries so effectively that the combatants could not hear each other any more and burst out laughing.

Although the critics did not seem to notice the new phrasing, one of them did notice something else: "Extremely enjoyable though it was, the attentive listener could not have failed to notice a slight tiredness in the beautiful voice of the singer."

It was hardly surprising really: after getting back from the USA and Spain Elisabeth had had to make up for her absence with many opera performances and concerts. Fortunately the summer holidays arrived.

They were spent in St Wolfgang in the Salzkammergut. It was not far from Vienna and near to Salzburg too, to the music festival – due to start at the beginning of August (1922 was the first year in which the Salzburg Festival was to be a music festival). But thoughts about performing there had to be pushed aside for the moment: now it was time to enjoy the peace and quiet of Lake Wolfgang.

Schnuck was there! He was staying for four weeks. The whole of the last year they had seen each other hardly at all. Elisabeth had for some time been turning for help about Gerd to Walther's wife Hertha, she had even put her under a slight obligation by arranging for free tickets for the Hamburg Opera to be sent to her. But even without this, Hertha understood what sorrow the separation from Schnuck was causing Elisabeth; for two years now she had been a mother herself, she had a little girl of her own. So every now and then, when talking to Walther, she put in a good word for Elisabeth. It was high time she saw her son more than once a year. He was eight now, and to him his mother was a distant fairy godmother who sent him wonderful presents.

Once or twice during their stay Elisabeth and Schnuck inadvertently offered their neighbours an amusing entertainment. People suddenly stopped their hay-making when they heard a woman's voice singing very high, bright notes, running up and down and as clear as a zither. And then a piping child's voice. Then they saw a lady coming round the corner with a boy. She stopped, put the boy's hand on her stomach, and sang quite delightfully; whereupon the boy held his own stomach and tried to produce similar beautiful notes. Elisabeth was teaching Schnuck how to sing one of the Queen of the Night's coloratura arias from *The Magic Flute*.

Schnuck grasped it quickly and Elisabeth was so enchanted she could not stop telling everyone: "This little chap can sing the Queen of the Night – at the right pitch!"

It was such a joy to have Gerd with her! She wrote to Lene: "He is so sweet, and I'm particularly glad that he is so attached to C – he hugs and kisses him ten times a day. . . ."

One day they crossed the lake to Bad Ischl, the elegant spa resort where the Emperor Franz Joseph had often stayed. As they were walking through the town Elisabeth suddenly cried: "But that's Rosé!" It was indeed Arnold Rosé, the leader of the Vienna Philharmonic Orchestra, and well known for his string quartet. Schnuck could hardly greet the gentleman properly, his eyes were fixed on the girl standing behind him – his daughter Alma. She certainly was the loveliest sight: brown hair framed an unusually animated face in which shone big dark eyes, so warm and friendly that one felt immediately drawn to her. The eighteen-year-old girl began a conversation with Schnuck, and he was simply enchanted by her personality. Elisabeth observed this with delighted astonishment, and at once she knew what he was feeling. She promised him that they would go to Alma's afternoon concert in Wolfgang in a few days' time.

They had seats in the front row so that he could see Alma well. She looked charming in her white dress, playing the violin so gracefully and beautifully. Schnuck wandered about in a dream afterwards, even on the next day too. He was in love! It was just as well that he was now off to Salzburg. They set off on August 5.

The town of Mozart's birth delighted Elisabeth at first sight: there could be no more beautiful town in which to celebrate the music of Mozart, her ideal. This visit in 1922 also meant her longest reunion with her mother since her father's death. Sixty-year-old Emma seemed astonishingly self-possessed and serene; Elisabeth realized that it was due to the release from the worry of nursing an asthmatic. Schnuck, too, was delighted with his grandmother who seemed to know so many card games. Once she had taught him several, he wanted to play wherever they were, even at the opera before the curtain went up for *Così fan tutte*.

But then the music enveloped him and there was a whole new world in front of his eyes – a great magic world, and in it the woman he called "Mummy". Now she really was a fairy godmother.

The success was boundless. Many, many times the singers had to reappear before the curtain with their conductor, Richard Strauss – again and again. Schnuck was allowed to watch from the wings and was surprised that Strauss was always there too. He said to him: "Why are you bowing as well? You haven't done anything!" To which Strauss replied: "Quite right, little lad, I've done nothing!" Perhaps he was partly serious; perhaps he had felt what a miracle the place they were in had wrought on the performance.

To be celebrated in Salzburg was quite special for Elisabeth. They were hardly any distance from Vienna yet they were performing to an international audience. Renown here meant world renown.

Her awareness of this may have played its part when, shortly after the Salzburg Festival, Elisabeth showed that she knew who she really was. In the following season in Vienna there was to be a new production of *Don Pasquale*, not in the opera house but in the ballroom of the Hofburg, where, during the time of the Kaiser, many masked balls had been held. One could not imagine a more beautiful setting for the old opera than this room with its magnificent tapestries and chandeliers. What was more, it lay in the same wing of the Hofburg as Elisabeth's apartment, which meant that she would be able to get into her costume and do her make-up at home and then slip through the corridors to the ballroom, as ladies and gentlemen must often have done in the past. The whole thing was a charming idea.

Then came the blow. One lunchtime C, who always had the latest theatre news, came home even more hastily and excitedly than usual (on arriving home he would always tear open all the doors calling hoarsely: "Elisabethchen! Elisabethchen!"), with the woeful tidings that she was not to sing in *Don Pasquale* at all until later on. Ivogün was singing. Elisabeth was only to take over when Ivogün was gone. Second cast!

At first Elisabeth took it calmly. But when she started to think about it the situation began to rankle. She had been in Vienna three years now, and her roles were always Sophie, Susanna, Zerlina, Marcellina, Micaela. Here was a new role at long last, and what happened? – she was placed in the second cast!

Strauss was in Garmisch so Elisabeth went straight to Schalk and protested. Not long after that a letter came from Strauss:

Garmisch, 23.10.22

Dear Schumännchen!
Direktor Schalk has told me of your complaints and justified wishes. I am in complete agreement about complying with your request for new roles . . . I hear that you have refused to sing after Ivogün. I most earnestly entreat you to reconsider on the following grounds: the performances in the ballroom need to have a sensational start if they are to continue to be a box office draw for some time. Works like *Figaro* and *Barber* do not usually need this. Not so with the weaker *Don Pasquale*, for the première of which not even the best house cast would be sufficient to cover costs in such a place as the ballroom.

Therefore I decided on the engagement of Ivogün who, with such a rare guest appearance in Vienna, would give the première enough sensation to allow 30 more performances in the ballroom with the equally good house cast. These are not artistic considerations but purely business ones. I beg you to respect these and to declare yourself willing after all to sing *Don Pasquale* after Frau Ivogün without feeling slighted, which is the last thing we would want.

Please be the good and sensible artist you always are! Please co-operate: I promise you that everything will be done to compensate in other ways.

With warmest greetings from all of us . . . to you and Alwin,

Your ever sincere and devoted

Dr Richard Strauss

Almost immediately Elisabeth's feelings changed. If that was the reason, these business considerations – well then. . . . Had she not vowed never to forget what he had done for her? And how near to his heart her wishes always seemed to lie!

Constant deprivation of her child was a far deeper cause of any unhappiness she might have felt at this time. Schnuck was now a real little person, a friend, and she hardly ever saw him except in the summer. Then, early in 1924, something happened which made Elisabeth and Walther suddenly start writing to each other very frequently: Gerd had developed slight tuberculosis in the glands and one lung. Elisabeth urged that no expense be spared and that they should both talk to the doctor about sending him to a highly recommended resort in Switzerland, Madulein in the Engadin.

For the first time in seven years Gerd's parents met. This, and meeting Hertha, posed no problem to Elisabeth whose chief concern was for the health of her child. She and Walther went together to consult the specialist, whose surgery gleamed with the latest X-ray equipment.

When the doctor greeted Elisabeth very warmly and took far less notice of Walther she realized that here was a fan, and that he would undoubtedly do all he could to help her. The two of them chatted amicably about Elisabeth's days at the Hamburg Stadttheater, and it was not long before they had agreed that Schnuck should go to a children's home in Madulein for a whole year.

Elisabeth and Walther parted again on the best of terms. Four weeks later Emma Schumann came to Hamburg, picked up Gerd and took him to Switzerland.

Thus it was that the spring of 1924 had brought about a change in Elisabeth's personal life.

CHAPTER 11

Italy, England and Vienna, 1924

WITH THE YEAR 1924 the really great time of Elisabeth's career began. She now embarked on fifteen years of intensive music-making in Europe and overseas, beginning with concerts in Rome.

Even Italy, favoured as it was with such beautiful singers, could no longer disregard the nightingale from the north. But Elisabeth was gripped with anxiety when the call came: such a musical people, such a discerning public! They were known to be keen whistlers, the Italians, especially if one did not sing in the Italian way. Into Elisabeth's despondency C flung his protest: "*World class* is what you will show the Italians, Elisabethchen! They'll like you so much they'll want to eat you."

There were to be two concerts: one in the big hall of the Augusteum with the conductor Bernardino Molinari as accompanist; the other in the charming little Sala di Santa Cecilia. In the latter at least, C would have to accompany her: to sing in Italy without his help – impossible! And the programme should include only those items with which she was assured of success, especially Mozart; and a few Strauss songs: not many could better her in those, she felt. And her voice: an overhaul was essential. Alma Schadow would have to come.

Elisabeth went to considerable expense by asking her teacher to come to Vienna so that she could work with her every day for two weeks. All because she had to sing two concerts in Italy!

The huge hall in the Augusteum was filled to capacity; part of the audience was sitting on the platform. Even members of the Italian royal family had turned up. Elisabeth was beside herself with nerves. As soon as she was on the platform it seemed to her that the Italians were only waiting to pick holes in this German singer from that hated old enemy, Austria. But as she turned to Molinari to give him the sign to begin, she saw in his look nothing but admiration and confidence. And things could not have started better: there was rapturous applause after each song.

Then Elisabeth felt she would like to sing to the people on the platform, as she often did in crowded halls. So before the next song she turned round. Suddenly there was a murmuring and whispering in the audience. What was the matter? Was there something wrong with her dress? She kept calm and continued with the concert. At the end the audience went mad with enthusiasm, and, after endless encores, Elisabeth sank exhausted onto the sofa in the artists' room. C was already waiting for her and bubbling over with things to say: it was unprecedented! Rome was shaken to its foundations. The greatest success of all time. And his Elisabethchen had simply turned her back on Their Royal Highnesses! All Rome was staggered!

So that was it! She had turned her back on royalty. It had not occurred to her. What would they think of her now?

The Italian critics were gallant and made no mention of the incident. "The Helen of Song", they called her. The public had also enjoyed tremendously the Schubert and Strauss songs which she sang in her second concert. According to Vienna "the whole of the Italian press is in agreement that Elisabeth Schumann is one of the most outstanding foreign singers to have charmed the public of Rome for many years. . . ."

Rome, the eternal city, had a stimulating effect on Elisabeth. For a start there was the language. She often had to sing in it, and now to hear it live was a pleasure. The people were so full of life and song, everywhere one seemed to hear beautiful natural singing voices and a great musicality in the simplest of people. And the antiquity – revealed in such splendour! Every spare moment she had, Elisabeth would wander among the ancient sights of Rome. With awe she visited the café where her beloved poet Goethe had sat writing in 1786 – he must also have drunk in all this beauty, one hundred and thirty-eight years before.

The scores of churches were unspeakably beautiful; it was part of the life of many Romans to spend time in them in contemplation and prayer. This made Elisabeth pensive. At that time she was not yet a believer. There was a Creator, she was convinced of that; a Steerer of Fate; but further than that she could not go. It was not until she lay on her deathbed that she believed, without knowing how near death was. But now in Rome, years beforehand, she was briefly touched by faith.

There was the chance of a private audience with Pope Pius XI. A gentleman from the Austrian legation informed Elisabeth that he could arrange things with the Vatican. She was utterly thrilled with this great honour, and to be able to see the private apartments not open to the public.

When she walked into the audience chamber with C, it was quite different from what she had expected. She could never really describe it later; she could only speak of a great and deep impression. Probably the Pope's personality played a large part: the head of this eminently learned man looked so intellectual; his eyes and gestures spoke of a true priestliness; and he was able to communicate with them in their own language. But that was not all. Suddenly Elisabeth was surrounded by a world of which she had never had any concept, but which was now so real and so powerful.

When the Pope gave her his hand, she bent over the signet ring and kissed it. No one had expected that she, as a Protestant, would follow this custom. But she wanted to touch St Peter's seal with her lips.

Elisabeth was somewhat given to imagining problems ahead. In Rome she had just had the greatest success of her life; now came a summons from the Royal Opera House, Covent Garden, in London – and again she had doubts. They were planning to put on Wagner and Richard Strauss during a "German season", the first really "German" season since the war. And she was to sing the Composer in *Ariadne auf Naxos*, and Sophie. If only she did not have to sing the Composer, a role which she did not know well, in front of those cool English people! Luckily C would be conducting *Ariadne*, and would be able to help her a lot. She would sing Sophie under Bruno Walter; that was no problem, she had sung it with him in Spain. Perhaps it would be rather fun after all: Lene Jung was coming too, to sing Annina and Dryad, and also Lotte Lehmann, to sing the Marschallin. But she still had terrible misgivings.

The contract had arrived, and C kept saying every few minutes that she must sign, that this was the chance of a lifetime. England was an important country, very important!

Elisabeth signed and, feeling so unsure of herself, decided to study the Composer with Gutheil-Schoder who was so famous in the role.

But as yet there was no time to study the role in earnest: first she had to go on a whirlwind tour of Germany: on March 25 a recital in Pforzheim; then a dash to Hamburg to see her child and talk to Walther about his health; in between she sang Mimi in Lübeck; on April 3 a recital in Hamburg with "Egonek" (Egon Pollak) accompanying wonderfully at the piano; then Dortmund, Cologne, Frankfurt and Berlin. Despite all this toing and froing, and success after success, dear old Merseburg was not forgotten, even if it did come last. And C was accompanying.

Elisabeth was to sing in Merseburg's casino! For weeks this had been the talk of the town, and at seven o'clock on April 16, despite pouring rain, it was pouring people – into the casino. The local paper reported the following day:

> Everyone with musical feeling and a feeling of pride for their home town wanted to be there when the great Elisabeth Schumann sang, the daughter of our town, of whom we are all proud, because she proves wrong the malicious rumour that nothing good ever comes from Merseburg ... after the first bars of the heavenly first [Handel] aria we were already done for ... the four Strauss songs at the end were anticipated with great excitement.... One had the impression of a perfect rendering, as if, in the case of paintings, one had for a long time had to make do with looking at reproductions, and now suddenly one was confronted, in all its freshness of colour, with the original, which disclosed infinitely more depth and detail than one could have guessed at.

At the end "Lisbeth" was greeted with cheering and storms of applause. Even outside the casino people thronged around her. "Hurrah!" they cheered when seeing her off with a huge bunch of flowers at the railway station. When the train began to move and Elisabeth sang "Lebetwohl! Lebetwohl!" out of the window, the good people forgot their respectability completely. Elegant ladies cried "Lies, Lies!" and waved their handkerchiefs ecstatically, and worthy gentlemen ran with the train, tore the hats from their heads, threw them up in the air and shouted "Hurrah!"

But London! It still hung like a millstone around Elisabeth's neck, and no sooner was she back home in Vienna than she started studying the role of the Composer with Marie Gutheil-Schoder. She got her to demonstrate every gesture, every expression, every smile, and memorized them rigidly.

She gradually began to feel more confident about London, but right up to the last moment she would rather have been able to wriggle out of this engagement in England – where her voice, her artistry was to become proverbial! Shortly before going there she had to sing in Switzerland, caught a cold and telegraphed C in London: "Bad cold cancellation possible?" He flashed back: "Impossible. Singing absolute must."

She went.

Was this what they called London – these endless rows of sooty, yellow-brick workers' houses next to the railway line? One terrace as miserable as the next, for miles.... In the city centre it was better: here and there imposing buildings, and a whole lot of lovely parks, and every now and then a grandly laid out thoroughfare; but only now and then, not like Paris. London seemed so untidy, much too sooty and higgledy-piggledy to be the capital of an empire. But there was also something solid and dignified about it.... And was this the Royal Opera? A house which did not even stand in an attractive open space, but was surrounded by the bustle of a market, by lorries with fruit and vegetables? Men were hurrying to and fro with carts piled high with potato sacks and orange crates. Tomatoes and cabbages were rotting in the gutters. Could the *Royal* Opera really be here? Could it really hold a discerning public? What *had* she been worrying about? As long as her cold did not slip down to her chest she would be all right. And *Ariadne* was not to be performed until she had sung *Der Rosenkavalier* three times.

Nevertheless Elisabeth worked very hard at the rehearsals. Lotte Lehmann, the Ariadne (but who had successfully sung the Composer in the world première of the opera in Vienna in 1916), watched her for a bit. Finally she said to Elisabeth: "All that acting you're doing – I never did any of that!" But Elisabeth was not put off, replying merely: "Every step from Gutheil."

Der Rosenkavalier was back at Covent Garden for the first time since 1914. This was a great occasion for London. May 21 1924, seven o'clock. The carts of cabbage and carrots had vanished. In their place all was elegance, as carriages and luxurious motor cars rolled up – not, however, without having to negotiate mounds of earth and deep ditches, for in honour of the start of the opera season the local authorities had decided to dig up the roads around the house, in order to make access as difficult as possible. "But Britons are made of stern stuff," wrote *London Opinion*, "and aren't to be put off by little things like that – unless, of course, the musical fare offered were English instead of German!"

135

Elisabeth had time during the first act to scrutinize the audience from the artists' box. What unbelievable elegance! All the men in dinner jackets. What an example to the Viennese! And the ladies with their incredible jewels – their dresses were not, perhaps, very chic, but the pearls and diamonds, and the wonderful tiaras in their hair! What a rich country this must be – an empire, in fact. Ladies and gentlemen were taking their seats in the royal box: Princess Beatrice and her guests.

Elisabeth was overcome by a wave of acute stage fright. That was what the unusual atmosphere did to her, this rich, glittering audience in this unremarkable opera house.

Nevertheless, this strange house was inspired to applaud with an enthusiasm which Elisabeth had seldom heard on the continent. A critic even wrote: "I have never heard the house 'brought down' as it was after the final act of *Rosenkavalier*. No one can accuse us of being insular where music is concerned." Yet some of the beauty of the opera did seem to have passed them by. How could they otherwise dismiss the role of Sophie in a few words? It was true that all agreed that the performance had been good, but *The Daily Telegraph* wrote of Sophie: "Miss Elizabeth* Schumann looked well and sang well as Sophie von Faninal." And *The Manchester Guardian*: "Mme Elizabeth Schumann sang Sophie most beautifully, and managed to infuse life into the rather colourless character."

Colourless character! thought Elisabeth indignantly. A naïve young thing, fresh out of a convent – Hofmannsthal and Strauss could not have depicted her better! And *The Morning Post* seemed to think the role should be sung more earthily: "Frau Schumann made a pleasant Sophie von Faninal, though one feels that her voice owes rather more to art, or at least less to Nature, than should that of the perfect singer."

Elisabeth bore no grudge. She had heard that foreign languages were not the forte of the English, and the beauty of Hofmannsthal's libretto was all-important in the appreciation of *Der Rosenkavalier*. And the English were so kind, polite and helpful, without imposing in the least; and everywhere one heard the word "sorry". How funny this seemed! "Sorry" meant "sad". So they were "sad" if they had not noticed you coming through the door behind them, "sad" if they touched you by mistake, or if they had run out of something in a shop!

---

*Elisabeth's name had been mis-spelt in the programme.

The shops were simply marvellous and inspired many a spree. Elisabeth and Lotte bought so much that they spent virtually the last of their money on extra suitcases to accommodate it all. Their friend, Maria Olszewska, also singing at Covent Garden, declared that they would end up in the gutter.

In fact living in London seemed quite pleasant, especially the feeling of great personal freedom. Otherwise the many parties to which one was invited from morning to night would have been unbearable. Everything was always so relaxed, one was never pressured into doing anything or staying longer than one wished.

Elisabeth was able to enjoy the next two performances of *Der Rosenkavalier*. On one of these evenings the last act could be heard live on wireless sets all over England. Even the role of the Composer went much better than Elisabeth had feared, *The Times* deigning to say that "it was beautifully sung by Mme Elizabeth Schumann". Another critic wrote:

> . . . in the prologue the noticeable feature was the singing of Elisabeth Schumann of the Composer. . . . As the action takes place very far back on the stage, and the orchestra was consistently too loud, the point of the jokes on the stage was mostly lost nor did Herr Alwin bring out much of the humour of the music.

On the whole poor C was pulled to pieces; almost nowhere did the critics have a good word to say about him. Bruno Walter enjoyed a wonderful press, perhaps because he was much better known. Unfortunately the two men did not get on well and had some quite heated rows, Alwin's self-assurance and lack of diplomacy no doubt contributing strongly. It was amazing to Elisabeth how self-confident he always was. Was this because he felt he had Strauss behind him? Yet even in Vienna he was regularly squashed by critics, especially Julius Korngold, who would criticize anyone who had anything to do with Strauss, even Elisabeth (it is possible that he resented the fact that his son, who was an accomplished composer and had been a prodigy as a child, did not get Alwin's post as conductor at the Vienna Opera). It was a sad fact that Alwin had rarely enjoyed good write-ups while working at any of the really prestigious opera houses. But to perform *Ariadne auf Naxos* after just a few rehearsals with an orchestra not in the Viennese tradition. . . .

Vienna. Elisabeth did begin to miss the warmth of the Viennese.

Londoners seemed so reserved. She felt that if she were to walk naked down the street no one would turn round. When the weather or animals were involved, however, they were quite different. One day Elisabeth saw a lady leading two Pekinese and could not stop herself from exclaiming with delight, managing to have a little chat with their mistress too. Elisabeth found the little round heads and the big brown eyes, with their look of loyalty and a little melancholy, particularly endearing. The thought of having such a little creature at home to look after was quite irresistible (her maid Luise could look after it when she was away). So she visited a breeder and bought a ten-month-old Pekinese. She called him Sorry in memory of her days in London.

Sorry, who to Elisabeth's delight attached himself to her very quickly, nevertheless did not seem to like leaving his homeland when the time came for Elisabeth, C and Lotte to return to Vienna. By Calais he had lost his appetite, and by Paris he had a high tempera-ture. They left the train in Paris to visit friends. Elisabeth hardly greeted them, all she could say was: "Someone must 'phone for a vet" echoed by C's: "My kingdom for a vet!" The vet diagnosed distemper, injected Sorry and prescribed "absolute rest". Elisabeth was beside herself. How could he rest when she had to leave for Vienna that very evening? They had a performance schedule to meet. The vet took C aside and said: "Monsieur, he is very ill, but I should give your wife a tranquillizer if I were you, she's in a worse condition than the dog!"

They had no choice but to travel on that night. The journey was terrible. Lotte had the berth above Elisabeth's. Neither she nor Elisabeth got much sleep those two nights. C, who had a berth in a nearby compartment, haunted the corridor driving the steward mad. "Hot water! Cold water! Some cotton wool, please! A towel!" All for a dog. It was enough to make a cat cry. Every few minutes C put his head into the compartment and cried: "Is he dead yet? If he is, throw him out of the window!"

But Sorry survived and quickly settled down in Vienna. Soon he was running between the legs of the huge Lippizaner stallions as they trotted daily across the courtyard. Whenever she called her dog Elisabeth was reminded of England, the country which was to become so important in her life. She had brought a bit of England with her, but not only in a canine form: to the surprise of her frequent guests she began to have her dinner table laid in the English fashion – with mats on the polished wood instead of a tablecloth.

Elisabeth was just thirty-six, and, despite feeling as young as ever (especially after a rigorous diet which she had imposed on herself for London) she disliked people seeing her date of birth in her passport, which one had to show so often these days, not only at borders but on occasion to any Tom, Dick or Harry of a civil servant. By means of a charming chat with a gentleman at the German Embassy in Vienna she was able to have the date of birth in her passport amended to June 13 1891. What a relief! Now, at least officially, she was three years younger. (In later years she even refused to give her date of birth to *Who's Who*.)

She needed to feel young. After the strain of London there was a lot to sing in Vienna. Then just four weeks holiday and at the beginning of August the Munich opera festival began, with, in between, a couple of performances in Salzburg. C was particularly overworked. "C is desperately busy, he's still got to put on the Bittner première [*Rosengärtlein* by Julius Bittner] on June 28 – madness! I wish it was all over – C really needs a rest," wrote Elisabeth to Lene.

After all the grind there was the sarcastic write-up by Julius Korngold attacking Alwin's première: ". . . The orchestra played under Herr Alwin, the reputable Bittner conductor. . . ."

Alwin knew there was no point in getting annoyed; this was simply a case of personal antipathy towards anyone in the Strauss camp – in a way almost a compliment. Even Strauss himself had the odd poor write-up: the Viennese critics absolutely slated the première of his ballet *Schlagobers*, whereupon he resentfully declared that he no longer wished to première his works in Vienna: his new opera *Intermezzo* (based on incidents in his private life, and for which he had himself written the libretto) would be performed in Dresden. He could hardly be blamed if he thought the Viennese ungrateful. In the five years he had been there opera had blossomed: the artists enjoyed working with him and the audiences packed the house. Times were uncertain, and while money was losing value, art seemed to gain it in the eyes of the people. Now, in 1924, money had become somewhat more stable, and the financiers, to many of whom artistic achievement was of little significance, were bustling about again and gaining the upper hand. Franz Schalk, Strauss's co-director, must have seen an opportunity in this: he seemed more and more to side with the administration. What has to be said is that he was the director who, behind the scenes, had to juggle with figures and try as hard as possible to balance the books at a time when huge amounts of money were being spent on lavish productions. Try as he would, there was always a deficit.

Could it ever happen that Strauss would be openly opposed in his methods of running the opera? It hardly seemed possible. The maestro's sixtieth birthday had just been celebrated with a "Strauss Week" in which the Viennese seemed to show their undying friendship.

Now, at last, it was time to rest – in Switzerland. Worries about Korngold and Schalk could almost be forgotten when one was resting one's eyes on the beautiful lakes of the Oberengadin and the blue-white snow of the wild, jagged mountain peaks.

Schnuck had joined them from his children's home nearby, looking tanned and livelier than ever.

Elisabeth was so enthralled by the beauty of her surroundings that she began to think of building a summer home somewhere in the mountains, nearer to Vienna, or even in the Bavarian Alps, which would be practical for the Munich opera festival. Perhaps when she was there she would have a chance to look around; she did not have much to sing this year – just Blonde and Cherubino.

These were to be unforgettable performances. Maria Ivogün sang Constanze and Susanna, and Furtwängler conducted. To Elisabeth his hands and arms seemed almost to glow as he took the tempi of *Figaro* unusually fast, to the delight of a critic who also commented: ". . . Elisabeth Schumann . . . portrayed Cherubino with grace and finesse, although the two solos were sung with little charm."

Elisabeth took critics with a fistful of salt. The things they cobbled together! And how much of an idea did they really have about how roles should be performed? Another critic had quite a different point of view: "Our guest from Vienna, Elisabeth Schumann, sang Cherubino with the clarity and loveliness needed for the portayal of this divine boy, while at the same time captivating us with her pleasantly cheeky acting."

During the festival there was an invitation from Strauss to visit his country house, "Villa Strauss", in Garmisch. How wonderful to be allowed to see him in his own home, and where so much heavenly music had come into being! – *Der Rosenkavalier*, *Salome*, *Elektra* and the many, many songs.

Tall, dark pines stood thickly round the site so that visitors could not see the white-walled house with its red-tiled roof until they were at the gate. There they had to say who they were into an electric gadget, then the creaking gate let them onto the paved path leading to the house.

If anyone held sway in Richard Strauss's country house it was his wife Pauline. The parquet floor was the first indication: it compared favourably with a still mountain lake – spotless and cool, it reflected everything around it. The concomitant row of felt slippers stood impressively along the wall of the entrance hall: one was kindly requested to choose a pair to pull on over one's shoes.

C looked so comical in those thick slippers! Even taller, and his legs even lankier. Of course he immediately started fooling around, intoning the giants' leitmotif from *Der Ring des Nibelungen* and making arm movements to suggest a tree trunk of a staff in his hand. Thus he slid with long skating strides into the drawing room. Even in the maestro's house he had to play the fool! But his boss let him do what he liked, and was even perhaps quite glad that these obligatory abominations of felt could allow a bit of fun in all this rigid orderliness. However, Alwin was quickly slapped down by the sobering voice of the mistress of the house: would he please sit down and stop this silliness; the parquet had already been polished, thank you!

The house was embarrassingly clean and tidy; everything was in place, there was not a bit of fluff to be seen; even the maestro's large study lined with books was in perfect order. The composer's grand piano was so polished it seemed to be laughing at one.

This great artist, confined in this regimented household! A wife who jealously watched over his everyday routine, who would burst in and call him out for his daily walk, who could not abide a minute's lateness at table . . . yet she herself was an artist. She had met him when she was a singer, Fräulein de Ahna, from the beer-brewing family Pschorr; a wilful little madam with a voice which had made him prick up his ears. According to Alma Mahler-Werfel[*] he is supposed to have proposed to her immediately after a rehearsal at which she had thrown her vocal score at his head! He rather liked her tactless, frank remarks and seemed to need a domineering partner. They gave recitals together, and he laughed at her objection to any piano postludes in his songs: "With your pattering postludes you ruin all my applause!" He would do anything for her, even compose songs without postludes! But life could not have been a bed

[2]In *Mein Leben*, S. Fischer, Frankfurt-am-Main, 1960.

of roses for her either; Elisabeth remembered how moody he had sometimes been in America, how hard, cold and snappish. Pauline was also up against another problem; she once asked: "What does one do with a man who, when he begins to get sensual, starts composing?!" Yes, he needed this woman who would not let him get away with anything.

But then he could be charm itself. No sooner had he gathered that his guests were thinking of buying a house in the mountains than he suggested: why not build one? And why not in Garmisch, near to him? What could be a lovelier spot, with here the wonderful view onto the Zugspitze massif with its wild, craggy rocks, and there the view onto the long range of the Wetterstein Mountains, which glowed in the evening light? The only sensible thing to do was to build. The farmers were always glad to make a bit of money selling a piece of land.

So Elisabeth and C found a patch of meadowland quite near the Strausses for their longed-for country home. It was to be a cosy little house, mainly for holidays of course, but with room enough for a piano – C insisted on that. Strauss wanted to give them his grand piano as a moving-in present, but they would not hear of it.

A building firm in Munich drew up plans for a wooden house with a balcony going halfway round the upper floor. But it was to cost a lot of money, which meant working very hard over the next months. The building should be finished by the spring, then they could spend their first summer holidays there.

Soon there would be chance enough to work. The time of the Vienna Music and Theatre Festival had arrived. It seemed almost like the days of the Hapsburg Empire again as the carriages, limousines and cabs rolled up. Admittedly it was a different kind of person who stepped out. There was virtually no aristocracy any more, only occasionally a member of an old family. Instead it was all the new, recently up-and-come people and, in addition, the many Vienna-crazy foreigners.

Only the beggars seemed to be of the old establishment. Like hermit-crabs in their surrogate shells they seemed to fit in the niches of palace walls and between the pillars of grand porches. But perhaps they had changed too; there were so many new beggars now.

In the Reitschulgasse too, the street where Elisabeth lived, two figures could always be seen at a certain time of the day. They would mumble "God bless you, ma'am" when the well-wrapped singer furnished them with a gleaming coin on her way to the opera: a sickly, pale woman out of whose black shawl a child's face always peered, and a "colleague" (as Elisabeth was wont to call street musicians), who was scratching a few little songs on his fiddle.

It turned out to be a plentiful September for these old friends, for Elisabeth went to the opera a great deal, not just to sing but to listen and watch as well. Strauss was putting on such a lot of interesting works, such as Beethoven's ballet *Die Geschöpfe des Prometheus* and his incidental music to Kotzebue's *Die Ruinen von Athen* which he was linking with a melodramatic scene of his own composition in the style of Beethoven. How wonderfully he had reworked, in his Straussian way, the theme from the last movement of the Fifth Symphony! It sent cold shivers down one's spine. In the ballroom of the Hofburg Strauss also put on examples of the classical singspiel and his *Der Bürger als Edelmann* (Hofmannsthal's version of Molière's *Le Bourgeois Gentilhomme* with Strauss's incidental music. This had formed part of the original version of Strauss's *Ariadne auf Naxos*).

This was all for the weeks of the festival and it brought with it a lot of extra little singing parts – with extra fees which went straight into Elisabeth's savings for the house in Garmisch.

On top of all the extra work there were irritating little worries at the opera house. Strauss would arrange the way things should be if he was away for a time. But when he was gone they would be done quite another way. For example, Strauss would often ask Schalk to start preliminary work on a new production, but when he returned he might find that no work had been done and that he would have to do all the groundwork himself. Schalk often seemed to lack initiative where new works were concerned. He would also sometimes make decisions which had not been authorized.

Then there were the endless carpings from Julius Korngold. With Elisabeth's Blonde he could find no fault, but it was not so with the new production of *Die Fledermaus*: he described her Adele as "a chambermaid from a good North German family" (whereas another critic wrote: "A better Adele could not be imagined"). But it was after the festival production of *The Magic Flute* that the poisoned pen really got going: "Frau Schumann . . . possesses neither the quality of voice nor the character to represent Pamina adequately."

No sooner was Elisabeth off on tour (singing guest performances in Hamburg and recitals in Hamburg, Kiel and Berlin) than

Korngold was commenting that the standard of cast in Vienna was just as high without her, that she was a "flitting, migrating bird", that she was "adequately replaced, more than adequately" by Frau Schöne. There were more cutting remarks about Strauss's *Schlagobers*, and also about his policy of taking stars from Vienna in order to perform his works elsewhere: Lotte Lehmann was in Dresden singing Christine in the première of *Intermezzo*. There were things that could be changed, he wrote, and they should be changed before it was too late. How confident the hostile camp seemed in its attacks! What was happening? The crunch was soon to come.

On her way back from her recital in Berlin (which had been accompanied by the composer Reynaldo Hahn, some of whose songs she had sung) Elisabeth was able to stop in Dresden, not only to see her best friend Lene Jung again but also to watch the final rehearsals of *Intermezzo*. Strauss and Pauline were there too, of course.

What an extraordinary sight: there was the drawing room of Strauss's country house on the stage! Everything was precisely in place, here the old cabinet, there the armchair where C had been told to sit down. . . . Was Strauss going to display his domesticity to all the world? What a pity that the parquet floor was missing! Elisabeth did hear that Strauss had been rather taken aback by the stark similarity, although he had allowed the set designer to visit the house, but he had been convinced of the necessity of it, for, after all, this opera was all about his life: Kapellmeister Robert Storch was none other than Richard Strauss himself. Friends of his were portrayed, and the prickly Christine was Pauline to a T. But it was clear that Strauss also saw his wife in a different light. That was the secret of his marriage. Pauline was not just as she seemed. Robert Storch explained it in a scene where he is playing skat:

> For me she is absolutely the right woman. . . . For what I have become I have you to thank, especially healthwise! . . . I need life and temperament around me. Every person has two sides, the difference being only that some people only show their good side; those are the people with an agreeable exterior. While she, she is one of those very tender, chaste creatures with a rough shell − I know several like that, they are the best! A hedgehog armed on the outside with spines. . . .

Pauline tender? Perhaps, after all. When Strauss sometimes read out letters from her in America there had been many tender words.

Lotte Lehmann was marvellous as Christine. Of course she looked quite different from Pauline, but when she flung scolding words about one really seemed to see that "tender, chaste creature with the rough shell". Korngold should see her now! In fact all the Strauss opponents should hear this work: the tempo with which the Strauss family life swept candidly across the stage, often in secco rectitative; the voluptuous orchestral interludes; and the way in which the orchestra flowed with a charming lyricism toward the cadences.

But it would have been fruitless. The enemies were already smelling victory. There was a rumour going around in Dresden that two officials from the Austrian Ministry of Education in Vienna had arrived; that Direktor Schalk had a new long-term contract; that Strauss was utterly stunned when they told him.

Perhaps that was why he had not turned up for the rehearsal – he did not want to be seen; and that very evening Elisabeth's train left for Vienna. . . . So they had decided against him. The Ministry of Education knew full well that Strauss could no longer work with Schalk. And they had to break it to him right in the middle of the last rehearsals for *Intermezzo*! What would the maestro do now? C was sure to know more.

Saturday, November 1. C was waiting to meet the train as always, despite the early hour. He shouted through the door of the still moving train: "A scandal about 'Robert' [Storch]!"

So it was true. All Vienna already knew about it: Schalk was to remain director, and Strauss had tendered his resignation.

But all might not yet be lost. The gentlemen of the Ministry of Education should be shown the significance of elbowing out someone like Richard Strauss. Others might go too, namely Elisabeth Schumann and Kapellmeister Alwin. Perhaps that would make them think again. Elisabeth's contract in any case ran out in five months' time, but it was better to leave now in protest.

It was a hectic Saturday. Friends came and went, told news, advised and prognosticated. The telephone was in constant use and C was soon completely hoarse. On top of all the flurry they had to think out the wording for their request to be released from contract. The row over Strauss should seem to be no more than the catalyst for the resignation, not the whole reason. Otherwise too tense a relationship with Schalk and the Ministry would be created, assuming that their request would not be granted, which was highly likely. No, Korngold would have to be given as the main reason – his ever more acrid press notices. Thus the real reason would become evident, but only indirectly.

At the beginning of the week nothing had changed in the slightest. The press would have to get more involved. Interviews should be given. The whole of Austria, the whole world, should be told that a great man was being unceremoniously booted out. The Ministry should be put under the pressure of public opinion. Perhaps it would also have its effect on the maestro.

On November 4 Alwin spoke out in the *Neues Wiener Journal*:

I find it immensely sad that things have got as far as they have. How I stand with Strauss is well known and my greatest pride. But in the judgement of most professional musicians and of the public, Richard Strauss, in his position as opera director in Vienna and as the greatest living composer, must surely represent the strongest force in this house. There must be a way of keeping Strauss as director for Vienna Opera. . . .

I deeply regret that the initially good understanding between Strauss and Schalk, who complemented each other so favourably, has broken down. I personally hold Direktor Schalk in the highest esteem in all respects. . . .

I personally have to say that I am very glad to be in Vienna. . . . But if it really came to the loss of Strauss as opera director, then I would never again be able to enter the opera house without the painful sensation that it had once held Strauss and had let him go. . . .

As yet I see no reason to resign . . . this report is only true in connection with my wife, Elisabeth Schumann. . . . Since my break in personal relations with Doktor Korngold neither I nor my wife have managed to evince a single friendly word about our work in Korngold's paper [the *Neue Freie Presse*]. . . . An indisputable, personally coloured, truly malicious condemnation robs my wife of the joy of working in Vienna; his standpoint is in such blatant contrast with that of the public and the rest of the press. . . . You cannot blame an artist, renowned in all the world and not least . . . in Vienna, if she would rather avoid attacks of this nature. My wife's resignation has been refused . . . in the friendliest possible way by Direktor Schalk, and my wife will therefore fulfil the remaining five months of her contract. The reasons for this attempted resignation . . . are not to be found in the opera house.

Most of the other newspapers supported Strauss, even those which had always been against the co-directorship. The public also had their moment of protest: on November 5, Alwin conducted Gluck's *Orfeo ed Euridice*. At the beginning of the third act he lifted his baton. . . . Suddenly there were cheers and cries for Strauss, getting

146

louder and louder. For minutes the whole theatre was in uproar. C had to lay down his baton; with bowed head he waited. Never before had he waited so patiently. He was proud that the ovation for his friend had broken out just when he was conducting.

It was all to no avail. Soon it became crystal clear what the Ministry thought and what had happened. Schalk was definitely to remain director. They at least wanted someone who would devote all his time to the opera instead of only five months of the year, and someone who would not keep "borrowing" its best singers for performances of his own works in other opera houses. The two officials sent to Dresden (one of whom had in fact been Strauss's friend, Ludwig Karpath, the Ministry of Education's theatrical adviser) had presented Strauss with a written instruction with clear demarcations between the directors' various activities, which, among other things, made it clear that, according to the terms of the new contract which Schalk had negotiated, the latter was authorized to make all decisions whenever Strauss was away. Strauss had merely remarked: "As long as Schalk is there the instruction is just a scrap of paper." The officials had been prepared for this and were authorized to accept his resignation.

To Elisabeth everything in the opera house now seemed rather subdued: the shimmering gold semi-circle with its sounds of applause; the brightness of the strings; even those almost heavenly moments when the orchestra was married to one's own voice; and the fiery emotions which flashed between conductor and singer. It was more peaceful, admittedly, but duller. Now there was not even the opportunity any more proudly to champion Strauss's cause. The battle was over.

C once said: "If I am ever remembered in musical history, then I should like it to be only as the loyal friend of Richard Strauss." Would he ever be able to thank Strauss again for what he had said about him while on the tour of America? In Washington he had been talking to his son Franz and to Elisabeth about the Jews. He had turned to Franz and said: "Just you try and find a man like Alwin among the Christians – he's no coward either, no lickspittle."

The man who had said that was gone, was no longer the benevolent, inspiring leader of the opera. So Elisabeth wrote to Lene: "What will happen to us? C does not get on well with Schalk, so for him it's hardly possible to stay here. Perhaps we'll go to Munich – I would go like a shot."

147

CHAPTER 12

Vienna, 1924–1925

ALWIN LEAVE VIENNA? As if Schalk would not want to avoid that at all costs knowing that it would mean also losing his valuable wife!

It was not in Elisabeth's nature to brood over things for long. It would all work itself out, as everything in life did. Besides, there was no time to worry. Whether Strauss was leading the opera or not, there was more trilling and warbling than ever to be done. Concerts too. Before Christmas there were recitals to be given in Hungary, Czechoslovakia, Germany and Switzerland. New songs had to be studied: it would not do to keep serving up the same menu each time. Elisabeth's routine with a new song was first to study and think over the text and music, then to try it out at the piano on her own, then with C, then over the following weeks and months to sing it again and again, twenty times, fifty times, even a hundred times. Until it "sat" properly no one should hear it. So there really was no time for worrying.

It was almost Christmas. Presents had to be bought – for C, her mother, Lisa and Milan Reitler, Lene, Lotte, Donner ("Thunder" – Elisabeth's regular taxi-driver), her dresser, ill people and beggars. And last but not least Schnuck! This time he was allowed to come to her. It fitted perfectly: on December 13 Elisabeth had to sing six Strauss songs with orchestra in Basle; after that she could take him back with her to Vienna.

Gerd was brought to the train by a teacher at a small town along the line from Basle. They had just two minutes to find the carriage before the train moved on. He got a huge hug, and his few bits and pieces were soon in the compartment. The whistle blew.

"And where's his passport?" It had been forgotten. What a frightful nuisance. They could well get stuck at the border, which was not far off.

148

At last, after an uneasy wait they could hear the sound of doors being slid open and shut. Passport control. If only she were at least an Austrian citizen and did not have a German passport!

In humble tones, with her self-assured charm, which could be so disarming, Elisabeth began to explain who she was, that she had to sing at the Opera the next day, therefore it was absolutely imperative. . . .

The man interrupted in a strong Austrian dialect, with animated surprise: Frau Schumann! He had heard so much about her from his cousin whose girlfriend had seen her on the stage as Adele in *Die Fledermaus*. The loveliest thing. It had said so in the paper too.

The game was won. Elisabeth did not have much more explaining to do. He wished them a happy Christmas in the politest terms and thoughtfully pulled the door quietly shut behind him.

In Vienna Gerd went to many of his mother's performances. Beforehand he always came with her to her dressing room to watch the astounding transformation wrought by make-up. His delight at the sight of all the frogs on the make-up table knew no bounds: wooden frogs, china frogs, some made of iron, some of lead, even silver – they hopped, swam, climbed – a huge glass toad stared with bulging eyes, and a band of frog-musicians played concerts to the rest. In the three-leaved mirror they became legion. Thus all frogs in the throat had been banished to the table, explained his mother. (Visitors on guided tours of the opera house would often ask about the frogs in Elisabeth's dressing room. Many, when they had heard of her superstition, promptly sent her another one. They came from many parts of the world.)

The year 1925 brought renewed hope with regard to Strauss, much to Elisabeth's excitement. The Minister of Education had to give way to public pressure; he sent Councillor Karpath to Garmisch to offer Strauss a new post especially created for him: chief adviser to the minister in all musical affairs including the State Opera and the Music School.

The maestro's response was cool: the new post would be a retrogressive step after having had, as director of the opera, unlimited power to carry out his plans whenever financially possible. Any advice he would now give would have first to be ratified by the minister, then agreed by the director, which would be a quite intolerable situation.

The door was closed. Now it was impossible for Strauss to return

149

permanently. Elisabeth would have to cope without her champion; she would just have to deal with things as they came along. And the next thing to think about was her new contract. On February 14 1925 she wrote to Lene:

> In the next few days I shall be signing for another 6 *years* – C has after all still another year of his contract. I have made the stipulation that I could give notice on 1st February or 1st June in the first year, so that if C's contract is not renewed I am free to leave with him. . . . Yesterday Sorry became a man. He was mated with a sweet bitch and, God willing, will be a father in 61 days.

Could there be a more splendid dog than Sorry? Well, it was true that Lotte's Pekinese Pizzi was strong competition; he came from a marvellous pedigree. But Sorry had something leonine about him, with his thick, bushy fur. And the shortness of his legs – Pizzi's were not quite ideal. Perhaps that was why *Das Tiermagazin** had asked for a photograph of Sorry; it was to appear in the next issue, in a picture series of famous Viennese dogs.

But when the issue appeared there was no sign of Sorry, only an almost life-sized photo of Pizzi! So Lotte had been asked for a photo too – and she had not said a thing about it.

The magazine was very apologetic and explained that the photos were both to appear, but in consecutive issues and in alphabetical order.

"But his name is Alwin," pointed out Elisabeth, "Sorry von Alwin."

Unfortunately the surnames had been understood as "Lehmann" and "Schumann".

The "dog war" even became a joke in the newspapers:

> . . . Since that day Frau Schumann suspects Fräulein Lehmann of malicious intrigue, and Direktor Schalk is entrusted with the diplomatic mission of persuading the two artists to appear on stage together. . . . It is hoped that nobody will believe that this basically true story will have any serious consequences.

The birth of Sorry's four puppies turned out to be rather timely. Elisabeth's mother, who was going to move permanently to the new house being built in Garmisch, was to be given Sorry's daughter Happy as a companion. The house, built mainly of wood in the

---

*The official magazine of the Austrian Society for the Protection of Animals.

traditional Alpine style, was due to be finished by May.

Someone sent a photo of the building half done. There were no walls yet, it was just a skeleton of props and beams. C thought it looked like a birdcage which had been built for his little canary Elisabethchen. It was not a house, at most a bird-house, a "Canarihaus".

But the "little canary" was not to be subdued either by the photo or by C: ". . . am enjoying furnishing the Canarihaus tremendously. All the upholstery, lamps, lampshades etc. are being made here, which means a lot of thought about the right colours and materials . . . and we move to Garmisch on the 10th [July 1925] . . . – let's hope I'm not totally bankrupt by then – it seems to be costing more and more. . . ."

The builders kept demanding new payments which had not been predicted. Elisabeth thought this must be normal and paid. The London season was almost upon her; the generous fees from Covent Garden would fill the coffers a bit. One hundred pounds a night, two thousand marks!

Yet fees three times as high could not have compensated for the hard work and stress of such a tour. To Lene went the complaint: "I'm dreading London – 4 weeks is too long – and without C or you either! I can't bear to think of it. How nice it could have been!"

But her Eva in *Die Meistersinger* was a great success, and her Sophie became the talk of the town; both particularly valuable, for great competition was singing this season. Maria Jeritza appeared in her famous roles of Tosca and Fedora, and more important – the idolized Australian diva, Nellie Melba, was making three appearances, so that London and the press were in a fever. And yet: "Oh Lene, I wish it were over, it's so dreary sitting here and singing 6 times in 4 weeks. Be glad that you're at home – I'd give a lot to be in Vienna now. One thing, thank God, we have found – a charming little hotel [Haymarket Hotel] where you really feel at home – the proprietor, an Austrian, reads our very wishes in our eyes . . . Lotte is in the next room to me. . . ."

One feature of the hotel Elisabeth found particularly charming. One day when there was a knock on the door it was immediately followed by the sound of a high-pitched voice; long drawn out, almost singing, it called: "Paaage!", and in came a little pageboy bringing the mail.

How delightful; she simply had to imitate it. She immediately

knocked on Lotte's door, letting out a very high, silvery "Paaage!".
To Lotte's delight she then tripped into the room with little pageboy
steps. After that she always announced herself in that way. Even
many years later, whenever Elisabeth telephoned her friend, the first
thing Lotte would hear would be the bright, silvery "Paaage!".

During that time in London the two of them became even closer
friends. She and Lotte would often amuse themselves by walking
through the elegant shops of Piccadilly and Regent Street.

Elisabeth was an unselfish friend. But if others did not repay her
in kind, they would get to see quite another side to her nature. Lotte
never forgot one occasion when she went for a huge shopping spree
during that London season. Elisabeth trotted faithfully along
through all the shops and department stores, helped to choose,
showed admiration, advised for and advised against. It was already
long past lunchtime when Lotte had everything she wanted. Now
Elisabeth wanted very quickly to buy some piece of "lovely old
silver" at a silversmith's two streets on. But Lotte groaned that she
was too tired to go with her. In a flash Elisabeth turned on her for
her unfair behaviour, after *she* had kept her company the whole
morning. Lotte was coming, or else!

And Lotte, speechless, meekly followed her.

Elisabeth was not able to go straight home after the London
season. Once again she and Alwin would have to wait a little longer
before seeing each other – oh, how often it was like that! But she
would manage Würzburg standing on her head: although she had to
sing three consecutive evenings there, in each case it was only a
question of doing three numbers, perhaps four or five if there were
encores. This sort of work had to be fitted in; all for the Canarihaus,
for the real life!

On her thirty-seventh birthday, on June 13, the train brought her
to the old town of the prince-bishops, Würzburg.

As a backdrop to Mozart's music the prince-bishops' residence had
been chosen, that unique rococo palace by Balthasar Neumann. And
the second evening was charmingly arranged: the music was to be
performed on the balcony with the audience in the garden. It was
beginning to get dark. The people down there, the flowers and trees,
were already becoming less clearly defined in the twilight. Only the
palace was clearly visible, for from its tall windows glowed the light
of candles and the white and gold of the rooms. The spinet was right
up against the balustrade so that Privy Councillor Zilcher was also

in the open air. Looking up at Elisabeth he read from her posture when he could begin. She had complete confidence in him; he was a fine, throughly schooled musician, one of the many good conductors and accompanists who could be found even in the provincial towns of Germany.

Elisabeth began the recitative to Susanna's "Deh vieni, non tardar" . . . The air was still soft from the afternoon rain; it seemed to carry every slight nuance of voice and music far away, into every corner of the garden. Only two things had clear dimensions in this twilight: Balthasar Neumann's palace and Mozart's aria. The spirit of the eighteenth century shone from the one, sounded through the other, and was held in a wonderful union; and Elisabeth herself, Mozart's instrument, was an integral part of it.

> Elisabeth Schumann ... sang ... with enchanting beauty through the sound-enhancing twilight of the evening. Herself overwhelmed by the strangely moving atmosphere, the singer's greatness and fame were much furthered by her performance. Quite unsubdued and unrestrained the bell-like, warm waves of sound spread over the eagerly attentive audience, who finally would not cease the storms of applause until the artist was prepared to offer another song. "Das Veilchen", which she now sang, was a dreamlike revelation! [She had also sung the songs "An Chloe" and "Sehnsucht nach dem Frühling".]

That evening in Würzburg was quite unforgettable. But yet, what a joy it was to be in the train, rattling back to Vienna, to C and home. It was almost holiday time too. The thought of one's own little house in the peace of the mountains!

As usual dear C was on the platform with Luise holding little Sorry, and C was gesticulating and calling out his excited greetings. But then he cried: "Scandal about Garmisch!" Something about Strauss again? But no, it was the Canarihaus. The building firm had gone bankrupt.

What news to be welcomed with! Naturally C had exaggerated, as he so often did. The firm had become insolvent but it was completing started buildings. Nevertheless there was now no question of moving in on July 10. Meanwhile the firm was demanding more money all the time. It was a good thing that there were so many music festivals to be sung at. At the beginning of July there were the thousand-years celebrations in Cologne, in August the Munich opera festival. Salzburg would not be possible this year: three performances of *Figaro* and almost at the same time seven performances in Munich

– it simply was not possible. In a sense the festival in Cologne was an extension of the Vienna season since a large number of Vienna artists – singers, orchestra and ballet-dancers – were performing on seven evenings there. Elisabeth was to sing Zerlina, Sophie, Marzelline and Susanna. Lotte was coming to sing the Marschallin, and the great Richard Mayr was performing Leporello, Baron Ochs, Rocco and Figaro. The combination of having friends around together with the glorious Rhine wine gave the stay almost a holiday atmosphere, despite the hard work.

Completely worn out after the most wearing autumn, winter and spring of her life, Elisabeth sat in the train which brought her and C to Munich. But there was no peace to be had, for C would not stop talking.

Gerd arrived in Munich at almost the same time as his mother. Then came an almost agonizing night of anticipation – to see the new house. At last, with the eight o'clock express, they were on their way to Garmisch. . . .

They had not even finished the staircase! Elisabeth had to climb up a ladder to the first floor, and up there, where her own bedroom was to be, all in white and canary yellow, it was a stark picture of bare beams and gaping holes. It would take at least another three weeks, if not four. And the local boarding house, Pension Kohlhardt, only had vacant rooms for another two.

Every day Elisabeth, C and Schnuck went on their "pilgrimage" to the building site to see how things were progressing; often they went twice a day. The workers had three-mark coins pressed into their hands in accordance with the motto that tips paid off. Every two days two crates of beer were delivered. Money flowed, especially in Pension Kohlhardt. Perhaps it was just as well that they had to leave it after two weeks and move into a much more modest and cheaper boarding house, but it meant climbing three flights of stairs. A crow's nest, C called it.

The longed-for holidays thus turned out not to be as restful as hoped for; on top of everything else there were some dreadfully hot July days. No wonder Elisabeth felt so feeble. But one day she suddenly felt ill as well. She was trying to get up to the "crow's nest" and had to pull herself up by the banisters. The unpractical C, in an agony of anxiety, pulled her up the last steps and plumped her down in a corner instead of laying her on her bed. Then he flew downstairs, yelled for a doctor, raced upstairs again, could not find

Elisabeth, rushed into the bedroom – she was lying on the bed smiling weakly.

The doctor diagnosed sunstroke and exhaustion and firmly prescribed a few days in bed. During that time the patient was not to be bothered with any professional matters, the Kapellmeister was not even to read about music and theatre from the newspapers. There should be no visits to the building site in the next two weeks. This meant absolute rest while there was still time before Munich. At first she stayed in bed, then she lay on the verandah. The slowly dragging building work was barely mentioned. C crept about on tiptoe; he read the papers quietly to himself, usually in Schnuck's room. But every now and then he could not contain himself any longer. He would leap up, rush next door – but Elisabeth only needed to put a finger to her lips and he would let the newspaper drop and would creep out again.

As always Elisabeth's natural vitality won. She travelled to the Bavarian capital in the best of health, rehearsed intensively and sang four roles: Despina and Blonde under Richard Strauss, Susanna and Eva under Hans Knappertsbusch.

Clemens von Franckenstein, General Manager of the Munich State Theatres, always invited Elisabeth and C to a dinner at his house every year. And every year they were given the same: venison with cranberry sauce. Elisabeth always had trouble keeping a straight face when the delicious game was dished up on a silver platter. If Schnuck was invited too, she always warned him before they entered the lovely old house: "For heaven's sake keep a straight face when the roast comes in. And don't dare look at me, or else I shall burst out laughing."

But over the venison of 1925 a very special offer was made. Solemnly Baron von Franckenstein suggested that since for some years Elisabeth had helped to a great extent to bring the Munich opera festival world renown, she should be rewarded in a more conspicuous way than by words, that was to say that he would be honoured if she would consent to his recommending her to the Minister of Cultural Affairs for the title of *Kammersängerin.* He already knew that the Minister would agree. Would she be inclined to accept such a title?

---

*"Court singer" – literally "singer of the chamber". A title bestowed by royalty or the artistocracy to denote a singer of excellence.

Titles did not mean a lot to Elisabeth. When the King of Denmark had declared after a performance that he would like to decorate her and asked her whether she would prefer a title or an order, she chose that which could be worn on a concert gown. So she was given the High Order of Art, a large medal of heavy gold on a red ribbon.

But this time she could not help but be pleased. Her first title – *Bayerische* [Bavarian] *Kammersängerin*! Bavaria, where Strauss came from; where Bayreuth was. Wagner, Ludwig II. And soon she would have a house in Bavaria.

Soon it really would be time to move into the Canarihaus. The paint was almost dry. One day Pauline Strauss breezed in and, as was her wont, was immediately ready with suggestions for improvements. You should do this, you should have done that, you shouldn't have done that. She left nothing uninspected. The built-in cupboards were opened and checked, the drawers of the brightly-painted chest of drawers were pulled open, the hand-painted and varnished table-tops were examined, even on their undersides, to check that they were sturdily and not cheaply made.

For quite a while Elisabeth accepted the situation benignly. She was hardly ever angry, but if she was, then it was a sudden and violent anger. This was what happened now. It suddenly rose up inside her, and Pauline was given a piece of her mind: those who wished to criticize and improve should please do so within their own four walls and not in other people's houses.

After that the relationship between the two women was always slightly strained.

August 21 1925: a milestone in Elisabeth's life. From this day on she was to enjoy the peace of her own house. No telephone could ring – there was none in the Canarihaus. For C that was a bit difficult, but soon he would get used to it and it would do his nerves good. All that could be heard of the village were the church bells; the crickets chirped in the meadows and occasionally a cowbell could be heard from the mountain slopes.

Elisabeth and Lotte were to appear with C in guest performances in November: "I'm already looking forward to Spain, that's to say to our being together, for I know that dirty country well enough already. It'll be such fun."

All too easily things could become too much fun when they worked together, so they might well have burst out laughing on stage at the Teatro Liceo in Barcelona had they not, fortunately, had almost no opportunity to do so: they were only to appear together in *Der Rosenkavalier*, and as Sophie and Annina they had hardly anything to do with each other. The performance seemed very foreign to them, as they had to sing Hofmannsthal's wonderful libretto in Italian. This in itself was enough to give them the giggles, but mercifully C was spared such an embarrassment. To be conducting *Der Rosenkavalier* in Barcelona was a wonderful task for him. He had also been asked to rehearse and give the Spanish première of *Intermezzo*. There was enough of an embarrassment in that première already, for when Storch's little boy, Bubi, has to protest from his cot that "it's not true, Father is good", a mature male voice rumbled from between the sheets: "*Non vero, Papa è buono!*" From the gallery came a sarcastic imitation in a deep bass voice; the hilarity in the whole house was great. Seemingly the Teatro Liceo had had insuperable difficulties in casting Bubi.

CHAPTER 13

Vienna, 1926–1928

IT WAS NOT England's fault that it did not become acquainted with one of its favourite lieder singers until 1926. Already, shortly after Elisabeth's debut at Covent Garden, the well-known London concert agents, Ibbs & Tillett, had asked whether she would like to give a concert in England. That had been grist to C's mill: whenever there was an opportunity, or even if there was not, he would always try to persuade her that she must sing lieder in England. But Elisabeth had still not quite thrown off her anxiety about anything to do with that country. It seemed so different from the rest of Europe, so far from home, so insular. And to sing in the concert season there, she would have to experience the English winter which she had heard meant damp, fog and inadequately heated rooms. Of course, these were just the superficial excuses: what she still really feared was the discerning English public.

It was Max Mossel who started the ball rolling. This Dutch-born violinist and impresario, always full of life and fun, had made a name for himself with his popular Max Mossel Concerts, performed in the provinces and Scotland to a very high standard. He often introduced artists from abroad, and he knew instinctively that the British would take Elisabeth to their hearts. He would be able to offer higher fees than those in Germany: £75 a night, i.e. 1500 marks (in Germany the average was between 800 and 1200 marks). Ibbs & Tillett would arrange the London concert.

Finally Elisabeth let herself be persuaded. In the middle of January 1926 she would make a start in the Midlands, then she would go to Edinburgh and Glasgow. For the London concert the ideal venue would have been the Queen's Hall, but the cost of hiring it, including publicity, would have been £150 against the £40 or £50 of the Wigmore Hall. Despite the fact that the latter was so much smaller

Elisabeth decided in favour of it: there was always a risk that she would not sell out at the larger hall.

In the first weeks of the new year of 1926 Elisabeth set off for England, travelling via Hamburg where she had a concert and a three-day stay. Soon she was travelling through the English provinces. The only ray of light in the gloomy prospect of an English winter was the enthusiasm of the public – Max Mossel had been right.

> Piccadilly Hotel, London
> 24.1.26
>
> Lene – it's dreadful here – the town is frightful in winter – always dark – always electric light! So far I have had 4 concerts with *unbelievable* success – tomorrow afternoon at 3 is my own lieder recital – you must cross your fingers for me because of course it's the most important one. So far I have sung in Manchester, Birmingham, Cheltenham and Liverpool. Now I still have to go to Glasgow, Bridge of Allan, Edinburgh, Oxford and Haslemere.... I'm not earning all that much here, and everything is so *expensive* – and what will my lieder recital cost me? Frightful – one sweats blood and tears and then has to pay for it into the bargain. Let's hope it will help my future career.

The next afternoon Elisabeth stepped onto the platform at the Wigmore Hall followed by her accompanist, George Reeves. The hall seemed even smaller with all the people in it. It was packed, even the balcony was crowded – London's musical world seemed full of anticipation.

Not many hours later C and Emma both recieved happy telegrams, and to Lene Elisabeth wrote:

> My London concert was a sensational success – press unanimous that such song artistry never before heard here.

The Daily Telegraph wrote:

> From beginning to end it was the work of one who is complete mistress of her art. Many people must have asked themselves, in Wigmore Hall yesterday afternoon, whether they had ever heard finer lieder-singing than Elisabeth Schumann's.

Elisabeth no longer had any worries about singing in England. She had even made a profit of £40 at the Wigmore Hall. A second concert was arranged for April 28, a third for May 5. Max Mossel was already planning tours for the coming November and for February 1927. With a light heart Elisabeth travelled to Scotland.

The Scottish public was equally enthusiastic, and *The Glasgow Herald* and *The Scotsman* praised her with: "... sang most wonderfully ... moulding her phrases in the most exquisite fashion" and "... with an intelligence and a sense of style which are rare among singers."

Elisabeth was back in London in time to see what Ernest Newman had written in *The Sunday Times*:

> ... She has a voice of unusual purity: it has no great variety of colour in it, yet it is not cold; its timbre has something of the quality of starlight, bright and clear. Her technique is so sound as to give her singing great assurance in the most difficult music.... Elisabeth Schumann, on Monday, could have sung to a much larger audience than the Wigmore Hall could accommodate.

Suddenly it was as if England and Elisabeth had found each other. And now His Master's Voice made its appearance. They wanted to record Mozart arias, since Elisabeth had had such a success at Covent Garden with the role of Susanna. Mozart arias in Italian: perhaps it still seemed too much of a risk to put records of German lieder onto the market. The wretched World War was still having an effect. But before April there was anyway no question of recording: after the last concerts in Oxford and Haslemere it was back to Vienna.

Next to her normal operatic work Elisabeth had some special tasks to fulfil: expected and unexpected ones. Bruno Walter was to conduct a Philharmonic concert at Easter. For it he had chosen one of his favourite pieces: Mahler's Fourth Symphony, with the soprano solo in the last movement, for which Elisabeth had been engaged. It was to be a midday concert, and midday concerts always presented the particular problem of what to wear. An evening dress was, of course, entirely ruled out. The only thing to do would be to have a dress made specially at Grünberger's fashion salon.

The result was a stunning creation, almost too "dressed up", but this could be softened, with a hat perhaps.

The creation became a sensation – because of the hat. In one or two press notices about the great musical occasion newspaper space was even wasted on it.

Before the third movement Frau Kammersängerin Elisabeth Schumann made an entrance in a purple dress with a matching hat.

As if she had just popped in from a stroll on the Ringstrasse for a moment, to sing about the heavenly life. With a hat. (Let us hope that Mayr will not appear for the Ninth in a top hat. . . .)

The unexpected special task was to be done for Richard Strauss. He was working on a new opera, *Die Ägyptische Helena* (*The Egyptian Helen*), for which Hugo von Hofmannsthal had written the libretto. He wanted to give his collaborator an impression of the music, not just by playing it on the piano but with the human voice. He wondered whether Elisabeth would be so kind as to learn Helena's first big aria, "Ein Feuer brennt, ein Tisch ist gedeckt" ("A fire is lit, a table laid"). He would then invite Hofmannsthal and one or two friends to his large house in the Jaquingasse to hear her sing it to his accompaniment.

March 27 was the date chosen. Not until the morning did Elisabeth receive the pages of manuscript with Strauss's tiny writing. She only had the melody line and the words. It was a highly dramatic aria, six pages long, an aria which she would never dream of performing on stage as a lyric soprano. And how was she to learn it in a few hours without an accompaniment? Alwin came to his wife's rescue, improvising an accompaniment in as Straussian a fashion as he could. By the afternoon's performance she was note-perfect and confident.

Hofmannsthal was spellbound by the music. The day after the little concert he wrote to Strauss from his home in Rodaun:

> The joy which this "Helena" music has given me is, I think, greater than that which any of your compositions have ever given me before, and I feel that I am justified in this, although I have not the means to express myself properly. But, poor though my ear may be, I evidently have some kind of sense of the essence of music, and this sense was most deeply touched yesterday. . . . The feeling this music has left me with is truly spellbinding; everything so light and bright, even in all that great, unalloyed solemnity. I am happy beyond measure.

Elisabeth asked whether she might keep the manuscript, and Strauss presented it to her with the droll dedication: "To the first Helena, Elisabeth, in memory of March 27 1926."

Countless times in her life Elisabeth was filled with deep joy when making music. Yet this short concert with the great composer – for him and for his librettist – always counted as one of the great experiences of her life. She felt that for these two creators of the opera she had breathed life into Helena; through her art a new character in musical literature had come into being for the very first time; this was not just performing, this was helping to create.

Set against such an experience all her other work almost seemed routine: singing opera, lieder recitals, even radio concerts. It was obvious that unusual, exciting happenings would become less and less frequent as her career progressed.

But England was still a relatively new campaign to be fought, and now, in the spring of 1926, she was determined to win. And how easily England yielded! The London recital on April 28 was completely sold out.

The next day His Master's Voice drew up a contract for a year's recording, and on the day after that, four Mozart arias were recorded. (When she heard them at her next recording session on May 19 she rejected two of them, being far readier to forgo a fee than to let an imperfect performance be published.)

At the next London recital, on May 5, so many people were unable to obtain tickets that yet another concert was arranged for June 10.

On May 10 the opera season opened successfully with *The Marriage of Figaro* conducted by Bruno Walter. Richard Mayr sang Figaro, Lotte Lehmann the Countess, and Elisabeth was, of course, Susanna. The Count was sung by the elegant Josef Degler from the Hamburg Stadttheater. Delia Reinhardt was Cherubino and Luise Willer Marcellina.

Two days later Elisabeth reported to Lene:

> The first Figaro was a huge success. Willer is here in your place – all Walter's people – if I hadn't had such success here in February there'd be another Susanna here too.

There was in fact also a second conductor: Robert Heger. He conducted *Die Meistersinger*. He was good to work with: he had a quiet, almost gentle way which could make the ladies quite shy of him, but not apparently Elisabeth and Lotte when they were fooling around in their hotel rooms – as usual. Lotte was a keen rider and must have wanted to show Elisabeth how one controlled a horse. At any rate, it happened that on one occasion Lotte was crawling round the room on all fours with Elisabeth riding on her back. There was a knock and Heger's head appeared gingerly in the crack of the door. At the spectacle which presented itself he merely said: "Oh, dear ladies, have I come at an inconvenient moment?" and closed the door again at once. He was followed by gales of laughter.

With great anticipation the production of *Don Giovanni* under Bruno Walter was awaited in that season of 1926, for London had perhaps never before had such a splendid cast for the opera:

Donna Anna	Frida Leider
Donna Elvira	Lotte Lehmann
Zerlina	Elisabeth Schumann
Don Giovanni	Mariano Stabile
Don Ottavio	Fritz Krauss
Leporello	Jean Aquistapace
Masetto	Pompilio Malatesta
Il Commendatore	Edouard Cotreuil

It was sung in Italian and the first performance was on June 7. The following day brought another great occasion for Covent Garden: Nellie Melba was giving a farewell performance in the form of scenes from operas; she sang Juliette, Desdemona and Mimi. Ovation after ovation followed the performance by the renowned Australian diva. At the end she made a little speech – in front of a sea of floral tributes and a kangaroo made of flowers. Elisabeth had sent flowers too, and a few days later Melba wrote to her:

Dear Elisabeth Schumann,
   Your flowers were too beautiful and I send you my loving and grateful thanks.
Yours very sincerely,
Nellie Melba
   I am coming to hear you tomorrow and adore your art.

This was not the first time this great lady had paid Elisabeth a compliment: the previous year, when they had also been in London at the same time, Melba had sent Elisabeth a photograph of herself under which was written: "To the Golden Voice".

Elisabeth was at last able to go to Garmisch. The arrival was almost the best part: having rattled along in the hackney-cab at an easy pace past the hotel fronts, over the foaming River Loisach, past the old farmhouses with the colourful pictures on their white gables, she would then move onto the narrow gravel road; over in the meadow was the crucifix, then round a corner – and there it stood, the dark brown, wooden Canarihaus with its green shutters. The two dogs,

Sorry and Happy, would rush towards each other in greeting. Mother's head of white hair appeared at the door, and she would smile widely, affectionately. Alwin would run towards his wife with a "ha!" and a "ho!", then rush to the piano in the living room and thunder out the march from *Aida*.

Altogether the holiday turned out to be quite lively. The conductor Hans Knappertsbusch and Marion, his gentle, angelic wife were staying nearby and often looked in. Strauss arrived with freshly composed music for his *Ägyptische Helena* which he played to them on the piano.

One kind of visitor was unwelcome: the fleetingly met and forgotten admirer who wished to bask in the light of their star. C could think of only one solution to the problem – a drastic one: he had a notice painted for the front gate which read: "Mornings unavailable, afternoons not at home". Elisabeth had to laugh about it, but she was also embarrassed by its grand and dismissive tone – so alien to her nature. Emma removed it after the holidays, and in the following summer it did not reappear.

The holidays were almost only nominally such, for Elisabeth had to sing both at the Salzburg and Munich festivals. She began on August 4 with *Figaro* in Munich. A week later she was there again to sing in *Così fan tutte*. The very next day it was Serpina in Pergolesi's *La Serva Padrona* under Schalk in Salzburg, with repeat performances on the 14th, 15th and 17th. Then it was back to Munich for *Entführung* on the 19th, and on 21st *Figaro* again.*

The summer seemed over far too soon. Elisabeth had to leave Garmisch on August 31 – the Vienna State Opera wanted to have something of their globe-trotting Schumann too.

We are leaving with heavy hearts – the weather just too heavenly.

But on September 5 Elisabeth was again in Munich to sing Eva in *Die Meistersinger*. For the return journey she took the latest and quickest form of transport: "... and *flew* back, which was simply wonderful."

---

*In the *Opera Annual 1954–55* Harold Rosenthal wrote: "I can recall two Despinas whose equal has not yet been seen at Glyndebourne. One of these was Lotte Schöne at Salzburg in 1927; another was Elisabeth Schumann about the same date at Munich (when Mme Schumann sniffed the cup of chocolate at her first entry, I remember how Richard Strauss, accompanying the recitative, used to play a crystalline upward flourish in illustration of her gesture).

If only travelling could always be so effortless, so swift. Instead it was an endless shaking and rattling in trains; leaving in the grey dawn, arriving just in time to go to bed; or, after a concert, climbing into a sleeping car to arrive all shaken up at a rehearsal next morning. Waiters in restaurant cars began to know Elisabeth and, remembering her generous tips, would rush to her service with greetings on their lips; customs officers recognized her and merely passed by with a friendly word. Now in the autumn it seemed that half her life was spent in trains and on railway platforms. From Vienna to a concert in Gotha; from Gotha to Berlin for a "radio" (broadcast concert); from Berlin to Hamburg, where she had to give two operatic guest performances and a recital. Then it was off to London, again for a "radio". From there to Manchester; then to the south coast to Eastbourne, and back to London for a big evening recital. After that the train journeys were directed north, to Preston, Edinburgh and across to Glasgow where she gave two concerts on consecutive days. Then back to Newcastle and Bradford and, via London, back to Vienna. And at the end of January 1927 she was off again for another six-week tour of England.

As part of the celebrations of the centenary of Beethoven's death Franz Schalk was putting on the *Missa Solemnis* in Vienna in March, and Elisabeth was committed to sing the soprano solo, which she had never even studied before, let alone performed. Important statesmen and diplomats were coming, and anyone who was anybody in the fields of art, science or commerce would also be there.

Elisabeth had rarely been so nervous at a performance before as during that "Missa". Towards the end of her life she wrote: "In the auditorium were the finest musical ears: Thibaud, Casals, Cortot, Elman. I was deathly white with nerves." But despite the pallor and the trembling knees, all went well. As usual her technique saved her.

Just as the lilac was beginning to blossom wonderfully in Vienna it was off to Covent Garden again for a few performances of *Der Rosenkavalier*, *Die Entführung* and *Parsifal* (in which she sang the first Flower Maiden). Although she wished heartily that Lene Jung had been engaged too, at least she had the company of Lotte Lehmann and Maria Olszewska. Maria had a hotel room very near to Elisabeth's, and the two of them often indulged in deep nocturnal discussions during which Elisabeth confided in Maria about her former love for Klemperer and the great blow which had followed. She was never able to be rid of the unhappy memory.

If Elisabeth and Maria were chatty on such evenings they were anything but that on days on which they had to sing. Then the two of them and Lotte would keep silence. If Maria came into the dining room a little later than the other two she would find them sitting at separate tables , and Maria would considerately seat herself far away in a corner somewhere. Although they ate well, Elisabeth and Lotte always had little pairs of scales by their plates in order to weigh what they ate. They allowed themselves to eat "everything", but only in restricted amounts. In the case of some dishes, this was very little.

Maria was full of admiration for her resolute colleagues until one day after lunch she bumped into them coming out of a confectioner's, happily munching away on chocolates. Oh, it was so difficult to starve oneself to slenderness. But it simply was not on to roll onto the stage like a barrel, the way some other singers did.

Even when Elisabeth was on holiday later in the summer she could not risk letting herself go. She went for many walks and always kept the scales on the table. Every few days her silvery voice would call out happily from the bathroom: "Another pound less! What slenderness! How wonderful it makes me feel!"

When she was slimmer her asthma was better too, and that was particularly important now, for at the end of October came her Paris debut. It was nine years since the end of the war, and there was still anti-German feeling, of course. But the debut was to be given within the framework of an orchestral concert under the direction of the French conductor Gabriel Pierné. Elisabeth was going to sing only *Exsultate Jubilate* and three Strauss songs. However, a few days later she was due to give a recital including some works by Berlioz she had never sung before, with C at the piano. How would the two Germans be received?

She need not have worried. A quarter of an hour after the end of the recital she was still being called back for encores.

Ten weeks later, in January 1928, Elisabeth again had to sing two concerts in Paris: an orchestral concert and a recital with C. In May she was there again, for something so important that Covent Garden had to do without Schumann for their 1928 season: from May 4 to 18 the Vienna State Opera was performing under Franz Schalk in the French capital. The operas to be presented were *Don Giovanni*, *Rosenkavalier*, *Figaro*, *Entführung*, *La Serva Padrona* and *Fidelio*. Before the first performance of *Fidelio* the ensemble was anticipating with trepidation the German dialogue they were going to have to speak. Since the war not one syllable of German had been heard on a Parisian stage. But no one hissed, and the ensemble was celebrated almost as never before.

Elisabeth received a decoration. On May 16 she and Lotte were both awarded the title *Officier de l'Instruction Publique* by the French Minister of Cultural Affairs. From now on the little mauve rosette could often be seen on Elisabeth's concert dresses or on the lapel of a jacket.

On June 6 1928 the première of *Die Ägyptische Helena* was to take place, conducted by Fritz Busch. The question of who should sing Helena was proving awkward: it was between Elisabeth Rethberg and Maria Jeritza. After months of indecision a compromise was made: Rethberg sang the Dresden première and Jeritza the Vienna. In Dresden Lene Jung had the part of the Sea-shell, Marie Gutheil-Schoder was artistic director, and Elisabeth's verdict of the performance was "glorious!"

Four days after the world première and the evening before the first Vienna performance, to be conducted by the composer, Elisabeth gave a huge reception in honour of Richard Strauss. It was June 10, eve of the maestro's birthday – he was to be sixty-four. The tall, gleaming white double doors between the large rooms in Elisabeth's apartment stood wide open, and the long suite of rooms was filled with about one hundred and thirty people.

It was an historic gathering. Hugo von Hofmannsthal had come, of course. He looked uneasy, as if he were suffering a little amongst so many people. Strauss on the other hand, tall, full of life and humour, seemed in his element. With his sixty-four years he was still slim, if a little stooped. Ferdinand Foll, that great artist and adviser in the study of Wolf songs, was among the guests. Ministers chatted with Elisabeth and Alwin, as newly-arrived foreign diplomats were led by liveried footmen across the cobbled courtyard.

1928 was turning out to be a wonderful year. And it was not only the French who bestowed an honour upon Elisabeth: on June 26 the title of Austrian *Kammersängerin* was conferred on her. It was quite something to be honoured thus as a foreigner (Elisabeth was still a German national). The document arrived in the holidays, in Garmisch.

Holidays is hardly the word for those weeks from the beginning of July to the end of August in Garmisch, for it was quite impossible to relax completely. Almost a hundred guests came and went during that time, and Elisabeth also had to work hard at the Munich opera festival. So the time was gone in a flash. After a few weeks' work in Vienna it was off to Paris again in October, and then to England.

A year had never seemed so full of those things which accomplished artistry can bring: success and honours. Something which Richard Strauss wrote to Carl Alwin towards the end of the year seemed to sum it up: "... our dear Elisabeth, crowned with glory".

CHAPTER 14

Vienna, 1929–1933

ELISABETH'S LIFE was more often "crowned with glory" than not, yet a time of many changes was now beginning, changes which were to go on for a decade and which were to alter her life radically, and not only in its outer circumstances.

It started with the economic situation, which was steadily growing worse. Although Elisabeth continued to earn well she was nevertheless aware of these hard times; she could not fail to be, with Alwin frequently rushing into her bedroom with the newspapers at seven in the morning saying things like: "Ha! The world is going bankrupt! The vultures are hovering – over us too, my little wife!" With that he would sit on the edge of her bed and rattle off the stock market news with almost gleeful sarcasm.

Elisabeth would not let this worry her seriously. She could see that she had to adapt; for example, she felt that in this discouraging climate she would have to do without her big receptions for a while and make do with dinner parties.

Elisabeth was never again to hold a reception such as the one in honour of Strauss. Of the Strauss-Hofmannsthal constellation she would anyway only have been able to invite the one star, Strauss, again.

At the beginning of July 1929 Hofmannsthal had almost finished the libretto of the new opera, *Arabella*. He was merely reworking the first act, at Strauss's request. He undertook this work under great stress of mind, for his older son, Franz, was suffering from a seemingly incurable depression. With an almost superhuman effort he managed to complete the first act and sent the manuscript to Strauss in Garmisch on July 10. On the 13th his worry about his son turned to deep grief: Franz von Hofmannsthal had, in his parents' home, taken his own life.

Monday July 15, was the day fixed for the funeral. It was sultry, the enervating *Föhn* wind was blowing. Hofmannsthal had to muster all his willpower to keep control of himself. Dressed for the funeral he went back into his study where a pile of unopened letters of condolence lay. Among them was a telegram marked "Garmisch". But he did not open it; he did not even want to read condolences from Strauss at this moment. He turned to go, and, in the doorway, collapsed unconscious to the floor. He had had a stroke. His wife and friends laid him on the sofa in the study. Hours later, never having regained consciousness, Hugo von Hofmannsthal was dead. A few paces away from his body lay the unopened telegram from Strauss. The latter had cabled on July 14, without knowing what had happened in Rodaun:

> First act excellent. Warmest thanks and congratulations.
> Yours truly,
>
> Dr Richard Strauss

Strauss was somewhat unwell at the time of the funeral, and Pauline, always looking after him with great concern, would not let him go, afraid that the stress would damage his health. His son and daughter-in-law were sent to Rodaun.

In public this was put down to a certain lack of feeling on Strauss's part. But some days after hearing the tragic news he suddenly set off for the Canarihaus. Up till then he had not had a chance to talk to anyone about his dead friend; to spare his health the name of Hofmannsthal was strictly taboo in his own house. But with Elisabeth and the loyal Alwin he knew that he would be able to talk about his friend and feel near to him again.

Elisabeth was entertaining many guests in the garden, including the Franckensteins, when he arrived, saying he would like to read a little from his *Arabella*. She could see that he would not want to face a large company, so she decided to sacrifice herself for her guests and to miss the reading. She returned to the garden, explained that C and the Franckensteins were asked to a discussion with Strauss, and suggested a walk with her for everyone else.

When she returned Strauss had gone, and C and the Franckensteins were clearly moved. They told her that Strauss had suddenly stopped reading and had broken down in tears. He had given vent to his grief for a long time.

In this time of great sadness Strauss found in Elisabeth and Alwin like-minded friends, and the bond between them grew stronger. Otherwise the death of Hofmannsthal had little effect on Elisabeth's life. Two other deaths in 1929 affected her more deeply.

Max Mossel, dear, charming Max, died in his homeland, Holland. London without him seemed impossible to imagine. Shortly after his death Elisabeth had to sing Sophie and Zerlina at Covent Garden. This time arriving at the station there was no sudden appearance of that white, smoothly-parted hair popping out of the crowd, and those artful eyes no longer laughed out of the bird-like face.

And in Vienna Ferdinand Foll passed away, that great and knowledgeable artist whose interpretation of Hugo Wolf had been a complete revelation to Elisabeth. He died of cancer a few days before Hofmannsthal.

Elisabeth was hardly afraid of illness, and she was no hypochondriac; but one thing made her shudder: she would say about her own death: "As long as it's not cancer. To end like that must be terrible."

At rehearsals at the Opera the loss of Ferdinand Foll was sorely felt. And other things changed too: Franz Schalk resigned his post as musical director. The administration of the Austrian Federal Theatres had increasingly restricted his artistic activities with regulations. For a man of his stature this was intolerable. The administration, which Schalk had once called upon for help against Strauss, had now become too strong, and he left. Wilhelm Furtwängler, already much loved in Vienna through his conducting of the Vienna Philharmonic in symphony concerts, was the favourite to succeed, but, not wanting to desert his beloved Berlin Philharmonic, who were in dire financial straits, he felt he had to refuse. On September 1 1929 Schalk was replaced by Clemens Krauss, who came from Frankfurt am Main.

Almost at one stroke the atmosphere at the Opera changed. The new director brought with him some of his singers from Frankfurt, among them the soprano Viorica Ursuleac and the mezzo, Gertrude Rünger. As guest artists he invited the wonderful *Heldentenor* Franz Völker, the buffo tenor Erich Zimmermann and the dainty, slender soubrette Adele Kern, so elegant on stage. He had worked with these singers before. There is hardly ever harm in fresh blood and there would have been nothing amiss with these additions had not the new director treated some of the trusty members of the company, such as Elisabeth and Lotte Lehmann, in a quite singular fashion.

Up to now Elisabeth had always been treated by musical directors with an almost reverent respect. Clemens Krauss showed no signs whatsoever of following that pattern. The arranging of rehearsal schedules, and indeed everything which had to do with her daily work at the opera house, was handled with little consideration. Treatment of Lotte Lehmann was similar.

The reason for this cannot only have been that the attitudes of Elisabeth and Clemens Krauss were diametrically opposed; it must also have been that she and Lotte represented to the new director a type of singer who belonged to the past, a past connected with the conservative, Mahler tradition. Since the war art had changed a great deal; Krauss and his producer Lothar Wallerstein were advocates of the new trends which they had followed in Frankfurt and which they now wanted to introduce in Vienna. No wonder Krauss had brought singers who had already worked under him. Thus it was that he tended to give them the roles in any new productions, letting the singers of the Strauss-Schalk era be cast in the routine ones.

Was there any point in defending oneself against such treatment? C was always saying that she should. But what would be gained by it? – discord. Her main work was now in the outside world rather than Vienna, where she had, after all, already made her mark.

C did not seem to notice that all Elisabeth really wanted and needed was peace. Not that he was not tremendously concerned for her welfare in other ways: helping her from a train he would cry anxiously: "Mind the step!" An old friend from C's student days, Trudchen Koch, who was by now a great friend of Elisabeth's too, witnessed such a scene of solicitude. "You see," Elisabeth remarked to her, "he worries in case I trip, but then he sends me into the great, wide world!" But with him she felt completely secure on a concert platform.

It was a blessing that he was able to accompany her to Spain in April 1930, for after a guest performance in Madrid she had to sing to the Spanish King and Queen. Shortly before ten in the evening she was led with C into the music room at the palace. Neither of them had ever seen anything like it before: the walls were of porcelain, giving an unbelievably pure acoustic behind which no faults could be disguised. On the dot of ten King Alfonso XIII and Queen María Cristina entered the room followed by princes, princesses and ladies-in-waiting. The two artists remained bowed until the noble audience had taken their seats. Although she had sung to the King before,

Elisabeth's heart was in her mouth; nowhere had she ever felt so exposed, so vulnerable to frogs, as in this porcelain chamber.

The royal couple were charmed. Afterwards the King talked to them for a long time. His Majesty being an admirer of Wagner's music, Alwin, who knew all of Wagner's operas by heart, played almost a whole new concert of his music to him on the piano.

Not many weeks later, on May 6, Elisabeth sang to another royal audience, but this time in a role: that of Adele in *Die Fledermaus*, at Covent Garden (where she also sang Eva in that season of 1930). King George V and Queen Mary were attending a German-language opera for the first time since the war, and never before had *Die Fledermaus* been performed at the Royal Opera House. Bruno Walter had always wanted to perform it in London, but had never been able to persuade the board of directors to agree. After having conducted it with great success at the Wagnervereeniging in Amsterdam, however, permission was finally granted. The sets and costumes were borrowed from Amsterdam, and Walter got an outstanding cast together. Lotte Lehmann sang Rosalinda, Maria Olszewska Prince Orlofsky and Eduard Habich was the gaoler, Frosch. Three other members of the cast were singing in London for the first time: Willi Wörle as Eisenstein, Karl Jöken as Alfred and the excellent Gerhard Hüsch as Falke. Walter added *The Blue Danube* to the ball scene. The evening was so successful that the King and Queen expressed a wish to see a repeat performance. This took place on May 21. In the second interval Their Majesties invited the artists to be received in the Royal Box.

There were no holidays to be had in the summer of 1930; requests from Argentina and Brazil had come – Elisabeth was to go on a two-month concert tour there. With the economic situation as it was she felt she could not refuse such an offer. The sea trip would have to serve as a holiday; and this time Mitzi was coming too, as lady's maid.

Rio de Janiero was a dream, but unfortunately a short one, for the work in Argentina could not wait. From there Elisabeth wrote nostalgically to a British admirer Joyce Fleming*: "My thoughts are often in Garmisch. I hope the time here will pass quickly."

No kind of success could compensate for not being in Vienna or Garmisch. Yet what successes she had! Elisabeth was amazed that in

---

*Joyce Fleming, who came from Edinburgh, had spent much time in Vienna and had taken singing lessons from Elisabeth, purely for pleasure.

a city like Buenos Aires so many recitals could be booked out, as she wrote to Joyce Fleming: "I have sung 10 recitals here in Buenos Aires – in four weeks! This public is quite something!!"

Now Sao Paulo and Rio had to be conquered. On such huge tours Alwin was invaluable. He never flagged, was encouraging and, if Elisabeth was at a low ebb, managed with his liveliness and energy to pull her through it.

And he always knew everything. If he had been with Elisabeth in Greece six months later, at the beginning of March 1931, she would never have made the dreadful faux pas in Athens. She was in Greece for the first time in her life and only for five days, every minute of which was filled with activity. There was more than enough work: an orchestral concert and two recitals, with all the rehearsals that went with them. And then the city with its ancient buildings and treasures! – every free moment had to be devoted to it. She arrived by train at six in the evening and, within a few hours, was standing on the Acropolis with the best guide one could wish for: the famous Wilhelm Dörpfeld, who had been Heinrich Schliemann's assistant at the excavations at Troy, had asked to have the honour of escorting her.

On top of everything else it rained invitations; it was quite impossible to accept them all. There was one from a "Monsieur Venisolous", or something like that. There really was no time to go to people whom she did not know at all. Nevertheless Elisabeth, conscientious as she was, hastily wrote a reply saying that every moment of her stay was fully booked and therefore, regrettably, she was unable . . . etc. She found out too late that she had refused none other than the great Greek statesman and prime minister, Eleutherios Venizelos. Of course the matter became public, and from C in Vienna came a telegram on which was written just one word: "Disgrace".

Standing on the Acropolis Elisabeth had felt as if she had been lifted out of the present. Only faintly could the maelstrom of people and vehicles at the foot of the rock be heard. Every now and then Dörpfeld said a few quiet words, but otherwise it was only the past of which she was aware, between the pillars and pediments, brightly lit by the moon. With C an experience like this would have been impossible: he did not possess enough inner tranquillity. Would another man be any better? Klemperer must have been in her mind at this time, for shortly after Athens she was performing Bach's *St John Passion* in Berlin under his baton.

His fiery and passionate interpretation of the music was just as it had been twenty years ago. Again their eyes met when a certain passage had gone particularly well; again they both gave their artistic all to the music in which they were collaborating. To work with him was truly heaven.

Klemperer went to the recital which Elisabeth gave with Alwin in Berlin on March 28. Shortly afterwards a letter arrived from him.

29 March 1931, Berlin

Dearest, I cannot tell you how much I enjoyed your singing. Your voice has got bigger without losing any of its special personal charm. Musically you are – and I must include your accompanist – natural and sensible, just as I like it. My favourite (as a composition too) was the first Brahms song. "Es träumte mir" ["I dreamt"]. A song like that is for ever. In "Feldeinsamkeit" ["Alone in the fields"] I was enchanted by the bit "mir ist, als ob ich längst gestorben bin" ["I feel that I have long since died"], because there was no trace of "gloominess" about it, Absolutely right. This is a "seliger Tod" ["a blissful death"]. Mahler's "Ich atmet' einen linden Duft" ["I breathed a gentle scent"] is not (as a composition) spontaneous enough for me, finely felt though it is and although one could (almost physically) smell the "liebliche Lindenduft" ["lovely scent of lime"]. Korngold's "Was du mir bist" ["What you are to me"] I liked very much. The other two [by Korngold]? You are much too good for those. – So now you have a "serious criticism" and a very good one too, haven't you?...

I am enclosing my König von Thule [The King of Thule] which I think you would sing beautifully. Please don't think it too slowly. Rather think of Goethe's note in Faust when Gretchen is "undressing": it must be sung as if "to oneself".

Best wishes for your days in Garmisch.
Ever il vecchio amico
O.K.

In May 1931 Elisabeth was again enchanting the London public at Covent Garden with her Adele and Sophie, and was soon to celebrate a triumph singing in a Mozart concert in Paris. On May 16 she made an important recording for His Master's Voice: the *Meistersinger* quintet with the London Symphony Orchestra under John Barbirolli (later Sir John Barbirolli). Friedrich Schorr sang Hans Sachs, Lauritz Melchior Walther, Ben Williams David and Gladys Parr Magdalene.

Unexpectedly this recording turned out to be quite problematic.

The long introduction, which Elisabeth had to sing solo as Eva, she managed beautifully; but no sooner had three of the other voices come in than Melchior came in wrongly. So it was back to the top. Again that long introduction in which one was so exposed. This time she did it almost better – but Melchior bungled again! So it meant singing for a third time what was supposed to sound blissfully happy, which by now Elisabeth was not really feeling. At least it was a way of warming up – they had not had a chance to do so beforehand. But that was not the end of it; Barbirolli had to tap his stand again, and for the fourth time Elisabeth sang: "Selig, wie die Sonne meines Glückes lacht, Morgen voller Wonne. . . ." ["Blissfully as the sun of my happiness laughs, the morning full of joy. . . ."]. And at this point the thought flashed through her mind: "Anything but a morning full of joy." With that the feeling for the music had completely vanished and she felt like stopping; but with an iron will she forced down the laughter rising up in her. She need not have made the effort, for Melchior, seemingly quite unconcerned, made his mistake again. Now it really was funny – but then, at the fifth attempt, the recording succeeded.

Working in England had been enjoyable again. Each time she came she liked the island-country more. Everything breathed great tradition, quality, history. And how pleasantly that English maxim "live and let live" was put into practice in everyday life: people were considerate, there was no pushing and shoving in the street, instead discipline and decent restraint. Now Elisabeth frequently referred to her "beloved England".

Although she had no notion of it, an important part of her life came to an end in this 1931 London season: her singing at Covent Garden. She did not realize it for many years to come, but her performance of Sophie on May 12 was her last appearance at the opera house. There were several reasons for this. First of all the economic depression brought the house, which was, after all, not state run, into financial difficulties. After much debate, the 1932 season only saw a four-week Wagner festival. Then the managing director, Lieutenant-Colonel Blois, died in May 1933 and a new body took over, the Royal Opera House Company Limited, with Geoffrey Toye as managing director. Sir Thomas Beecham was by now artistic director. Wagner and Italian operas continued to be performed; more English opera was encouraged. For years there were very few operas with suitable roles for Elisabeth, besides which her concert career was taking up more and more of her time. Finally, the political events preceding the Second World War were a decisive factor.

Back at home Elisabeth found Sorry quite unwell. The poor little dog had itching sores where the fur was falling out. All night long there was the sound of thud-thudding on the floor as he scratched himself. The vet seemed unable to help; Elisabeth was in despair.

Then a lady in the opera house administration said that her nephew, Dr Krüger, was a skin specialist – would Frau Schumann perhaps consider consulting him? He would certainly not refuse such an artist of the Opera.

Elisabeth made an appointment with the surgery by telephone, but did not mention who the patient was: that had to be done face to face. With mixed feelings, Sorry on her arm, she attended Dr Krüger's surgery, which lay in the beautiful old Schottenhof. It consisted of quite a suite of treatment rooms and radiation cubicles. Suddenly she felt that perhaps she had been a bit rash in bringing a dog to such an obviously important specialist. But she hardly had time to worry for she did not have to wait one minute.

Dr Krüger was a highly cultivated man, Elisabeth could see that at first glance. Tall, about her age, still quite slim, with an impressive, high-domed forehead beneath thin, receding hair; the dark blue suit was respectably elegant.

When she explained rather nervously that it was her dog who was in fact the patient, his face remained professionally and discreetly impassive.

They entered a kind of special consulting room which was furnished in a very homely way. The antiques immediately caught Elisabeth's attention; she even forgot her pet for a moment.

Everything was "earlier" than her own treasures. There was some Renaissance and even a Gothic carved Madonna. Dr Krüger told her where he had found it and where it probably came from. He spoke quietly, without haste, and for a good while they were both engrossed.

Dr Krüger prescribed a spirit to be applied to the dog's skin. He also recommended ultra-violet radiation, should the spirit not be adequate.

In fact Sorry was quite recovered after a week, but there could be no harm in some radiation – then one could always have a nice chat about antiques and art treasures. So Elisabeth bought Sorry some dark goggles and brought him regularly to the Schottenhof for radiation.

Elisabeth now began to think seriously about her complexion. There was definitely room for improvement; all that make-up did not do it any good. Ultra-violet rays would surely do something for it. What was embarrassing, though, was that Dr Krüger would never take a fee. If she started to protest he would always quietly say: "Well, I am doing it for art." It sounded gentle, but also so firm that there was no point in objecting.

Now, whenever Elisabeth was in Vienna, she would regularly visit the Schottenhof. Each treatment was followed by a most interesting half hour. Other patients had to wait while Dr Krüger introduced her to a new *objet d'art*, showing the indications which proved its period, and telling her about the craftsmen of those days. He always spoke quietly but with expression, vividness and absolute authority.

One evening as she went before the curtain, Elisabeth suddenly saw him in a box. He was standing tall and upright and was applauding, or rather he seemed to dispense applause, for he clapped gravely, in accordance with his quiet, sedate manner. She bowed to him and smiled. She liked him tremendously. From now on she always gave him that little greeting whenever she sang in Vienna, for he came to every opera or concert performance of hers; for years he had been doing this, and even since she knew him he never talked about it. He seemed to be a quite extraordinary person.

However, Elisabeth did not do much singing in Vienna in the autumn of 1931. After the summer holidays she was at home for barely four weeks and then it was off on tour again – to Switzerland, England and France. And then America! At the end of October Elisabeth travelled with C to the USA to give concerts at their own expense. A daring exploit, for it was ten years since she had been in that fast-living country where bad times were now just beginning to be felt. What with all the travelling expenses, accommodation, hiring of halls, and publicity, they knew they could end up with a big deficit. But Elisabeth none the less allowed herself the luxury of taking Mitzi with her again – a necessary comfort on such a stressful tour.

Elisabeth was in a state of almost complete panic before her first concerts. After the New York concert was behind her C wrote a report to Lene:

From the New World a thousand warmest greetings! Just think, we had a *phenomenal success*. I have never seen Elisabeth in such a state in all my life. Like a *mad woman* in the artists' room; you should have seen it. As a man I had to control myself very much to keep a straight face. But she still sang phenomenally. – It's working; we're already negotiating dates for the next few years. The press is phenomenal. Whole columns. *New York Times* . . . writes that it would be worth *travelling from Europe* to hear "Nussbaum", "Aufträge" [Schumann] and Schubert sung and accompanied like this.

Just think, *such* programmes with German songs haven't been heard here for *10* years.

Elisabeth would be worn out without me, helpless – ha!... Goodness, the city; – the buildings are so small here, – ha! *32* floors. And the speed of things; but I'm still faster. . . .

I'm already taking a look round; when everyone is bankrupt back home we'll emigrate. – *Poor* Germany, – *rich* Germany! – Let's hope Elisabeth stays well.

She did. Her strong constitution survived even these exertions.

Joycechen! It couldn't be going better. Colossal press! Great successes and everywhere great understanding of German song. – We are flying suitcases. . . . On 18.XII. Paris – 20.XII. Vienna!

Christmas in Vienna and an end to the rushing about.

It could have been perfect had not C's restlessness been so great; after a couple of days of peace it had started again, worse than ever. If he was not on the telephone, he was talking, or thinking aloud; he had to tell Elisabeth everything that was in his mind. If something seemingly important occurred to him in the middle of the night he did not hesitate to go into her room, wake her up and tell her about it, even if it was one or two in the morning.

Soon it was necessary to be travelling again: the days of walking Sorry, writing to friends and reading Goethe were at an end once more – and the chats with Dr Krüger, which Elisabeth really began to miss when she was away.

Yet another new country was to be discovered: this time it was Romania. Already on the first day in Bucharest, on January 25 1932, Queen Marie, mother of the reigning monarch, enquired whether Elisabeth could sing a few songs to her privately. She did not hesitate; she could never refuse royalty. Years later Elisabeth wrote about her visit to the country seat of Queen Marie:

This wonderful lady, who loved music so much, could not believe that

179

a singer could ever get tired. Apparently she was starved of music, for she requested almost the whole lied repertoire. After that she talked with me, we also talked a great deal about my homeland Thüringen[*], where she had spent her childhood (Coburg). Because of her naturalness and easy manner one could quite forget that one was conversing with a queen.... When, after about an hour's conversation, she allowed me to go and, with queenly bearing and gesture, wished a lofty "bon-soir" to the other people present, I was again conscious of her immense dignity. She was wearing a long, flowing gown, and no one who had ever seen her could forget her beauty. Her lady-in-waiting Irène Procopin then asked me if I would like to see her private apartments, and I was happy to have this unexpected opportunity. Her bedroom impressed me no end. It almost had a mystical atmosphere. The Byzantine bed was partitioned off on one side with a wooden trellis; steps led up to a little niche in which she apparently had breakfast; there were heavy brocades on the walls and the most glorious, overpowering scents of flowers.

A further honour was bestowed on Elisabeth: King Carol II (Queen Marie's son) conferred the title of Knight of the Cultural Order of Merit, Class IIa on her.

The spring of 1932 was more full of engagements than ever before. Frequently she had to cross from one side of Europe to the other (although this time she did not go to England); to Vienna she made only fleeting visits, and she was only able to have a short break for Easter in Garmisch.

At last, at the beginning of May, all her foreign engagements had been fulfilled and she could stay in Vienna for a while, occasionally appearing at the opera, and visiting friends, particularly the one to be found in the Schottenhof.

Dr Hans Krüger had long been an ardent admirer of Elisabeth, and she was irresistibly drawn to the cultured, harmonious and peaceful atmosphere of his home, and impressed by his quiet respectfulness and his distinguished appearance. It was therefore not surprising that in these spring weeks of 1932 this friendship turned into love.

Elisabeth's life was completely changed. At last that life-long yearning for a man of tender soulfulness was assuaged. But how rarely they could see each other. Sometimes their only

[*]Elisabeth often said she came from Thüringen, though strictly speaking it was from neighbouring Saxony.

communication for days would be in thought alone, or perhaps a quick smile across the auditorium of the opera house. And then there were still the odd journeys away from Vienna which meant separation.

The summer holidays, normally so longed-for and enjoyed, now meant being far from Hans, and Elisabeth had never before looked forward so much to the day when she had to leave Garmisch for Vienna. At last, on September 1, she was back home, and a week later she wrote to Lene, who already knew how things were:

> You cannot have any idea how happy I am – I have never before in my life found a man like this. His tenderness, his tact, – to be loved so – cannot be imagined. I was with Hans again for 2 hours this morning – Oh Lene – it's so hard to find the time. . . . Hans gave me today (because it's a week since our reunion) a belt buckle from the time of Hans Sachs, gold – very large, I could only ever wear it as Pamina or Eva – on a white band which his mother wore – oh – I was so touched – he just gives me so much – you can't imagine – I am quite *lovesick*. I have never before been in *such* a state of happiness. . . .
>
> Goodbye for now – I can't settle down to anything – I know you understand.

Almost two weeks later a shadow was cast over Elisabeth's happiness. In the evening she went to the opera house; as always Sorry, full of beans and wagging his tail, ran after her to the door, begging to be taken too. If only she had taken him, as she sometimes did. When she returned home he was dead.

A door, just an ordinary door, had been his downfall; normally it stood open, but today it had been shut. He had run full tilt into it in the dark corridor and been killed outright. The next day Elisabeth wrote to Joyce Fleming:

> You can imagine my pain, because you know how much I was attached to him and how loyally he loved me. Never again will I have a dog – and I would never be able to find such a dear animal again.[*]
> I had him for eight and a half years, and now everything around me is so quiet – I miss him terribly. My eyes are hurting from so much crying – hence this short note.

Sorry, who had brought Elisabeth and Hans Krüger together, had had an untimely death. Was this a bad omen? No, as far as her love

---

[*] She did have another dog, but not until seven years had passed.

was concerned, Elisabeth could see no sinister connection, not for one moment. Her life now seemed to consist of two states: being with her beloved, and not being with him. On November 15 she wrote to Lene from Amsterdam:

> I talk with Hans on the telephone almost daily – we can't think of anything except the 6th December, when we see each other again. . . . Just think, on that day C will already be in Budapest. He thinks that I am arriving in Vienna early in the morning of 7th – but actually I'm arriving on the evening of 6th (am singing on 5th in Stuttgart) and will stay the whole night with Hans. Then on the afternoon of 7th I'll travel on to Budapest, where we are giving a concert on 8th. Well thought out, isn't it?
>
> . . . Oh Lene, then I'll only be in Vienna until 20th Dec. which therefore means a long separation until 1st March. I'm really dreading it. You can't imagine how Hans is already suffering from *this* separation, but America is of course much worse – you can never telephone, and letters take 10 days – before you get a reply 3 weeks have passed. Next year I'll arrange things quite differently.
>
> From Stuttgart I'll send you all the letters – records of love – wonderful! Never before has anyone written to me like that – never before has anyone loved me with such devotion. Oh, how will it all turn out – sometimes I wish that C will find me out so that something is done! And he was so touching during our last tour [in England], and he is being so deceived, God, Lene, if he knew!! . . . .

And on December 10 Elisabeth sent the following words from Vienna to Joyce Fleming (whose command of German was perfect):

> Joyce, Joyce, Joyce – *it was the happiest night of my life* everything worked out perfectly – I was here at 3.30 on the afternoon of 6th and came to the Reitschulgasse next morning at 7 – oh – Joyce, how wonderful that I *dared* to do it. Of course it was a risk, but what a reward! . . . . One never forgets a reunion after such a separation. – – – *Please destroy this letter.* – . . . Joyce, we want to do *the same* when I leave [for the USA] as when I came. I shall set off and then turn back at St Pölten – oh – it is terrible, unassuaged longing. . . . I went to a sculptor here today, he is making my left hand in bronze for him! him! him!
>
> Now farewell – I am quite mad, but truly
>
> Your excessively happy
>
> Elisabeth Sch.-A.

And then the hour of separation struck and the "excessively happy" Elisabeth embarked on the American steamer *Albert Ballin* on December 22 as a very subdued Elisabeth. Even the fact that Maria Olszewska was on board did little to change her mood. When the ship docked in England Elisabeth sent a few lines to Joyce:

> Oh Joyce, I'm finding it indescribably difficult to be going so far away – so I want to cancel the February concerts over there (there are only three) and then come back to Vienna *1 month* earlier.... The 2 weeks in Vienna were *spellbinding*! Joyce, soon it will be spring – farewell, my child – – – all the best for 1933, ever
>
> Your Elisabeth Schumann

In America hard reality destroyed her dream of returning home sooner.

> In the train to Los Angeles
8.I.33
>
> My dear Lene.... There is unfortunately no question of leaving sooner. I *must* hold out, otherwise I would be sued and not allowed out of the country. So I'll have to give in. On 24.II. I'll have finished, but there is no ship before 1st March, so I won't have my Hans again until 10th at the earliest.... I'm sure I'll have a good time now in California – I'm not worried about it either – I'm only dreading February now – it's too long.... Addio....
> With a hug from your
>
> Elisabeth-Lümmel [Elisabeth-rascal]

Rascal – that was how Lene often described Elisabeth now; and it was not written only in jest; for Lene was anything but thrilled about her friend's affair of the heart. She liked Alwin far too much, and believed that he was absolutely the right husband for Elisabeth. Although she said nothing about it to Elisabeth she had been disappointed in Dr Krüger when she had met him at the end of 1932. She considered him to be fawning but at the same time stubborn; in short, someone radically different from Elisabeth and to whom she was in no way suited.

But Elisabeth thought that her love was something ordained by destiny, and when in San Francisco she heard about a clairvoyant she went to her immediately to find out how fate would steer her love affair in the future. What the lady revealed to her made a great impression. Immediately after the consultation she wrote everything down. Lene was sent a copy straight away:

183

San Francisco,
Wednesday, 25.I.33

... You are married for the second time, your present husband (I see him playing the piano) will have gone out of your life at the latest in a year. You will marry a third husband, a doctor with the initial "H". You love him, he is waiting for you, thinking of you all day long – he was married, his wife died when his son was 4 months old. He loved his wife, but there is no comparison with his love for you. He sees an angel in you. In one year you will be divorced, your husband will marry again, also a singer, but a completely different type from you.... In four years' time you will *marry* the doctor, give up your career and live with him happily for many years.... Your mother is unwell. In 1 – 3 years she will no longer be alive.... Your present husband *knows* that you love another man, he only does not say anything because he thinks it will pass over, but after your return you will discuss it....

C knew ... they would discuss it ... in one year he would be out of her life.

Again and again these prophecies went round Elisabeth's mind as she travelled to Canada, back to New York and Europe. They gave her the impetus to act.

On March 6 1933 Elisabeth arrived in Vienna on a train from Paris. A whole party of friends had gathered on the platform to meet her: C of course, Karl Wisoko*, Trudchen Koch and other friends and admirers. The Vienna Boys Choir had arrived from Paris on the same train. Reporters and press photographers were waiting, and a choirboy presented Elisabeth with a bouquet of carnations.

In the taxi, as C was trying with his usual impetuousness to draw her to him, she managed to stammer out the words: they could no longer go on as before.

He was flabbergasted, he had not suspected a thing, and he pestered her, as always quite uninhibitedly, with scores of questions: why? when? how?

The fact that he was so amazed almost completely annihilated Elisabeth's resolve. Shame, fear, the wish to spare his feelings – all prevented her from making her confession. She merely gave him

---

*Karl Wisoko, a high-ranking civil servant, was one of the Alwins' most intimate friends.

some peripheral reasons: his incessant restlessness, her need of peace and quiet.

Alwin did not lose hope, of course not, that would have been absolutely against his nature. Convinced that their marital relationship would re-establish itself, he surrounded Elisabeth with care, did everything he could think of to move her and make her turn back to him.

All his efforts were fruitless, besides which she was not able to stay in Vienna very long: at the beginning of April she was travelling again. Thus the marriage smouldered on, with nothing decisive happening.

On April 30 1933 Elisabeth wrote from Athens:

> I have had some discussions with C – oh Lene – it's ever so difficult! And he just doesn't want to understand. . . . It's like a dream here, Lene – Athens – and in the spring too – but with yearning in my heart! Sweetest sorrow! . . . . One can't telephone Vienna from Athens – sad for the heart, but good for the purse. Ha! . . . . Hans's birthday is on the 27th June, I want to be in Vienna then – oh, and then no separation at all, if it doesn't *have* to be.

On top of the homesickness and heartache came a great worry about Emma who had been suffering increasingly since the autumn from diabetes. A few days later a telegram arrived from her sister Frieda saying that her mother was dying. Elisabeth cancelled her last concert in Athens and took the next train north – an endless journey through the Balkans. In Vienna there was just time to reach the three-o'clock flight to Halle and for a quick telephone conversation with Hans.

Too late. Her mother's eyes had closed for ever by the time Elisabeth approached the sickbed. All she could do was decorate the coffin with lilies of the valley, her mother's favourite flowers, and follow it to the Merseburg cemetery where a grave had been prepared beside Alfred's.

In later years Elisabeth wrote about the experience:

> I had the feeling that I had lost the ground from beneath my feet. My house in Garmisch could from that moment on not be the same as it had been when she had had the run of it and, with her beautiful white head, had been the loveliest ornament of the house. I only mention this in order to convey what a change enters the life of a child who is suddenly without parents.

A change indeed. And hardly was her mother buried than another journey had to be embarked upon, to England and France, in order to stand up in front of people, sing and look happy – but with such a heavy heart. It was as if fate had unhinged everything, except for the one reality which was her love for Hans.

Beset by such feelings it was then impossible for Elisabeth, on arriving home, to keep the truth from C any longer. As with many decisions in her life she made it early one morning. It was not yet seven o'clock. Mitzi had brought her morning coffee to her bed, and C came in in his dressing gown to say good morning. Elisabeth then told him everything.

At first he seemed more astonished than upset. "What," he cried, "that stubborn man, that mule!" How anyone could call such a calm and gentle person as Hans stubborn was beyond Elisabeth's comprehension.

C soon saw that he alone could achieve nothing with his wife. Wisoko had to come! Their mutual friend should be mediator. Without more ado he flew out of the room and out of the front door, just as he was, in his dressing gown, and asked the janitor to call a taxi, drove to Wisoko's, woke his friend up by ringing the doorbell and demanded that he should come at once. The latter protested that he was still in his pyjamas, whereupon C retorted: "What of it? So am I!" Thus they both drove back through Vienna in their dressing gowns and sat themselves down beside Elisabeth's bed.

Wisoko saw at once that the marriage was past saving. Elisabeth said several times during the ensuing discussion quite calmly to C: "I could have gone on deceiving you with Krüger for ever and not told you anything, but we are adult people after all."

Alwin, normally never at a loss, was now totally crushed. He told Elisabeth that very day that he would let her go, but in his helplessness he ran to friends and acquaintances and poured his heart out to them. Even in the opera house he announced the news to all and sundry.

Gerd was also very sorry about this turn of events and tried to change his mother's mind. He liked C very much, while Krüger's manner and ways did not impress him favourably.

For only two or three days was C bewildered. Then his practical sense and vitality triumphed and he began to think and act so realistically that it seemed almost grotesque. Though he had wanted to wait for a divorce, at all events until the autumn, yet he was already thinking in terms of a new marriage: he went to "look over" a widow in her thirties and took with him Schnuck who happened to be in Vienna, for his "Jungchen's" opinion meant a lot to him.

"How wonderful for us!" wrote Elisabeth on June 12 1933. "By doing this he has taken the final burden from us."

But now Alwin put an extra burden on Elisabeth's purse. For, although he was agreeing to a divorce, he demanded compensation for the material disadvantage to himself caused by the breaking up of their life together: Elisabeth should provide him with an apartment, pay him a regular allowance for two years and also buy from him the small piece of land in Garmisch which was his.

At first Elisabeth was absolutely straggered by these demands. She considered that a man should be chivalrous, whether he was in the wrong or not; men were supposed to earn a living to support their wives and themselves, not the other way round. But for fourteen years it *had* been the other way round: C had lived off his wife's money in a style which could not normally be afforded by a Kapellmeister.

But was she not happy and he unhappy? And did one not have to try to turn a wrong into a right? In any case it was so wonderful to know that she would soon be free. So she yielded to all C's demands, and he left the Reitschulgasse before the summer holidays. At the same moment as he was saying goodbye, a friend, Suze Rueff, was coming to visit from London for a few days. Her suitcases were being carried up as his were being carried down. C called out to Suze: "You are moving in, I am moving out!"

In November 1933 the divorce was made legal.

CHAPTER 15

Vienna, 1933–1936

Although she and Hans Krüger were still living in their separate homes, there now followed the happiest time of Elisabeth's life. She loved a man with all her heart and was sure that she could be happy with him for ever, just as she had thought she could be with Klemperer. But this time she was not tied to another man, was free, could live her love out in full and did not need to hide anything before the divorce came through, for C had told everyone already. Thus she was, for the first time in her life, completely happy. Even the yearning that she had sometimes felt when she thought of Klemperer was now stilled. Being Jewish, he had left Germany on April 4 1933, and when, in November 1933, she sang four of his songs in the Queen's Hall in London, she did it to demonstrate on behalf of this outstanding conductor and all the other Jewish artists who were now forbidden to work in their own fatherland. Klemperer wrote to Elisabeth on December 16 1933 from San Francisco:

Mia Carina! What a joy! Your letter! And the good news! I've been meaning to write to ask how it went with the little songs ["Paternoster und Ave Maria", "Ich denke Dein", "Schlaflied", "Chanson russe"]. Now I am reassured that it *sounded* good (in the accompaniment). I am sorry that "Ich denke Dein" made no impression. For the fact that "Chanson russe" had to be repeated I am sure I have to thank the "artist", and I do it herewith with *my whole heart.* . . . I have a lot to do, which is for the best. Every week a new programme. Otherwise – my God, my God, I had no idea there could be such a lack of intellectuality anywhere. This is an absolute desert. In Los Angeles I have one or two friends, no one important. I am reading Mozart's letters; could there be anything more delightful? If you do not know the letters you must get hold of them, but *all* of them, not a selection. Also I am getting to know Berlioz's music better here, at the same time reading his gripping memoirs. Do you know his scherzo "Queen Mab" from Romeo? That is an absolutely perfect work. Yesterday I conducted his Fantastique in Los Angeles. – I'm really homesick. – they say that the orchestra in L.A. will probably fold, that the patron won't pay (or can't). I hope to be able to travel back on the *Paris* on 28th April and am counting the weeks. – Be good. Sempre il tuo vecchio amico.

O.K.

Otto Klemperer really was now only a friend from the old days. That great experience at the beginning of her career had now been driven from Elisabeth's heart by her new-found love.

But she had to pay for her happiness. If she wanted to work through a new song with an accompanist or re-learn an old one, it was no longer simply a case of "C, let's just go through this one together" and the obliging husband leaping to the piano; now she had to use a *répétiteur*, and that cost money. She chose Leo Rosenek, an outstanding *répétiteur* at the opera house, who had learnt conducting under Bruno Walter in Munich, but whose greatest talent lay in piano accompaniment.

Elisabeth also had to pay for her happiness with the loss of something irreplaceable: the friendship of Richard Strauss. For the rest of her life Elisabeth always assumed that his wife Pauline had decreed that Schumann was no longer a respectable person, and that all contact should cease, but it was probably largely out of loyalty to Alwin that he now avoided all contact with her. The political developments of the next decade were to make separation inevitable in any case, and Elisabeth only met him twice more in her life: once by chance on a mountain path near Garmisch, when they exchanged little more than a polite greeting, and once, right at the end of the composer's life, in London.

But Elisabeth felt in her heart that the admiration which she and he had felt for each other would always remain, that nothing stood between them except his loyalty to Alwin and to his wife. She continued always to defend him if he was criticized in her presence: sometimes his conducting was said to be a little uninspired, to which she would respond by pointing out "with what economy of movement he could conjure up wonders, especially with the expression of his eyes; perhaps he *was* sometimes a little bored, then he would start working with his elbows, and, while still conducting, turn back a few pages in the score in order to look at something which he found interesting; but otherwise he was quite unique!"

Elisabeth happily consented when asked by His Master's Voice to sing Sophie in a new, much abridged recording of *Der Rosenkavalier*. It was made in the September and November of 1933. Robert Heger, Kapellmeister at the Vienna State Opera, conducted the Opera's orchestra, the Vienna Philharmonic; the Marschallin was sung by Lotte Lehmann, Ochs by Richard Mayr and Octavian by Maria Olszewska – an historic recording of several mature talents, which became one of the great recordings of the century. (It would have been even more historic had HMV agreed to pay Richard Strauss the fee he demanded to conduct it!)

Elisabeth was not only immortalized on the recording as Sophie but also, for a few seconds, as the Marschallin. The producer had overlooked the fact that after the trio in the final act the Marschallin still has to sing the short phrase "Ja, ja" ("Yes, yes") between the two verses of duet between Sophie and Octavian. Lotte Lehmann was therefore not called to that recording session and, when the mistake was realized, it was impossible to find her. There was no question of postponing a session which involved so many musicians and technicians. No one knew what to do. But Elisabeth had always been quite a good mimic, and while it was being debated what could be done, for fun she sang the phrase "Ja, ja" a few times in just the way Lotte usually did. That was the solution! Frau Schumann must sing it in the recording! And so she did, very creditably. She would always say about it later: "I made my voice nice and warm, like Lotte's."

A good six months later, when Strauss became seventy years old, she honoured him publicly by singing (without a fee) a group of his songs in a special celebratory concert which the Vienna Philharmonic gave on June 10 1934, the day before his birthday (the composer was not present).

A week later she wrote to Joyce Fleming:

> On 10th sang the Strauss concert under Furtwängler with huge success, and the Philharmonic conferred their *Ring** (of Honour) on me, which pleased me very much.

Her pleasure was greater than with any other of her decorations, for was it not as if she now belonged to this famous old orchestra, the glorious Vienna Philharmonic, and had gone down in history as

---

*The first woman ever to receive the Vienna Philharmonic's *Ehrenring* was Lotte Lehmann in 1933.

one of the many great musicians who had made Vienna the famous musical centre that it was?

In April 1934 Elisabeth had, at the age of almost forty-six, signed another contract with the Vienna State Opera for five years. She had made it a condition that she would have more time for concert tours and would only work for four months a year in Vienna. Clemens Krauss had not been party to the contract – Elisabeth would not have dreamt of discussing one word of it with her musical director. He had in any case begun to lose influence. Despite his systematic work and excellent achievements he had never been popular in Vienna, indeed resistance had grown up against him. His contract was running out, and the governing bodies in Vienna were hesitating to renew it, with all the conditions which he was making. Political developments, causing ever increasing tension throughout Austria, also played a role in this hesitation over the German conductor. Hitler's Germany lay close at hand and was exercising an ominous influence on public life. The State Opera did not escape this – far from it – for many guest artists came from Germany. For a long time now it had been necessary to exchange singers and conductors with the German Reich in order to keep the opera going. Thus it was that very soon after Hitler's seizure of power, that glorious institution on the Opernring was already affected by the tension and unrest which was increasingly to affect the whole population during the next five years up to the *Anschluss*.

When Vienna did not renew Krauss's contract, a place became vacant in Berlin in December 1934 due to the resignation of Furtwängler as musical director of the State Opera. Furtwängler, after his defence of the composer Hindemith against the Nazi state and his subsequent denunciation by the Nazi press, had felt honour-bound to resign. Krauss did not hesitate to accept an offer from Berlin. It was a post with state backing and facilities which a musical director could hardly have found anywhere else. (In fact Krauss did not make many friends in Berlin either and moved on to Munich after just two years.)

Clemens Krauss did not leave the Vienna Opera alone: "his" circle of singers went with him to Berlin, which left Vienna somewhat bereft. That such a thing could be allowed to happen shows how unpleasant circumstances had become.

Vienna now turned to Felix von Weingartner, who had already

been musical director there for three years after Mahler, and was now coming from a less demanding post in Basle.

Elisabeth was delighted. Vienna would be very tolerable with him as director. She was now glad that after Strauss had resigned she had not gone to Munich, the hub of political activity.

Little interest though Elisabeth had in politics, she nevertheless did rebel against the regime in the German Reich with her whole nature. She once said why: "I want to be able to sing what I want, to say what I want and to love whom I want." Those things she could not do in Germany. She was no longer allowed to have Mendelssohn songs in her programmes, for example. And to have to be careful what one said and in front of whom! Worse still: not to be allowed to love him who was worth every bit of her love! To give up Hans because he was a Jew! Not to be allowed to have as one's friends people whom one had grown to love and who had become the spice of life, simply because they were Jewish! It was quite plain: where such principles held sway one should no longer perform.

Thus Elisabeth sang in the German Reich less and less. 1934 was still an almost normal year. She gave about five concerts in Germany and took part in the Munich festival. The latter she did partly in order not to leave the manager, her friend Clemens von Franckenstein, in the lurch. This meant disrupting her holidays considerably, so that on August 2 she wrote from Garmisch to Lene:

> I haven't really had a single day of rest for I gave the Spanish girl 20 half-hour singing lessons,[*] was in Scheveningen [The Netherlands] for a week, have already sung 4 times in Munich, have to do *Figaro* once more, sing a radio [broadcast] and an evening concert in the garden of the palace and have not noticed any holiday so far.

On top of these engagements came an unexpected emergency one from Franckenstein. Elisabeth was sitting with Schnuck at lunch when a messenger from the Hotel Post arrived: Herr von Franckenstein had telephoned asking urgently whether Frau Schumann could take the place of an indisposed Eva that very afternoon; *Die Meistersinger* was to start at four o'clock.

It was almost two o'clock. The little Opel cabriolet which Elisabeth had given Schnuck happened unfortunately to be in the garage, ten minutes walk away. It took one and a half hours to drive

[*]Elisabeth's first pupil.

to Munich if one drove fast. Elisabeth wavered. "Schnuck, what d'you think?" He was burning with eagerness to be off. He was sure they could do it, he would fetch the car at once while she got her make-up together. With that he took off at a sprint to the garage, shouting to the messenger to telephone Munich to say they were on their way.

They made it. About ten minutes before curtain-up Elisabeth opened the car door in front of the Prince Regent Theatre. Among the theatre-goers who were still sauntering about in front of the theatre in evening dress and dinner jackets, there would hardly have been anyone who realized that the Eva of the evening, the famous Schumann, was the lady climbing out of the little car. Franckenstein, who had been waiting in an agony of anticipation in the entrance, recognized her at once, of course, hurried down the steps and thanked her with all his heart. Elisabeth accepted his thanks with a smile and said: "But do not forget my son. He has saved the performance."

As a reward Schnuck was given an exceedingly interesting seat for the performance. In his lederhosen he could, of course, not appear in the public area of the theatre, so Franckenstein arranged a seat for him in one of the lighting boxes close to the front of the stage and halfway up. From there he could see what hard work it really was to give a performance. How wide and shining his mother's eyes seemed to be – it had to be nerves; and how often she swallowed and discreetly cleared the frogs from her throat, especially before her very first entry; on top of that, she did not know where she should be on stage, since she had not rehearsed this production, so that she was having to watch the other singers intently. Then, after a particularly difficult bit, he noticed an almost imperceptible sigh of relief. Now Schnuck understood why his mother so often cried: "What a profession!" or "It's hard labour!"

As far as hard labour in her homeland was concerned, Elisabeth's career was virtually at an end in that summer of 1934. In the spring of 1935 she sang on the radio in Mannheim and did a concert in Nuremberg and one in Frankfurt. In 1936 she was only heard in Breslau, and then only as part of an orchestral concert. In 1937 she cancelled her only two concerts in Germany, which were to have been in Hamburg and Berlin. From then on she did not sing in her homeland again, except for a very few concerts after the war.[*]

[*]This is perhaps why she is hardly known in German today.

The city of Frankfurt am Main asked her to sing for them again before the war, but this time the authorities there required to know whether she was of Aryan origin. Elisabeth replied that she was Aryan, indeed her family tree could be traced back to Henrietta Sontag*, and for that she demanded a special fee. She named a sum which must have been far too high for Frankfurt, for she did not hear from them again.

Elisabeth had enough work at home and abroad without going to Germany. Every now and then there would be a major musical landmark for her, as when Toscanini came to Vienna and Budapest in October 1934. "Toscanini is here," she wrote to Lene, "Hans and I were at his rehearsal yesterday – heavenly. – Lotte is doing a concert with him today – I'm singing the [Beethoven's] 9th [Symphony] with him on 20th and 21st here and on 22nd in Budapest. On 24th I'm travelling to Switzerland."

Now America was beginning to play an ever greater role in Elisabeth's life. It was true that she had not been there during the winter of 1933–34, but in the spring of 1934 she had signed a two-year contract with the New York concert agent Annie Friedberg who had agreed to find as many engagements for her as possible, none at a fee lower than five hundred dollars. Thus the connection with the United States was now firmer and more businesslike than ever before – and tougher: Annie Friedberg demanded twenty per cent commission on all fees, which was twice that taken by Ibbs & Tillett in England.

In the autumn of 1934 Elisabeth was obliged to prepare herself for a journey to the USA and Canada. "Oh, how I'm dreading America and the separation until 27th January. But what can I do?" she wrote to Joyce Fleming at the end of October.

Once in America the tour did not seem so bad after all. There were some unforgettable evenings such as the three *Rosenkavalier* performances, on November 30 and December 1 and 4, with the renowned Philadelphia Orchestra conducted by Fritz Reiner. (In these performances Lotte Lehmann was singing the Marschallin in America for the first time.) In a letter home Elisabeth admitted to a friend that the time seemed to be flying by quite quickly. "Hans is longing for me and let me go with a heavy heart . . . but one can't just drop America completely."

---

*The prima donna who sang in the first performance of Beethoven's Ninth Symphony. For years the family mistakenly believed that Emma Schumann (née Sontag) was descended from her.

Elisabeth should not have "dropped" America to any extent, on the contrary she should have been making every effort to conquer the New World. For indications of the ultimate evil back home were getting ever stronger. In the summer Chancellor Dollfuss had been assassinated. The National Socialists were gaining more and more support in Austria, causing bitterness and hatred among the people. The country was in a ferment, and Hitler's Germany was threateningly close at hand. Nevertheless Vienna seemed to Elisabeth immovable and indestructable, her home for the rest of her life. Even if she had seen the political indications more clearly, they would have been blurred by her love for Hans and the happiness she enjoyed, living in the charming old Stallburg.

Her yearning for it never lessened. By the end of her American tour she was more than ready for Vienna.

> Minneapolis, 9.I.35. 9 p.m.
> Dearest Lene, I'm sitting here – far, far away from you dear people. But soon I will have done here – I'm counting the hours.... Hans writes with every ship – the dear man misses me dreadfully, and I find it really touching how patiently he is waiting ... my recital on 30th [December] in New York was a sensational success, a huge press and what an atmosphere in the audience. Fantastic! And all my colleagues were bursting with envy. I was in unbelievably good voice, completely without frogs – oh, then it's a joy to sing.... I'm longing to know how things are getting on at the opera – the new director [Felix von Weingartner] – it's amazing that at the age of 71 he has got a 5-year contract! There's hope for us yet....

Back in Vienna prospects at the Opera took on a surprising new form. Together with Lotte Lehmann, who had also just returned from America, she studied the rehearsal schedules which had been given to them. With astonishment they saw that they had been cast in roles which they had not sung for many years, roles like Aennchen and Agathe in *Der Freischütz*. They were expected to gambol about the stage again like young things! But as Clemens Krauss had taken some of the singers with him to Berlin, Elisabeth and Lotte had to help the Opera out of a casting fix and take on the "young" roles.

Not without mishap, however. It happened in *Der Freischütz*; Lotte was singing Agathe, Elisabeth Aennchen. At the point where Elisabeth, referring to Agathe and her love, had to sing "These young lovers are a bit of a worry", she could not help thinking of the womanly maturity of Lotte-Agathe, wanted to burst out laughing

195

and could not utter another sound. Because her next phrase was to be the last in that scene she simply ran off stage. But Weingartner was waiting for the cue, and a longish pause ensued before the orchestra started playing again.

With Weingartner as musical director Elisabeth now began to enjoy another particularly happy time at the Vienna State Opera. Vienna became again for Elisabeth what it had been before: as well as her home, the focus of her art. She and Weingartner respected each other greatly, which meant that they worked harmoniously together. This also showed itself outside the Vienna circle. During the Krauss era Elisabeth had not taken part in the Salzburg Festival at all; now, under Weingartner, she performed there again.

It had to be now, of all times, that Elisabeth, normally so healthy, was unable to sing in Weingartner's new production of *Die Entführung*. Perhaps she had really overdone things this time: shortly after the American tour, in February 1935, she had had to go off again, this time to Holland, France and England; then, at the end of March and beginning of April, there was a rushed visit to Budapest and Bucharest. She was hardly back from Romania when she was knocked sideways by a particularly nasty flu. On April 16 the first night of *Die Entführung* took place without her. It was not until the day after that she was even able to go out into the fresh air for a short while. Still weak, she had to set off on April 22 for The Hague, England and France. She should have taken more care.

Scheveningen, 2 May 35

Dearest Lene,
   Your letter was forwarded to me here, where I have come for convalescence, because I simply could not recover from the flu. My trachea wouldn't get better – vocal cords were perfect, that's why that idiot Wiethe [her throat specialist in Vienna] let me travel, and in two concerts I became completely hoarse and had to stop. Went for treatment in London too, and then on an impulse to the sea. And now I am as newborn, sang a recital yesterday in The Hague in particularly good voice, am travelling to Paris tomorrow, where I have a concert on 4th and will then be back in London from Monday 6th to 8th inclusive. Perhaps I will be able to get out of Florence and would then be in Vienna on 10th instead of 13th.

With her zest for life returned and her fears for her throat set aside Elisabeth was in an almost reckless mood. In a jewellery shop in London she was shown a diamond tiara – and she bought it. Its sparkle was almost subdued, not too vulgarly glittering, and in a few easy movements it could be turned into a necklace. She had hardly ever before been so pleased with a piece of jewellery.

Now she did not feel she needed to cancel Florence; with her newly-found energy she could cope with any strain. The city itself would have been compensation enough for anything untoward. From there, on May 11 1935, she wrote to Joyce Fleming:

> Arrived here safely – what a wonderful city! – Yesterday I spoke to Hans on the 'phone – he is *thrilled* about the tiara, but only if he is allowed to give it to me as a present. So I said "yes" straightaway. – Monday morning at 8 o'clock at home – oh, who could be happier than I am?

Gone were the days when Elisabeth had to buy everything for herself. But of all the things Hans had ever given her the tiara was the most beautiful. Another report went off to Joyce about it, this time from Vienna on May 20:

> Thank goodness I'm home again now – and Hans has seen the tiara and is *enraptured* by it. I wore it at my recital on 16th (a colossal success) and the whole of Vienna was saying: "But that tiara is surely *not genuine*." What do you think of that! In London no one would doubt it. Oh yes, "no prophet is accepted in his own country"! . . . Vienna is enchanting now in May with all the lilac, and I am happy to have some peace at last.

Now she could stay in Vienna until the holidays and find the leisure to do something which she had been wanting to do for a long time: Hans owned a stylish country house of the Biedermeier period[*] in Mauer, just outside Vienna. He hardly ever used it, for it was not very comfortably furnished – the house of a widower who did not have time to bother about it. So, in this heavenly Vienna spring of 1935, Elisabeth leisurely took it in hand with skill and delight. By the beginning of June they were able to move in. "We are living in a world of Renaissance and baroque" wrote Elisabeth to Joyce during that summer. She wanted to stay in it as long as possible; she did not even want to travel to Garmisch ahead of Hans: "We will not be coming before mid-July," she wrote to Lene, who was invited there too, "for I don't want to be separated from Hans as well this summer."

[*] Early nineteenth century.

But then Elisabeth's maternal resources were called upon. Gerd wanted her. He had been called up to the obligatory labour service which the National Socialists demanded of all young people. In Königsberg in East Prussia he was accommodated with hundreds of young men in a huge, old locomotive shed, and each morning he had to get up very early to do heavy work on a railway line. The unaccustomed primitiveness and roughness of his life, which lacked everything intellectual, was getting him down, and he was looking foward tremendously to his twenty-first birthday for which he had obtained two days leave. His father, step-mother and sister Minka were going to visit him, and he hoped desperately that his mother would be able to come too.

Thus Elisabeth did leave Hans for a while and went on the long and awkward journey to East Prussia. In fact she felt no inclination to meet Walther (although she had not seen him since 1924, when Schnuck had had tuberculosis), for she knew that there might be some disagreements about her son's career, which had already been discussed to some extent. Who would have thought that he, who had heard from his father quite a lot of arguments against musicians and the theatre world, and who by now, like his father, was a keen sports pilot, would declare his intention of becoming a film director! At first Elisabeth had not been able to believe it.

Walther insisted that his son should first of all have a decent academic education, as he himself had had. One could then build upon that education. Gerd was in fact quite taken with the idea of student life and offered no resistance; he chose subjects which would later be of use to his career: theatre studies, literature and art history.

For his birthday he had asked his mother for something very special. He had got to know the young organist Traugott Fedtke and his wife Edith, who played harpsichord, at concerts which they gave in a nearby church. He had written to his mother asking if she would not like to give a little concert with them, just a private one for him and perhaps a couple of music-loving comrades.

Elisabeth agreed and took the task very seriously. She chose the programme carefully with Fedtke and rehearsed with him. They were to perform several sacred arias with organ accompaniment but also some secular, for, as there was a grand piano in the church, Schnuck had particularly requested "Morgen" and "Traum durch die Dämmerung" by Strauss.

The recital was unforgettable. The day of Gerd's birthday,

Sunday, had passed harmoniously. They had all spent it on the Baltic coast. Not a word about Gerd's education had passed anyone's lips; they had sat on the beach, sunned themselves and bathed, gone for walks, joked, laughed, and eaten and drunk in style.

Then, in the wide space of the baroque church on that mild evening, mother and son held a more private celebration of the birthday. In a light-coloured dress she stood up in the organ gallery and sang with all her heart down to the man in his brown uniform, sitting listening with his two friends.

As they went alone afterwards, arm in arm, to Elisabeth's hotel he could not find the words to thank her; he merely squeezed her arm once or twice. They had never felt so strongly before how much they belonged to each other.

The summer of 1935 was not particularly restful. Having at last arrived in Garmisch Elisabeth agonized about whether she should shorten her holiday, as her commitments actually demanded. She no longer had C's driving force behind her – he would have put such thoughts straight from her mind. (They hardly ever saw each other now, only at rehearsals and performances in Vienna. He had married again – the lady whom he had "inspected" with Schnuck.) Hans was proving to be the absolute opposite of C in this respect: he clung to Elisabeth and tried every argument against her going away.

The extremity of his behaviour gave her extra strength of mind, and she tore herself away, left Hans and the beloved little country house before she had really had a proper taste of the summer, and travelled to London. Her sense of duty had prevailed, especially regarding the English public, who had become so attached to her. Besides, Sir Henry Wood was conducting the Promenade Concert for which she was engaged; to refuse him, who had brought the Promenade Concerts into being and which he put on every summer in order to awaken the love of classical music in the hearts of the people, would have been quite out of the question.

Thus the whirlpool of work spun again and sucked Elisabeth into it. When England was over, there were just three weeks in Vienna, and then it was living out of suitcases again. Hundreds of times she wondered whether all this singing was really necessary any more. For twenty-six years now she had stood on stages and platforms, and with her forty-seven years she could surely be allowed to slow down a bit. Just before Christmas she came home, and on January 3 1936 she was due to set off for America again. It did not bear thinking about! And America was not always that profitable: the hugely successful recital in New York on December 30 1934, which Elisabeth had financed herself, had brought a deficit of 570 dollars!

Suddenly Elisabeth made up her mind. Despite the fact that her first concert in America was then postponed to the end of January she wrote to Joyce Fleming on the 2nd:

> 1936:
> I sent you all the best for 1936 and the news that I have *cancelled* America. I can't make up my mind, want to live a little, not only work. Just think, Gerd has been here since 19th and is staying a few more days [before returning to university]. Christmas was heavenly – I am blissfully happy to be at home with my loved ones.

And on 9th:

> . . . Oh, I am so happy to be here. Gerd had to return to Hamburg yesterday – so today I am suffering a bit from heartache. – But [you] must also know that I have been given the Legion d'Honneur and am *very* proud of it.

Chevalier de la Légion d'Honneur, knight of the famous order founded by Napoleon. To belong to the host of select people who had excelled with outstanding achievements in military, artistic or scientific fields (including her beloved Goethe), was truly an honour.

Now at last there was an opportunity to enjoy some rest and to "live". In those first two months of 1936 Elisabeth could not even bring herself to sing at the Opera. To Lene she wrote:

> Now they are pestering me at the Opera to sing Adele on 2nd [February] – I haven't agreed yet – but I think I shall *have* to – they are beside themselves that I am here and don't want to sing. . . .

So she did agree to do the *Fledermaus* performance, but otherwise she sang not a note in two months. In the end she had to admit to Lene that doing nothing was not a good thing: ". . . I am so depressed, the way one is after a long rest."

Why should all that uninterrupted time with Hans have made her depressed? They had now been able to enjoy their love freely for nearly three years. The hot passion had cooled down to a warm, homely love. Now they were actually living together for a far longer period than ever before, and it was during this time that Elisabeth was sometimes seized by the feeling that even this man was not the right one for her. She had to have a person with whom she could feel quite free, and with whom she could, quite uninhibitedly and spontaneously, exchange ideas. During this first period of living together for so long, there was often a lack of light-heartedness between them. Of course it was touching how Hans looked after her, but it was getting to be too much of a good thing: "For heaven's sake wear your fur coat, Elisabethchen" (although it was not cold, so that it was just a nuisance); "And please make sure you put on your scarf" (the air could not have been milder); "No, please, please close the window, it's so easy to catch cold in a taxi" (pointing out that there was no draught was always pointless). Gradually Elisabeth began to see what C had meant when he had cried: "What! That stubborn man, that mule!" It also often seemed to her that Hans regarded her as his personal property. That would not do at all; she had to feel free.

In her letters her tone, when referring to Hans, began to change. On February 22 1936 she wrote to Joyce, referring to a concert tour of Egypt, Switzerland, the Riviera, Algiers and France, due to begin at the end of February:

> I simply must do some work again – my voice is quite rusty, and Hans is so spoilt having me here that he's already moaning about the 5 weeks' separation.

"Spoilt"! "Moaning"! How different her choice of words now was! How lucky, she thought, that she had been loath to marry again immediately. Although this did leave her open to proposals of marriage – from men like "Hirschi".

Hirschi had always come back to the artists' room after the concerts in California (in January 1933), and finally he had invited Elisabeth to spend one or two days on his ranch. She had expected a grand estate with servants and every comfort, but had found instead a big log hut which was surprisingly primitive. What was more: apart from Hirschi there was not a living soul there, not even a servant – she was all alone in a wilderness with her admirer. And he was such a peculiar chap – the way he would look at one from beneath his thick eyebrows.... what a bit of luck that she was able to lock her bedroom door! More than relieved, she had left the following day. She had answered Hirschi's letters occasionally after that, but after his proposal of marriage she never wrote to him again.

After almost eight weeks of rest, when Elisabeth was preparing to leave for Egypt at the end of February 1936, she felt depressed, was having doubts about her relationship with Hans and was worried that her voice would no longer behave itself.

But these gloomy thoughts were not to last for long.

CHAPTER 16

Vienna, 1936–1938

THE TRIP TO EGYPT soon put an end to Elisabeth's negative thoughts. The beautiful spring there was intoxicating, and once again she was surrounded by magnificent ancient buildings. On March 5 she wrote to Joyce: "It's a dream here, and I would never have thought *such* success possible." She was amazed at the enthusiasm of audiences which could hardly have had much experience of German song. The fact was that the concert-going public of Cairo and Alexandria had not yet been spoilt with regular concerts of good music.

An added bonus was that Schnuck was on vacation from university and was able to join her for two weeks after she had completed her engagements in Egypt. They met in Zürich, from where they travelled together to Monte Carlo and later to Nice, Marseilles and over to Algeria.

She thoroughly enjoyed showing Gerd Monte Carlo. She took him dancing in the exclusive Sporting Club; went for drives with him; frequently accompanied him to the casino, gave him money and showed him how to play roulette. She was just as excited as he was. In fact she made a marvellous companion.

During the crossing to Algeria they tried their luck at gambling again. In the ship's saloon roulette was being played, and also a kind of horce-racing with knee-high horses which looked rather like chess pieces. Of course Elisabeth chose the horse with her lucky number, but the thirteen never came anywhere near the first three positions. After several games they lost interest and went off to have coffee and cake. Suddenly the croupier made an announcement and they could just make out that the next winner would take a particularly high prize. So they had another go.

After a promising start they noticed to their amused dismay that thirteen was losing more and more ground. They had gambled away several thousand francs. But oddly enough, although several horses had already reached the finishing line, the croupier did not stop. Perhaps the placing of the horses mattered? But thirteen fell further and further behind, until at last it stood all alone on the field. The croupier bundled together a large number of banknotes and cried: "Numéro treize! 72,000 francs!" What did it mean? Thirteen the winner? A pageboy brought them the fat bundle of notes. This time it was the horse which came last which was the winner. Elisabeth curled up laughing, and did not recover for a long time.

That summer of 1936 Joyce Fleming was able to join them in Garmisch for a few days. While she was with them Elisabeth could not resist asking her to read Gerd's palm – she was so good at that sort of thing. So, sitting up on the mountainside, resting after a walk, she looked at his hand and declared that he would meet the woman of his life within the next fortnight. Elisabeth was intrigued and excited, but Schnuck just laughed: he already had his girlfriend Ria with whom he was well on the way to being engaged. His mother could be taken in by things like that if she wanted, but he was not!

In July 1936 Elisabeth and Schnuck travelled to the Salzburg Festival together. Elisabeth was to sing in *Cosí fan tutte* under Weingartner and in *The Marriage of Figaro* under Toscanini. To sing with a genius like Toscanini was an experience. In fact, Toscanini's feelings about Elisabeth were similar; he wanted her at all costs. Once in the past she had had to cancel; to do that again would have been out of the question. On that unfortunate occasion her telegram had been handed to him during a rehearsal. He had screwed it up, thrown it to the ground and stamped on it.

In Salzburg Schnuck came to the rehearsals, the performances and to the parties. Mother and son visited the house of Mozart's birth, where Elisabeth became very quiet and contemplative.

Almost every afternoon they would have a coffee at the Café Basar, a favourite haunt of artists and musicians. On one occasion Schnuck was struck by a young girl with thick, black hair, a clear face, brown eyes and the finest features. The young lady was standing at a table saying goodbye. Elisabeth also thought she looked unusual. Two days later, when they were in the Basar again, the dark beauty was having coffee in the garden. "Look, Schnuck," said Elisabeth, "there are friends of mine with her at that table. Come on, we'll join them."

But only for a few minutes could he enjoy her company. She was an English girl – she was introduced as something like "Miss Blackton". Yet one could have sworn that she came from a Mediterranean country. And she spoke excellent German. He could find out nothing else, for everyone was joining in the conversation, and very soon Miss Blackton had to leave.

The next day Schnuck could find her nowhere, and the day after that he had to leave Salzburg. He asked his mother to keep a good look out for her and find out where she lived; and Elisabeth, who would have done anything for her son, especially where his heart was concerned, did try her utmost, but without success: no one could tell her anything, and the friends who had been sitting with the girl had left town.

Two months later, at the end of September, Schnuck came to Vienna for a week's visit before the start of his term. He had been there for less than forty-eight hours when Elisabeth, coming home for lunch after shopping, rushed in and cried: "Schnuck, guess whom I've just met! The young English girl from Salzburg, and I have her address!"

Elisabeth had been at her milliner, trying on hats. Suddenly in her mirror she had seen another mirror in which was reflected the face for which she had searched so diligently in Salzburg. In the reflection their eyes met. Elisabeth nodded a greeting which was shyly returned. In an instant Elisabeth turned round and declared: "Aren't you the young English girl from Salzburg?" And when Miss Blackton affirmed this, astonished that the great Schumann should recognize her, Elisabeth came straight out with "My son liked you so much. He is very young, admittedly, but perhaps you would go out with him just once?"

Schnuck rang Elizabeth Blagden (not Blackton) immediately, but she said that she was fully booked for a week, as she had a friend from England staying with her. And even when that week was over, Miss Blagden still had little interest in going out. But then Schnuck found out from her that she was studying singing, so he lured her out of her reticence with tickets for a Lotte Lehmann recital in the Musikvereinssaal.

Elisabeth went too. The concert was sold out and she had to sit with Schnuck on the patform, where extra chairs had been placed. As a guest Miss Blagden got the best of their three tickets: she sat in a box at the side of the stalls, so mother and son saw her mostly in profile; only occasionally would she turn slowly towards them with a shy, fleeting smile. "The prettiest thing about her," said Elisabeth, "is her little nose."

She was almost as happy as Schnuck about finding her again, and she was overjoyed when she noticed that the girl was falling in love with him. Not one word of criticism about the object of his worship passed her lips – not even a mention of Ria; she made him feel that she was in complete agreement with his choice, although in fact she had some doubts, for Biddy (as she was always called) was three years older than Schnuck. Elisabeth once wrote to Lene:

> You must love without scruples the women or men chosen by your children or else you lose your children – and be in agreement; perhaps one can never agree absolutely with the choice – one has always imagined or wished for someone different.

Elisabeth was very glad that Biddy came from her beloved England. There was only one embarrassment: that she was learning singing. Sooner or later Biddy would be bound to ask for her opinion, and what if she did not consider the voice to be worth training? She would hate to have to disappoint her. There would be other worries as well about Biddy and Schnuck in time to come, but always loving worries, never any annoyance or the slightest jealousy. To empathize with a person, to be obliging and kind, whether with her own child, a friend and admirer or any of the many people who came into the artists' room after a concert, was a strong feature of Elisabeth's character.

Members of audiences who came to say an admiring word to her often became firm friends for life. In this very year, 1936, the foundation of such a friendship was laid: a friendship which was to be of great importance towards the end of her life. And this time it was not with a young admirer like Joyce Fleming, but with a person of her own age.

Miss Winifred Hall was nanny to a family called Armstrong; she had been with them for many years and had become more of a friend than an employee to her two charges and the widowed Mrs Armstrong. The family had a record of Elisabeth Schumann singing the Strauss song "Freundliche Vision", and Winifred could not hear enough of it. On November 14, 1935, Mrs Armstrong gave her a ticket for an Elisabeth Schumann recital in the Queen's Hall.

She returned from the concert completely entranced and eagerly wishing to give something lovely to Elisabeth to thank her for the joy that she had received from her.

At the end of April 1936 Winifred saw a picture of Elisabeth in the *Radio Times*, with the news that she was to give a radio broadcast on May 3. Then she took her courage in both hands and, without telling a soul, she wrote to Elisabeth via the BBC, asking her if she could make anything for her, and what would she like?

A reply came very soon, a photo of Elisabeth and a little letter (in English, of course):

> Thank you for your sweet letter. It is very kind of you to want to make me a present, although I do not like you to have so much work for me. I leave it to you to do as you like.

After much deliberation, and discussion with Mrs Armstrong, Winifred decided to make a more wonderful dressing gown than even an Elisabeth Schumann could ever have possessed before. Winifred was extremely skilled with needle and thread, an artist in sewing and embroidery. A miracle of a dressing gown was created – pink and with lace ruffles cascading down it like foam.

The great moment of presentation approached – on November 20 1936, when Elisabeth was singing in the Queen's Hall again. With wildly beating heart Winifred went to the artists' room after the concert. There was such a huge queue of people at the door that her courage almost failed her. Even when the people had at last all gone she did not dare to go in. Then Elisabeth opened the door, went along the corridor and disappeared into a kind of lounge. Winifred said to herself: "It's now or never," went after her and knocked almost inaudibly at the door. Elisabeth could not have heard it, but at that moment two ladies came out. Shy and trembling Winifred stood at the open door. Elisabeth looked at the timid figure and asked: "Do I know you?" Now the poor woman did not know whether to say yes or no, but suddenly Elisabeth exclaimed: "It is Winifred!" And with that she pressed her warm cheek against Winifred's, giving her the courage to say: "I brought you a present. Shall I open it?" But her hands were shaking so much that she was not able to without Elisabeth's help. Their combined efforts finally revealed the garment. Elisabeth was enchanted – she had truly never before possessed such a beautiful, finely worked dressing gown. "I hope it is the right colour," Winifred said anxiously. But she could not have chosen better, for Elisabeth loved pink and, with her voice slighty hoarse from singing, cried: "Oh yes, always pink!" When Winifred very soon made a move to go Elisabeth said: "You will hear from me."

Six days later another photo arrived with the words:

Dear Miss Hall,
   I must tell you how *touched* I am to work for me such lovely things.
It is really too nice.
   Again my thanks and I would be very glad you enjoy the photo.

With best regards,
Yours sincerely,
Elisabeth Schumann

Winifred was, of course, not the only person who had to be thanked. After a big concert in London there were always many flowers and tokens of admiration, and Elisabeth never failed to acknowledge them. In this November of 1936 she was, in fact, so busy that she hardly had any time to be with Lene Jung who had come with the whole Dresden Opera ensemble to London to perform at Covent Garden, among other things *Ariadne auf Naxos* which Strauss was conducting himself. On November 16 Elisabeth wrote to Trude el Bedell, a cousin of Hans Krüger, with whom she had become great friends:

   . . . I found the whole ensemble so comic – you know, *so* bourgeois, *so* German – not a word of English – what a scream. And they all looked like housewives who get 20 marks housekeeping money a week. I wonder if I looked like that when I came to Vienna!

Thirty years before, the members of the Dresden ensemble had seemed to the little student, Else Schumann, to be godlike beings whose achievements were unattainable.

Elisabeth's first task in 1937 was a concert tour in the USA for which she set off in January. Her first engagement after arriving was to have been to sing at a reception at the White House, given by President Roosevelt. But the illustrious party had to do without Schumann in the end. In an interview on American radio, Elisabeth explained what had happened on the sea crossing:

   Oh, it was awful. We were one and a half days late, first because of storms and then we were three hours in a fog in New York harbour. When my manager 'phoned to the White House that I was marooned on the ship, President Roosevelt asked: "Can you not push that boat?" Of course, nothing could be done and I missed the concert.*

---

*A year later Elisabeth did give a concert at the White House, on January 6. She shared it with Percy Grainger who played pieces on the piano including two of his

There were plenty of other concerts to be given, for the tour took her to many provincial towns and then via Florida to Cuba. She also had to give two concerts in New York.

In the middle of May, when Elisabeth had been back in Vienna for many weeks, a letter arrived from Joseph Hofmann, Director of the Curtis Institute of Music, Philadelphia. He asked whether she would be interested in joining their faculty as teacher of German lieder in the winter of 1937–38; he assured her that the timetable of lessons would be fitted around her concert schedule.

This was the famous institute where the great Marcella Sembrich had taught. She had died in 1935; perhaps they were looking for a replacement. Elisabeth could not make up her mind immediately, she knew how boring teaching could sometimes be, but she had to think of the future, of a time when her own career would be slowing down. So she accepted the offer in principle and asked for terms.

Meanwhile – and it was almost like a sign of things to come – there were changes in the household in the Reitschulgasse. Mitzi, Elisabeth's perfect and ever cheerful lady's maid, was getting married and would have to leave. The wedding was to be on May 23, and Elisabeth did everything she could to make the occasion a special one. A week before the event she wrote to Lene:

> The wedding dress will be made with the gossamer which you gave her last year ... the dress will be made by *my* dressmaker – so everything will be tiptop. I shall of course sing in the church – although she doesn't know it – afterwards there'll be a big feast at my place, all her relatives are coming; the table will have wedding decorations, there'll be garlands at the door, and I'll have flowers strewn in the courtyard for her....

It was a sad farewell, but Elisabeth was lucky: Mitzi's place was taken by Lotte Lehmann's well-trained Resi, for Lotte was hardly ever in Vienna for any length of time these days.

Although things had changed in the Reitschulgasse, life in Garmisch in the summer of 1937 was almost the same. Of course Mitzi was missed, and Gerd could not come as he had to do part of his military service during the university vacation, training as a pilot.

---

own compositions. Arpad Sandor accompanied Elisabeth, who sang songs by Mozart, Schubert, Langstroth and Strauss. The President presented her with a large photograph of himself, framed with wood from the original roof of the White House.

But Lene was able to come and stay for a while, and later Elisabeth was there alone with Hans.

On July 13 a telegram arrived from the Curtis Institute offering fifty dollars a lesson, six lessons a week for three months. A salary like that on top of concert fees was not to be sneezed at; besides, the offer had arrived on the 13th, which had to be a good sign. Elisabeth accepted.

When she shut up the Canarihaus after six weeks at the end of August she felt sadder at leaving than ever before. It was pouring with rain on the evening she left; as she was being driven off to the station she looked back, and the sight of the little house, empty and abandoned, filled her with an unusually intense yearning. What she did not know was that she had just spent her last summer in the Canarihaus. A new life was about to begin.

On September 1 1937 she wrote to her friend Suze Rueff:

> I am not quite satisfied with Resi – am playing with the idea of locking up the apartment completely on 1st November and of looking for new staff in the middle of April. Since Mitzi has gone I don't feel so happy in the apartment any more. . . .

It was almost as if she were already moving into that new life and inwardly cutting herself off from her beloved home. In the end she did not reduce it to a state of hibernation but let the household carry on through the winter.

Nothing had really happened to produce these feelings and misgivings. Everything, life and work, went on as before. In fact it was in this very year of 1937 that the Viennese excelled themselves in showing "their" Elisabeth how indispensable and how immensely appreciated she was. On June 17, a few days after her forty-ninth birthday, Education Minister Pernter created her an Honorary Member of the Vienna State Opera; Erwin Kerber, who had replaced Weingartner as musical director, sent her the document with a most respectful and admiring letter. And in the autumn, when Elisabeth was singing in the final rehearsal for Bruckner's *Te Deum* with the Vienna Philharmonic under Bruno Walter in the Théâtre Champs Elysées in Paris, the bassoonist and President of the Vienna Philharmonic, Hugo Burghauser, stepped up to the conductor's stand and made a short speech: he said that he was delighted to declare her an Honorary Member of the Vienna Philharmonic Society – the only woman to have been awarded that distinction.

"In all the years during which we worked with you, your voice – never failing, never dimming – went before us like a shining star. . . ." When Professor Burghauser then walked up to Elisabeth and presented her with the document, the orchestra gave her a standing ovation.

She was in her fiftieth year, yet her voice was still as silvery and fresh as ever when, on October 31 and November 1, she sang the first Flower Maiden in *Parsifal* at the Vienna Opera. Little did anyone taking part or listening know that these two evenings marked the end of an era: the Honorary Member of the Vienna State Opera was singing her last operatic role. A week later, when she set off for England and America, she left her operatic career behind. It was a few years before she herself knew that this part of her artistic accomplishments, which had begun twenty-eight years earlier with small roles in Hamburg, had ended with a small role in Vienna.

To leave the stage in this manner was absolutely to Elisabeth's taste. When, three and half years later, Lene Jung had to say goodbye to the theatre, Elisabeth, who had by now firmly decided never to sing in opera again, wrote comforting words to her friend:

> You won't miss playing about on stage for *one* single day – admittedly it means the passing of an era, but that's life. Of all things one should not have a farewell performance or farewell recital – these things make everything so difficult – to depart without fuss – that's the right way, believe me. I didn't know that I was giving my last performance in November '37, and I'm so glad I didn't.

If Elisabeth had been more politically aware, she might have realized that things could not go on as they had been for much longer. If she had still been with C, who had much more of an instinct for such things, she would have known that they were living on a volcano.

After she had had her first teaching experiences at the conservatoire in Philadelphia she wrote to Joyce Fleming:

> My first two hours at the Curtis were desperately unhappy ones, I was straightaway given *three* men to audition – I said at once of course that I never teach men. Now I have 6 female students, 5 of them are very gifted and have good material. I only teach *style*, not technique, and that's really rather pleasant, it's more like *making music* – no scales, although I often tell them a lot of technical things like how to colour a note, how they can help themselves with this and that etc.

I only go to Philadelphia once a week, teach from 11–1 and from 2–6, then back to New York – dead tired of course.

But the new activity was more promising than at first thought; ten days before Elisabeth travelled back to Europe she wrote to Joyce:

Everything is going wonderfully here. At the Curtis I'm such a success that they want me for the whole season next winter. I agreed to 6 months with double the number of lessons!! Triumph all along the line! My recital here was a great success, – at first I thought I would have to cancel, had an abscess on my left tonsil, it was lanced and I had 8 painful days. So alone too – it wasn't very nice.

This was how Elisabeth saw her immediate future, as she wrote further:

My ship leaves on 24th [February]. It's the *Deutschland*. Early on the morning of 3.III. I'll be in Cherbourg – then quickly to Vienna for 6 days. On 11th back to Paris, then Monte Carlo, Bordeaux, Lausanne, Chaux de Fonds, Marseilles, Algiers, Tunis, Oran, Casablanca, Rabat, on the way back Cannes again, then on 12th April at last in Vienna until the end of the season. Unfortunately not London this time, I think I won't be there until August (Prom).

While Elisabeth was still singing and teaching in America, on February 12 the Austrian Chancellor, Dr von Schuschnigg, went to see Hitler at his mountain retreat, the Obersalzberg near Berchtesgaden. And then, one month later, when Elisabeth was able to be in Vienna for five days, the desperate measures of the Austrian government were made known – the decision to appeal to the people. Leaflets were distributed for a plebiscite (which was later cancelled). Fate was allowing Austria three days' respite, days full of paralysing tension. Elisabeth, the born optimist, inclined to the view that everything could come all right in the end. She knew Schuschnigg and thought highly of this cultured music-loving man. But now, as Austria's last hours ticked away, with radio and newspaper reports chasing on each other's heels, Elisabeth felt a terrible anxiety, for she knew only too well what it would mean for Hans, his son Heinzi, and many friends, if the National Socialists came to power. She would not leave Hans's side; she did not have to sing during those five days, so she stayed with him in the Schottenhof. Any little differences they had had during the last few years were now brushed aside by the threatening political danger.

On March 11 1938, that black Friday in Austria's history,

Elisabeth and Hans sat hand in hand listening to the report of Schuschnigg's resignation, demanded by Hitler. At the State Opera Carl Alwin conducted the last performance of old Austria: *Eugene Onegin*.

Next morning, on March 12, the day German troops marched into Austria and were euphorically welcomed by the people, it was time for Elisabeth to depart again: the concerts in France and North Africa had to be sung. Although she did not know that the following day Hitler would declare Austria to be part of the German Reich, never before had she left Vienna in such depressed spirits; she had often sighed, finding it hard to tear herself away, but she had never been so deeply troubled. And it was strange that Mitzi, who by now had her own household to run, turned up early that morning in the Reitschulgasse. She did not want to be deprived of helping her beloved former mistress with her travel preparations and of saying goodbye. As faithful Donner's taxi, with Elisabeth inside, began to move off from the courtyard of the Stallburg, Mitzi burst into tears – as if she had not said farewell to her dear lady dozens of times before.

CHAPTER 17

1938: Emigration

AT FIRST IT DID NOT OCCUR TO Elisabeth that she would not be back in Vienna in a month's time: that was her home and that was where she was under contract to sing; and there was no question of abandoning Hans and Heinzi in these changed circumstances.

But soon she had doubts. A new power was controlling the opera house – and the whole country. Would it be possible to work and live under these people? Lene Jung had been doing so for years in Dresden, although she was no friend of the Hitler regime. It was true that she was not such a public figure and did not have an "undesirable" man at her side. Hans was in fact Elisabeth's greatest problem. What would happen if she were to continue to admit her liaison openly in this new Austria, or "Ostmark", as Hitler had named it? But the Austrians were such friendly, easy-going people and admired her so, they were hardly likely to make problems for their Schumann, especially as the Nazis rated art so highly; and the thought of leaving her home, possibly for ever, was too awful to contemplate.

Then the newspapers in France began to print disturbing reports from Austria. The easy-going Austrians were turning out to be particularly energetic followers of Hitler. Jews were forced to scrub the pavements; shops which belonged to Jews were badly damaged, their windows smashed and the goods destroyed.

Not a word came from Hans, only a little news about him came through his cousin Trude el Bedell, who was an American citizen; he himself did not dare to write, being convinced that post would be opened by the secret police.

On March 19 Elisabeth was singing in Bordeaux, and heard eye-witness accounts of the events of the last few days in Austria. A whole ensemble of banished artists had collected in the French city for a guest performance, among them the soubrette Irene Eisinger

214

(who had had to leave the Berlin State Opera as early as 1933), and from the Vienna State Opera the conductor Josef Krips. He had been dismissed in Vienna at once (as had Carl Alwin).

It was almost impossible to believe all that was happening in Vienna. Leading politicians, whether Jewish or not, were arrested. Gangs of youths with swastika armbands dragged to prison Jews who had held high posts in the economy or in the civil service. Then they "cleaned up" the homes of these Jews: furniture, pictures and carpets flew out of the windows, pianos crashed down the stairs. The heavy boots of the swastika bearers could also be heard echoing through the corridors of hospitals. They were looking for Jewish doctors and took them away unceremoniously – snatching them from bedsides, X-ray departments or operating theatres. Anyone who dared to resist or protest was roughly manhandled and set to scrub a pavement straight away with a corrosive solution harmful to their bare hands.

Fortunately Hans practised only privately and the name Krüger did not sound Jewish. But so many other good friends in Vienna were living in fear, were not free to make purchases in the shops of their choice, were not allowed to use lifts in their own apartment blocks and could not sit on a park bench if it was marked for the use of Aryans only.

In Bordeaux the small circle of artists in which Elisabeth found herself gave vent to their feelings against Hitler and Germany.

Many years later Irene Eisinger told Schnuck how quiet his mother had been at this time. She had thought that this behaviour was all part of Frau Schumann's elegant refinement. But no, it was not that: the horror which was creeping upon her made her taciturn. It was there in Bordeaux, one week after the *Anschluss*, that she felt she could not bring herself to return to Vienna. And Hans? It was clear that he and Heinzi would have to try to leave Vienna as fast as possible. It would be much easier to help them with affidavits and visas from outside the Reich.

But it was dreadful not knowing where one belonged, to have to live out of a suitcase in expensive hotels, to hasten from one engagement to the next and to commute between Europe and America because earning more money was so essential. Of course, after the North Africa tour there would now be a huge gap: Elisabeth should have been singing in Vienna, but now there would be no engagements from the middle of April until the summer holidays.

From Lausanne Elisabeth wrote to Ibbs & Tillett in London on March 22:

> Yes, poor Austria!! It was terrible exiting [sic] the few days in Vienna. I believe I don't go back to Vienna and stay after my tour which is the 11th of April finished in *London* till I leave in October for America. – – So – if you can arrange as many engagements in England during the season and later, as possible, do it please. I think, there would be a BBC, a "prom", a few At Homes, perhaps I could go to Bournemouth or Brighton – you will see, what is to do.

This was almost like begging; Elisabeth had not written a letter like this since her very first attempts at getting engagements. But in extraordinary times extraordinary measures had to be taken.

An ominous letter arrived during the journey through North Africa. Elisabeth's concert agent, Dr Artur Hohenberg, to whom the letter was addressed, had sent it on to her for her information. It was from the "Ravag", the Austrian radio broadcasting company, but with "Deutschösterreichischer Rundfunk" (German-Austrian Radio) rubber-stamped over it.

Vienna, 19 March 1938

Dear Sirs,
    We refer to your esteemed letter of the 12th inst. and have to inform you with the greatest respect that the lieder recital by Elisabeth Schumann planned for Easter Sunday unfortunately cannot take place.
    With German greetings,
                    Deutschösterreichischer Rundfunk

Not one word more. The two signatories were keeping quiet about the reason for the cancellation. After all that she had heard it was not difficult for Elisabeth to guess what it was: Hans. A singer who was connected to a person of that kind could only corrupt her national comrades with her art, however great it was and however widely renowned. She was not wanted.

As it happened Hans himself came to the conclusion that for Elisabeth to return to Vienna was out of the question. Schnuck had discussed everything with him and wrote in a long letter to his mother (using riddles and false names, since letters were being opened by the authorities) that Hans did not want her to return on any account: terrible things were happening there. He urged his mother to have her registration as a resident of Austria cancelled, so that, as a German with a foreign place of residence, she would the more easily be able to make return visits. But he also reported that "Marion's husband' which meant Hans Knappertsbusch, who often conducted in Vienna, had advised continuing to meet one's commitments at the opera until the end of the season (as if the authorities would have allowed that now!).

Up until now the opera administration had given no indication that Elisabeth's contract should no longer be fulfilled. Simply to stay away would be a breach of contract; and with these new authorities that would probably not only mean a fine and loss of pension but also confiscation of all financial assets and possibly the apartment in the Reitschulgasse.

As if all this was not bad enough, Elisabeth was stricken with an extremely unpleasant stomach bug while in North Africa. For days she could swallow nothing but tea, and she became very weak. She knew she would need some time for convalescence, and this seemed suddenly to be the answer: officially to declare herself unfit to sing at the opera house for the time being.

Lene in Dresden seemed now to be living on another planet. The only friend to whom Elisabeth could pour out her heart was Joyce Fleming in England. The sea journey back to the Riviera at last afforded some time to write.

7 April '38

Dearest Joyce, I have no idea where you are – I've heard nothing from you, and I hope that this letter will be forwarded to you at once. You know that I went to Vienna for 5 days after America and witnessed the coup during that time, which I found awful. You know that I have never been a supporter of the movement, besides which Hans and Heinzi and many of my friends have been severely affected by it, and I was very, very sad when I left Vienna on 12th March, for I had to sing in Paris on 13th and then my African tour began which has finished today, and I shall be at the *Hotel Majestic, Cannes* early on 9th. In the meantime I have heard from Vienna that I shouldn't return there, they might take my passport away etc., at any rate vex me in every way they can. I can't appear at the Opera any more because I'm tied up with Hans, which doesn't bother me in the slightest, since to sing at *that* opera house, the way it is run now, is neither an honour nor a pleasure. Only one thing makes me immensely unhappy: that I cannot go *home*. I was so looking forward to my lovely apartment – you know how I love it – and the thought that I might also not be

217

able to go to Garmisch later makes me feel quite ill. I have now taken steps to cancel my registration as an Austrian resident, and, if that succeeds, to register as a German with a foreign place of residence. Then everything is easier, and I'd be able to go to Garmisch too in the course of the summer. – Hans proposes to go to America with me in October – we got quite close again during those days in Vienna. . . .

Always to have to go on stage with such a heavy heart and to try to give people pleasure! After a recital in Cannes on April 10 she was handed a telegram at the hotel: "Kammersängerin Schumann". That had to be from Vienna – was it bad news from Hans? "Recommend short extension of leave Kerber." Thank goodness it was only that! Elisabeth had written to Trude el Bedell (being an American citizen there was less likelihood of her letters being opened) and had requested her to ask the musical director's advice. She had evidently done so. Then a letter came from Trude. She had spoken to Kerber. He had not only recommended that Elisabeth should request extension of her leave but also that she should write another letter saying that she was very attached to the opera, but that certain circumstances had made it awkward to work there and that she particularly wished to spare the administration any embarrassment, and that she kindly requested relief from duties with a pension. Knappertsbusch had apparently paved the way for Trude, for Kerber had been so helpful, but she urged Elisabeth to write quickly, and most politely, since letters like this would be used as evidence.

It was a long time since Elisabeth had written a letter as difficult as this one, not since her letters to Walther about Schnuck had she had such a hard task. Just at this time she also had to move. On April 12 she took a room in a comfortable boarding house in Nice, which was much cheaper than the grand Hotel Majestic in Cannes. On her first day there Elisabeth wrestled with her petition to Direktor Kerber, writing and rewriting it many times.

My dear Herr Doktor,
    Having only just requested an extension of my leave, I find I must write to you again, for after much consideration I have decided to ask you to allow me to take early retirement with a pension.
    I cannot put into words how difficult this step is for me, for you have no doubt noticed with what love and devotion I was always attached to the most glorious of all institutions. The time that I was able to serve art in that place was the most glorious of my life. And

the fact that I was so privileged as to be able to carry the fame of it to all the artistic centres of the world remains for me the greatest satisfaction and finest reward of my career.

I do most earnestly ask you to direct my petition to the right quarters with your support, and already thank you warmly in advance.

The letter did achieve its aim in part: she was informed that she would be allowed to retire.

Apart from some correspondence from her solicitor about cancelling her registration as a resident of Austria she now heard nothing at all from Vienna or even London for almost two weeks. She had written on April 11 to Ibbs & Tillett again:

Just to tell you ... that I will arrive in London on the 26th April.... I have the idea to give for two months a master course for *Lied style* – can you help me with the announcement? It has to be in the papers before I arrive, don't you think so? Please, send me a line as soon as possible....

In fact she was unable to travel to London when she planned. It was proving very complicated obtaining affidavits for allowing Hans and Heinzi into the United States. The American Embassy in Nice needed all sorts of documents from Elisabeth and the two Krügers: photographs, birth certificates in duplicate, medical certificates, even Elisabeth's divorce certificate in duplicate, and a copy of her contract with the American concert agent Annie Friedberg. All this involved express letters, telegrams and telephone calls to Vienna, Merseburg, Hamburg and Löbejün (where her sister Frieda lived) – and then waiting.

On April 28 a sobering letter from her solicitor arrived: it seemed that the question of a pension had been approached wrongly and that the most she might hope for would be repayment of her pension contributions.

At last, at the beginning of May, all the necessary documents for the affidavits had arrived, and on May 7 Elisabeth arrived in London. But prospects there were far from rosy: Ibbs & Tillett had not yet been able to arrange a single concert, there was just the possibility of an At Home in June. The advertisement for the lieder course had appeared in the newspapers, and Elisabeth wrote to Joyce in the middle of May:

I'm not singing here at all ... am not giving *any* lessons (in the lieder course) – about 15 applied, but they almost fainted when they heard the terms, only *two* signed on, but I haven't yet made a start with only the two.

Nevertheless Elisabeth continued to live in the expensive Hyde Park Hotel; a small flat, which Elisabeth had hoped Joyce might be able to find for her, had not yet turned up. And now Gerd had to have a room in the hotel too. He had finished with his training as a pilot for the time being, and at last he was free to join her for one glorious week! He had his breakfast by her bedside; she went shopping with him and took him to eat at the famous Scott's Restaurant. They saw the latest films, about which Schnuck always had plenty to say. Money was just flowing away. . . .

They discussed what should happen about the Canarihaus. It did not seem advisable to leave it in Elisabeth's possession after she had been guilty of "Reichsflucht" (flight from the Reich), as it was so nicely called. The best plan seemed to be to pass it to her son as a gift. While they were arranging this with a London lawyer and by telephoning a solicitor in Garmisch, Schnuck never heard the slightest word of complaint from his mother, who was, after all, now homeless; and, while concentrating all her efforts on helping Hans, his son and a number of friends, was on the point of losing her own hard-earned property and possessions. For him she was the same vivacious, fun-loving mother he had always known. Neither did she make the slightest attempt to persuade him to leave Germany. He should finish his studies, that was important. His beloved Biddy, the English girl from Salzburg, was near him now, for she was studying singing in Berlin. The two of them were planning to spend the summer holidays with Biddy's parents in England – this young woman was for Schnuck a strong connection with a foreign country, with freedom.

One day mother and son were wandering along Piccadilly when Schnuck suddenly caught sight of a racy two-seater, an MG, in the huge showroom of University Motors – a smart little car, black with a green radiator, upholstered in emerald-green leather, the doors cut sportily low, spoked wheels – Schnuck could not take his eyes off it.

Elisabeth said: "Schnuck, I'm giving it to you as a present." With that she pulled him into the shop. The MG Midget cost £222. "Listen," said Elisabeth to the smartly dressed salesman, "I am Elisabeth Schumann. How much discount can you give me?" The young man looked serious and said nothing; he obviously did not recognize the name, not being one of the more musical car salesmen of this world. Elisabeth gave him a little clue: "Most firms give *artists* a discount." This firm did not. But after some hesitation they declared themselves willing to allow payment in three instalments. Schnuck was surprised that his mother wanted to stagger payment; it did not occur to him that she was having to be careful with her money.

One of the motoring trips they made in the new car was into the countryside, to the seat of Elisabeth's rich admirer Mr van Geldern, who lived in the county of Sussex. The conductor Wilhelm Furtwängler was also a guest there as well as two young ladies, one a brunette, the other blonde, both delightfully pretty and charming; good company for Schnuck – and for Furtwängler. He even joined the young people for a bathe in Brighton. They all had to change behind a rock, first the ladies who, after they had swum, lent the men their costumes to wear. Furtwängler hesitated about getting undressed, but the ladies persuaded him until he dared. He re-emerged from the rock looking very long and thin, almost like a giraffe with his long neck on his drooping shoulders; the lady's costume was very tight and he had had to roll up the top part around his waist. His head, with its tonsure, was impressive, giving him a somewhat learned, ascetic look.

His appearance was deceptive, however, at least as far as asceticism was concerned, for there was no question but that he flirted with the blonde girl. He did it with the self-assurance of someone who is accustomed to being surrounded by admiring females.

That evening Elisabeth told her son that Furtwängler was a great lady-killer. She had bumped into him in Egypt where he had told her of his many children scattered around several countries. When she had asked him whether they came to his concerts he had replied: "Oh well, some of them are still too young for that."

How quickly the golden days with Gerd flew past. He returned to the "Reich" in the MG without the slightest misgivings, with the carelessness of youth. It was a comforting thought for Elisabeth that at least he was not suffering. . . .

Shortly after Schnuck had left, Elisabeth went to look at a little studio flat recommended by Joyce Fleming. It was a charming furnished flat, complete with grand piano. At first Elisabeth felt that the rent was too high for her, at £4 a week plus 10s 6d service charges, so that she might as well stay in the hotel, but in the end she simply could not resist taking it.

Having a grand piano was particularly important now, for Leo Rosenek had arrived in London with his wife, and Elisabeth had a number of His Master's Voice recordings planned, for which she had chosen Rosenek as her accompanist. Until now Elisabeth had had an unwritten agreement with George Reeves that the latter should always accompany her when she was in England; but she had explained to Reeves how absolutely vital it was for Rosenek as a refugee to be allowed to work in England and to start to build up a new existence. Reeves had agreed at once and, while Rosenek had waited in Amsterdam, Elisabeth had acquired a work permit for him through HMV and sent him £10 for the journey to England. On June 7 she wrote to Joyce:

> Work daily with Rosenek. And *one* pupil comes three times a week. Ha ha! Then I'm going to make records, on 29th an at home – oh, how time flies. – Was at Glyndebourne, marvellous: *Macbeth*. [Fritz] Busch [conductor] fantastic, [Carl] Ebert [producer] wonderful – unforgettable! What artistry!

During that June and the beginning of July 1938 Elisabeth made about thirty recordings in a total of six days. Eleven of them were of Brahms songs – almost half the total number of Brahms songs she ever recorded; there were six Schubert songs, songs by Strauss, Liszt, English songs and some songs in a lighter vein. Although these were some of the best recordings she ever made, she always maintained that at this difficult time her voice had already lost some of its "Blütenstaub" – bloom (literally: pollen).

During these weeks of work, news from Hans came seldom. It was not certain when he and Heinzi could leave Austria; all they kept saying was that it would be soon. Elisabeth waited impatiently, not only because she missed Hans and wanted him safe but because a big decision had been made. On May 14 she had confided to Joyce: "And then! – we will be *married* here in London – but no one must know, so keep quiet!"

To marry Hans was of course a risk, that had showed itself clearly in the years after their first great love; but to live alone in America when one was not so young any more would surely not be all that pleasant in the long run, and if Hans was going to have a career there, his position in society would have to be made respectable. But would Hans be capable of such a huge change? Would the completely different way of life in the New World perhaps make living with him even more difficult than before?

Elisabeth's English friends and admirers were not happy that she was planning to move to America, and she was often asked: "Why don't you honour our country?" To Joyce, Elisabeth wrote in explanation:

> My child, New York is the only possible new home for us. First of all I've got a contract with the Curtis for 8 months, 2. Hans will have it much easier there than here. Of course, in my heart I only want to live *here*, but I suppose it is not to be. . . .

On no account should either Hans or Heinzi be "unemployed" for too long. Elisabeth had heard chilling news from Lotte Lehmann, as she reported to Joyce on June 7 1938:

> Lotte wrote a *very* unhappy letter a week ago. Otto[*] is also in Cap Martin, the children[†] are being looked after in Monte Carlo. They haven't a penny – Lotte has to earn for all of them – too much for two vocal cords!! She finds Otto very unwell. Oh, how sorry I am about that – on top of all the other worries.

And on July 1, lying in bed at 7 o'clock in the morning, Elisabeth wrote to Joyce:

> . . . Hans and Heinzi are still not here – it's supposed to be any day now, but they don't come. Heaven only knows what sort of problems they are having! On 9th, a week tomorrow, I'm going to Abano near Padua – perhaps we can meet up there first. . . . Everything is still unsettled and won't be decided until they are out at last. I've got lots to do here, a thousand invitations. London in the season is mad – but wonderful! I love it dearly. . . . I miss you very much – often have lots to talk to you about – am a little anxious about the marriage and would rather things remained as they are. I wonder what's written in my palm!

It seemed that Elisabeth wanted to know what fate was going to decree so that she could decide accordingly. She even had Hans's

---

[*]Lotte's husband Otto Krause.

[†]Krause's children from his previous marriage.

handwriting analysed. A whole lot of character traits were presented on five typewritten pages. None of them were very positive or really very negative. It made the decision even harder, although such a mixed character – if the analysis was correct – spoke against marriage.

Abano was a pleasant distraction from these problems. The mud-baths were strenuous, the heat great; Elisabeth became quite lethargic and hardly had the strength to worry. But best of all: Lene had come! That meant there would be plenty of laughter.

Elisabeth's and C's friend Karl Wisoko joined the ladies in Abano too. He was very unhappy that Elisabeth was no longer intending to sing in Vienna, but whenever he tried to dissuade her from her decision she would reply that under present circumstances Vienna was more foreign to her than Timbuktu. "Germany and Austria don't exist for me as long as the Nazis are there."

When it was time to depart Elisabeth and Lene hugged each other in tears, as if they knew that they might not see each other again for a long time.

On July 29 Elisabeth arrived back in London. Then it was only a few days before Hans and Heinzi finally arrived. The young man was immediately lodged with a family in order to learn English: Joyce had arranged that. Hans lived with Elisabeth in her flat, although they were not sure if it was the done thing.

But in London hardly anyone bothered about what their neighbour was doing; people living in the same building often did not know each other by name, since it was not customary to have one's name written on the front door. It was quite easy to pretend that they were married, especially as they did not have to register anywhere as residents. That was typically English: freedom of the individual. In America that would not be so easy: it did not help to live together permanently in an unmarried state, and to live apart would cost far too much. Besides, the name of Schumann could be of more use to Hans in his career if he were married to it.

This was an argument in Hans's favour when he was urging Elisabeth to marry him, and he spoke of it constantly.

Just at this time, at the beginning of August 1938, Schnuck came on a short visit again; he had just spent a holiday with Biddy Blagden and her parents in Devon. Now mother and son walked arm in arm up and down in front of 5 Thurloe Square, where the flat was. Suddenly Elisabeth asked: "Schnuck, should I marry him – Hans?"

For him there was no doubt: "Mummy, if you ask that, then it's obvious that you shouldn't marry. One only marries when one is absolutely certain." For a while she said nothing and then said she thought he was probably right.

A few hours later Schnuck drove off back to Germany in his MG. As the car moved off he looked up to the first floor; Elisabeth was standing rather rigidly at an open window, waving. What Schnuck did not know until much later was that at that moment Hans Krüger was kneeling behind her with his arms clasped around her knees, imploring her, almost in a whisper, to marry him.

On August 15 1938 they got married in a registry office. They had chosen the town of Redhill for the ceremony, for near there lay the beautiful home of Mr van Geldern who acted as witness and as host to a wonderful wedding breakfast afterwards. Thus the press did not get wind of the event.

Elisabeth was relieved to have made the step at last. Radiant with happiness she sang, three days after the wedding, a group of lieder in a promenade concert at the Queen's Hall in London. The effect she had is shown in a letter of August 19 1938 from the widow of John Galsworthy.

Dear Elizabeth [sic] Schumann,

I, an old woman, always greatly devoted to music, and to a fair extent trained therein, would like so much to thank you with all my heart for your lovely singing at last evening's Promenade concert. It gave me more pleasure than any singing I have ever heard; in all my long experience I have never heard the exact middle of each note touched so surely and musically, never known such perfectly lovely phrasing, never heard such wonderful endings to every song. Could one ever forget that last "mein Knab!" in "Vergebliches Ständchen"? I had for a moment the (perhaps ridiculous) feeling that if you had put forward the toe of your shoe, the whole audience would have moved forward to kiss it!! . . .

Sincerely and gratefully yours
Ada Galsworthy
(Mrs John Galsworthy)

On August 24 Elisabeth, with Hans and Heinzi, went on board the Cunard steamer *Aquitania*. A day before their arrival in New York Elisabeth wrote on a postcard to Joyce: ". . . the crossing is heavenly, and we three are so happy."

Elisabeth only had three weeks to arrange everything in New

225

York, for on September 22 she was going to have to leave for Europe again. The three of them stayed at Hotel Meurice which was respectable but not too expensive, and where they could live for six months or more without using up too much money. Elisabeth arranged English lessons in a language school for the men. In order to practise medicine, Hans not only had to pass a medical exam but also one in written and oral English. With Heinzi things were easier: he had commerical interests, it would be best if he started work in a large firm. Elisabeth exploited all her contacts, wrote letters, telephoned, had lunch with people, invited out to meals anyone who could be of help.

In the midst of all this activity news came that Hans's furniture was on its way to New York and could arrive any day. Elisabeth's furniture could not be released until the question of her "Reichsflucht"-tax had been settled, and that could take a long time. Storing furniture in New York would have cost a great deal, so now it was necessary to find an apartment at once; it could be furnished while Elisabeth was in Europe. Hans's cousin Trude el Bedell, who was also now in New York, was longing to do it for her. In fact a pleasant apartment was found before Elisabeth had to leave; it was in a building with "only" eleven storeys: 171 West 57th Street, not far from Central Park.

With her mind at rest, Elisabeth set sail on the *Ile de France*. When she arrived in France on September 29 the country was in the grip of high political tension. Immediately upon arrival Elisabeth tried to telephone Gerd, but neither he nor Biddy were to be reached in Berlin. The next day, September 30, brought some relief at least: peace! Chamberlain had signed an agreement with Hitler in Munich which fulfilled almost all of the dictator's demands and left Czechoslovakia practically defenceless. But at least there might be no war now – or so a born optimist could feel.

When Elisabeth arrived at the Hyde Park Hotel in London on October 3 a letter from Schnuck was waiting for her. He had been called up and was being trained to fly large aeroplanes. Before that, during the political crisis when war had seemed likely, he had driven Biddy and her friend Jean Howard, who was also studying singing in Berlin, in the little MG in a dramatic dash as far as the German border at Aachen (there was room for three if one of the passengers sat on the transmission shaft!). The two young ladies had then proceeded in the MG to England alone while he had reported for training. (Biddy in fact returned to Berlin a few days later, when the crisis was over.)

So it was now clearly impossible to see her son, as Elisabeth had hoped. However, she finally managed to telephone him in Berlin at a weekend.

It was a happy conversation, and a few days later Schnuck wrote to her that he had felt they were incredibly near to each other. But increasingly Elisabeth was getting the feeling that the two of them were living in two different worlds. The wish that he would leave Germany preoccupied her more and more. For a long time she had kept silent about it, but now on the telephone she had asked cautiously what he would think about working at the Curtis Institute. He had understood at once that she was hinting at eventual film work in Hollywood, and had reacted very negatively: what he had heard about the American film industry had put him off going there; besides, his English was not good enough. No, he wanted to get lots of practical experience in the German film industry before he thought of moving anywhere else.

When she was at parties Elisabeth found that most English people thought there would be no war; they thought that Hitler had acquired so much territory he would be satisfied with what he had got. That cheered her up a bit, but she could not help the nagging worry coming back from time to time. The words of the songs she had to sing were extremely poignant for her at this time: words about peace, about loneliness, about far off places and a yearning for the homeland. She even recorded, with nostalgia, some German Christmas carols for HMV in October.

At this time it was still possible to market recordings of German carols; and on October 24 Elisabeth was still singing in German on French radio: as yet the world was ten months away from catastrophe.

Paris made Elisabeth almost happy again for she was staying with her friends the Spitzers, where she gave an At Home. To her great joy she met Lisa Reitler there – her dear friend from Vienna. The Reitlers were also planning to emigrate to America, and when Elisabeth went on board the *Paris* in Le Havre at the end of October she had the feeling that she was not going to be parted from many friends for long.

Seldom did Elisabeth enjoy an Atlantic crossing more. Lene was sent a report from on board:

... yesterday there was a big gala concert for the widows and orphans – fantastic, because there were first class artists on board – a tenor and a lyrical soprano from the Chicago Opera, then Myra Hess, the wonderful pianist, who accompanied me, and afterwards cabaret artists, a banjo player who's just done a big tour of India, then a pair who did some apache dances – it was just like being in Paris. . . . Delightful ship. I felt very well – and the weather was fantastic. For seven days a floating restaurant!

The most important thing now was to make a home again. It had only changed location: giving concerts in Europe simply meant a rather longer journey than before. Engagements in England were already planned for 1939.

In a way it seemed that things were just going to go on rather as they had before.

CHAPTER 18

1938–1945: Exile and War

IN NEW YORK everything immediately looked promising. The new home in the western part of 57th Street was most beautifully furnished with the select pieces from Hans Krüger's apartment in the Schottenhof. Professionally speaking, too, the New York season could not have begun better. Elisabeth had hired the New York Town Hall for November 13 and gave a recital with Leo Rosenek, at her own expense.

> My recital on 13th was a huge success – I'm really on top form this year – touch wood – press unbelievable, am enclosing the most important *Times* notice.

In it Lene could read that in Schubert's "Liebesbotschaft"

> every phrase of the lyric was a thing of perfect beauty in itself . . . there was a caressing quality in the voice throughout this remarkable bit of singing, a tenderness and eloquence in the projection of its message that were indescribably effective.

Elisabeth felt that this good start would soon have its effect: now there would be more concert and broadcasting engagements, and pupils would apply for lessons.

Instead what followed was like a cold shower. The "hugely successful" New York recital made a loss of $508 which Elisabeth had to pay out of her own pocket. The concert had only been "very well attended", not sold out. The great effect which Elisabeth's artistry had seemed to have, had apparently been lost on the wider New World. Engagements did not turn up.

> There is a vague possibility of a radio [broadcast] . . . they pay well and I would be very much helped by it. In January and February I have a couple of concerts – but it's all not enough to keep me going through the long summer. . . .

Elisabeth Schumann

Lene also learnt in this letter of December 1 how things stood with teaching:

Then I suppose there will be a lot of requests for lessons – but – my God – no one wants to pay my fee (25 dollars for a 40-minute lesson), *all* hope to get free lessons at the Curtis – so far not the *slightest* sign of private pupils queueing up. For 50 dollars a month I give the singer Farell from the Metropolitan (special price for a colleague) 4 lessons – so far that is my only extra earning besides the Curtis. Leo [Rosenek] has not given *one* private lesson so far. It will all come with time, but it's so slow.

One person who could not complain of such problems at this time was Lotte Lehmann. She had been in America a great deal and had often sung at the Met, where she was still performing regularly. She was therefore well occupied and was not only able to pay for the treatment in a sanatorium of her fatally ill husband but was even able to support C who had also come to America. She did not have to for long because, as Elisabeth heard from him in a letter, he was soon touring with singers in the south – but only for two months. It was going to be hard for him too.

Elisabeth's own situation was such that she was having to make a completely abnormal request of her friend:

I wanted to ask you to send me *nothing* for Christmas and not to be cross if I send your watch later, perhaps for your birthday ... Lene, I simply haven't the spare cash at the moment, and if friends can't tell each other such things sensibly, who can? Taking the apartment, the servants etc. has made my budget quite a different one from what I anticipated, so that I really have to do my sums.

It was clear that if Elisabeth and Hans had stayed in the hotel they would have saved more money; keeping servants was a considerable expense, but Elisabeth would not have dreamt of coping without them. And why was she not getting more singing engagements?

She began to realize that she had neglected America far too much in the past. She had sung opera there during one season only: 1914–15. Lotte Lehmann and Maria Olszewska had come over far more frequently, giving concerts and singing at the Met or the Chicago Opera House. The larger part of the American public had never heard of Elisabeth, even the concert agents who were not located in the East almost certainly did not know who she was. Critics had to explain: "Elisabeth Schumann, the famous Viennese

230

soprano." In England that would almost have been an insult.

In addition to these problems was the medium itself through which she performed: the lied, that small-scale, subtle art form which had been born in the culture of Europe. In the huge, fast-moving New World this miniature musical form did not have the same appeal, and therefore the demand for lieder recitals was not great.

Elisabeth was also recognizing something else: America had changed a great deal in the last ten years. Between 1930 and 1937 the economy had managed to drag itself out of the slump following the crash of 1929. By mid-1937 the production index stood higher than at any time in ten years. The national income had risen 75 per cent in just five years. But in August 1937 a decline began. Production dropped, shares fell and the number of unemployed rose to about ten million.

When Elisabeth had been in the United States in the winter of 1937 – 38 she had not been there in order to find a new home; perhaps that was why she had been unaware of the economic climate, or at least what she had noticed had made little impression on her. Thus it was that she had, in the summer of 1938, believed so confidently that America was the "only possible new home" for her: the land with the greatest possibilities. For Hans this was true. Conditions for immigrant doctors were far more favourable here than in England. But for the "famous Viennese soprano" things were different.

Elisabeth no longer had any illusions about her position; she even played with the idea of going to Europe in the summer, where she would be more likely to have some concerts. Hans did not agree with this plan, blaming all of his wife's misfortune on the incompetence of her manager. Elisabeth had been looking for a new one for some time, but no one seemed interested. She had even enlisted C's help, for he was constantly in and out of managers' offices in search of work for himself.

But the beginning of the year 1939 gave her a lift. On January 8 she sang a radio concert for the so-called RCA Victor Hour, "Magic Key". "The first since I've been in America," she wrote to Lene a few days later, "it's a very important show here, quite apart from the publicity there is a huge fee."

Also in January were the long-arranged concerts in Cleveland, Philadelphia, New York and Detroit (at all of which Leo Rosenek was the accompanist). These produced healthy fees, but the New

231

York recital unfortunately afforded no major publicity: it was a concert for the Young Men's Hebrew Association, at which there were no critics. However, the concert in Cleveland – that centre of American Germans – brought not only many detailed write-ups but also, before the event, a great wave of publicity in the form of notices and articles in the English and German-language newspapers.

It seemed almost as if the American ice was broken. But after the end of January there were at first no more engagements. Two months later she took part in two performances of Beethoven's Ninth Symphony under the baton of Fritz Reiner, and on April 24 she contributed to an orchestral concert in New York's Carnegie Hall. At the Curtis Institute, as Joyce learnt in letters, all was going well: Elisabeth was particularly delighted with the voices of six of her pupils, two of whom were outstanding.

Since she taught there in the winter months she would be free to go to Europe in the summer. Her manager in Paris, Friedländer, declared his willingness to arrange concerts in Paris, Monte Carlo, Vichy, Ostend and Scheveningen. At her request Ibbs & Tillett were going to try and arrange engagements in England. They also, incidentally, requested her date of birth, needed for an entry about her which was to appear in Grove's *Dictionary of Music*. Elisabeth's reply was: "I am sorry – I will not allow to include my age for the Grove's Dictionary. That is too much asked for a woman and rather I prefer not to be named." At this difficult time, when she was struggling to get engagements, the last thing she wanted was for people to know that she was already fifty. Thus it was that the editor of the dictionary did not know her date of birth until a much later edition, and for years Grove's, probably having heard that she tended to take three years off her age, *added* three years by giving the year off her birth as 1885 instead of 1888.

As far as getting engagements was concerned there was one avenue which Elisabeth had not yet explored: advertising herself commercially in true American fashion, as Lotte Lehmann had done. Elisabeth had never set much store by advertisements, which she tended to ignore. Nevertheless, at the end of 1938 she did allow herself to be persuaded by Annie Friedberg to have "glamour" photographs taken for an advertisement in the high-quality journal, the *Musical Courier*.

In those first months in New York Elisabeth did not really grasp that the name "Schumann" did not as yet mean much to the

Americans. Instead of trying to remedy that with a concentrated campaign of publicity and performing, she kept thinking about concerts she could give in Europe. She was also longing to see Gerd again. He was all set to marry his Biddy Blagden, something which he had already "confessed" to her in a letter of the previous October. He had admitted that what spoke against the marriage was the fact that he had no career yet; on the other hand, the last thing they wanted was to be separated by war, should it come. During the Munich crisis they had therefore decided to get married within the next few months. On January 12 1939 Elisabeth wrote:

> Oh Lene, what madness to tie oneself down so young and before one is earning – it will surely make his life much harder. And I'm convinced that he never wanted it but that Elizabeth absolutely forced him to it.

Although Elisabeth believed this of the young English girl, she was very kind to her: she corresponded with her, sent her a beautiful brooch for Christmas, in fact behaved as if Biddy were already an inseparable part of her Schnuck; she had to love anyone who made him so happy.

When, on February 1, she returned to New York from her concert in Detroit, Hans handed her a telegram which had arrived the previous day: "Married. Potsdam Palasthotel. Biddy Gerd". Elisabeth seemed dismayed and several times said between her teeth "Schnuck, the rascal" whereupon Hans, the experienced medical specialist, commented: "Syphilis would have been worse than this early marriage."

A few days later a long letter arrived from Biddy which she had written five days before the marriage, when the registry office had not even been booked yet. She wrote how unjust the suspicious attitude was which Gerd's father and stepmother had towards her, little knowing that in writing about it she was dispelling suspicions which Elisabeth had also had.

> ... I do not think that the Puritz family should talk as if *he* [Gerd] was falling into such terrible danger. They have a funny attitude. They believe that I want a man at all costs and have therefore snapped Gerd up. That is of course ridiculous, for I am after all not *that* revolting that I couldn't get a few men with plenty of money if I wanted to. On the contrary, for Gerd I'm not only embarking on a very frugal life but am also giving up my country, my home and my nationality (I do it gladly for him).

Elisabeth was very tickled. One could not hope for a better daughter-in-law than a woman who could write about herself with humour. Elisabeth's letters to her friends about the event were full of joy; she was particularly happy at the bride being English: that meant that her grandchildren would be half English – but she hoped she would not be promoted to grandmother too soon! She had imagined the wedding of her only child quite differently: how wonderfully they could have celebrated it in London! She still wished that Biddy would give up her singing; she had heard that she was planning to give singing lessons as a living. Elisabeth dreaded the day when Biddy would sing to her and ask her advice. Little did she know how long it would be before the opportunity for that came and how wrong her misgivings were in one respect.

And what about Elisabeth's own marriage? All that she reported to Lene about it was: "Life with him is working out wonderfully" and "We are marvellous together – no differences of opinion – you wouldn't believe it." Elisabeth had long since given up thinking in terms of blissful happiness. As long as there were no tensions and domestic peace reigned she considered herself happy.

Hans was having to work hard. At nine o'clock in the morning he went to a language school and came back at four, studied until supper time and afterwards into the night as well. He could not enjoy peace of mind now that he and his son were financially dependent on Elisabeth, something which he found almost intolerable, for his attitude was that his wife should belong to him entirely (not that she had done so in Vienna). Now it seemed that he belonged to her, and the thought that she had married him more to help him than for any other reason rankled. He saved every bit of money he could, eating 10-cent lunches in a cafeteria, shaving himself instead of going to a barber, in fact not spending anything on himself except for bare essentials. Even when Elisabeth was getting a more regular income he lived no less frugally. Saving became an obsession: he would not only eat cheaply at a drugstore, he would also eat too little and then raid the fridge when he got home.

Elisabeth could be grateful when she thought of Lotte, whose husband Otto Krause had finally been released from his suffering on January 22 1939. A month later a letter from Lotte ended with: "Oh Elisabeth, my heart is so heavy. Give my regards to your Hans – be happy as long as you can and hold onto what is yours. . . ." Elisabeth felt she ought to be happy considering she still had a constant companion and, what was more, one who had shared the wonderful times in Vienna. Yet Hans seemed to have drawn a line underneath his former life, for when Lene sent him a book full of photographs of Vienna Elisabeth replied to her:

> Hans sends you many thanks through me – he understands your kind intentions but just think, Lene, he has not looked at it *once*. I'm sure you can't imagine how the once inveterate Schottenhofer does not want to see *anything* from there, but believe me, it is so. I enjoyed myself thoroughly leafing through it. . . .

The prospect of enough engagements in Europe to make a summer trip worthwhile was beginning to look very poor. Friedländer had hardly been able to arrange anything in France, and Ibbs & Tillett had been unable to find anything in addition to the busy English tour in November, which had already been planned for some time. It seemed as if everyone, before making additional financial arrangements with foreign artists, wished to wait and see whether the political situation would improve.

The thought that Elisabeth might not see Gerd for a long time was almost unbearable, and she missed Lene terribly. No amount of persuasion would induce Lene to emigrate, leaving her beloved Weimar and her brother's family, with whom she had a very close relationship.

Summer had come, Elisabeth was finished at the Curtis Institute until the autumn, and her lean months of "unemployment" were upon her. Yet the outlook for the holidays suddenly did not seem so grim after all: an invitation from English friends in Vancouver came; after being with them for July she was to travel down to Los Angeles where Lotte was longing to have her to stay in the house she had rented. So Elisabeth's only outlay in the summer would be travelling expenses – or so she thought: on June 17 a telegram arrived from Gerd: "Suddenly have leave July 15 to August 20. . . . What to do? Kisses."

Immediately she telegraphed back saying that he should come over with Biddy, she would treat them to everything, including the journey out and return, second class. She was wild with joy; all thoughts of saving money were forgotten; Vancouver and California were cancelled. Now she would have to rent a country house outside New York. The emigré conductor Fritz Reiner had just had a lovely house built near Westport, Connecticut, and he knew of the very spot: Goggin's Place. Elisabeth wrote about it to Lene:

1½ hours from New York. This area is a dream – to get into the little town for shopping it's 10 minutes (car), to the sea 15 minutes – the house stands completely in the woods, isolated, peaceful, memories of Switzerland: a rushing stream in a gorge – magical.

The white wooden house, built in the English colonial style, was rented until the middle of September, a car was bought "for without a car life is impossible in this countryside," and then, on June 30 Elisabeth moved out there with Hans and waited for her Schnuck.

How short those three weeks were, from July 20 to August 11, from the moment when she, standing on the pier, saw the huge *Bremen* gliding slowly up the Hudson River and suddenly discovered Schnuck, who was wildly waving his white Panama hat – he had already spotted her several minutes earlier. The separation of almost a year was over. How quickly the time then sped to that last minute on board the *Europa*, when he, happy and full of everything which he had experienced and with many exposed spools of film, was on the point of returning to further study and further creativity (so he thought), and his mother was flinging her arms around him once more and kissing him, and with the words "No long farewells, please!" was hurrying out of the cabin, drying her eyes.

The three of them had wandered along the Atlantic shore; they bought fresh lobsters from the fishermen and feasted on them in the evening in front of the open fire where they then remained a long time talking; they drove in the new "cheap" Pontiac to Fritz Reiner's estate and bathed there in the swimming pool; they sped to the World Fair, which was being held on Long Island.

Elisabeth was much amused by an incident which happened to Biddy when she was driving Gerd to New York in the Pontiac one day: unaccustomed as Britons were to speed limits on highways in those days, Biddy was stopped by the police for speeding. The policeman, evidently much impressed by the beauty of her English accent and no less of her person, waived the fine on condition that the young couple bought tickets for the forthcoming police ball.

Even when Hans was able to join them at Goggin's Place everything went well.

There was not the slightest misunderstanding (woe to Hans, had there been!), but his manner gets on their nerves. . . . Thank goodness Hans did not notice *anything*, but if they were together for another three weeks, who knows! For E. [Biddy] has little patience, and above all she possesses the urge to contradict.... *I* have the patience of a saint, Lene, and close my ears whenever I want. And with me *alone* everything works perfectly....

Elisabeth wrote these words to Lene while her "children" were packing upstairs in the house. The next day, August 11, the *Europa* sailed. Hans was due to go to stay with an American family in a few days' time: he had failed his language exam.

Then I shall be all alone in this big house and won't know what to do with myself ... I've had such happy days, I'll just have to feed on their memory.

At least there was the chance of seeing Gerd again in England in November. Once or twice she had spoken to him about the political situation in Germany, had asked him if he did not feel the need to escape the Hitler regime. He did not. Brought up by his father, indoctrinated with ideas of German nationalism, he considered it quite right that an end had been put to the Weimar Republic with its many splinter parties. In his political indifference and naïvety he did not believe evil of Hitler and the other great political animals.

Elisabeth had one comforting thing left to remind her of her children: the colour film which Gerd had made as a birthday present for her. It was a film of his and Biddy's honeymoon visit to the Canarihaus in Garmisch – a film showing old haunts and conjuring up beautiful memories for Elisabeth.

It was to serve for a long time as a substitute for seeing them again.

When, on August 21, it was made known that the Soviet Union and Germany had signed a non-aggression pact to last ten years, Elisabeth believed that a war would not come. But soon things looked different. At the almost daily tea and cocktail parties which she attended it emerged from conversation that this pact had almost made the situation worse. Now England, France and Russia could not stand together against Germany, and Russia was giving Germany a free hand – in Poland, for instance. Poland was the obvious next victim after Czechoslovakia had been overrun, and Great Britain had pledged to support Poland.

On August 25 Elisabeth wrote to her admirer Winnie Hall in England: "My children had to go back on the 12th August, but I am looking forward to see both again in November in London. I hope nothing worse happens!"

Only one day later, on Saturday August 26, when Elisabeth was sitting on the terrace of Goggin's Place eating her supper, unpleasant things were already happening to Gerd and Biddy in the middle of the night. They were woken up by their landlady knocking at the door: call-up papers had come for Gerd; he was to report without delay to the military airfield of Oschatz in Saxony; mobilization was in full swing.

"We quickly packed," wrote Biddy four days later to Elisabeth, "then we lay down to sleep again until 6 in the morning, then off to the Anhalter Station. There we learned that there wouldn't be a train until 8.47, so we had a frightful wait. It was so lovely in Goggin's Place!"

Elisabeth did not receive this letter until September 18. In the meantime she had enjoyed no more peace at Goggin's Place. Normally not very interested in politics, she now heard every news bulletin, leafed through every newspaper for reports about Europe.

When, on Friday September 1, Elisabeth got up at seven as usual and switched on the radio for the next news bulletin, it was to hear that the Luftwaffe had bombed Polish airfields and railway lines at dawn. German tank and motorized divisions, followed by the infantry, had crossed the German – Polish border.

Now she knew that there would be war. Her only child was separated from her. Had she not suffered enough during his childhood? Paying the price for her freedom from Schnuck's father never seemed to end.

Just at this weekend of all weekends, with all its tension, Elisabeth had to prepare an important concert with Rosenek. It was to take place on the evening of September 3 at the home of the founder and President of the Board of Directors of the Curtis Institute, Mary Bok.* Her home, Lyndonwood, was a beautiful place, and almost everyone of any importance in the musical world of the eastern United States would be there.

---

*Mary Louise Curtis Bok Zimbalist was the daughter of magazine publisher Cyrus H.J. Curtis. She married first Dutch-born Edward W. Bok, then – after his death in 1943 – the violinist Efrem Zimbalist, Director of the Curtis Institute 1941 – 68.

In her agonized state of mind Elisabeth was having to prepare three groups of lieder and Schubert's "Shepherd on the Rock" (with clarinet). Cancellation was out of the question: she could not have done such a thing to Mary Bok, who had always done her utmost to make work at the Curtis Institute as pleasant as possible.

On the afternoon of the concert the dreaded news came through: England had declared war on Germany. Once again Elisabeth had to put on a brave face for a performance. After the concert there was a glorious buffet supper. But for once Elisabeth did not feel like enjoying it, and she said her farewells as soon as she politely could.

Dreadful days followed. Elisabeth sent telegrams to Biddy and Schnuck in Berlin to ask for news. At last, on September 8, a telegram came from Biddy:

> Do not worry, Gerd only called up for the reserve, visited him at weekend, is well. Kisses Angel.

Not for nothing had she got that nickname from Gerd and his mother: Biddy was an angel; she could feel what was in her mother-in-law's heart.

Not until September 15 did Elisabeth feel able to sit down and write a letter to her friend Lene:

> I'm desperately worried [about Gerd]. On top of that there is in this war the risk of bombs on you as well, Berlin, Dresden – oh, how dreadful it all is. I think so much now of 1914 when Gerd kicked happily in his bath and I often thought: "Oh, what a good thing that I will not have to experience him going to war." . . . Lene, write *often*, even if there aren't many ships then I'll just get a whole lot of news at once, but it is all we have left, for there's now no question of seeing each other in November. I would go like a shot of course, I'm not frightened of mines, but of course there are no concerts. . . .

"Of course there are no concerts." Horror at the war had made musical life in England come to a standstill. Only gradually did it revive again, when the first shock was over and the war became part of everyday life. If Elisabeth had then lived in England she would surely have had a lot of singing to do. As it was, she was living far from the centre of things: between her and England lay an ocean which was to be infested with mines and submarines. The thick curtain which was to hide Elisabeth Schumann from the eyes of Europe for a long time had come down.

Now it was time to concentrate on making an impact on the American musical world again and to make up for lost opportunities she had had in the past in this huge country. And she could still, in her fifty-second year, charm with her art. "Elisabeth Schumann enthralled the large audience" wrote the *New York Times* after the big recital in the Town Hall on November 11 1939.

> ... the inimitable grace of outline which Miss Schumann invariably brings to every number she attempts. This factor was again ever present yesterday, as was the depth of human emotion in every tone.... Taken all in all, a recital of exceptional worth....

On the night of the concert Lotte Lehmann wrote:

> Your concert was so heavenly, Elisabeth, I have to say it to you again. My goodness, what miserable little beasts those are who are against you! There is really *a whole world of difference* between your art and the "new".... It was an experience for me, with the understanding I now have of lieder, to feel the unbelievably sweet and tender art which knows how to sublimate every expression so unspeakably finely that everything comes out of the ether and is made to float, released from all earthly heaviness. Believe me, you do not know on what a lonely pinnacle you are standing.... Oh, one complains and sighs about one's lost youth, but someone who is capable of giving something of *that* calibre, which you gave today, is beyond youth or age.... Admittedly, that lovely unconscious bubbling over which youth gives us is wonderful too ... but to perform with such complete perfection, as you did today – that no young person can do.

And yet, barely four days before the concert Elisabeth had written to Lene: "Will be glad when it's over, you know the problem: youth has gone, and art and technique are just delusion now."

In the spring of 1940 she explained to Lene:

> You ask whether I still give plenty of concerts. Of course, I take on whatever is offered, which isn't much any more, but I no longer have the slightest pleasure in singing. I find that the voice has weakened a lot – I just don't have any strength any more. So a recital like the one on 11th November has to be helped in every way possible, I have electric treatment and a strychnine throat spray beforehand so that I am brought back up to scratch – then it goes just about all right, but on tour, when I don't have a doctor it's a big effort. I would not have thought – when all's said and done – that my voice would be finished so soon – I must have sung too much and too often with my bronchial catarrh, which, incidentally, has been bothering me again

for weeks. I'm sure it's also a big mistake that I almost never practise any more, but the idea sickens me so much that I simply cannot do anything about it. I'm happy enough with the Curtis [Institute], I've had enough of singing.

Yet she could well have done with the extra earnings which singing brought in. Hans's sisters, both older than him, now had to be provided for. After a lot of shilly-shallying by the authorities they had been let out of Austria and were able to sail in an Italian ship from Trieste to New York. Rosa, the younger, was a widow, and Ida too was heavy-hearted because her husband had not yet been able to leave Vienna.

Elisabeth was now having to provide for a proper little family: Hans and his son Heinzi, her two sisters-in-law, occasionally also cousin Trude el Bedell; they were spread over two apartments, for both of which rent had to be paid. Admittedly Heinzi was beginning to earn a bit now, but sometimes Lotte Lehmann's words echoed in Elisabeth's mind: "too much for two vocal cords", and Lene was to hear many complaints that these were no easy years. Yet her standard of living was kept as high as it had been in Vienna, except where clothes were concerned: with these she had to be very economical. She longed for the time when Hans would be able to start his practice.

> You cannot imagine how difficult the exam is and how much energy he is having to put into all that learning. But I haven't heard the *slightest* complaint from Hans – I think I would have thrown the books against the wall a hundred times by now.

Later she was to say that "during the war I dried up", but it was not true that her voice was "finished". At her annual New York recital on November 9 1940 she actually sang a difficult song which she had never included in a programme before. And she could obviously still enjoy singing, for she wrote to Lene shortly after the concert:

> . . . was effortlessly in good voice, and it must have been one of the best concerts I have ever given. It was like the old days, or rather the young days – at the end I started all over again because I did ten encores, not just little ditties but including songs like "Vergebliches Ständchen", "Morgen", "Ständchen" etc. And with the "Junge Nonne" I created a sensation. Yes, they've always heard it being bellowed here before – please take a look at Schubert and see what dynamics he

wrote. There are two little fortes in it, not *one* fortissimo, and mostly piano or pp or even ppp. I am enclosing some press notices. Of course the fellows always write about x years ago, how the voice sounded then etc., but what maturity and art one can produce now instead! And why should a voice not give after a while, get older! We get wrinkles in the face after all! But otherwise the press was fantastic.

So Elisabeth was still able to experiment. Later (in November 1945) she even made a gramophone record of "Die junge Nonne". Leo Rosenek had encouraged the "experiment", and the day before the concert Elisabeth had been so plagued by doubts that she had almost left the song out of the programme.

"During the war I dried up." Her worry about Gerd naturally had a lot to do with this: it sapped the energy needed to sing. Admittedly Biddy and Gerd wrote that he was still being trained and would have to pass an exam before joining a squadron at the front. So there was still no cause for worry. But how long would that last? Were the children perhaps making the situation sound less serious than it was in order to reassure her?

On January 16 1940 a letter came with very happy tidings: Biddy was expecting a baby in July. But within a week or two Biddy had had a miscarriage and was in hospital. When news of this arrived in New York weeks later Elisabeth wrote:

> You know, Lene, perhaps it's a sign from above. In these times! I am rather glad than sad. And what a burden for the two of them. And Gerd a father! You know, I didn't really want to think about it – it's better like this.

In these times: the Germans entered Denmark and Norway in April 1940. Elisabeth was dreadfully worried. Then two letters from Gerd came at once, both two to three weeks old, but Elisabeth was in transports of delight. Then came the attacks on Holland and Belgium, and the French campaign. It was frightful. But as Elisabeth wrote to Lene: "I . . . wrote to Gerd that I am behaving with *dignity* – I never complain and no one knows when I am worried."

After the fall of France, England seemed to be in great danger too. Her beloved England! As she wrote to Winnie Hall in October 1940:

> My most treasured memories are all connected with your lovable, delightful country, and in these dark days my attachment to those fair islands has only grown deeper and deeper. . . .

The summer holidays offered a welcome respite from war worries. Elisabeth was usually invited to the summer music school of the Curtis Institute during July and August. It was held at Rockport in the beautiful East Coast countryside of Maine State. Any of the teachers or students of the Institute who wanted to could spend their summer holidays there by the sea. There was always music-making in Captain Eell's Boat Barn, a beautiful old boathouse decorated inside with fishing nets. Famous musicians came to perform in it, trying thereby, as Elisabeth put it, "to restore the gentle traditions of peacetime for a better future, which, I hope, is not too far off."

Elisabeth loved the ocean, the mountains, the lakes and forests, the riding lessons she took in the mornings, and especially she loved the well-known, delicious lobsters which could be bought and cooked at every street corner and then consumed, looking at a view of the Atlantic.

Of course Elisabeth would have to give a recital in the Boat Barn, but the whole atmosphere which Mary Bok, President of the Curtis Institute, had created and which lay over everything, was so attuned to the music and so stimulating that Elisabeth was glad to make the effort.

There in Rockport Elisabeth Schumann and Mary Bok became friends. In a newspaper interview the singer said of the magnanimous patron: "Mrs Bok is a quite unique person. Whatever she does enriches immeasurably the musical future of American youth. I am proud to be able to call her my friend."

Two weeks later Elisabeth sang in the B Minor Mass in the Berkshire Festival.* Serge Koussevitzky conducted. The huge 6000-seat music shed was open at the sides, and a full moon lit up the countryside. The following day she wrote to Winnie Hall in England: "During the majestic music of Bach my thoughts were wandering over the ocean where so many people mourn and suffer now."

In the autumn Biddy was pregnant again, and by now in the fifth month. The singing grandmother! Elisabeth found the idea of Schnuck being a father even funnier. If only letters travelled more quickly! Telegrams were no longer allowed out of Germany and letters were being held up by censorship. It was not until April 24 1941 that a letter at last arrived from Biddy, written in pencil, obviously in childbed:

*Held on the Tanglewood estate, near Lenox, Massachusetts.

Dearest Mutti[*],

On 30th March at 1.45 at night our little boy came into the world. He was 2 weeks early ... he is delicate but quite healthy ... unfortunately Gerd cannot be reached at present, he has just gone off again and I cannot find out his new address yet. Oh, if only you were here, Mutti!

It was quite hopeless, of course. All that Elisabeth could hope was that Lene might be able to visit Biddy at some stage and then report about little Christian, as her grandson was called. Lene might have more time on her hands soon for, at the end of the season, she was to take her leave of the Dresden Staatsoper, quietly and without a farewell performance, and return to her home town Weimar to take up singing teaching at the Musikakademie. Elisabeth thought of the relative drudgery which lay before her best friend.

Elisabeth only had to travel to Philadelphia once a week, but she had to take six lessons running with only a twenty-minute lunch break. It became so exhausting that she had to arrange to spend one night in Philadelphia and spread the teaching over two days. But it was wonderful to teach where the great Sembrich had taught. Elisabeth wrote to Winnie Hall:

I came to fill her place and I am very proud of it. I teach in her room – a very good portrait, golden framed, is hanging over the fireplace – I often look at it and wonder if I will be – once – on the other side, at least silver framed.

On June 22 1941 Hitler's troops marched into the country of his ally Stalin. Schnuck was now with a squadron at the front, and had already taken part as a transport pilot in the Balkan campaign and in the invasion of Crete. Some months later Elisabeth guessed he was in Russia, from a letter in which he was only allowed to hint at where he was. She lived from day to day waiting for news. Letters from Gerd and Biddy or Lene seemed to be the main events of her life at this time. Suze and Leon Rueff, banker friends in London, lost Markus, their only son, in North Africa. Lene sent news of other mutual friends who had lost their only son. Elisabeth wrote back: "Poor things – their only son – life has no meaning any more."

She did not realize that after that letter, which she wrote in October 1941, her contact with Germany would be broken off

[*]Mummy.

almost completely. Before she received a reply, the Japanese attacked Pearl Harbor, and the USA joined the war against the Axis powers. Elisabeth had the dreadful feeling of being totally cut off. There was no mail; one could only send messages through the Red Cross, a maximum of twenty-five words. In neutral Switzerland her good friends the Reiffs still lived – in Zürich, where, during the First World War, she had first met Richard Strauss. Lilly Reiff would surely be glad to forward letters for her.

Months passed, winter was over and no word came from Germany to 171 West 57th Street. The USA had been in the war five months when, on May 6 1942, a letter came with a Zürich postmark. In it were a few lines from Frau Reiff and a letter from Lene, many weeks old but fat. The same evening in her reply she wrote: "Friendship is the most beautiful thing on earth – it is everlasting – and separation cannot shake it. . . ."

Happy is the person who can write this, one might say. Yet what bitter recognition actually lay in these words, for they did not spring only from the happiness caused by getting the letter: the happiness itself showed Elisabeth quite clearly that this friendship was the only human relationship in her existence which was completely fulfilled, which was without worries and would so remain as long as they both lived. It was even more beautiful than the relationship with her child, where, despite all the love, there was still the generation gap and the gap between the sexes. It was an even richer relationship than any she had had with the men she had loved, however dearly; it never died, whereas the love for them had.

Even Hans, while he still considered her to be his for ever, was no longer truly close to her heart. She had felt until now that she must be sensible and try to live in harmony with the partner with whom she had started this life in the New World. But now, just when she was cut off from family and friends, and when her companion ought to be making up for her loss, that meagre basis for a reasonably harmonious life together trickled into the sand. His old stubbornness showed itself ever more frequently and more strongly.

Hans, after three and a half years of study, had passed his exam in the spring of 1942, was now working as a specialist in a large clinic and was earning again; he would also be starting his own practice soon. A character trait which had appeared early on in their relationship in Vienna was now showing itself again: his very quiet yet obstinately persistent determination to dominate, which was unbelievably aggravating.

245

There was something else too: never did Hans speak one word about Gerd, although he knew perfectly well how worried Elisabeth was about him. He never asked her whether she had had any news, and if she got post from Gerd and was cheerful he said nothing. Elisabeth admitted to Trude el Bedell that Hans's relationship with her must be quite wrong if he took no interest in someone who was so dear to her. Sometimes Elisabeth asked herself whether there was the slightest spark of straightforward, natural humanity in this man. Then she realized what a chasm of difference lay between them and wondered how on earth she could have loved him so much. She remembered how amazed C had been that she was attracted to this mulish man.

Divorce? For a third time? In the American "divorce-paradise" Reno it was very easy: one only had to live there in a hotel for a few weeks, and then it all went swiftly through. But now Hans was earning at last, her voice would not last forever and engagements were few and far between – it was too much of a financial risk. There was nothing for it but to continue living with him and to tolerate his personality with good humour.

Gustl, son of a dear Viennese friend Käthe Breuer, who was now serving in the US army, had lunch in the Krüger-Schumann household at about this time. He could not make out what was going on. There was a tension at table which he would never have thought possible in Elisabeth's company. Dr Krüger hardly spoke a word, hardly looked up, the conversation was extremely forced, and Rosie, who kept house for Elisabeth, shot with exaggerated attentiveness from one to the other in order to cover up the oppressive atmosphere.

In the summer of 1943 when they were both staying in Rockport again, it came to the point where Hans began to ignore her completely when she spoke to him. Soon she gave up trying to get a response from him and did not speak to him either. In the end they avoided each other as much as possible, and this was then perpetuated in New York. They had in any case always had separate bedrooms.

This estrangement from her husband was not dramatic in the way her estrangements from Walther and C had been: there was no other man involved. Perhaps that was what made it so particularly oppressive: her *joie de vivre* was being paralysed. Her depressed spirits made her especially vulnerable, and in the autumn of 1943 she suffered a severe cold which dragged on and on.

Then, on November 17, a telegram came from England. The sight of it alone was a shock: private telegrams from overseas during the war always meant bad news. And it was from Biddy's mother too:

> News dated September. Elizabeth expects baby November. Gerd rather serious accident, now convalescent and legs will be alright. Love Hannie Blagden.

At first Elisabeth could not put her thoughts into any sort of order; all she could see in her mind's eye was that terrible vision which had so often plagued her: a smashed aeroplane, and in the wreckage, bloody and lifeless, Schnuck. In despair she sent a telegram to England begging for a letter with more details.

For days Elisabeth was in a state of anxiety and uncertainty, hardly doing anything except think of Gerd. On December 4 she was due to give her big annual recital in the New York Town Hall. It seemed impossible to sing now, especially as she still had a bad cough. But she could not even find the strength to cancel. She gave the recital, after insufficient rehearsal and still not feeling well. Only her confidence in her technique and in the magnificent Rosenek allowed her to go before her public with eight Schubert and eight Wolf songs. She herself announced at the beginning of the concert that she was suffering from a bad cold, and that reassured her somewhat; but it was still a battle right up to the last note of the last encore, and sometimes she was not able to give full voice. Yet she had particularly wanted to sing three songs very intensely. One was "Ellens erster Gesang" by Schubert, the words translated from Sir Walter Scott: "Soldier, rest! Thy warfare o'er. . . ." She had already put this song in the programme before she had known of Schnuck's wounding – it was almost a premonition, for surely the war would be over for him now. And she had wanted to stress, in Hugo Wolf's "Ihr jungen Leute", the worry of the women about their loved ones going to war. The penultimate song, Wolf's "Tretet ein, hoher Krieger", was supposed to have been a warning to the world to cease wars and murder. The press wrote:

> Though troubled by a cold, Elisabeth Schumann gave an artistic song recital . . . Schubert's "Dass sie hier gewesen" and Wolf's "Wie glänzt der helle Mond" may be singled out as illustrating the soprano's skill in the projection of mood. Her voice today is a very limited one but she remains a persuasive interpreter.

In the middle of December a letter arrived from Biddy's mother which had taken four weeks to reach her and which only half reassured her:

Nov. 19th – 1943.

My dearest Elisabeth,

I got your cable in reply to mine this morning and I am now going to write you a little more in detail. My only news came on a postcard from a mutual friend in Lucerne, and I will now copy out what she says:

"... Yesterday I had a letter from Biddy, she and Christian had two very bad days (Hamburg raids!). Now, however, they are happily settled with her cousin Oscar Henschel and will stay there indefinitely. Her husband had a pretty bad accident, his legs rather smashed up but apparently he will be able to walk again, but the healing process will take some time. He feels rather rotten, because he had a lot of fever and the worry about his family, as he had no news of them for some time. He is in a hospital rather far South and travelling for Biddy is rather difficult at the moment as she is expecting a baby in November. Christian and she are both very well, have good food and lovely country air. As soon as her husband is out of hospital, he will join her for his convalescence. She is longing for news of you all...."

Then yesterday ... I had a Red Cross message from Biddy herself, but that was dated earlier still and runs: "Had to leave home. Happily settled in Oscar's country house. Gerd rapidly recovering from accident in hospital. All well. Tell Mutti. Dearest love. Biddy."

So that is all I can tell you, my dear co-mother, and I think you need not worry about Gerd now. Poor boy. But just think how grateful we two, you and I, ought to be, that they were both so protected, and we will now hope that our new grandchild has arrived safely, the dear pet! I am so glad they are in the country....

Elisabeth replied at once:

December 17th, 1943.

My very dear Hannie,

Now I have the details and I cannot tell you how grateful I am that you sent them so quickly. I am horrified that poor Biddy had to go through two such days with little Christian, and in her condition. I can't understand at all why she was in the town and not in the country house of her father-in-law, and I feel like blaming him. If there wouldn't be any room, one of them could have slept on the floor and given her the bed.* Poor, poor darling! What terrible experiences she must have had. I only hope that she had a good confinement and that it had no effect on the baby.

---

*In fact Biddy had been keeping house for her father-in-law in his apartment in the Curiohaus. The raids had been unexpected.

Above: In Paris with Richard Strauss in 1921, on their way to America.
Below: Singing lieder in 1926 or '27, accompanied by Carl Alwin.

In her Vienna flat, with Carl Alwin, in 1927.

Radiantly glamorous in Vienna, with Sorry, in 1932.

Above left: with Lene Jung and Hans Krüger at the Canarihaus, 1934.
Right: Hans Krüger. *Below*: With Gerald Moore and his wife in 1938.

With her son Gerd, the author of this book,
on their way to Algiers in 1936.

Above: Rehearsing with Bruno Walter for their Edinburgh Festival recital in 1947.

Below: With Lotte Lehmann at a radio interview in New York.

bove: Schloss Falkenberg, where the family
as re-united after the war; and Elisabeth
i her ENSA uniform.

elow: With her accompanist Hubert Greenslade, on their triumphant tour of
outh Africa in 1951; and receiving her American citizenship from Judge Knox
i November, 1944.

Above: Teaching at Bryanston; and with her daughter-in-law Biddy, in America.

Below: With Gerd and his family at the seaside in 1948. *Inset*: The only photograph of Elisabeth with her granddaughter.

My only wish and prayer is that both of our children will be now united. I believe so strong, Gerd will be well enough to have joined her by now!

Of course, this postcard sounded very depressing, but Biddy's message cheered me up enormously. You are so right – we have only to be grateful every minute. . . .

Life somehow went on. There were so many other people around Elisabeth who were suffering too, after all: refugees from Austria who could not find their feet and needed help and encouragement. Even her pupils, those at the Curtis Institute and her private ones: she could not only look after their voices but had to deal with their emotional problems too. They frequently poured out their hearts to her and needed advice and sometimes practical help. Someone who had seen Elisabeth in action when teaching in New York and in Rockport, Janos Delej, the son of a good friend of Lene, wrote about Elisabeth to Winnie Hall in those last difficult weeks of 1943:

She is not only such a gentle, charming, wonderful person but also one with immense self-control. I have never heard her worrying about her own problems but always busy with the problems of other people.

If Elisabeth had heard this eulogy she would have laughed and said that it was simply by nature that her optimism always kept the upper hand.

The amazing thing was that things did always work out somehow. For instance, the Curtis Institute was now offering her a new three-year contract beginning in October 1944. Unfortunately the delightful Josef Hofmann had been replaced as director by the violinist Efrem Zimbalist in 1941 (whom Mary Bok had married two years later) and Elisabeth found it difficult to form anything but a chilly relationship with him. But Mary Bok was still president and still a good friend, the atmosphere at the Curtis was delightful, the teaching rewarding – altogether she felt she was secure there.

New Year 1944. Still no further news from Germany, not even whether Christian had a little sister or brother; the beginning of the New Year was marked only by many greetings from friends and a resolution with Hans to try and improve their relationship.

For a while things went quite well. But how could they forget? It was almost as if each of them was waiting for the other to start the nastiness all over again; and very soon everything was back the way it had been, though now it seemed worse.

But at least one delightful thing happened that New Year. A great admirer of Elisabeth, Harry Goddard Owen, who in civilian life had been a university dean and now held a high rank in the navy, thanked her for the album of records which she had sent him for Christmas, and wrote further:

> This morning I received a letter from a friend of mine [Donald Stauffer] now at New Guinea – in the midst of things! He has taught at Breadloaf* and is one of the most brilliant professors at Princeton. His letter, dated Dec. 17, came by air and this is what he says:
>
> "It was good to hear from you and what makes me reply so soon, apart from the letter, was Elisabeth Schumann's voice this afternoon floating in out of the jungle, in the most brilliant sunshine – evidently from some Australian radio station, picked up by one of our sets. Made me want to weep, as it did when I heard her at Oxford and at Breadloaf and at Middlebury. She sang 'Der Nussbaum' and 'Voi che sapete' and lots of the songs I love. You should have heard the boys shout at the end of each song."
>
> Isn't that quite an experience – to be singing to the Marines in the jungles of the South Pacific!
>
> I have just played the Mozart again and I am sure that if Mozart could have heard you sing he would have written more for the soprano.

In the middle of March – at last! – a letter from Hannie Blagden again. Full of happy anticipation Elisabeth tore it open only to stiffen with shock as she read the first lines – and Hannie's writing was so difficult to read: "This letter follows the wire I sent you yesterday. I thought over carefully whether I could tell you all about our children on the wire...."

Great God! What had happened? What telegram? The letter was dated February 18, almost a month old, the telegram must have gone astray.

> ... and then I came to the conclusion that, as his mother, you should know every detail possible, so that you can help him.... Your healing, loving, constructional thought will do so much for them.† I only just got the bare facts that Gerd had had his leg amputated ... how far up his leg, my friend did not say, but I will quote the actual words she writes...: "Had a letter from Biddy after Rupert was born

---

*An American summer music school.
†Hannie Blagden was a Christian Scientist.

(an easy birth). She tells me that after her husband's crash, his leg has had to be amputated; he is getting on well, and as soon as he is able to travel, he will join Biddy and the two boys. . . ."

My American friend who sends me the news, tells me that, as a new American law has come out forbidding American citizens to communicate with the enemy country, there will be no further correspondence between them, which is rather sad for us, dear Elisabeth, isn't it? Never mind! Courage, we will go on! . . . So now we have two little grandsons! There are some good things left to us, aren't there? . . .

Yes, the new grandson – but it was difficult now to enjoy thinking about him. Elisabeth had so been looking forward to hearing about the birth, but now the news had come in the same letter, in the same minute, as the other news. He would be a cripple for the rest of his life; he, who had been so athletic, had loved dancing, skiing, driving and flying – was that all to end now? What had he been through and what was he going through now? Hobbling about on crutches! And was it really only one leg, or was Hannie trying to spare her more anguish? It was dreadful not to know, and with the new American law there would only be news through the Red Cross now, which often took months.

But unexpectedly some more news arrived at the end of April. Hannie had heard about Gerd and Biddy through a friend of her sister in Sweden:

Gerd is *quite well again*! That sounds good, doesn't it? . . . He is building up and will be as splendid a man as ever before, and even more so, for he must have learnt a great deal in that most difficult and bitter experience.

And with regard to Biddy's attitude to her crippled husband Hannie wrote comforting words: "She has a gift of loving tenderness to those in trouble, which she always had, even as a small child."

Still Elisabeth was not completely reassured. How badly Gerd had really been injured was a lasting, nagging worry. She found she was unable to bestir herself to much activity, she hardly even wrote to anyone – it took her a month to answer Hannie's letter.

Only where Hans was concerned was she beginning to feel decisive. More and more she felt that now, when almost all her thoughts were daily with her child, he did not belong in her life.

One evening in June, not long before the end of the semester, she was in a more relaxed mood than she had been for many months;

perhaps the news of military successes by the Allies in France had cheered her up. So, when Hans came home from the practice, she was able to approach him with equanimity, even warm friendliness, but above all without embarrassment or fear about what she wanted to discuss with him: she insisted, during the course of a long conversation, that the only possibility for them both was a permanent separation.

The following morning she went to Philadelphia to teach. Towards evening she received an express letter there from Hans, a touching yet unrealistic letter in which he exaggerated the importance of remaining together.

When Elisabeth returned from Philadelphia her resolve was unchanged and Hans yielded; he even offered to get rid of their apartment during the summer months. In the short time before the holidays it seemed as if a weight had fallen from his mind and he could breathe easily again now that the decision had been made. Everything proceeded without difficulty or drama; the atmosphere had cleared perceptibly. They both discussed moving from the flat, they even discussed the divorce and decided that, in order to facilitate it, Elisabeth should stay in Reno from the middle of September until the end of October.

In Rockport, without Hans, the realization of what a torture the last few years had been really hit her. This time she had taken Rosie with her, and her little Pekinese (another "Sorry", whom she had acquired as an eight-week-old puppy at Christmas 1939) was also a constant and lively companion. Now for the first time she could feel completely free again.

Towards the end of August good news of Gerd came from Hannie:

> July 29, 1944
>
> I have just had a Red Cross message from Biddy, and I will write it down here for you to see:
>
> "Had heavenly six weeks. Gerd here well and jolly. Wound not yet quite healed. Rupert christened, Jack [Biddy's brother] as Godfather. All happy and loving you.
>
> Biddy."
>
> (sent off from her on 26th June 1944. Received by me 28th July). . . . So this is all *very good news*. I am sending this off immediately!

Elisabeth cabled Hannie at once: "I am the happiest mother in the world."

But it was as if a price had to be paid for this happiness. In Rockport Sorry was hit by a car and had to be put down. Elisabeth could hardly take it in that he was dead. All her pupils mourned with her – almost the whole Institute.

She was rather glad to leave in the middle of September. At first she returned with Rosie to New York. There she had to wait for some time: in wartime it was not so easy to book a berth on the Pullman to Reno. But Goddard Owen used his influence as a highly-placed person in the navy to get a reservation for her. It was a long rail journey: days of travelling almost all the way across the continent to Reno in Nevada State, the "marriage and divorce paradise". When she arrived, on September 26, she was pleasantly surprised, for Reno seemed almost like a holiday resort, lying at about 4000 feet in beautiful countryside with the peaks of the Sierra Nevada not far away.

But then the weeks did seem very long after all. Soon Elisabeth had seen all the films; and now, during the war, there was practically no good music. So all that remained to be done was going for walks and reading, following the news of the war which still would not end, enjoying the food, which was quite passable, and chatting to fellow "sufferers", with whom the Riverside Hotel was thickly populated.

Elisabeth could not wait for the war to be over and to see her family again. The divorce seemed so unimportant now. Even looking for a new flat, normally such fun, seemed a burden when she was back in New York again.

The annual recital in the Town Hall was drawing closer. Because of Elisabeth's stay in Reno it was not to be held until the beginning of December. This time it would be an American citizen who mounted the platform. In January 1944 she had applied for US citizenship and it had taken months; she had written to President Roosevelt but had had a reply from the Department of Justice saying that they still needed to investigate her case. By November 22 it was settled.

Thus, on December 2, a "brand new" American citizen stood on the platform of the Town Hall, and on her dress she had proudly pinned a tiny American flag made of diamonds, rubies and sapphires, which her friend Lisa Reitler had given her in honour of her new nationality. She did not have a cold, she was in good voice, and this time there were no warlike songs on the programme, but romantic and hopeful ones by Schubert and Strauss.

253

The first Strauss song was "Mit deinen blauen Augen". Next to it was an asterisk with a footnote: "Sung in honour of the 80th birthday of the composer." Strauss's birthday had been on June 11, but this was the first suitable opportunity Elisabeth had to honour it in front of the American public. But was it not a bit risky, during this bitter war against Hitler's Germany, to honour publicly a living German composer who, it was said, had come to terms with the Nazis?

It was to the credit of New York's musical life that there was no word of protest. The press concentrated on the artists' achievements. *Musical America* wrote:

It would be fatally easy to take the consummate artistry of Elisabeth Schumann for granted.... How few singers there are in the world who have her unerring instinct for the poet's and the composer's meaning, her ability to color and project vocal tone without losing the shape of the word and her exquisite sense of phrasing! There is no need to waste time on the limitations, wisely self imposed, of Mme Schumann's singing, the reduced scale of tone and occasional dramatic constraint which goes with it. She is fortunate in having the collaboration of Leo Rosenek, whose piano playing is on the same high plane as her vocalism. Their performance of Schubert's "Im Frühling" was as close to perfection as music by mortals is likely to get.

Shortly after this concert, which had lasted two hours with all the encores, Elisabeth sang on the radio a Christmas programme in German for the "Invitation to Music" hour of the Columbia Broadcasting Corporation. From the estimated thousands of listeners came a solitary protest:

Gentlemen:-

I would like most emphatically to protest about the Christmas program sung by Elisabeth Schumann at 10.30. To think of a Christmas program, in America, being sung entirely in German, while the German soldiers are mowing down our captured and disarmed boys is just more than I can stand. Can you for one moment imagine such a performance in Germany in English?

Yours in disgust
Leah G.H. Buss
(Mrs Raymond Buss)

Elisabeth could well understand how this woman felt. But, she wondered, should politics be allowed to limit art?

Christmas was made particularly happy by the fact that Elisabeth received some snapshots of Gerd, Biddy and the boys. Lene's nephew, who was an American prisoner of war, had sent them on to her. From these she could see that Gerd really had lost only one leg and that the boys were "too sweet for words".

In the first few months of 1945 no more news came from the family. All Elisabeth could do was to follow the gradually weakening struggles of Germany against the Allies – as far as she could: a lot was kept secret.

At last in April a letter came from Hannie Blagden with a copy of a letter Biddy had written to a friend in Switzerland. The latter was dated December 21 1944 and read:

> ... Gerd's wound has healed at last ... he is ... bursting with health. He is also far from being inactive. Apart from being a kind of man-of-all-jobs here – because he is clever with his hands – he has spent some months now in writing a book, and is still at it with great zeal. He also does sport, can drive a car with a contraption he made himself, and has even flown several times in a glider, using a makeshift wooden leg, also of his own construction.... Both children are frightfully energetic and lively and, consequently, very exhausting, but still it is lovely to have them.

It was another four weeks before the German forces finally capitulated. May 8 1945: VE Day. The following day Elisabeth received a touching letter from Mary Bok, who had tried in vain to telephone her on the great day:

> ... I wanted just to say I'm thinking of you, all this wonderful day – knowing what it means to you – and that I am deeply happy for you – You have borne the years of dreadful anxiety *so well*! Thank God your son lives – and you will surely see him and your little grandsons within the year. I do rejoice for you.

The problem was: how was she to contact Schnuck? Elisabeth telephoned here, there and everywhere, but even people with influence could not help. What was certain was that the family was living on a country estate called Schloss Falkenberg, not far from Kassel, in the US occupied zone. Its owner, Biddy's cousin Oscar Henschel, was a wealthy industrial magnate, so she could assume they were comparatively comfortable; but letters could be sent only through US military personnel, and this was frowned upon as fraternizing. So it was a question yet again of wait, wait, wait.

Ibbs & Tillett asked whether they could arrange concerts for the autumn in England, there had been several requests already. The loyal English public! Perhaps this would afford an opportunity to visit Germany; by then one might be able to travel more freely again.

On June 1, three weeks after VE Day, Elisabeth received a letter from Gerd which had been forwarded by a Captain in the US Military Government, where Gerd worked as an interpreter: a channel had been found through which Elisabeth would be able to communicate with her family after all. It meant writing in English, for the sake of the censors, but that was a small price to pay.

June 1 1945: it was as if on that day the gates of life were beginning to be unlocked. Now all Elisabeth's efforts would be concentrated on flinging them open again – as wide as possible.

CHAPTER 19

New York and Europe, 1945–1947

ENGLAND, DEAR, GOOD, LOYAL old England! Suddenly it was there again, almost impetuously demanding of Elisabeth that she should, after seven long years, simply carry on where she had left off and say yes to every offer of an engagement: concerts in London, Hull, Cambridge, Leicester, Harpenden, Reading, Lincoln and more.

This loyalty was touching, but it was also a little nerve-racking. Just a few weeks ago the English critic Beverley Nichols had written of the contralto Olive Gilbert, who was singing in a new musical by Ivor Novello: "She could sing beside Elisabeth Schumann without blushing, and if anybody wants greater praise than that, they will not get it this side of the grave." The English were evidently expecting the Schumann of old, instead of which they were going to get an old Schumann, in her fifty-eighth year and a grandmother to boot. But, more than anything, this grandmother wanted to help her family, and that meant sing, sing, sing. Gerd had no career yet and would certainly need financial support for at least another two years. The weeks between Elisabeth's first concert in the Royal Albert Hall in London and the beginning of semester at the Curtis Institute would have to be filled with hard work. This was the end of hibernation.

Varied programmes had to be worked out with Rosenek; Elisabeth decided, out of respect for all that the English people had suffered at the hands of the Germans, to include more English songs in her predominantly German repertoire. Her wardrobe would have to be spruced up, but not a lot before she had started to earn well again. Thoughts like this reminded her of the terrible shortage of everything in Germany now. Gerd had written:

Things we need most, and that may sound funny to you, is soap . . . next comes shoes for the children as it is hardly possible to get any. . . . But, of course, after nearly six years of total war, we have practically a shortage of anything you can think of. . . .

Elisabeth was very grateful to Gerd's communication channel Captain de Nubla, who was prepared to forward anything. This meant that a large parcel could be sent off to the family every week. Soon Red Cross parcels could be sent too, which meant that she could send goods to all sorts of friends and relatives in Germany and Austria. Money flowed.

It was by no means certain that Elisabeth would be able to visit the family when she was in Europe; travelling into the occupied zones was strictly limited to military personnel and people with other essential business. Besides, with all the concert engagements, there would only be a short gap of two weeks or so when Elisabeth might be free.

Even booking the passage to England looked grim at first: the few passenger liners had been booked up for months. But once again Goddard Owen came to the rescue and procured a cabin in a freight steamer, the *Prometheus*, which was due to sail at the beginning of August. With accommodation in London Elisabeth also had some good fortune: Suze Rueff, who had not only lost her son in the war but who was now also a widow, offered to let her stay with her in her flat. She was an interesting person to know: she had been a devoted friend of the great French tragedienne, Sarah Bernhardt, and had some good stories to tell.

On August 8, the siren of the *Prometheus* hooted and she was off. It seemed a pleasant, clean ship; her cabin was small but neatly furnished. There were only four other passengers, and Elisabeth was the only woman on board.

Quite late on the evening of August 14 a strange commotion ran through the ship. As the sounds came nearer what sounded like "peace! It's peace!" could be heard. Cabin doors were flung open, and the five passengers and any off-duty crew members went up on deck to hear the momentous news which had come over the ship's radio.

Japan had surrendered.

The men slapped each other on the shoulders, jumped for joy and hugged each other. Sailors dragged crates of flares and signal rockets up and starting setting them off until the sky was cracking and popping and brilliant with red, white and green light. Hardly had the light dimmed when singing and piano-playing could be heard from below: "The Stars and Stripes". The old honky-tonk piano, not too badly out of tune, had been woken up from its dusty sleep.

Elisabeth's voice joined in with the rest – high and clear above the men's voices and the tinny piano. There were shouts for a solo, and the song which came to Elisabeth's mind, the song seemingly made for this evening, was the gloriously peaceful "Nacht und Träume" by Schubert.

No one wanted to accompany, so Elisabeth sat herself at the old upright: "Heil'ge Nacht, du sinkest nieder...." ("Holy night, you descend upon us...").

Elisabeth spoke about that audience some time later in an interview: "I will probably never again in my life have such an attentive and deeply moved audience."

Having landed in Liverpool on August 21 and reached London safely, Elisabeth telephoned Ibbs & Tillett and heard that her first concert, in the Royal Albert Hall, had been sold out for weeks. His Master's Voice also contacted her at once, in the person of Walter Legge, who managed their international artists. He was already a man of great influence in English musical life, although he had not yet brought into being the Philharmonia Orchestra and Philharmonia Chorus, for which he was to be particularly well known. Elisabeth immediately got on well with Legge; she felt that he was a person to be relied upon, and this proved to be true.

Very soon he had convinced her of the necessity of making more records. But who could be her accompanist? Rosenek was unfortunately in America; George Reeves was also not available; but Gerald Moore, who had played for her once or twice before at recordings, had developed into a specialist of the lied. A rehearsal was to take place in the Ritz Hotel.

It was over eight years since Elisabeth had worked with him, and she could only vaguely remember him. Now, on seeing him again, she remembered how she had been struck by his strangely unartistic appearance: rather thickset and with roughly hewn features. But how he played, how he understood the nature of the lied! He also seemed to understand her difficulties so marvellously; without needing any hints he sensed the places which she no longer found so easy, and dealt with them, immediately and very discreetly.

On August 29 and 30, at 3 Abbey Road, Elisabeth made recordings again for the first time in almost six years. She performed eight songs by Haydn, Mozart, Schubert and Wolf, including the charming Mozart song "Abendempfindung".

259

Elisabeth was surprised how relatively little London had been changed by the war. Things looked slightly drabber, and there were large bombed-out areas in the City, but places like St John's Wood, where the studio lay, seemed almost the same. A great sadness for her was the destruction by bombing of the beautiful Queen's Hall, where Sir Henry Wood had started the famous Promenade Concerts. What triumphs she had celebrated there! The huge Royal Albert Hall, holding over 5000 people, would not have the same intimacy so necessary for artsong; she had also heard that the acoustics there were not all that they should be. And that was where she was to give her first performance, and it was to be broadcast too, for it was one of the BBC's Promenade Concerts. But at least that meant that it would be a varied programme and that she would only have to sing a few numbers: two Mozart arias and two Schubert songs. "Deh vieni" and "Voi che sapete" were to be accompanied by the BBC Symphony Orchestra and conducted by the fine, considerate Sir Adrian Boult. The piano accompaniments for "Ave Maria" and "Die Forelle" were to be performed by the excellent Myra Hess. She would be well looked after.

But at the rehearsal on the morning of September 12, the day of the concert, the vastness of the cavernous hall did seem rather daunting to Elisabeth, who had to stand quite low down and look up at tier upon tier towering above and around her. But then she was reassured by the sound of her voice carrying in the huge space.

The concert was fixed for 7 p.m. Already in the afternoon huge queues formed at the box office. The seats had already been sold out, but the "Promenaders" were queueing for their standing places in the arena. Even after 7 o'clock people queued still, hoping for returned tickets. Those who had driven to the hall and were too late for tickets sat in their cars with the radio on. Large groups of people soon began to gather around the cars to hear what they could.

While the orchestra played Schubert's Unfinished Symphony the person to whose singing so many people were eagerly looking forward, was pacing up and down in the bleak artists' room like a caged animal. And the thermos flask with hot lemon was also constantly in use. Gracious Heaven! These people were expecting the Schumann of 1938 and she did not exist any more!

All of a sudden the terrible and so often experienced moment had arrived: the moment when you had to pull yourself together and, despite extreme nervousness, walk out smiling and with dignity.

Hardly had the huge mass of people caught sight of the long purple dress moving through the orchestra than it burst into an applause which grew ever more enthusiastic until it seemed as if thunder were rolling round the huge hall, for mixed with the sound of clapping came a wild stamping of feet. London's musical public was celebrating the return of Elisabeth Schumann before she had even sung a note. For minutes on the end the applause roared. Elisabeth could do nothing but stand on the podium, deeply moved, occasionally giving bows of acknowledgement. Not that this did anything to quell the enthusiasm. Sir Adrian had to raise his baton ostentatiously several times before, at last, the first gentle phrases of "Deh vieni, non tardar" rose up.

> Your voice sounded more beautiful and glowing than ever before, and I would have given anything to have been there in the auditorium to add my small acclaim to the host before you.

An American sergeant, Richard Weagly, had heard the broadcast live in France. His most earnest wish, to get leave to be able to fly to London for the concert, had not been fulfilled.

> I did not know that the programme was to be broadcast and it was an unusual stroke of fortune that I happened to enter my office ... this evening and turn on the radio just as you were beginning "Deh vieni". The applause was terrific after this number and I held my breath, for fear that this was your closing number.... Then the strains of "Voi che sapete" began and I knew that the treat was to continue. At the end of this the cheering and applause became so great, I felt you had to sing again. I could see you receiving the audience's welcome with that graciousness and sweetness with which I have so long been familiar ... I am moving to Wiesbaden, Germany, on September 21st, and my greatest hope is that you will be able to sing near there....

It was as if Sergeant Weagly had guessed what had happened just recently: since her arrival Elisabeth had asked friends, acquaintances, colleagues and anyone with influence whom she met, how she could get to Germany. Then one day Walter Legge tentatively asked her: "Elisabeth, would you by any chance sing for ENSA? It's true they don't pay well." This was the Entertainments National Service Association, and Walter Legge quickly explained that the organization brought entertainment to the troops in the form of music, theatre and cabaret, by sending artists to them, during the war sometimes almost to the front line. By those involved, ENSA was often jokingly referred to as "Every Night Something Awful"; but usually the artists were top class. These had to "join up" in a sense and wear uniform, for civilians were not allowed into the occupied zones of Germany.

Elisabeth was immediately game. She would be willing to sing without a fee, and in uniform and a steel helmet if necessary, as long as they let her into the American zone.

It took Walter Legge no time at all to discover that ENSA was interested in Elisabeth Schumann, extremely interested in fact. Several concerts were waiting to be fixed in many towns in Germany, but all of them were in the British zone.

But, optimist as she was, Elisabeth went straight to ENSA Headquarters at the Theatre Royal, Drury Lane, and agreed to give concerts in the British zone for two and half weeks from about October 24. Her pay would be a mere £15 a week, all expenses paid; she had not been paid so little since she was a beginner, but that was not important now. Once in Germany she would surely find a way to get to Falkenberg. In the meantime she must concentrate on all her concerts in England: fourteen in the next six weeks.

After her huge success at the Albert Hall, Elisabeth received a letter which she was least expecting: it was a demand from the Inland Revenue for over £430 of arrears in income tax for her earnings as a singer in Britain just before the war. She was staggered. To pay that off she would have to sing at least five concerts. After six years and a world war they were coming with their tax demands! As always, Ibbs & Tillett had the answer: they would gradually deduct the money as she earned it with her forthcoming concerts. (The result of this unexpected financial drain was that she returned to New York at the beginning of December with a clear profit of only £450, although she had earned £1500 in concert fees.)

What had happened to Winifred Hall? Why had Elisabeth not seen her at the Albert Hall? With some difficulty she found out the telephone number of the farm where Winnie was living and rang up. Winnie was ready to sink to the ground when she realized that her idol, the great, heavenly Schumann, had bothered to think of her. When she had recovered her composure she explained that she had been too buried in the country to hear about the concert. Elisabeth insisted that she must come to her next one, at the Cambridge

Theatre in London. "I can't send you a ticket, because there is no room. But come, I'll put you somewhere."

She came, of course. She came carrying a little basket saying it was just a little greeting from Mrs Armstrong and the farm. A little greeting! – a dozen fresh eggs and honey! Great luxuries in rationed England.

The only place which could be found for Winnie was in the wings, but she was richly compensated for this awkward position by being passed by Elisabeth each time the latter came on and off stage, each time getting a tap on the shoulder and a roguish smile.

After repeated enquiries and requests Elisabeth at last heard at the end of September that she would be able to give a concert in the American zone at the end of October, at the Liberty Theatre in Kassel. She could not have got nearer to Falkenberg if she had tried. What was even better: the other concerts were so scheduled that she could spend four whole days in Falkenberg! Gerd wrote excitedly:

> Darling Mutti! . . . I'm counting the days until the 28th of October.
> I feel like a child before Xmas. And I'm looking forward to the concert
> so very much – I can't tell you . . . come soon into my arms. . . .

In the same letter Gerd asked whether she could somehow manage to bring with her an important spare part for his MG, a new cylinder head; he had not been able to drive for a long time, and they needed the car desperately. Elisabeth was sure she could grant this small favour – until she found out that the cylinder head weighed thirty pounds! Luggage would be strictly limited in the military aircraft taking her to Germany, and something so unimportant to the army could not go as freight either.

Somehow she would have to get the help of the army. Jack Blagden, Biddy's brother, was now a lieutenant-colonel in the British military government in Germany. Elisabeth consulted Hannie Blagden who suggested that her nephew Willie Blagden, a brigadier involved with army supplies, could perhaps procure the cylinder head, and, after Elisabeth had paid for it, send it officially to Jack, who would then somehow get it to Gerd.

No sooner said than done. Elisabeth lunched with Willie who promised to do what he could for Madame Schumann and the husband of his cousin Biddy. Thus it came about that some time later the British Army helped a "big bad German" to obtain a new cylinder head.

Elisabeth was kitted out with her uniform at the ENSA headquarters. Although she was, as "Star Artist", allowed to have a well-fitting uniform made of the best material (Walter Legge had insisted on the latter), she felt quite out of place in the rather plump-making brownish-green clothes. But she cocked her peaked cap cheekily over her right ear, slung the haversack over her shoulder and marched up and down in front of the mirror, whistling and trilling a march from *Carmen*. She even had herself photographed in uniform and wrote on the backs of the photos "My latest role! First performances October-November 1945".

At last it was dawn on October 24. Elisabeth woke very early and was already in her uniform when Suze's cook came to wake her. She could hardly eat any breakfast, which was not like her at all, and waited for the car which was to drive her to Croydon Airport.

It was a windy day and the aircraft was anything but a luxury liner. There stood an old Dakota, just like the many thousands which had been used to transport troops during the war. Inside it was very spartan, with metal frames for lashing goods in transit securely, and uncomfortable seats which consisted of metal rods with canvas seats and backs. Elisabeth was almost forced to leave some of her luggage behind, for, what with all the presents for the family, she was over the weight limit. She pleaded and made all sorts of excuses about needing extra things as a singer, but it was not until she pulled out the copy of her contract which talked about "Madame Schumann . . . celebrated prima donna proceeding to BAOR [British Army of the Rhine] to give special performances . . ." that they suddenly found that, all told, the aircraft was not overloaded.

The flight was not cosy. Quite apart from the seat, the autumn wind was giving the Dakota a thorough shaking, and unfortunately some of Elisabeth's fellow passengers were not good travellers.

After about two and a half hours they landed near Hanover where the only transport available for getting to Bad Oeynhausen, the BAOR-Headquarters, was a three-ton army truck. Although Elisabeth was fortunate enough to get a seat in the driver's cabin, the din of the engine was incredible, and it was a frighteningly bumpy ride along badly kept roads.

Since there was no question of holding a conversation without endangering the precious vocal cords, Elisabeth was able to look out of the window at her leisure. The little villages which lay along the route seemed untouched by the war, only the shop windows looked empty and bleak. And the people! – thin, with grey faces and worn-out clothes; many still wore bits of old uniform; even women wore coats, jackets and skirts made of uniform material. Almost all of them carried huge bags or rucksacks around with them and stood in queues in front of food shops. And there were so many disabled men hobbling around on crutches! Perhaps Schnuck looked like them now. . . .

At Bad Oeynhausen a soldier came up to her, slim, in his mid-thirties, with an aquiline nose, and, what was most striking, dark sunken eyes behind thick horn-rimmed spectacles. In a rather thin, husky voice which reminded Elisabeth distantly of C, he introduced himself as her accompanist, Hubert Greenslade. Elisabeth had been expecting a pianist in civilian clothes carrying a music case under his arm, but of course, he was in ENSA too.

As she stood opposite him she suddenly seemed to hear Lene's voice, in her strong dialect, saying: "What a crazy get-up to be bringing your singing back to your homeland in!" She would gladly have translated this for Hubert Greenslade and explained why she now began to laugh so much. But she could only hang onto his arm and say, choking with laughter: "This uniform and everything – too funny!"

This light-hearted attitude to their concert tour made Hubert, who had been somewhat apprehensive, feel at ease. He felt even more so once he had started making music with Elisabeth. If ever she sensed that accompanists were afraid of her great ability and experience, she always knew how to make them feel that they were playing exactly as she wanted. It was like that now, although Greenslade played very well. He had a slight tendency to hardness and thumping, but with great discretion and consideration she was able somewhat to bend his interpretation to her way of thinking. He was acute enough to realize how much he could learn from her and made the best of this opportunity. He also proved himself an excellent courier; being lively and energetic and very conscious that he had been sent to make the unfamiliar military milieu as pleasant as possible for the great Schumann.

The days up to October 28, the day of reunion with the family, went by if not in a flash then almost in a dream. Suddenly, at Iserlohn, she was singing her last concert before the great day and spending a last restless night. The eagerly awaited transport was again a truck, but a smaller one with a canvas-covered platform onto which Hubert had to be stowed with all the many parcels for the family, which Elisabeth had additionally managed to obtain from the NAAFI (Navy, Army and Air Force Institute).

It was a frustrating journey with many wrong turnings. Hubert got quite indignant with the driver, but Elisabeth, being so full of joyful anticipation, merely said: "It does not matter – don't rush, we get there."

They did at last reach Kassel, but a long time after lunch. Hubert was to stay there, but for Elisabeth there was no time to eat: the parcels and luggage had hastily to be packed into a car which was waiting to drive her the further thirty-five kilometres to the country estate of Schloss Falkenberg. This journey was also not without its delays and problems, but at last they drove into the courtyard of the grand half-timbered house with its stone tower.

She had no eyes for its comfortable beauty; her heart was bursting with anticipation, and as she climbed out of the car she said firmly to herself: "Don't look shocked, whatever he looks like."

Two little girls heralded her arrival loudly as she was led upstairs by a servant into a pretty room with a low, beamed ceiling and low windows giving onto the park. Then – there was Biddy, slim as always, her black hair almost unchanged, and in her dark eyes the same kind, loving look. They fell into each other's arms and then walked to the window, still holding hands and without saying a word. Elisabeth took off her cap and laid it on the windowsill. Now Gerd's voice called from next door: "Mutti, Mutti! I'm coming, I'm coming!'

Biddy said: "He's just quickly putting on his leg. You see, we didn't know when you'd be coming."

As the door opened Elisabeth did not immediately look in his direction. He was quite close to her when she turned – and fell into his arms. After quite a while she lifted her head, smiled at him, tears still in her eyes, and said: "Isn't this get up frightful? I'm not nearly as fat as this uniform makes me look."

Children's voices could be heard coming from the corridor, one very high-pitched: "Omi* is here! Omii! Omiii!" The door burst open and the boys scampered into the room. Christian first, tall for his four and a half years, with soft blond hair and dark eyes. Not in the least bit shy, he danced up to Elisabeth. Behind him waddled almost two-year-old Rupert, stockier than his brother, with a funny little nose, blue eyes and amazing charm for such a youngster.

*Granny

Both were familiar with their granny through stories and the many packets which had arrived from her, and this brown-green figure, which whooped for joy and knelt down to take each of them in one arm, held no fears for them. "Christian! And Rupchen! My sweet, sweet, *sweet* ones!"

Now it was time to unpack and show the two of them, who were hopping around in excited anticipation, what she had brought for them: wonderful toys, not to be found in Germany for love or money, picture books, the most heavenly sweets and exciting new clothes.

Elisabeth was so happy that her family was safe and contented and in such good company. Gerd in particular was in need of this to help him cope. He seemed to be in good cheer, but his artificial leg gave him trouble: having been hurriedly made by overworked limb-fitters it did not sit properly and made him sore. Elisabeth had already made enquiries about a big limb-manufacturing centre in London and suggested to Gerd that she should try to procure an artificial limb for him there. The only problem would be to persuade a British firm to supply a German national so soon after the war. "My child," she continued, "just let me do it. I'll invite the director to lunch. Everything in this world can be arranged over lunch."

She was horrified when she heard the details of Gerd's "accident". Frightening though the story was, she felt she had to know at least something about it.

He and the flight of Junkers 52s he led had been dropping supplies by parachute onto the northeast corner of Sicily. It was a beautiful day and Gerd had left the controls to the co-pilot and taken the gunner's place at the rear so that he could film the operation in the open air. Suddenly, out of the sun, British fighters had pounced. Gerd hurriedly handed his lovely camera to the gunner and grabbed the little-used machine gun – which jammed after the first two volleys. Within seconds shells and bullets were whizzing through their machine, hitting Gerd in the leg and the man with whom he had changed places in the chest, killing him outright. Their aeroplane dived in flames into the sea, turning upside down as it hit the surface. Gerd was trapped in the gunner's position but managed to dive further underwater and then up – but not before he had had a frightful tussle with a cable trapping his leg, which had almost meant drowning. After an hour in the water, clinging to the remains of a badly holed inflatable dinghy, Gerd and those members of his crews who had survived, were picked up by Sicilian fishermen. (That had

267

been July 25 1943. That very night, in Hamburg, Biddy had experienced her worst air-raids of the war.) Then had followed the long, hot journey by train north through Italy. In Innsbruck, Austria, he was too ill to be transported further and it was there that doctors had tried in vain to save his leg before amputating. Biddy had sat for six weeks at his bedside until he was out of danger and had then returned to Falkenberg to give birth to Rupert.

What had her poor children been through! Elisabeth could hardly bear to think about it.

The honoured guest from America was offered the best that could be found in the way of food and drink. Fortunately the farm produced enough, if uninteresting, food, but the wine cellar had almost run dry. An American Pioneer Unit, billeted for weeks in the house, had seen to that. During that time the occupants of the house had had to find temporary accommodation in the village. Elisabeth heard with indignation that during the celebrations on May 8 the men had also broken open cupboards and drawers, stolen jewellery, dressed themselves in the women's clothes they found and jumped into the pond.

For years Gerd and Biddy had not heard Elisabeth sing, not since 1938. They had not even been able to play the two records which they had managed to rescue, for their gramophone was broken and there was no question of obtaining spare parts. They tentatively suggested that she could perhaps sing something to them.

The recital was to take place in the evening of her second day in Falkenberg. Hubert had agreed to drive over from Kassel to accompany her. Soon there was a feeling of excited anticipation in the house, a festive feeling like Christmas. In the large, low-ceilinged hall on the second floor sofas and armchairs were arranged to face the grand piano; in the stone wall of the tower, which curved into the hall, the heavy, carved door stood open, revealing the elegant proportions of the spiral staircase; bunches of autumn flowers adorned the carved wooden pillars and both sides of the open fireplace.

Once the children were in bed the adults gathered in their evening dresses and dinner jackets; Detta, the children's nurse, was in her snow-white uniform, and the butler, Franke, looked immaculate. It almost seemed to Elisabeth as if she was just about to give a big concert, and, while Franke served some of the champagne rescued from the Americans, she even began to feel the familiar nervousness, especially as they were all waiting and waiting for Hubert.

Suddenly the telephone rang. He was still in Kassel and simply could not get anyone in the army to drive him up.

No one else could play well enough, Biddy was quite out of practice. There was a feeling of anticlimax.

"The only thing to be done is for me to accompany myself," said Elisabeth. Spirits rose immediately. Oh please, yes! everyone cried at once.

Elisabeth warned them that the concert would not be nearly as pleasurable, especially as she would have to choose songs with easy accompaniments.*

But what did it matter? What did it even matter that they could not see her expression as she sang? Beside this voice there seemed to be nothing of importance any more. The singing, that glorious sound, seemed to come from another, a heavenly, world. The misery of war seemed left behind in unreality. At the end of every song the cessation of this glorious sound was like a shock, and the clapping was like the din of everyday life intruding again.

German nationals were not allowed into the concert for American soldiers in Kassel, so although Gerd drove his mother to Kassel and back in his little MG (as a disabled ex-serviceman he was allowed to use his car), he was unable to hear her there.

The four days in Falkenberg flew by and soon Elisabeth's last evening had come. Hubert had managed to get a lift from Kassel to join everyone for this farewell dinner. Everyone shared the hope that Elisabeth would come again as soon as possible, but for her the most important thing was to get the family to America somehow. Here they were just vegetating. In the meantime they simply had to visit Biddy's mother in London as soon as ever possible; Elisabeth personally would try to find out about visitors' permits.

An announcement that the gardener was outside the door was greeted with some surprise. He made an entrance not unlike that of the gardener in *The Marriage of Figaro*, clumsily and in his working clothes and heavy boots. But instead of a broken flowerpot, he held in his hand a perfect orchid. Elisabeth, not a great lover of orchids, was nevertheless impressed when the man slowly said: "It only flowers once – and only for one night. And that is now."

---

*Among the songs she sang were "Wie bist du, meine Königin" (Brahms), "Freundliche Vision" and "Morgen" (Strauss).

269

The miraculous flower was placed in a lovely glass on the dinner table. Hubert wanted to know its name.

Queen of the Night.

"It must have felt that Madame Schumann was here," he said.

Elisabeth responded by bursting into song, and one of the coloratura passages sung by the Queen of the Night in *The Magic Flute* poured out in a silvery stream.

Early the following morning, on Friday November 2, an army car pulled up at the house, and a few minutes later Elisabeth was out and about in the big world again.

Now, for the first time since 1934, Elisabeth was on her way to sing in Hamburg, the city where C had come into her life and married her. By a strange quirk of fate it was at the ENSA Headquarters in Salzuflen, only a few hours away from Hamburg, that she found a letter telling her that C had unexpectedly died of a heart attack on October 15. It had happened at his home in Mexico City, where he had been a conductor at the Opera Nacional.

Soon she was looking across the water of the Binnenalster at the familiar silhouette of Hamburg's city centre with its many church spires, thinking of the man who no longer was, the man with whom she had begun the most important part of her career, who had been such a capable helper and amusing companion for those many years of rewarding work and great triumphs. Transience.

Transience was affectingly visible now in the silhouette of the city which was looking quite unreal, like stage scenery, for many of the once so solid-looking office blocks and business premises were nothing but empty shells with hollow windows, and among the church spires the graceful baroque tower of St Catherine's Church was missing. It was affectingly visible too at the Stadttheater, the starting point of a career and showplace of many triumphs – now half burnt down.

But some things had not been ravaged by transience. The Curiohaus, for example, where Schnuck had been born, was still standing and – it was a miracle – a lot of the beautiful old furniture from Vienna was there. Only one thing spoiled it: British military personnel were making themselves comfortable on it – the Curiohaus had been requisitioned by the British Army for offices. Proving that the furniture belonged to an American citizen and organizing its removal to storage as soon as possible involved a lot of toing and froing.

About the rest of the furniture, stored in Dresden, there was no news. It was to be assumed that it had all perished in the bombing shortly before the end of the war. Elisabeth could not feel too badly about it when she saw all the misery around her. But what was upsetting was the fact that she had heard absolutely nothing from Lene, who was in the Russian zone. Trying to get permission to enter the zone would have been like hitting her head against a brick wall. All she could do was to keep writing to her friend and hope that one day something would get through. At least there was some hope that Lene might hear Elisabeth on the radio: the concert in Hamburg, on November 3, was recorded and to be broadcast on the 16th.

The next stop was Berlin. When Elisabeth arrived by aeroplane on November 4, a cold she had been nursing had by now slipped down her throat and there was no possibility of singing to the troops there. All she could do was to wait until there was a chance to catch another aeroplane out.

Spending two days with nothing to do in the old capital of the Reich was very depressing. There were endless rows of empty shells of buildings and bomb sites on which men, and even more women, were moving rubble like a lot of ants. Most of the people in the city had the typical grey, emaciated faces she had seen before; but every now and then, standing on street corners or in doorways, people plumper in face and figure could be seen – the smugglers and black marketeers.

Once back in London, on November 8, Elisabeth did not forget her promise that she would try to get a better artificial leg for Gerd. Perhaps Van Geldern, at whose house she and Hans had enjoyed their wedding breakfast, would be able to help to make enquiries at one of the limb-manufacturers at Roehampton through a friend of his, who had also lost a leg.

Van, who Elisabeth had reason to believe might be hoping to marry her, had immediately contacted her on her return to London and invited her to lunch at the Dorchester. Despite her lingering cold she had accepted and, talking quietly so as not to strain her voice, was soon recounting her experiences to her pleasant companion, who sat opposite her reminding her rather of a walrus. She talked a lot about Gerd and about how she wanted to help him. Could Van help?

In his reply Van's voice sounded no less pleasant, if rather quieter. He said that anyone who had fought for Hitler ought to put up with the consequences.

271

If it seemed that she hesitated for a moment it was only because she had not immediately been able to believe her ears, for it was quite clear to her how she should react. Without a word she laid down knife, fork and napkin, stood up and, without deigning to give him another glance, walked with measured tread out of the restaurant.

That was the end of the acquaintanceship of many years with Van. Elisabeth never heard from him again.

As it happened, Elisabeth had no trouble in persuading the director of Hanger's to have a leg made for Gerd, albeit in his brother-in-law Jack Blagden's name.

The journey to New York was set for December 2 1945. This time Elisabeth decided to travel from London to Southampton in luxury by hiring a chauffeur. On December 1 they set off in fog which became so thick that Elisabeth did not climb the gangway of the *Queen Elizabeth* until the early hours of the next morning.

She felt tired for almost all the journey because of all she had crammed into the last few weeks in London. With the daily help of Dr Alfred Alexander, a throat specialist of Viennese origin recommended by Hannie Blagden, Elisabeth had managed to be on top form for another big concert in the Royal Albert Hall on November 19. From then until her departure she had had to sing almost daily: radio broadcasts, a concert for the Free Austrian Movement, concerts in the provinces and two days of recordings. In between there had been the inevitable parties, friends to visit, purchases to be made . . . .

Now, in contrast, New York seemed almost quiet. This time there was not the excitement of a big Town Hall recital – the long European tour had left too little time for that. Before Christmas there were only two radio concerts to sing, and of course there were her private pupils and the Curtis Institute.

Elisabeth enjoyed once again the quiet afternoons and evenings in her flat at 520 East 90th Street when friends came to visit her. There was C's older brother, Kurt Pindar, who reminded her a little of C but was really quite different: thickset, quieter and calmer, a good listener and with a marvellous dry humour. If Hugo Burghauser was there too – the bassoonist and former President of the Vienna Philharmonic Orchestra, who positively radiated merriment – there was no end to the laughter. Young Gustl Breuer, who had now left the army and was working in a publicity firm, and music-loving, ever helpful Harry Goddard Owen were also frequent visitors.

Despite her friends New York did not seem to be the place it used to be for Elisabeth; her focus had shifted to Europe, to her family. It was now of the utmost importance to Elisabeth to try to get her children to America. If only President Roosevelt were still alive, for it seemed that only victims of political persecution were being allowed to emigrate from Germany. Elisabeth tried writing to his widow, but even this failed, and she also heard that Gerd and his family would have to wait quite some time before even a visit to England would be permitted.

There was nothing more Elisabeth could do for the time being, so she concentrated hard on her teaching again. The Curtis Institute had given her a new two-year contract and there were plenty of private pupils too. She was a kind, encouraging teacher, idolized by most of her pupils, but she could be strict too: sometimes pupils were allowed to practise nothing but exercises for a week; if after six months she felt that a pupil was not singing the way she wanted her to, then that pupil had to leave her: time was too precious to waste on someone who would not learn – she would rather have someone else in their place.

The arrival of summer 1946 meant returning to Europe with the hope of seeing the family again. But this pleasure would have to be paid for by lots of singing which, luckily, was mostly to be in England where Elisabeth felt loved. Even the younger generation contributed admirers. When seventeen-year-old Lionel Miller had heard that she was coming to England again he wrote, in February 1946:

> I can't tell you of the joy I felt, when I heard that you would be visiting England. I recall now, quite vividly, that night of September 1945, when I, like so many others, packed the Albert Hall to hear you sing. You were the first artistic fruit of peace. It will remain an event in my life, that I will never forget. The beauty of your voice brought tears of pleasure to my eyes.

She heard once again how hardened soldiers had come to love her singing. Shortly before she was due to sing in a broadcast of Mahler's Fourth Symphony in June 1946, she had a boost to her confidence (always reassuring before a performance) in the form of a letter from a colonel still serving in the British Army. He had spent many years in Japanese prison camps. After a long struggle the prisoners had been allowed to have "concerts" of gramophone records.

273

Among our original forty records was a recording of you singing Böhm's "Still wie die Nacht". As our concerts were usually held in the open and finished about 7.30 p.m. just as the Japanese switched on the perimeter lights and we had to go inside, this record became one of our favourite methods of closing our concerts for nearly three years. It was certainly the best loved record of our collection and enjoyed alike by the high-brows, low-brows and even the jazz enthusiasts. I can hardly express to you what it meant to exiles so far away from our homes to hear your lovely voice just when the hush, which comes with the tropical sunset, was falling. I know that I, for one, used to go to sleep feeling calmer and more secure for having heard your record. . . . I feel that you ought to know how much joy you brought to one Japanese prison camp. . . .

It seemed to Elisabeth that that summer of 1946 was the time of her true come-back in Europe. She felt that her voice had really come to life again and that she was able to work as hard as she had in her youth.

At first this come-back was only in England; there were almost no invitations from other European countries, until suddenly Vienna made a peremptory request for her services. Elisabeth suspected that she had Walter Legge to thank for this, for he, as one of the first civilian foreign visitors to the city on the Danube, was at that time searching for talent for His Master's Voice. Vienna was putting on a charity concert for children's welfare in October; Elisabeth was also asked if she would be interested in two opera performances (these would be held at the Theater an der Wien instead of the opera house, which had been bombed).

It was a difficult decision: "I'm so afraid of going back to Vienna," she wrote to Trude el Bedell, "but I suppose I shall have to do the concert." She had no trouble in deciding against the two guest performances: she felt that she was too old to take on young, soubrette roles any more.

Perhaps a visit to Arnold Rosé would clarify her feelings. It would be good to talk to him about Vienna.

It was August 6 when Elisabeth drove out of Central London to Blackheath to see the old, sick erstwhile leader of the Vienna Philharmonic Orchestra and founder of the Rosé Quartet. How ill he looked! His wonderful beard and head of white hair had all but disintegrated.

Vienna – the name brought only the faintest flicker of memory to his eyes. His brother, Eduard, was uppermost in his mind – where he was, whether he was still alive, had he perhaps died just like . . .? He could not say the name, but Elisabeth knew it just the same – Alma, his daughter. That beautiful, talented young violinist with whom Schnuck had fallen in love twenty-five years ago in Bad Ischl, had died in a concentration camp.

It comforted Rosé to know that Elisabeth would make enquiries about his brother in Germany and Austria. He died on August 25.

Through ENSA Elisabeth received another impetus to go to Vienna. They suddenly announced that they wanted concerts for the soldiers in the theatre of the beautiful palace of Schönbrunn at the end of October. Walter Legge gave the final push. He arrived in London for a few days in August and, over lunch, told Elisabeth enthusiastically that plans were afoot to raise money for the rebuilding of the opera house. He had suggested that putting on concerts with prominent artists would be a good way to start, and who could be more suitable than Schumann?

When he saw that she was almost won over he began to outline his ideas for the programme: something English to start with, Purcell perhaps, then Mozart; in the second group Schubert; the third and fourth groups could be Wolf and Strauss.

Elisabeth was really quite happy about going; it would mean seeing the family again. Although she had managed to visit them in July, it had been only for three days.

Before she left for Vienna she wrote to Lene: "I shall be staying at the Sacher Hotel opposite the ruins of the beloved opera – my heart already aches. I don't know whether I shall venture into the Reitschulgasse."

In the event any feelings of nostalgia upon arrival were pushed right into the background. Miserable weather spoilt all the plans for her arrival; the aeroplane landed just two hours before the start of the recital in the big Musikvereinssaal. In her agitation during the drive into town, most of what she saw passed in a blur: sometimes she recognized something, the next moment there were just unrecognizable ruins. She quickly got ready at the hotel and rushed to the brief rehearsal. The accompanist Heinrich Schmidt, a complete stranger, seemed very good and sensitive.

Now she was going on stage – there had been no time to get nervous. Then – thunderous applause, for minutes on end: Vienna was greeting its Schumann again after almost nine years. How thin and grey-faced the people looked, all wrapped up in many layers of clothing against the cold of the unheated hall. But after "Deh vieni, non tardar" and "Das Veilchen" the sadness and worry on the faces grew less.

The success! After every song a storm of enthusiastic clapping. At the end encore after encore. During her very last song Elisabeth could see the tears running down the people's faces. It was "Morgen" by Strauss: "And tomorrow the sun will shine again", "which," wrote the critic Heinrich Kralik, "will be to us a message of promise, a comforting cheer from the other shore."

The artists' room teemed with old friends and acquaintances. Former colleagues from the opera had sent wonderful flowers and were almost all present, some of them very aged and almost unrecognizable. The joy of reunion could not completely disguise the look of depression on most faces. Only Wisoko, thank heavens, had not lost his humour.

Those three days were like a dream. Every morning Mitzi came into the Sacher Hotel and looked after and spoilt Elisabeth as of old, which also meant a pleasant chat for half an hour. From nine o'clock Elisabeth hardly had time to turn round – the telephone rang nonstop. But she gave herself a little time for the Reitschulgasse. She went there quite alone, passing over the Albrechtsrampe, where she had so often walked Sorry. Timidly she walked underneath the archway and opened the wicket in the heavy oaken door. On her left in his box was a strange porter. She asked after the old one, whom she had known so well – dead. To the left there was still the old court apothecary, but straight ahead across the courtyard the stables were closed and barred and completely silent – no neighing or pawing to be heard: the stallions were gone, for the time being anyway. And upstairs on the first floor, in the once so stylish, noble rooms – office desks, typewriters, files, stale air.

What had been would never be again.

Walter Legge invited Elisabeth to lunch in the Kohlmarkt; he wanted to introduce her to two young, up-and-coming stars.

Judging by the richness of delicacies available despite the hard times, the establishment in the Kohlmarkt (Coal Market) seemed also to be in the middle of the black market. Trust Walter, the gourmet, to find it! The two young ladies were Elisabeth Schwarzkopf and Irmgard Seefried. With Walter's talent for sniffing out talent one could be sure that they would make it to the top.

The party soon became relaxed and cheerful. The young Seefried plucked up courage to ask Elisabeth: "Where do you get that fabulous C sharp from?" The experienced singer then pointed to the heaviest part of her anatomy and said, "From the bum, dear child, from the bum!"

Elisabeth overcame her qualms and went to have a look at the largely burnt out ruins of the opera house. She stood in the central box (where the Kaiser would have sat) and looked into a yawning emptiness – through to the Sacher Hotel.

Then she left Vienna and wrote to Lene a few days later:

> Everything is really like a dream. . . . I am glad – it's all behind me
> – I went there with such a heavy heart, but I had to do it for the
> children.

To be able to see them again, no price was too high for that; after the mad turmoil in Vienna the heavenly peace of Falkenberg, with its quiet, hilly woods in autumn colours, did her good. Gerd was able to come on walks too, for Elisabeth's efforts at Roehampton had paid off: with the English leg made of light metal he was walking much more easily.

The family had by now applied for visitors' permits for England: conditions had been relaxed and German husbands of British women were being allowed to make long visits. But although they had sent all the necessary documents in the summer they had heard nothing as yet. When would things get back to normal? Elisabeth was not even allowed to go to Weimar to see Lene. At least she had started getting letters from her in July again, but they sometimes took weeks to arrive. Elisabeth still hoped that she would be persuaded to emigrate to America.

She proved very useful in connection with Elisabeth's furniture which had been stored in Dresden. By some miracle the warehouse, situated in the old part of the city, had remained unscathed in the terrible bombing raids. It was true that the Russians had been through the warehouse like a swarm of locusts, but a lot of furniture remained, if damaged. The removal firm wrote that some of it could be repaired; at the same time they sent a fat bill for the previous years of storage. Lene offered to pay the bill for the time being and arranged for repairs to be done.

Was all this not going to cost far too much money? Would the plan to ship all the furniture over from Germany perhaps remain a dream?

Many things were now questionable since the unexpected shock of the letter from Efrem Zimbalist, director of the Curtis Institute, which had arrived in October. No one knew of its contents except Suze Rueff to whose address in London it had been sent, registered. Elisabeth could not bring herself to tell anyone, not Lene, not the family – certainly not them – not even Walter Legge. She needed to come to terms with it herself first.

September 24 1946

Dear Elisabeth,

Your cable prompts me to write and tell you that we find your decision to defer coming to the Curtis Institute until November 11th so very disappointing.

Last year we had difficulty in keeping your students in line and I do not doubt that it will be be same again this year.

Somehow, dear Elisabeth, your association with the Curtis Institute is not working out well and, most regretfully, I must tell you that at the expiration of the present school year your contract will not be renewed.

Apart from business, you may always be assured of our great admiration for you as an artist, and affection for you as a friend.

Sincerely yours,
Efrem Zimbalist

As well as the shocking significance of this letter – no longer would $6000 be coming into Elisabeth's bank account each year – the tone of the letter seemed to her so school-masterish: she was being ticked off for being a naughty girl. The reason for it seemed so silly: the Institute had a seven-month season while she was only engaged to teach there for six; of what consequence was it whether her pupils had no instruction during the first or the last weeks of the school year?

This was the worst humiliation of her career, her first real failure. Did they not like her teaching? Had not her pupils always done well at the end-of-semester concerts? They should be glad that they had someone who could still reap triumphs on the concert platform! But perhaps that was it: she was away too much, she did not attend the summer school in Rockport any more either. Perhaps her dismissal was also an economy measure, Efrem was good at those: he had cut salaries during the war. But would he not have said if it were only that?[*]

[*]It was noticed over the years that Zimbalist, possibly in order to ensure his complete power over the Institute, tended to dismiss people who had a close friendship with, or influence over, his wife.

It so happened that she did not see Zimbalist for some time, but Mary invited her to tea very soon. To this older, almost motherly friend Elisabeth was able to confide her hurt feelings. Mary was clearly unhappy and in disagreement with her husband's decision, but in the interests of the Institute she felt she could not go over his head.

When Elisabeth went back to her studio she was confronted by the portrait of her predecessor Sembrich in its gold frame. The slightly mocking, amused smile suddenly struck her. Now she knew that her own portrait would not hang there, not even in a silver frame.

It was now that Elisabeth began to cherish the idea of moving to London, possibly spending just a few months each year in New York. She suddenly did not feel as if she belonged in New York any more. This Christmas time was particularly depressing; most of her friends were away, and she did not even have the pleasure of buying presents for Christian and Rupert: she had arrived back too late for them to be sent in time, and in London there had been no time to do anything about it either. Erna Samuel had offered to buy something and send it via Biddy's brother Jack to Falkenberg.

Erna and Jacques Samuel were new friends Elisabeth had made in London, Viennese and great lovers of music. After one of her London recitals they had turned up in the artists' room – Erna, whose clear, melodious voice made one look up at once, and the quietly-spoken Jacques who always seemed to be on the point of breaking into a mischievous grin.

Elisabeth had not regretted accepting an invitation to dinner: the Viennese cuisine served in the most tasteful manner had been exquisite, and their little flat was charmingly furnished with antiques. Most exciting of all was Jacques' collection of letters written by famous people, mostly musicians: letters from Wagner, Liszt, Clara Schumann – he kept pulling out more and more delights. There was even a scribbled note from Goethe which said something like: "I need urgently to talk to you further about this."

Luckily Elisabeth soon had things to think about other than her longing to be near the family: the big recital on January 14 1947 in the Town Hall of New York. Although success was now even more vital, since the shocking news from the Curtis Institute, Elisabeth took the event completely in her stride. Giving concerts was once again routine and straightforward, not like during the war when every concert had been a huge mental and physical effort.

The last day at the Curtis Institute drew near. Mary was to have a present, something to show Elisabeth's friendship and gratitude to this great patron of music. After much thought Elisabeth found a fitting gift, although she hesitated to give something away which was so precious to her: Helena's aria, text and melody line written in Strauss's hand over six pages and with the composer's dedication: "To the first Helena, Elisabeth, in memory of March 27 1926." Mary had a wonderful collection of manuscripts and autographs of musicians; this manuscript would be a perfect addition to it. In the letter which Elisabeth put with it, in which she explained the origin of the manuscript, she indicated that she was really giving it to Mary alone, Mary and her Institute.

It was to be a complete surprise, and Elisabeth kept the gift until the last day of the semester at the beginning of May. As Mary Curtis Bok Zimbalist looked at the Strauss document all she could do was shake her head in wonder and delight. The two women hugged each other.

Efrem looked into the room briefly, showed his admiration for the gift, and he and his former employee parted after all on what seemed to be friendly, even warm terms.

CHAPTER 20

New York and Europe, 1947–1950

B ACK IN LONDON in May 1947 Elisabeth had plenty of concerts in England already arranged.

At the beginning of the month Ibbs & Tillett had cabled to New York asking if she would give some performances of Sophie and Pamina at Covent Garden. The idea of a portly almost sixty-year-old grandmother trying to portray innocent young girls seemed to Elisabeth too absurd; besides which she did not feel she would have enough stamina for the performances, several of which were close together. Ibbs & Tillett were instructed not to accept opera engagements on her behalf any more.

At first she put up in the Hyde Park Hotel again, where some of the staff still knew and respected her. But soon she was able to move into a small, pleasant flat near Primrose Hill found for her by Erna Samuel. It belonged to a pianist, Vera Benenson, who was letting it while she was on tour in Africa for six months. The flat formed part of the ground floor of a building called Wellington House, and from the drawing room, where Elisabeth could practise at the grand piano, there was a pleasant view onto the garden.

ENSA no longer existed and Elisabeth wanted to visit the family, of course. Somehow a way had been found to arrange concerts for British soldiers in Germany: two in Hamburg and one in Bad Oeynhausen. They were so well scheduled that Elisabeth was going to be able to have three weeks holiday in Falkenberg.

When, on July 2, Elisabeth alighted from the airport bus at the Hotel Atlantik in Hamburg she saw Gerd hurrying towards her with his funny little hopping steps. He had made it! He had managed to get enough petrol to drive up from Falkenberg in a larger car borrowed from an old friend. Gerd was able to attend the concert in the Musikhalle; now, two years after the end of the war, Germans were allowed to come to events put on for the allies. When Elisabeth looked for Schnuck from the platform she saw something quite unexpected: Walther was sitting next to him, little changed since she had last seen him twelve years before at their son's twenty-first birthday party; thinner in the face after all the privations of the war, but that did no harm to his looks; his white hair was as full as ever and still cut too short at the sides, so that he had not the slightest look of an artist.

"She still sings fabulously," said Walther to Gerd in the interval.

However, he did not go to the artists' room after the concert; the last time Elisabeth was ever to see her first husband, she did so only from a distance.

Two days later Gerd drove his mother to Bad Oeynhausen, where she had to sing before travelling on to Falkenberg. Gerd was able to be with her the whole time. After the concert the commanding General of the British Army stationed there invited Elisabeth to a banquet in the casino.

"My dear General," said Elisabeth, pointing to Gerd, "this is my son. Can he come too? But he is German." The General did not hesitate and gave his permission at once. Thus Gerd may possibly have been one of the first former Luftwaffe officers to dine in a British HQ, with its officers and their wives, after the war.

At Falkenberg Elisabeth found some presents which Lene had sent her from the Russian zone: some beautiful Dresden china and a new biography of Richard Strauss. "What an idiot of an author!" Elisabeth wrote back to Lene, for neither she herself nor Lotte Lehmann had been mentioned in the book. In the same letter she begged Lene to try her hardest to visit her in Falkenberg.

On July 22 Elisabeth was called to the telephone. Lene had arrived at the railway station at Wabern. She had come over the *grüne Grenze* – the green frontier – which meant that she had crossed illegally, for the last part in the Russian zone she had needed a guide. She was going to have to return in the same manner. But now she wanted someone to fetch her.

There happened to be no petrol available for driving, so Moritz, the good old horse, was harnessed to the cart as quickly as possible, and a friend acted as driver for Elisabeth and Gerd.

In the meantime Lene had set off on foot in the direction of Falkenberg. Thus it was that the great reunion took place on the open road.

For quite a while the two friends hugged each other tightly.

Emotional though the scene was, Lene could not help noticing the funny side: "Golly, Elisabeth, skinny old me – I'm almost invisible next to your graceful corpulence!"

Elisabeth was almost ashamed. But she had planned to go to Abano in Italy for a couple of weeks in August to get rid of her catarrh once and for all and there she would diet a few pounds off herself.

It seemed as if nothing had changed in the last nine years; the friendship was as close as ever and the separation seemed as if it had been much shorter. Only one thing slightly marred Lene's visit for Elisabeth: it was clear that Lene did not want to emigrate. Now that her brother had died she did not want to desert her sister-in-law, and she loved her apartment in Weimar.

After three happy days Gerd drove Elisabeth back to Hamburg. The journey did not go without a hitch. Halfway there one of the tyres started losing air. Gerd got up quite a sweat changing it, while his mother trilled and whistled and, every now and then, told him to calm down: "If we don't arrive today then we'll arrive tomorrow, my child. The 'plane isn't leaving until tomorrow midday." The spare tyre was not much better, it seemed that they would have to get a new one from somewhere – on a Saturday afternoon!

After much searching they at last found a garage from which a dour man emerged in response to knocking. At first he wanted a coupon for the tyre. He looked suspiciously at this strange couple in the old Hanomag: the civilian was obviously a war-cripple, and the woman was in a British uniform. Allied personnel didn't drive around in broken-down German cars, they could get anything they wanted. But with her usual charm Elisabeth explained the situation, gave the man a packet of coffee and some cigarettes, and they ended up being given a tyre for free.

At three o'clock the next morning Elisabeth and Gerd arrived dead tired in front of the Hotel Atlantik. But where was Gerd to sleep? Only allied personnel were permitted to enter the hotel. Elisabeth had an idea. She announced her arrival to the night porter and said that her son had driven her there and would just help take the luggage up to her room. He would surely be allowed to refresh himself a little before he left?

The porter looked doubtful but said nothing and helped carry the luggage up. After a fat tip he shut the room door behind him. "Room number 346, which adds up to 13," said Elisabeth, "we're in luck again."

It was a suite of two rooms, and Gerd headed straight for the one with the sofa. But Elisabeth insisted that he take the bedroom after having driven so far (which, as usual, he had done with crossed legs, since he could only use the accelerator and brake with his good leg, the left one). No amount of protesting would stop Elisabeth from settling herself with a cushion and a couple of blankets on the sofa.

Late next morning, after she had been awake quite a while, she woke Gerd and ordered breakfast to be brought up. She was tremendously bucked at the trick she had played, and said once or twice: "Schnuck, you here with me in the Atlantik, where only British and Americans are allowed! What a hoot!"

Within twenty-four hours Elisabeth was far away from anyone she knew. There followed the very boring cure at Abano, in terrible heat. The mud baths were tiring, the inhaling was irksome, and she was lonely: no Wisoko or Lene, as there had been in 1938. There was not even the possibility of consoling meals: she had to diet and she lost eighteen pounds.

A telegram arrived from Ibbs & Tillett. Lotte Lehmann was indisposed and had cancelled her trip to Europe; would Elisabeth be able to take her place at the Edinburgh Festival, giving a recital with Bruno Walter? At first she was none too keen on agreeing to perform only as "first reserve". But this being the first year of a major new international festival (to which the Vienna Philharmonic was also invited, she remembered), there was really no question of refusing.

Two weeks later Elisabeth was also singing a BBC programme in Lotte's place. Then Bruno Walter came to Elisabeth's little flat in Wellington House to rehearse for the Edinburgh concert, with press photographers in train. Once they had gone, the music-making was intensive, for Walter often went over certain passages several times. It was the first time that he had worked with Elisabeth as accompanist, rather than conductor. He became visibly excited and did not seem to want to stop, playing beautifully. The little flat in Eton Road witnessed quite a performance, which was then repeated with great success in Edinburgh.

There was so much going on in England: an ensemble of the Vienna Opera and the Vienna Philharmonic were in London giving performances. This meant the possibility of seeing old friends again, but in fact Elisabeth had so many concerts to give in the provinces at that time that she only managed to fit in a *Don Giovanni* and a *Salome*. She noticed how high the standard of the Viennese artists still was, and their great success showed how starved of good music the Londoners were at this time.

For Elisabeth the cultural highlight of that autumn in London was going to be the concert in the Albert Hall by the recently formed Philharmonia Orchestra conducted by Richard Strauss. The eighty-three-year-old composer had come to London without his wife – flying for the first time in his life.

At the end of the concert, in which *Don Juan, Burleske* and *Sinfonia Domestica* were performed, Elisabeth was moved almost to tears. She wanted to leave at once but friends held her back, old Viennese colleagues and London friends crowded round her. "You must go to him! – You must!" they cried at her from all sides.

Strauss half turned as he heard someone coming into the artists' room. He was completely exhausted, just looked at her and did not recognize her. Elisabeth wished the earth would swallow her up. Then he asked: "Who are you?" When she quietly replied "Elisabeth" he brightened and said: "Good God, Schumann! I hear you still sing so well."

After very few more words Elisabeth quickly left. For a long time she could not bring herself to tell anyone what had happened. Finally, months later, when Lene had repeatedly asked her about it, she described the scene adding: "With 'great Richard' it was so disappointing because I was completely alone with him – and he did not recognize me! It was very embarrassing, and I wish I had never gone to see him."

Back in New York Christmas had soon arrived, and on Christmas Day Elisabeth telephoned Gerd in Falkenberg. He told her that the family had permits to go to England as long as they obtained exit visas from the Americans.

Luckily Elisabeth had a string to pull. At a concert she had given in Germany in 1946 she had met a man who had been quite charming: the United States Political Adviser for Germany, James W. Riddleberger. With his help the family knew by February 18 that their exit visas were being issued.

Elisabeth heard the happy news a little later, and with it came some more happy news: Biddy was expecting a third child in September. This time it had to be a girl!

Leaving Germany was going to be only half the battle. To get the family to America would be another difficult step. It had occurred to Elisabeth that Mexico might be quite a good stepping stone. There was even a growing film industry there. So she had arranged to give three concerts as well as two radio broadcasts there, with a view to sounding things out while she was in the country.

This exploratory journey came within an inch of being cancelled, for, a few days before departure, Elisabeth was suddenly overcome by the most terrible pain she had ever experienced in her life. It exploded through her body and brought her to a complete standstill: even the slightest movement caused pain which almost made her faint. There was no question of reaching the telephone to get help, she just had to wait until Rosie came back from the shopping and found her huddled up in a pathetic ball. Could lumbago be as painful as this?

The doctor gave her injections and, with some bed rest, the problem subsided and the flight to Mexico was possible after all.

Elisabeth felt very much at home staying with Lisa Reitler's sister, who welcomed her warmly. She looked around as much as time would allow. She was fascinated by the towns, the architecture and the landscape with its snow-clad mountains in the distance and brilliant sunshine. As a stepping stone at least, it would be pleasant enough to live here, and, judging by the success she was having with her concerts and broadcasts, Elisabeth would probably be able to find enough engagements to combine with visits to the family. She did, however, notice that the people's interest in the lied as an art form was somewhat limited to the lighter, jollier songs. No wonder C had enjoyed living here, with his sparkling, energetic way of making music. Twice Elisabeth went to his grave, taking a sheaf of the glorious flowers that proliferated here. He lay in a beautiful cemetery, high up, overlooking Mexico City. The companion of her happiest years had found his resting place in this beautiful spot, and yet "poor man! *So* alone in this for us so foreign soil!"

A telegram chased away sorrowful thoughts. From Gerd! They needed her to send the money for their journey in dollars as soon as possible. Departure was set for April 1. Arrival in London in little more than two weeks! And they even had somewhere to live: a roomy house in St John's Wood which belonged to an ailing aunt of Biddy's who was now living in a sanatorium.

April 2 arrived but no telegram from London. Then, some days later, a telegram arrived from Hannie: "Boys down with measles journey postponed."

Elisabeth began to wonder who would reach London first: she or the children. But on April 28, the day before her departure, another telegram from Hannie came: "Safely arrived all well love Hannie."

After what seemed like the longest Atlantic crossing of all time Elisabeth finally arrived one morning in the smoke, dust and crowds of Victoria Station in London. Almost at once she saw Schnuck hopping towards her along the platform, behind him the already plumper figure of Biddy holding the boys by the hand.

Of course the family was invited to have lunch at Wellington House, for Elisabeth had brought so much food with her: chicken, ham, sausage, cheese, cream, chocolate, sweets, marzipan. Most of it had travelled over in the refrigerators of the *Queen Elizabeth* – her good friend the purser had seen to that.

It was a memorable day, that May 5 1948. It seemed that on this day they were reunited for ever; there would be no long separations any more, they lived in the same world again.

In June Elisabeth travelled up to Edinburgh to give a concert and to visit Joyce Fleming. Gerd and his mother travelled up together in the Flying Scotsman.

It reminded them both of their train journey from Switzerland to Vienna shortly before Christmas 1924; they had the same feeling – that they were good friends.

In the compartment Elisabeth pulled a sheaf of typewritten pages from her suitcase and gave them to the surprised Gerd saying: "I'm supposed to look through this, the translation of my book."

A London publisher had persuaded Elisabeth to write a book about German song. Now she watched with amusement as she noticed her son reading with increasing puzzlement and consternation. "But Mutti, you don't write like this!"

She confessed, even more amused, that not she but a ghost-writer, namely Rosenek, had written it. They had discussed the contents in detail, of course, and many of the ideas had come from her, but he had done the writing. Schnuck thought it was a pity that it lacked the light touch she would have given it. His mother was not bothered; she anyway found it difficult to write about something she preferred actually to do.

The Edinburgh audience heard Elisabeth's last concert in her fifties. On June 12 she and Gerd returned to London, and next morning he came with his family to Wellington House for the big birthday celebrations. This was the first time Gerd had ever celebrated his mother's birthday with her since the time when he was too young to know what it meant. How young she still seemed as she delighted in the presents and flowers friends from all over the world had sent.

Despite her sixty years there were plenty of concerts to give. At last the continent had woken up to her again. Paris wanted her, and Amsterdam, Copenhagen, Helsinki: not a bad thing for the money coffers and, as far as she could tell, she was still in good voice. What was now becoming a problem was stamina. Sometimes it seemed as if she would not be able to sustain a note and let it spin on, holding the tension. It was a terrible feeling, as if one were sinking, trying to clutch onto something. Electric treatment did not have a lasting effect on her vocal chords.

Once again she asked the help of Dr Alexander, and he came up trumps. After noting that all was physically sound he prescribed some pills which worked wonderfully to keep up her strength throughout a whole concert. Now she could really enjoy the concert in Paris on June 28. "My God, this city is breathtaking!" she wrote to Erna Samuel. "How beautiful Europe is." In the same letter: "What will the winter bring?"

Elisabeth was getting worried about Gerd's position. Emigration to the USA was going to be difficult to achieve, and in the meantime he had no work and was draining her resources. Biddy was planning to write to Prime Minister Attlee to ask him if Gerd could not be allowed to remain in Britain longer than six months and obtain a work permit. Biddy's father was no longer alive, but Attlee had sometimes played tennis with him in the past; perhaps he would remember the name.

At the beginning of August the BBC rang and asked if Elisabeth would be interviewed for the Austrian Service and perhaps sing one or two songs too. She recognized the polite and friendly voice from the time she had given a recital for them before, it was Martin Miller, also originally from Vienna. (Poor Mr Miller had found it so embarrassing at that time telling her what her fee would be: the External Services of the BBC, paid by the State, had a limited budget.)

Having agreed to the engagement, Elisabeth asked him if she could see him about a possible job for her son. She thought that he wrote quite well and it would be good for him to have some work while he waited for emigration to America.

Ten minutes before the appointed time for meeting Mr Miller

Elisabeth arrived at Bush House and waited in the big entrance hall for Gerd. When he arrived four minutes late she was obviously displeased. Nevertheless she lectured him quite gently: "My child, unpunctuality might make you very badly thought of one day. Now *I* will have to take the blame and tell Mr Miller that I was late. I find it very embarrassing."

Mr Miller took Gerd to the German section. Everything was very friendly and to the point. No one was going to grant him any favours just because he was the son of Elisabeth Schumann; nor had Elisabeth expected that. He would have to show what he was worth by writing a talk for them to look at.

Elisabeth was very much hoping not to be away from London when Biddy's child was born and "I do hope it will be *pink* ribbons and bows . . . I'm very much afraid it may be a son again – Biddy looks too well to be carrying a girl . . . ."

When Elisabeth flew to Copenhagen on September 8 "Isabella" (as the baby was called at that stage) had not yet arrived. So, despite the great success of her concert and many social invitations, she turned her back on the good food and merriment and hastened back to London.

The baby kept her waiting another week after that, and then Gerd telephoned her in the small hours one morning.

"A girl, a girl!" he shouted. So it had all been worth it.

They talked for a long time, laughed, made plans. If Isabella's voice was like her grandmother's then her granny would have to train her, maintained Gerd. "My child, how old will I be then? She could start at fifteen – that would make me seventy-five; then Isabella will keep running to her mother and saying: 'But I can't learn singing from Granny, she's all doddery and keeps nodding off.'"

In the afternoon they visited the baby. The next day Elisabeth wrote to Trude el Bedell:

At last, at 3.15 yesterday morning, Joy Elizabeth came into this dreadful world. I hope she will have much happiness in her life. She was just as ugly as all small babies and one could not see any likeness. I can't say that my heart leapt with joy, it was just quietly glad that all went well and that both are in good health – I was almost sad, thinking of what this frightful world might bring to this poor little creature, and of all the worries and sorrow one has to go through on this earth. But that is the lot of mankind, I suppose, we all have the same fate and – in the end – we enjoy living and don't want to leave this planet.

Now began a few weeks of intense family life for Elisabeth. The boys had gone to their English school for the first time on Joy's birthday, but every day after school they were with their grandmother while Biddy was in the clinic. The idyll did not last long though; soon she had to be off on tour again to earn money for the family of five. Paris wanted another concert,* and Holland three.

> Lene, this month I'm working like a twenty-year-old . . . I'm having truly fantastic success. Paris was beside itself again, and it was like that in The Hague yesterday. With the new generation of singers people just aren't used to the real thing any more. Amsterdam has been sold out for weeks – The Hague was the same – Paris sold out – in Liverpool the platform was filled to the last corner – I think the public is starved of good music and art. . . .

Back in London there was good news about Gerd: the BBC had liked his script and he was to broadcast it in a few days. Also, Biddy's letter to the Prime Minister had done the trick: Gerd now had an unlimited residential permit and a work permit. It would be such a good thing if he could get regular work from now on; the hundred pounds with which Elisabeth had to subsidize the family each month was making a large hole in her purse.

The day before the recording of Gerd's talk Elisabeth was attending a concert with him at the Albert Hall. He spoke very little but occasionally cleared his throat very quietly. When Elisabeth asked him what the matter was he said he was afraid of getting hoarse. She found that highly amusing: "You see," she said, "now you know how we poor singers have to suffer!"

Just a few days later Elisabeth was reminded of other unpleasantnesses singers – even famous ones – had to bear. She had already experienced the like in America, but in "her" England, in London, where she was so loved, it had never happened before: the concert on October 26 in the Central Hall Westminster carried a deficit of over forty pounds. Was it perhaps too large a hall? But the Wigmore Hall would have been too small. If only the lovely old Queen's Hall had not been bombed! This Central Hall had no warmth, no atmosphere. Perhaps the London public's hunger for concerts was being satisfied now; every evening there were so many good concerts to go to.

Back in New York Elisabeth found a lovely new flat to rent: 2 East

*In the Salle Gaveau, on October 10 1948, accompanied by Maurice Faure.

75th Street, right by Central Park and Fifth Avenue. Unfurnished and expensive. It was a charming ground-floor flat with a garden which led off from the bedroom through French windows. Lisa and Milan Reitler lived just five minutes walk away. She could not resist it.

She moved in in December. One of the nicest features of the flat was the large open fireplace which covered almost completely one of the living-room walls. Elisabeth's few pieces of furniture looked quite lost in the large rooms. If only the furniture in Hamburg would come at long last!

In the middle of her happiness with her new home a sad event took place: Milan Reitler, friend of so many happy years in Vienna and then in New York, fell seriously ill and died after only three days. Just when Elisabeth had moved so close to the Reitlers! But the worst thing was that Lisa was now, quite understandably, intending to join her brother in California.

But Elisabeth managed to secure another neighbour: young Gustl Breuer was looking for a flat, and, with influence and a bit of bribery, Elisabeth managed to get him into another flat in the same house as hers. Now at least she had one close neighbour who was a friend.

Cheering news came from England: the BBC were thinking of employing Gerd full time. And Winnie Hall was also about to have a change in her life: her employer, Mrs Armstrong, was going to pension Winnie off and give her a house to live in. "If I get a house, would you like to stay with me?" wrote Winnie, and Elisabeth, who knew how fabulously Winnie kept house, replied: "I'd like nothing better."

In February there was a sudden rush of engagements from Europe. In London two programmes for the BBC; Switzerland was wanting her, for the first time since the war, at first for three concerts, later it was six in all; Paris and Holland were asking for her again; Norway, Finland and finally Germany too. "Oh Lene, will I manage it all? It lies before me like a mountain. . . ."

Was Lotte Lehmann finding singing hard too now? She still gave many successful concerts. Her reply reassured and alarmed Elisabeth at the same time:

Yes of course I find singing much much harder than in the past. God, how can you ask!!! I'm absolutely dead after a recital and also have to be very careful in my choice of songs. It's getting more difficult all the time because the dramatic things tire me too much – but how can one build up an interesting programme without contrast? I have to make use of "humorous" songs more and more, but it is difficult to find them. Last season I sometimes sang things that were too strenuous – oh, it's difficult all right.

Well, at least she had the same problems, that was some comfort, but how rapid would further decline be?

At least Lene was free of that worry, now that she was only teaching. She had not been well and Elisabeth wrote to her on March 18 from snow-covered Montreal, just before a concert.

Today I'm singing almost only Goethe texts – oh, how I shall think of Weimar! It's almost time to get changed.... Now farewell, my dear friend, I'm too nervous to write more – stupid concert – get better soon, and don't worry, it will all be all right soon.

Yes, optimism was what one had to have. Elisabeth certainly needed it as she saw herself gradually getting into financial difficulties. The new flat was as expensive as it was agreeable, and there were always things she still needed for it. Then there was the huge bill from the Hamburg furniture depot for storage, insurance and packing of her furniture. During the winter Jacques and Erna had been kind enough to lend the money needed for Gerd and his family. She had £300 to pay them back now! Niggling at the back of her mind was also the thought that she still had to pay back Lotte $1000 which she had lent when Elisabeth was still looking after Hans's family. Lotte would rather have waived the debt, but she could not afford to either; she suggested Elisabeth could pay her off gradually, a little each month. But she was not even in a position to do that yet.

A sudden request to give a concert in the Albert Hall on May 17 meant cancelling her booking on the *Queen Elizabeth* and flying to London instead. But the concert would be a good start to the summer.

And Winnie Hall had her new home. The house in Barnes had been chosen carefully with Elisabeth's needs in mind: where would her music room be, where her bedroom? Would it get enough sun? Would the garden be big enough for the boys when they came to visit?

It was quite ready when Elisabeth moved in on May 13. And what a grand entry it was! Gerd and his family, including eight-month-old Joy, had met her at the airport and brought her to Barnes where she was led into the house, celebrated with much noise from the boys.

As always she had brought all sorts of wonderful food: ham, butter, chocolate, sweets and, for their first feast together, frankfurters. Winnie, her cheeks flushed with excitement and happiness, scurried into the kitchen with them. Having looked all round the house and rearranged some of the furniture in the living room to her satisfaction (rearranging furniture was one of her passions), Elisabeth began to wonder what had happened to Winnie. On entering the kitchen she saw a very red-faced hostess frying something in a pan which did not seem to want to turn out right. The frankfurters! They were beginning to look very shrivelled and charred. Poor Winnie, on this special day! Being an Englishwoman through and through, and from the north too, she had never heard of sausages which one cooked in hot water.

"Winnie, how funny," cried Elisabeth. "I can teach *you* some cooking, I who cannot do an egg!"

But the rather dried out frankfurters tasted well enough, especially on such a happy occasion.

Now Elisabeth had to cope with a terrible load on her mind. The £300 owed to the Samuels had to be paid back on May 18 as they were planning to move back to Vienna. If they had known what straits Elisabeth was in they would undoubtedly not have asked for the repayment yet. But she could not bring herself to tell them.

The night from May 17 to 18 was a dreadful one for her. All sorts of thoughts went through her mind. Perhaps the record company could give her an advance; perhaps she could get one for the master classes, due to start on June 2. It had been absolute madness to rent that new flat in New York. Asking Ibbs & Tillett for a loan was a possibility, she could say vaguely that she was wanting to save her dollars, but on no account should they know that she was hard up. If that failed she would have to pawn her diamond tiara. Life seemed harder than ever. How ironic, just when she was so happy to have Schnuck again. This happiness always seemed to have to be paid for dearly.

Next morning she walked to the nearest telephone box to avoid Winnie overhearing what she had to say to Ibbs & Tillett. After the short conversation the tortures of the night began to seem rather silly. When she had aksed Mr Tillett if, exceptionally, he could help

293

with a loan since certain unexpected expenses in connection with her family had cropped up, he had just said in his quiet, calm way and without the least hesitation: "For you, Madame Schumann, I'd do anything."

Another blow fell: the master classes had to be cancelled through lack of applicants. How would she last until September, when her concerts started again? But the situation was not as desperate as it might have been. Gerd was to be employed by the BBC from the beginning of June, so he would be needing less money from her. A very good friend who happened to be in London for two days lent her some money and Walter Legge arranged for the Gramophone Company to pay an advance of £200. Meanwhile dear Winnie had offered her £25 as a little help, which had been accepted rather reluctantly but with relief. Elisabeth had not been able to hide her troubles completely in the end; but Winnie was led to believe that it was only a temporary problem connected with transferring money from America. It was all extremely unpleasant.

During this summer the recording of "Frauenliebe und -leben" had to be finished. Walter Legge had suggested some years previously that she should put the famous song cycle by Schumann onto record, had talked about it again and again and finally pushed her unwillingly into it. She had made a start with recording in October 1946, when she had recorded the whole cycle but had been dissatisfied with several of the songs. She attempted recordings of these songs again in the Octobers of 1947 and 1948. She was still only partly satisfied, and by June 1949 she still had two songs to record, including "Du Ring an meinem Finger", the beginning of which lay so badly for Elisabeth. It was not as if it was so terribly low (they had in any case put some of the songs up a tone), but the opening phrases did not have any notes on which her voice could really shine – her voice even sounded thin and rather brittle.

On June 20, a week after her sixty-first birthday, she gathered all the strength she could muster for another try. What a good thing that Gerald Moore was accompanying; he was not only good at his job, but his whole way was so comforting, so understanding and he had humour. Schnuck was there too, giving encouraging signals from where he was sitting. The nervous tension was therefore somewhat reduced, which was a good thing, for it took almost all morning before Elisabeth was satisfied with that one song.

When she had heard the whole recording Elisabeth said she would really rather it did not come out on the market after all. But, for whatever reason, it did, and although it was published on 78s rather than the new long-playing records which had just come out (and on which Kathleen Ferrier had also just recorded the cycle), it was a sensational success. It was highly praised by many musical journals: what was particularly noticed was the intensity of feeling in her interpretation and also the convincing change from youthfulness to maturity as the cycle progressed.

Until a recital in Cambridge on August 14 there were no more concert engagements or broadcasts in Elisabeth's schedule. There was no question of taking an expensive summer holiday.

Fortunately an invitation came from Holland, from Desi von Saher (the daughter of the famous soprano Selma Kurz) who lived alone in a beautiful seventeenth-century mansion in the countryside south of Amsterdam. The journey would not cost too much, bed and board would be paid for and she would be earning a little too, for Desi wanted some singing lessons.

How quickly time seemed to fly. Joy could stand now. She was eleven months old and grandmother and granddaughter were able to spend plenty of time together in August: Winnie was looking after her while the boys, who had whooping-cough, had gone to the seaside with Biddy.

> 28 August 49
>
> Erna, you wouldn't believe *how* charming Joyli is ... today it's Goethe's 200th birthday – how must he have looked in his cradle? And the proud parents had no idea what a genius they were giving to the world and posterity. At a quarter to ten in the evening I'm singing only Goethe texts on the BBC, in the same concert there'll be the Egmont music live from Salzburg conducted by Krips. How lovely and festive! Am very happy to have been chosen to contribute to it.

To sing Goethe poems in his memory and broadcast them throughout the world, was almost like re-creating the work of the great man. From the piano Ernest Lush occasionally looked solemnly across to her. Goethe perhaps did not mean so much to him, an Englishman; he seemed nevertheless to be gripped by the significance of the occasion. It was a uniquely moving musical experience for Elisabeth.

On September 8 news came through that the kidney disease from which Richard Strauss had been suffering had got much worse. The following day the unhappy news was spreading round the whole world: that early in the afternoon of September 8 the great man had died in Garmisch. At home – at least it had been in his home where he had created so much. "My poor Strauss! Am very sad – what a loss!"

Gone, completely gone. . . . He had been far away for a long time now, had long since ceased to be part of Elisabeth's life. But at least he had always still been "there" and might perhaps one day have been able to come "here". . . . Now it was too late. That silent hope, which had been in vain for so long, was destroyed for ever. Only through his music was he still present.

It was time to travel again, to Finland, Norway, Denmark and Germany. The journey to Finland was fraught. During a stopover in Harkhalen a defect was found in the aeroplane which was not mended for hours; in the meantime the connecting flight from Stockholm had gone. This meant spending the night in Harkhalen – a bad night in a noisy hotel near the airport. Gone were any hopes of getting to know Helsinki a little before the concert. Instead Elisabeth did not land there until the following afternoon at two o'clock, dead tired. And there was still the rehearsal to do, which lasted until five. After that there was not time for more than a quick lie down, nerves preventing a real rest. Would she never get rid of those nerves?

It seemed astonishing to Elisabeth that despite her worries she still seemed to have such success. Could people living so far north really display such Latin enthusiasm? They could. And the press the next day was tremendous – at any rate, so she was told; it was all in Finnish, of course. After that a radio broadcast was fixed for the following day.

Yes, all the concerts were a success, but the rate of exchange against the dollar of all these European currencies meant that the fees were effectively very low, quite apart from the fact that these countries could not afford high fees, anyway. But beside the need to be near the family, it was important to remain in people's memories until better times. And when the concert agent in Berlin, Hans Adler, asked her if she could give a recital there in November, this had to take precedence over returning to New York. Trude would just have to find other tenants for her flat until she returned.

Of her two London recitals the second was on a Saturday afternoon, on October 29. This was a wonderful opportunity for letting the boys hear her perform.

The next day she asked for their verdict.

"Well, did you enjoy it?"

The "yes" sounded more dutiful than convincing.

"So you didn't really enjoy it?"

"Oh yes we did," said Christian, "the man played the piano brilliantly."

"And your Omi?"

"You sang things to us," said Rupert now, "but not like in the evenings at bedtime." And Christian added frankly: "That's more fun. In the Wigmore Hall it took so long."

She was highly amused and promised more bedside singing.

To Elisabeth's delight Lene was able to see her in Berlin. After they had embraced Lene held her at arm's length and exclaimed: "My goodness, you look like a dollar-princess!" Elisabeth almost let the truth slip out, that life in New York could hardly continue unless a miracle occurred.

Lene had heard her friend sing on the radio a few times since the war, but for the first time she was going to hear her in the flesh and at close quarters again. This opportunity was afforded by two recording sessions in the radio studio, to which Lene was invited. The husband of the soprano Maria Ivogün, Michael Raucheisen, who was also booked for the recital at the Titania-Palast,* was accompanying. Elisabeth could not have asked for a better man, he was almost a Gerald Moore.

The music-making had made a great impression on Lene: she said repeatedly afterwards: "Goodness, Elisabeth, your voice is still fabulous. And the expression, the feeling – it was never better. Amazing how you can still do it."

Elisabeth was feeling quite nervous about the recital in the Titania-Palast, especially as the whole family "caravan" was turning up. She positioned herself discreetly with Lene in the entrance hall of the Dahlemer Hotel to watch the arrival of this procession, so as to be mentally prepared for the reunion.

An elderly, white-haired lady pushed herself through the revolving door, muffled in a voluminous but old fur coat. Heavens! It was her! Friedchen . . . wearing her mother's coat . . . . Yes, and right behind her was Elisabeth's nephew Walter Paarsch, lively as always, happily flashing those smooth Schumann teeth. Behind him a line of cousins

---

*A former cinema, used because the Philharmonie concert hall had been bombed.

from Merseburg, including her favourite, Locksch. She had always been charming, and now, when Elisabeth spoke to her, she found she had not changed. But Friedchen! Her own sister − how was this possible? She had become either clueless or just plain stupid, it was difficult to decide which. She had become a nerve-grater who left one's patience in shreds, and who wanted to be in on everything. It was only with difficulty that Elisabeth could retire for an hour before the concert.

It was sixteen years since she had last sung in Berlin. Waiting to go on stage seemed longer than ever, but she was met with storms of applause. Berlin had not forgotten.

The critics wrote some nice things, but they were not as enthralled and unlimited in their praise as the Scandinavians had been; she was, after all, a prophet in her own country and had to be criticized in detail.

Anyone who has heard this spellbinding voice in its heyday now finds only a fainter likeness of the original. But what this artist does with it! One is almost tempted to say: the greatness of a singer's art is only proved when she can then still build palaces with it . . . With inimitable refinement she changes the power of expression. . . .

Der Sozialdemokrat 18 November 1949 G.Pl.

The Voice has to be handled carefully like very thin glass. But with what superior mastery this is achieved. . . .

Berliner Anzeiger 18.11.49 el

Extremely cautious in the use of her means, she limits her performance to a cultivated piano of small dimension. Even if our generation can learn from the technique of this artist, the affectation of this sugary singing should nevertheless alienate them.

Neues Deutschland 20. Nov. 49 slf

After all the farewells, there was endless waiting at the airport at Tempelhof. Fog. No aeroplane could fly beyond the Channel. At last, at seven o'clock in the evening, one flew as far as Hamburg at least, and the next day took off for Amsterdam. Then even more waiting.

18 November 49
2 o'clock in the afternoon
Dearest Lene, well, what a journey. . . . The first 'plane to Paris doesn't leave for two hours, so I won't get there till about five − the

broadcast was supposed to be at three – I cabled, asking whether it can be in the evening perhaps – if not, well, there's nothing to be done. I missed you so much yesterday . . . but was relieved to be rid of Frieda – oh, I always try so hard to be patient with her – but it is too difficult. Who on earth does she take after? I think of my mother – what she was like at 70. No, it is too incredible . . . It is sad that we have absolutely no kind of relationship with each other. . . .

There had been one good thing about being stranded in Hamburg for a while: despite the late hour she had managed to see to the final arrangements for sending her furniture to New York.

Soon it was only a few days before the departure for New York. Elisabeth rather dreaded the financial situation waiting for her there, yet there was a possibility of two new pupils, and her old ones would be waiting impatiently for more lessons. Somehow things would sort themselves out. A fortune-teller in Denmark had recently told her: "You will maintain your standard of living until the end of your life." Schnuck had looked somewhat surprised on hearing this. Why should Elisabeth Schumann not be able to? She was very glad her family had no notion of her financial plight.

On the *Queen Elizabeth* was Clarisse, the wife of Baron Alphonse Rothschild. Elisabeth spent a lot of time with her, and wrote to Erna:

She has just seen Pauline [Strauss] in Montreux – she [Pauline] has the same room that she always had with Richard – and sits in the chair where he used to sit, and *cries* all day long. She is apparently so broken down that one can only be sorry for her. (Not I, for I consider her to be a miserable character, who used to mock unfortunate people and never did a kind thing.) But it is remarkable that she is, after all, being forced to notice how alone she has been left without the great man . . . . I was extremely interested to hear all this – she could just as well have been in pink and powder blue, on the hunt for new suitors, one can expect anything from her.

But when Pauline died a few months later Elisabeth wrote:

Yes, Erna, poor Pauline, she could not live without her Richard after all – she surely died of a broken heart. It moved me sadly, despite everything.

Among the first people Elisabeth telephoned on her return to New York was Leo Rosenek. The programme for the Town Hall recital on February 4 had to be decided. He was very curt and would not talk to her properly. When she asked him what was wrong he said he could not and would not have anything more to do with Elisabeth Schumann.

It was unbelievable. And then it all poured out of him. Raucheisen! With that big Nazi she had given a concert, had gone on stage with him in Berlin, with that Nazi!

Elisabeth quickly explained to Leo that Raucheisen had been denazified and that nothing had been proved against him, otherwise he would not have been allowed to play in public. And Dusolina Giannini, who was a Jewess, had just given a concert with him too!

Then over the line came the inconceivable: he would not play for anyone who had performed with Raucheisen, not ever!

Elisabeth slammed the 'phone down. How could he accuse her of fraternizing with Nazis, he who knew only too well how she felt about them and whom she had helped to leave Austria, by insisting that he instead of George Reeves, should play for her; and he who, when Elisabeth had wanted to help Reeves when he was in America, had not been prepared to give up a single concert for him?

She had lost a friend and a wonderful accompanist.

Elisabeth tried George Reeves, but he was unfortunately not available for the date of the recital. Then she had a brain wave: Bruno Walter! They had got on so well together at the Edinburgh Festival. She wrote to him at once and he gladly accepted.

She decided to dedicate the concert to Goethe again and to sing only his texts. Annie Friedberg wanted to know the programme immediately after Christmas. The easiest thing to do would be to repeat her Wigmore Hall programme exactly. The songs had been carefully selected as being ones well within her present capacity. Bruno Walter would surely understand when she sent him the programme with a few explanatory words.

But she did not send him the programme, for just then the furniture arrived from Hamburg. It all looked wonderful and Elisabeth felt as if she was in Vienna again. She spent hours moving and re-moving everything around until she felt satisfied with her arrangement.

Then a letter came from Bruno Walter in Beverly Hills asking her what her programme was to be. Full of apologies Elisabeth quickly wrote back, enclosing the proofs of the programme which she had by now received. A few days later she had his reply.

16 January 1950

Dear honoured friend,

I thank you for your kind letter and for forwarding the programme. In all honesty I have to say that I very much regret your having planned it according to your English concerts without having given me the opportunity to comment on it before printing. In general it is quite problematic choosing a programme from a literary point of view rather than a musical or singing one, and it is doubly so here, where a Goethe poem is in no way on such a high pedestal as "over there". Nevertheless the Goethe Year had significance here too and I could understand your intentions, however I cannot refrain from saying that my heart only partly agrees with your choice. I do not want to make any difficulties for you or depress you, – so I am accepting herewith this fait accompli. But I must at least tell you that in the long years in which I worked with Lotte Lehmann in such concerts she never fixed a programme before having shown it to me for consultation and approval. . . .

Indeed, it would have been better if she had not let Christmas and the furniture distract her from writing to him sooner. Now at least she could give him some explanation:

New York 19.1.50

Dear friend,

Before you arrive here I must quickly answer your kind words. I wish there . . . to be not the slightest misunderstanding between us. I understand your point of view fully and completely, but please do not think that I wished in any way to bypass you in the choice of the programme. At my age there are purely physical reasons which are decisive in the choice. But I can explain all much better when we meet and I hope that I can, with my singing, draw out the full approval of your heart.

This indeed she achieved at their rehearsal in her apartment on January 29. The musicality with which the "Schumann silver" was manifested wiped all programme doubts from Bruno Walter's mind. Bruno Walter wanted to go through everything carefully. The comment "oh, we don't need to practise that any more" he dismissed with the words "you may not, but I do". Some of the songs, like "Schweizerlied" were new to him.

The news of the forthcoming concert, in which Bruno Walter was to play for Elisabeth Schumann for the first time in New York, caused a big stir in the city's music world. Journalists rang up wanting interviews. Among the statements she is alleged to have made were:

[Of Bruno Walter] A great artist, a great man, a great friend.

How he manages to find time between conducting assignments to play for me I shall never know.

Musical life in New York is unique. I always find the winter in this city artistically very stimulating. Young people's enjoyment of jazz does not prevent them from appreciating opera or lieder. And you have such talent here, my goodness! But why do all your singers try to get voice training while they are working all day long in offices, factories and so on! It is impossible to get anything out of lessons taken during lunchtimes, between hard daily sessions of earning a living . . . I would recommend part-time jobs. . . . Physical and vocal health are virtually one and the same thing and exhaustion from arduous labors is not the proper state in which to receive instruction . . . I wish that the young people would realize that.

Interviews like that posed no problem for Elisabeth, but Gustl Breuer had arranged a musical radio quiz for her. In vain did she protest saying "oh, don't bother me with it, that won't fill a single seat in the concert, it'll just take some of my energy away". His answer was, publicity started to pay off two years later. And anyway, it was not right that the people of New York should think that Schumann only came over from Europe for the odd concert. They needed to know that she was one of them.

So she had to give in. It was a great strain, the concentration which was needed and speaking English in public too – she would rather have sung ten concerts!

And it was such an embarrassing disaster, it was almost funny. Neither Elisabeth nor indeed any of her musical colleagues on the panel could answer many of the questions (except Elisabeth did recognize some of her own Brahms recordings!); they even failed to name a march which sounded infuriatingly familiar. A lady in the audience triumphantly gave the answer: the soldiers' chorus from *Faust*. That lady was the star of the show, getting most of the answers right. One of Elisabeth's team colleagues said afterwards: "Wasn't it awful, Madame Schumann, none of us knew anything and this lady knew everything!" Whereupon Elisabeth replied: "Yes, my dear, but can she sing?"

Even the German-language section of the Voice of America invited her into the studio for a programme for Austria about "Madame Schumann's life and work in America". Voice of America also planned to record the entire Town Hall concert for broadcast some days later.

A second rehearsal with Bruno Walter took place on the eve of the concert, and then the great day had come. Elisabeth's voice was on top form and she was not too nervous.

On February 4 1950, a few minutes after three o'clock, she went onto the platform. She was wearing her best dress and a lot of jewellery – this time she would really show what she was worth!

The hall seemed to be filled to capacity. That was because of Bruno, not the publicity; the great conductor as accompanist had drawn the crowds.

> Entering to a greeting of prolonged applause, the performers conducted themselves with the gracious dignity that keyed the whole event: Mme Schumann accepted repeated tributes with gentle smiles at one time gesturing modestly as if it were almost too much. Dr Walter declined to share her bows except at the ends of groups.
>
> Musically, the event gave the deepest sort of pleasure....

Winnie, my dear, the concert last Saturday was a triumph. I was in top form, the house sold out and Bruno played *very* good – some thought he was a little loud, but I like better a little more support than too less.

The flowers I got, were not to believe – there was no room on the platform, they had to put a lot in the artist room and my home looked like a flower shop. I am *so* happy that I gave this recital, it was high time to show myself again on the platform. The press is *very* good, and we have also already engagements for Toronto, Chicago and another town in Illinois – only a few days after the recital – so there will come more – I am afraid Walter can't do many – he is too busy with orchestra concerts and wants to be back in California at the end of March. But wait and see!!!

It seemed that the miracle had occurred after all. Things certainly began to look up. A New York recording company Allegro, offered to record songs by Mendelssohn and Franz. It was apparently quite a new company which was already producing long-playing records. HMV rapidly and generously gave their permission for Elisabeth to work with them. Things really did go allegro; and they made things so easy for one! They came with three contraptions to Elisabeth's apartment and recorded one or two songs which they then played back immediately. The results with the long-playing method seemed marvellous; there was no need for a studio, and they even provided a passable accompanist. The songs were recorded in three afternoon sessions. The records were to go on sale a month later. Allegro!

A miracle? – but what happened to it, where did it go? Weeks, months went by and nothing happened. Annie Friedberg had not been able to turn the enquiries from Toronto and Chicago into firm engagements. This was partly due to the unavailability of Bruno Walter. No other cities made enquiries; the press interviews had only really reached New York and its environs, and the recording of the recital had been broadcast only overseas.

But at least there were more pupils now, and with the inevitable drudgery of teaching came occasional rewards in the form of promising material. One young American, a delightful, attractive girl, was bound to have a career if Elisabeth was not mistaken: Claire Watson. Then there was the mezzo-soprano Gladys Swarthout, the wife of Gustl's public relations boss, Frank Chapman; she was already a singer of some standing. Both were highly talented and quickly made great strides.

Gladys Swarthout, with the backing of Frank Chapman's public relations organization, gave a big party in the Sherry-Netherland Hotel. Everyone who was a name in the music world was invited.

When Lawrence Tibbett, the great baritone, heard that Elisabeth Schumann was among the guests he suffered a confusion of feelings. He wished so much to get to know her, but he had something awful to confess. As excited as a schoolboy he pushed his way through the guests and introduced himself. She recognized him of course, she had heard him at the opera; plucking up his courage he said to her that he had always regretted not having heard her sing in the flesh, but that he owned all of her records. To this Elisabeth replied: "Ah, my dear, that is much better. You can always turn them off if you don't like them."

Frank Chapman was now busying himself writing to all the music academies he could think of: Elisabeth had to find a teaching post. From everywhere came either polite refusals, non-committal phrases, or silence.

Lisa Reitler had now gone to Paris and there seemed to be a great emptiness in Elisabeth's life. Christian and Rupert wrote: "When are you coming, Omi?" She longed for the children with all her heart. Until she could let her apartment she could not afford to go to England. She had no notion how the summer would arrange itself. Ibbs & Tillett had one single concert engagement for her so far: August 6 in Bournemouth; apart from that she was only engaged to teach at the Summer School of Music at Bryanston.

Then Elisabeth had a bit of luck: out of the blue a friend suddenly turned up in New York on business and agreed to stay in her apartment until he could find tenants for it after she had gone.

On June 10 she sailed for England in the *Caronia*. It was a pleasant voyage. Some friends who had once been neighbours of hers in the Curiohaus in Hamburg were on board too. On the 13th came a flood of telegrams. Everyone had remembered her birthday and cabled the ship. Her Hamburg friends invited her to a champagne cocktail. "So it was a lovely day. Yet another year gone by."

CHAPTER 21

◆━━◗◦⟨ତ⟩◦◖━━◆

New York, Europe and South Africa, 1950–1951

ANOTHER HAPPY FAMILY reunion! It was worth living and working just for that. The little "dolls' house" in Ruislip, the suburb west of London where the family had now moved, was teeming with life.

When Elisabeth rang Ibbs & Tillett the news was bad: so far they had not been able to arrange any more concerts in England; there were only a few concerts in Switzerland in the autumn. It was as if the initial post-war hunger for music had been satisfied. Apart from the week at the Summer School of Music at Bryanston and a concert in Bournemouth she would have nothing to do this summer. Even the one or two faithful pupils she had were on holiday.

There was, however, one cheering bit of news: South Africa seemed interested in the possibility of her doing a concert tour in the spring of 1951. They wanted twenty-five concerts in eight weeks, with lots of travelling in between. She wrote: "But Lene, I hardly think that I shall do it. Perhaps it'll be my swan song."

The day which Elisabeth had always dreaded came: the day when Biddy sang to her. As the latter went through her song with trembling knees, Elisabeth had a sad look on her face, a look which Biddy came later to associate with bad singing. At the end Biddy asked whether there would be any point in having her voice trained. Very gently Elisabeth delivered the blow: "I couldn't say, my child. It certainly isn't very pleasant now."

Christian's talent on the piano was extraordinary. Much of his achievement was due to Biddy's teaching: she had great pedagogic ability. When, some time later, Elisabeth praised her for it, Biddy took the bull by the horns and made a suggestion she had been longing to make for some time: she thought she could perhaps teach singing too, if Elisabeth would teach her and if she thought it was

306

worthwhile; then, teaching Elisabeth's method, she might eventually assist her and take over some of her pupils when she had to go away on concert tours.

Elisabeth's reply came without hesitation: "I think that is a very good idea. We'll start at once."

The first thing Biddy had to learn was to breathe properly. "Singing means, above all else, correct breathing, my child." Biddy's hand was laid on Elisabeth's abdomen. "Push out the abdomen, like this – – " the plump abdomen had suddenly extended outwards and felt incredibly firm. "Now the bottom of the lungs are filled; not until now should you expand your chest. As you breathe out, empty your lungs from below, so you are expelling the air by pulling in your abdomen. That is how your voice gets the necessary support." This was like a revelation to Biddy, whose previous teachers had never mentioned the breath. All at once she knew and felt: this is the basis of all singing.

Now it was Elisabeth's turn to be surprised: in no time at all Biddy had adopted the breathing technique and was using it correctly in her singing exercises. To understand and apply this so quickly was something Elisabeth had never experienced with any pupil before, whether at the Curtis Institute or with her private pupils.

Some lessons later they tried a song – one of the Italian *arie antiche*, Italian being an easier language to start singing in than German or English because of its pure vowel sounds. Elisabeth sat at the piano and demonstrated some of the more difficult phrases.

When Biddy had sung the song Elisabeth stood up and embraced her new pupil saying: "You have understood perfectly."

Thus she had gained a new pleasure: teaching her daughter-in-law singing. And what a joy it was! Having studied singing before, Biddy was able to discuss points with quite a knowledge of the subject, and knew the expressions in English too, which was a great help.

This was a godsend. Biddy would need only a couple of months of teaching and then she would be able to give lessons herself and take on Elisabeth's English pupils, who always complained when she had to return to New York. It would not be a bad thing if Biddy earned a little as well as Gerd.

Elisabeth could not help having money on her mind. The Inland Revenue wanted £2000 in income tax from her. One evening, as she sat eating supper with Winnie, the doorbell rang. Winnie returned from opening the door and said, looking very worried: "Someone from the tax office." Elisabeth calmly took another mouthful – her appetite was not easily disturbed. "He's come to look for the two thousand pounds," she said lightly, as if she were trilling a little song, and went to meet the gentleman in her winning, yet perfectly natural way, greeting him with the words: "My dear sir, what can I do for you?" as if she truly wished to help him.

The man was completely disarmed by this and could barely stammer out that he had come merely in order to draw her attention to the large outstanding debt. As soon as he had been assured that all would be seen to, he withdrew with copious apologies.

Soon, however, the Inland Revenue stepped up their activities and informed both Ibbs & Tillett and HMV of the situation and demanded that all Elisabeth's fees should go straight to them, otherwise they would instigate legal proceedings. Since it had happened before, Elisabeth did not feel too humiliated that her employers knew what dire straits she was in; and the Tilletts and Walter Legge were such good friends by now. They demonstrated this fact by, between them, paying off the tax, so that Elisabeth now owed the money to them rather than to the Inland Revenue. She would see no fees now for a long time, she would have to say yes to the hard work in South Africa. . . .

Bryanston was upon her and she was worried: apart from the master classes the director of the summer school, the pianist and music critic William Glock, wanted her to give two lectures on "vocal art". It would be difficult to talk about that, especially in English. Elisabeth had never been one for theory of singing, but she could understand that people were curious about it.

William Glock immediately inspired Elisabeth's confidence with his wide forehead, blue eyes and sensitive mouth. He was full of understanding for the needs of a poor, tormented singer: "There's no reason why you shouldn't give a lesson in your lecture." But no, she knew that was cheating.

Winnie dearest . . . Tuesday the "lecture"!!! But that will pass over –
I hope *I* don't!!!

The concert for the first evening was given by the Amadeus Quartet. This would afford an opportunity to take a look at the school. . . .

It was the venerable building of a public school which would serve for a few weeks as a summer school of music. The concerts were held in the big hall, and the classrooms and studios were used for lessons and practice. With all the young (and not so young) people eagerly intent on their music, the atmosphere was lively and friendly.

The Amadeus Quartet set a very high standard. Elisabeth hoped she would not let herself down when it was her turn to give a recital. But she did not, partly because William Glock proved such an excellent accompanist, despite the fact that he did not often play in public. When he got particularly carried away he did sometimes hum along a little, but what did that really matter?

The master classes were a great success and not without amusing incidents. The music critic and broadcaster, John Amis, who attended at Bryanston that year, remembers:

> She was giving a lesson to a very young-looking girl who was singing a love song. Elisabeth Schumann said: "Ach, my dear, I must stop you, I think you don't understand the words." The girl replied: "Well actually, Madame Schumann, I am German, I am a refugee." "Oh, ahso, but it is a love song, perhaps you have never been in love, my dear." And she said: "Madame Schumann, I may look very young, but I've got three children." "Ach, my dear, just sing, I say no more."

So soon, it seemed, it was all over, and everyone was asking about next year. "You must come back, Madame Schumann, you absolutely must!"

> Lene, for a week I worked at a summer music school, giving two recitals, two lectures (I sweated blood) and lessons. It was a lot of work but a huge success. My lectures were rather unconventional – with humour – and gave much pleasure. I spoke about "vocal art" – in the second one I ran out of material, and I talked about my life, my experiences, a lot about Strauss, etc. One has to know how to help oneself.

The concerts in Switzerland – in Berne, Basle and Zurich – were a great success, although Elisabeth had had to be one of the judges at an international singing competition in Geneva shortly beforehand, which was very tiring. The singing often went on until midnight, after which there were discussions. She was very saddened by the low standard of performance of the young competitors. Some of the Mozart and Bach she heard was almost unbearable to her. She considered that no first prize should be awarded to the men, only a second. The other judges did not agree. But what would happen to singing if one did not set high standards? Elisabeth argued in vain.

Her voice was also on top form for a recital, shared with the violinist Joseph Szigeti, at the Albert Hall in London on October 6. She sang songs by Schubert, Schumann, Wolf and Mahler, and was accompanied by Gerald Moore. It was good publicity – Ibbs & Tillett already had enquiries for the following year.

> RMS *Queen Elizabeth*
> Oct. 19th 1950

Dearest Winnie,

Now are already hundreds of miles between us, and I hope you don't feel too lonely and too sad since your beloved friend went off "again over the ocean". Was it not wonderful to be alone at the station? I think it was a marvellous idea to keep off "the fans". . . . My purser friend, who was *very* disappointed about my going cabin class, telephoned at once with the purser in the cabin class to give me the best what he was able to. . . . Funny enough my name is not in the passenger list, and through this I am not bothered at all, only the stewards know me. I read almost the whole day . . . go to bed at nine and up at eleven – so I will have power enough at my arrival in N.Y.

In Southampton . . . the shoe case was not to find, absolutely lost. The custom man was so kind to examine my luggage *without* the case . . . (you must have every luggage piece before he is allowed to do it), then I had another porter who began to search after it, and where was it? In the first class! Under S. I believe the case was disgusted to travel Cabin! . . . Myra [Hess] is on board, but I didn't see her yet – hoping only we have no concert – it would be terrible. . . .

On the pier in New York stood a regular reception committee of Elisabeth's friends: Trude, Pindar, Gustl, Goddard Owen, Rosie and Purghauser. How wonderful it was to have friends, to feel that one could give joy to so many people. In a cavalcade of motorcars they drove their recovered prize home.

From Biddy there was already an airmail letter:

> I found our parting particularly difficult this time, and I still always get a horrid shock when I think that six weeks must pass, and another six, before we will have you here again. Blessed as you are with your voice, an even greater blessing is the atmosphere of happiness and harmony which always surrounds you and which you yourself radiate.

Almost immediately Elisabeth was back into a packed routine of teaching and socializing. Otto Klemperer and his wife, both recently returned from Australia, came to lunch. . . .

He looked wonderful, seemed to be the old Klemperer. He still had the impressively slender, towering figure, in no way sunken or shrivelled. He carried his head high and looked even more like a huge bird than ever with those penetrating eyes, from which a sparkle of irony and amusement could often shine. A few years before, after a brain operation, it had seemed that his career was at an end; but now a great concert tour in Australia lay behind him.

Elisabeth was very keen that Klemperer should hear her star pupil, Claire Watson. It took some time to awaken his interest. "Very promising" and "lovely, warm timbre" hardly seemed to make an impression, but "charming, lively young woman" caught his attention and he began to ask questions: still young? American? Sings German well? And finally: "Let her sing to me."

This was achieved within the week. And now true talent was demonstrated, for, although Claire was not feeling very well and was also terribly nervous, her voice quite clearly charmed the conductor. With Claire everything came naturally: a lovely timbre, great musicality, a feeling for performance, and good nerves. Klemperer was immediately willing to work with her the following year in Switzerland. Now she was really on her way.

One night Elisabeth awoke to the most terrifying sounds and sensations. There was a rushing, thundering and howling. The lights flickered, the bed shook and so did the whole house. Was it the wind? Perhaps it was an earthquake. But that banging of the windows and doors could only be a gale. Suddenly there was a great crash and the howling gale was in the room sweeping leaves, twigs and dirt before it. The door had burst open despite the safety lock. Elisabeth struggled to push an armchair in front of it to stop it opening again. This must be what the end of the world was like. Thank God the wireless was still working – a human voice; it was telling everyone not to go outside: a hurricane was swirling glass, slates and bricks through the air, trees and street lamps were falling. . . . At last it began to get light; now it did not seem so bad.

Everything in America was on such a huge scale. To Winnie Elisabeth wrote about the storm: "Oh, what a country. Everything comes like skyscrapers." To Suze Rueff she admitted: "Suze, I thought the world was ending, the atom bomb cannot be worse. . . .

311

Well, everything passes, as did this happening in the elements."

No, the world had not ended, and now Elisabeth had to see to earning a living, and not just by teaching. She knew that she should be arranging another Town Hall concert, preferably with Bruno Walter again. Without having to be prodded she asked her agent to find a suitable date – but Walter was not available and it hardly seemed worth the effort to do the concert without him. A compromise solution was found by the publicity manager Frank Chapman: she could sing just three songs in the Concert of the Year of the AGMA (American Guild of Musical Artists) to be held on January 7 at the Met! It was to be a charity concert to boost the welfare funds of the AGMA, and many prominent artists would be performing, among others the violinist Yehudi Menuhin and the bass Cesare Siepi. It meant no fee, but she would get her publicity.

At the Met, that huge house, for the first time in thirty-six years! The last time she had been a rising star, now the star was gradually setting. George Reeves accompanied and Elisabeth sang songs by Schubert: two cheerful songs with a soulful one between: "Die Forelle", "Nacht und Träume" and "Liebhaber in allen Gestalten".

"Die Forelle" was a blessing. It just flowed effortlessly. But then came "Nacht und Träume"; with her nerves in front of this sea of faces, would her breath last the first phrase? . . .

The people were beside themselves, even jumping out of their seats. Someone threw flowers. Gustl! But they did not allow that here. . . . What a blessing that there could be no encores, otherwise it would have been a whole recital.

The whole of Frank Chapman's publicity office was gathered in the artists' room even before the concert had ended.

"Madame Schumann, your songs are the sensation of the evening! And this is quite something with people like Menuhin and Siepi taking part."

And Gustl: "You looked fabulous, with that purple cape waving in the air. And Elisabeth! Right to the back, up at the very top, you could be heard perfectly! I went to listen from various places."

Gustl, the wretch, had checked to see if her voice had carried everywhere.

"Well, and 'Nacht und Träume'! How wonderful it sounded, quite unearthly! Lawrence Tibbett had tears in his eyes!"

Elisabeth protested that she had been so nervous she had had to take a breath during the first phrase.

312

"But, Madame Schumann," cried a young man clutching an autograph album, "why worry about a little breath? Lotte Lehmann takes a breath not only after any old word but in the middle of words!"

Indignantly Elisabeth turned to him and fired: "Yes, young man, but what a voice Lehmann has got!"

On January 20 Douglas Watt wrote in the *New Yorker* about the Concert of the Year:

> ... I would like to mention what was for me the best thing of the evening. That was the enchanting singing ... of Elisabeth Schumann.... Despite the imperfections wrought by time, the quality of her voice was uncommonly sweet and musical. She was a delight.

Unfortunately, despite this success, no other concert engagements were forthcoming. But Elisabeth was cheered up by hearing that Biddy had given her first singing lesson. She had been terrified at first – until her pupil had sung to her: hearing such an untrained, breathy voice had made Biddy at once feel that she was master of the situation.

> My dear Lene,
> I am 19,000 feet up and am wafting over the clouds to England. Am in one of the newest 'planes [Stratocruiser] with all the trimmings – wonderful bed overnight, breakfast served in bed – a wonderfully comfortable washroom with delightful little gift packs of Elizabeth Arden make-up – there is a bar on board to which one has to walk down a few steps – just amazing. Where will this end? Next thing we'll be having baths too. 10 hours to Ireland, a short stop there, then 2 hours to London, where I shall have my dear ones close to me for three days.

The whole family was there to meet her, even Joyli on Biddy's arm, was waving.

Only three days with the children, but what wonderful days, despite the cold and wet.

In no time at all, it seemed, Elisabeth was hearing the sound of aircraft engines again and beneath her lay brilliant white fields of clouds, golden strips of desert, snowcapped mountains, dark green carpets of luxuriant vegetation – Africa.

Hubert Greenslade, travel companion and accompanist, knew South Africa. He had been born in Cape Town, taken to England as a baby, but had twice been back to give concerts – a wonderful country: heavenly climate, the people friendly and hospitable.

Down the steps of the aircraft and the air was warm and dry. Johannesburg was a tonic after the damp cold of London. It enlivened so much that Elisabeth felt almost certain that singing here would be easy.

And the publicity! She was handed a fat parcel of newspaper cuttings by Ernst Schütte, the impresario of SAMUT (South African Music and Theatre Company).

FAMOUS SINGER DUE NEXT MONTH
WORLD FAMOUS SOPRANO TO SING IN CITY
EMPRESS OF SONG ON WAY TO UNION

They really had thought up some amusing headlines. Even in Afrikaans they wrote *"Keiserin van die Lied"* ("Empress of Song"). But the best was *"Kanarie van Wenen"* ("Canary from Vienna"). Or perhaps even funnier was the photograph of Elisabeth as Sophie during her time in Vienna. Underneath stood: "Elisabeth Schumann as Rosie in Der Rosenkavalier"!

The suite in the Carlton Hotel certainly was fit for an empress, and it had a wonderful view of the city.

As Elisabeth unpacked she noticed to her extreme alarm that her make-up bag, which also contained her stamina pills, had been left behind in London. It was now Friday and on Monday she had her first concert here in the Town Hall in Johannesburg; it had been sold out for three weeks! Winnie would have to have a telegram the next morning asking her to take the pills to the airport and send them by express airmail. The thought of going on stage without those pills, which kept her going through a concert, was too appalling.

The SAMUT did not let up. On Saturday morning the reporters arrived for what was virtually a press conference. They wanted to know all sorts of details about her life, even her childhood and parents. Elisabeth noticed that no one seemed astonished that she already had three grandchildren. They scribbled and scribbled and were much amused when she told them that she had left her make-up in England (she did not mention the pills, of course).

The director of SAMUT, Mr Steyn, and his wife gave Elisabeth a wonderful reception at the Carlton that afternoon. The room was full of the most beautiful flowers; wine and all the delicacies and fruits which Africa could offer were here – this country seemed a paradise. Only the receptions she had had in America with Strauss came anywhere near this one. The mayor was also there, and there were speeches, to which Elisabeth gave a brief reply – her first speech in her life: "I am a singer – I cannot make speeches, but already I am much touched at the kindness and friendliness of everybody I have met. And your wonderful climate!"

The reception was reported in the papers. In *Die Vaderland* the report began with the words (in Afrikaans) "But she is so natural!"

The pills failed to arrive. The hotel receptionist did all he could to track them down – in the hotel and at the post office, but to no avail. Elisabeth immediately cabled to Dr Alexander to send a new lot by air, so that she would at least have some for the next concert on Thursday.

As she mounted the "gallows" on Monday evening Elisabeth's nerves were terrible. How extravagant this country was: the platform was beautifully decked out with rubber plants, gladioli and dahlias.

Not a single hand clapped as she walked to the piano, but the air seemed charged with tense expectation; no one moved. Elisabeth gave the slightest bow. Suddenly the spark was there and four thousand hands thundered applause. Yes, here was a piece of England, of Europe; the people knew after all whom they had before them.

As she sang Mozart's "Das Veilchen" in the first group Elisabeth thought perhaps it really was not going to be such an effort to perform on this tour after all. But as the concert progressed she noticed that she was getting tired. Singing in town halls was never very satisfactory either; real concert halls with good acoustics were much easier. By the end the low notes were getting quite weak; she certainly would not sing more than two encores.

Yet it was a success, and she was laden with bouquets, baskets of flowers, and finally a little coloured boy dressed as the page in *Der Rosenkavalier* came and presented her with a silver rose. The audience went mad with enthusiasm. It was a real rose; only the tips of the petals were painted silver. Holding the silver rose she sang her last encore, Schubert's "Liebhaber in allen Gestalten". It was a strange experience to be holding up a silver rose and to be singing Schubert instead of Strauss.

"A great and courageous singer". The critic of *Die Vaderland* had hit the nail on the head, for he was endowed with acute hearing:

Towards the middle of her recital she began showing signs of tiredness ... but in spite of this a wonderful atmosphere was created.... Mr Greenslade succeeded in creating a beautiful unity between voice and piano and contributed in no small measure to the success achieved by the courageous Elisabeth Schumann....

"... it is a long time since we were privileged to welcome an artist of this calibre ..." wrote the *Dagbreek*. So Elisabeth really did have a task to fulfil here. To this country, which seemed so young culturally, she must give the best of her art.

If Dr Alexander had got the telegram she would get the pills either at East London or by the 26th at Port Elizabeth. That name could only mean good luck, and the date, 26th, was twice 13! And all the digits of the date, 26.2.1951 added up to 26 too. How could luck fail now!

Port Elizabeth, February 26, 1951

Winnie, my dear,

I got just in time the pills for the concert today. Oh, I am so happy now. You have no idea how important it is for me and what I suffered without these pills in such an important concert like Johannesburg. Now everything is all right and I begin to relax.

Although East London had not been such an important concert Elisabeth had felt very tense during the long train journey there. And the concert had been quite a struggle, for, on top of everything else, the concert hall had had a smoky atmosphere, because the audience was allowed to smoke during the interval. The critic of the *East London Daily Dispatch* condemned this practice and mentioned nothing about tiredness in the voice. Perhaps he had put it all down to the smoke!

The car journey from Port Elizabeth to Cape Town – almost 700 kilometres as the crow flies – began at dawn; but it was a pleasure – the countryside was like a wonderful dream. And Cape Town was like a fairy-tale, the pearl of South Africa. It was breathtaking to look down onto the bay from high up on the slopes, to see how this vast continent ended here, plunging into the ocean. And when Elisabeth turned round she saw the most select little domestic world you could wish for. She had her own suite of rooms in the house of the Misses M. and H. Holt, sisters of the London concert agent Harold Holt. In her drawing room she had a wonderful grand piano, which had apparently been chosen by the pianist Wilhelm Backhaus.

The telephone hardly stopped ringing for Elisabeth. Press photographers swarmed in to take photos of the "Queen of Singers" posing at the Backhaus grand.

In fact it was not yet Cape Town's turn for a concert: Elisabeth was only here this time to give concerts in two smaller, neighbouring towns, Paarl and Stellenbosch.

How happy she now felt singing was reflected in the press notices she received. The *Cape Times* wrote:

> A vast audience in the Stellenbosch Town Hall was carried away with enthusiasm ... by Elisabeth Schumann, that queen among singers.... The effortless freedom with which she articulated her words was in keeping with the liquid beauty of sound....

Elisabeth felt so happy that she was even moved to replenish her wardrobe somewhat. It was so long since she had done that, and the Misses Holt could recommend an excellent dressmaker in Cape Town.... Life was so wonderful, if only the family were experiencing it all with her. Perhaps she should come to live in this country and teach at a music academy; life seemed so much easier here.

Bethlehem, Sunday 11. March 51.

Dearest Trude [el Bedell],

... Everything is going to plan – the concerts are *all* sold out and extremely successful. The people know what I am bringing them, and the press always writes that I am the first singer to give the same programmes which I sing in Paris, London, Vienna, Berlin or New York. And *that* is what they really want – even if they certainly do not understand everything, but they are so proud and only want to have the best served up.... Cape Town was a dream, and the place where I stayed! Fantastic! Am returning there on 7th April – how lovely! The social events nearly finished me off – dinner with the British High Commissioner, lunch at the House of Assembly – everything official – in the small towns like this one there is, thank God, nothing so exciting. I'm enjoying the tour, it's wonderful, oh, and what a change from all those lessons.

March 1951

Lene, my dearest, this is just so you know I'm still alive. Am up to my 10th concert and am as fresh as a daisy ... did you read in the newspaper that Lotte announced after her last concert in February that she wasn't going to sing any more?...

Did she really have to retire, thought Elisabeth, when she is only a few months older than I am? But when she read the letter which

Lotte Lehmann wrote to her about it, she realized that her friend was right.

Santa Barbara, March 1951

Dearest Elisabeth,

Yes, it was both a wonderful and a sad farewell. I felt a little as if I were dead and just about to be buried. . . . But on the other hand I'm so glad that I can stop now. Look, with you it is quite different: from you no one expects any *dramatic* songs, but that I, who once sang Fidelio, am glad when I find enough cradle songs to sing – that's more than I can stand. My middle range, which was always the best part of my voice, does not obey me any more. Sometimes it is quite clear and then suddenly it's all husky. It was such torture to sing that I now feel free and happy. . . .*

The Easter break was approaching, and Elisabeth ended the first half of her tour with two splendid orchestral concerts: one on March 22 in Pretoria and two days before that she sang in Mahler's Fourth Symphony in Johannesburg. "I'm causing a revolution here" she wrote to Trude el Bedell. Sitting in the Carlton Hotel at Easter with suddenly nothing to do was quite an anticlimax. She had never enjoyed a tour so much or found one less tiring; a month had gone by like one week. What was more, she knew that by her ninth concert she had paid off her tax debts; and she had heard that Rosie had managed to let the New York apartment. Another boost to her income was now to be the making of records for the SABC (South African Broadcasting Corporation), who wanted to take the opportunity of Elisabeth's Easter break to fit them in. She daringly demanded a fee of £900 for twenty records, which was agreed to; but in the end she only earned £300: her tonsils swelled up, and after making six records she decided she must save her voice.

Cape Town was thrilled with its Elisabeth Schumann concert. Afterwards the newspapers were full of adulation and triumphant headlines:

IMMACULATE ARTISTRY BY GREAT SINGER
ELISABETH SCHUMANN DELIGHTS WITH
CONSUMMATE ARTISTRY

*In a letter to Elisabeth of October 14 1951 she wrote further: "Even though the public was so faithful to me and turned a blind eye to all the imperfections, I myself cannot tolerate these imperfections. Every concert made me *deeply miserable* in these last years. Success or non-success, I suffered like a dog. It is really tragic that, just at the time when I understand singing so profoundly, the ability to do it the way I would like is taken from me."

The critic of the *Cape Argus* was nearer to the truth:

Time, inevitably, has touched the voice itself – but how gently. As if to compensate, the serene charm and warmth of the singer's personality has deepened. All the impeccable musicianship remains.

Elisabeth was so enchanted by Cape Town – its beauty, its climate and, above all, the high standard of living here, that when it was suggested that she might be offered a contract to teach in the music department of the university for six months a year, she thought so seriously about it that she even mentioned it to friends in her letters. But she decided to wait another year before making up her mind. Nevertheless the press, inevitably, got hold of it and started mentioning that she was thinking of coming to live in Cape Town. The gossip columns also had a wonderful time writing about what she got up to when she was not singing. *The Star* wrote on April 12:

On one occasion a picnic luncheon was arranged for her during a day's motoring from one singing engagement to another. It began to rain heavily. But, nothing daunted, Madame Schumann insisted on finishing her alfresco meal under an umbrella with the rain dripping from the tips.
   Madame Schumann has revelled in the beautiful scenery of South Africa, particularly that of the Cape, where she half expected to see a lion behind every bush. One of the "musts" of Madame Elisabeth Schumann's visit to South Africa is to see a lion. She says it is as much as her life is worth to go back to the United States without having done so.

It was quite true: the thought of returning to England and America after two months in Africa, and having to admit that she had not seen even the tip of a lion's tail was too appalling.

16. April 1951

Lene, my dear . . .
   The penultimate concert today [at Potchefstroom] – oh, what a feeling! Tomorrow for three days to the famous Krüger Park. We will be sleeping in bungalows, will have our food with us – will be getting up at four in the morning to observe the life of lions, zebras, giraffes etc. It is supposed to be quite an experience – am *so* looking forward to it . . .

19. April 1951

Erna darling –
   Have just come back from the Krüger Park, where we were for three days. It is uniquely beautiful, and we saw 16 lions, giraffes, cheetahs, everything there was to see – in the wild – you can't imagine it. An experience . . . tomorrow is the last of the 25 concerts [at Heidelberg]

319

and on 21st, the day after tomorrow, Hubert and I are flying back to London. I can hardly wait to have the children again. . . .

At the end of a fortnight in London it was back to New York in time for a charity concert (in aid of the Musicians' Guild) with Rudolf Serkin at the Waldorf Astoria Hotel on May 9. All she had to sing were ten songs, by Schubert and Wolf, so why, oh why did she feel so tired? Her voice sounded it too. Was it reaction after the tour after all? She could tell that Gustl had noticed it too, although he would not admit it.

It was a pleasant surprise to hear that Ibbs & Tillett had got moving – on July 26 a concert with orchestra in Liverpool – that meant she would have to leave again for England on about the 15th. The pupils would complain: they would only have had her for two months.

June 13 1951: Elisabeth's sixty-third birthday! Even Ernst Schütte had remembered it:

> . . . and I must humbly express my deepest gratitude for your visit to South Africa and for all you have meant to our public and to me personally. . . . Everything and everybody still keeps reminiscing on your last tour. You have left nations of friends behind. . . . And now your birthday on the 13th June. How can I wish you or express in words what I would like to be your blessings for the future. . . . May you, above all, be spared to come back to us. . . .

It almost sounded as if she was in mortal danger – "may you be spared". And why no more word about a possible teaching post in Cape Town?

Good news had come from Claire Watson. She had an engagement to sing Desdemona in Verdi's *Otello* in Graz. It was no small thing to sing such a leading role as a debut! Elisabeth wrote to Claire on 2nd July:

> Give Klemperer my best greetings and tell him that I envy you to work with him and to listen to his concerts and, even more, to the rehearsals. Oh, what a genius!

Annie Friedberg telephoned (a rare occurrence these days) to say there was an offer of two concerts on August 2 and 3 – and at the Berkshire Festival, the most famous music festival in America; four groups of four songs in each, and for fat fees! That would mean leaving for England a month later. When Gustl heard the news he was very excited for her: Liverpool would definitely have to go by the board. Tanglewood was the Salzburg of America (it had gained in reputation since she had sung the B Minor Mass there in 1940), she simply *had* to go. All the top musical people would be there (as well as the top unmusical ones!). This would be excellent publicity.

The small theatre where she had to give the two afternoon recitals, the Berkshire Playhouse, was charming. It was completely made of wood and had a marvellous acoustic. It was no wonder that Koussevitzky and the Boston Symphony Orchestra had chosen Tanglewood for the festival. The climb up the steep, narrow, winding stairs, which Elisabeth and her accompanist Franz Rupp had to do from the stage to the artists' room, was quite an effort though – at least it was *after* one had performed! And the elderly Fritz Kreisler, the great Austrian-born violinist, laboured up those stairs in the interval to see her. He wanted to say how lovely her singing had been: what came out of her mouth transported one to another world. . . . The interval bell sounded. He begged her not to start the second half until he was back in his seat. abeth sent Gustl down to give the sign when he was ready.

Within a few days of her successful concerts at the festival, Elisabeth was sailing to England on the *Caronia*.

> RMS *Caronia*
> 13. August 1951.

Lene, my dear child . . . here on the ship it is heavenly . . . I go to bed early, sleep *ten* hours, and in the day also take a nap – so you see *how* tired I am. The *Caronia* will take seven days, so it will be a wonderful rest. . . . This time in London I want to work with Schnuck at my book. Schnuck is going to write it. I find it *so* difficult. My life has to be told as it really was – otherwise it will be deadly boring. And that is not always easy!!! . . . Schnuck will look deep into my heart – although I don't think there are any more surprises there for him. My English publisher said last year – surely my *son* could not write my book – I replied: my son knows everything about my life.

Elisabeth was asked to do a programme in the series "Desert Island Discs" with Roy Plomley on the radio, to be broadcast in December. It was quite a problem choosing the records. The BBC wanted her to use many of her own recordings, but that seemed far too conceited. Not a lot could be fitted in, what with talking as well, so

321

in the end it was quite easy to put something together: Hans Hotter singing Bach, Arthur Schnabel playing Schubert, the Prelude to Act III of *La Traviata* and, on a light note, "The cab" by Xanrof. She allowed a bit of her own *Rosenkavalier* recording, since it really was one of her favourites: the final trio and the Marschallin's monologue. Of her own recordings she also chose the *Meistersinger* quintet and a rendering of "Abendsegen" from *Hänsel und Gretel*. She thoroughly enjoyed herself and found her interviewer quite delightful.

Biddy was an excellent chauffeur. Elisabeth thought that everyone at Bryanston would be most surprised to see Madame Schumann driving up in the little black sports car (which the family now called "Black Beauty") – still going strong after all those years since its rather rash purchase in Piccadilly.

She was very glad she had asked Biddy to come with her to the summer school this time. She did not tire her in any way, and she was able to make the composition of the obligatory lecture so simple. This time it really was a proper lecture, not as amusing as last year's perhaps, but now the audience would really learn something.

Elisabeth could see how grateful her audience was, it hung on her every word. She saw how much she meant to these English people. How different from America! Had she made a mistake by not settling in London in 1938?

1. Sept. 51

Trude . . .

In two hours we are leaving here in our little Black Beauty. These days with Biddy have been a delight. . . . I worked frightfully hard here this week, but *what* a success – you can't imagine. . . . Everything is going wonderfully. I'm feeling gay and happy. . . .

Once in London Elisabeth received an unusual telephone call, from someone called Bernard Miles. He asked her to sing a recital in such an unusual venue, that, despite all her money problems, and the fact that she did not know him, she agreed to sing gratis. He had founded the Mermaid Theatre, not an ordinary theatre by any means, and one which was to show unusual plays. He was trying to raise money for it. He was eager for his theatre to be associated with great names, and Ivor Newton, the pianist who was to accompany Elisabeth, had suggested her.

The theatre was in Acacia Road, St John's Wood, the same street where Gerd's family had lived when they had first come over from Germany. But this Regency-style house was considerably larger and set back from the road. There was a narrow drive, but the setting was very attractive, almost park-like. The little theatre had been fitted into the house very cleverly; the entrance hall with the sweeping staircase could be incorporated into the set or partly used as auditorium. Now the audience was sitting closely packed on the stairs, and the little rostrum seemed almost like a pulpit, as if one were singing a sermon.

"What's the next song, Ivor?" Elisabeth asked during a short interval.

"Der Nussbaum."*

Oh no, not "Der Nussbaum" again. It seemed as if she had sung that one at every concert in her life; she only had to hear the title and she would feel quite ill.

Many years later Ivor Newton wrote in his autobiography.[†]

> But a few moments later she went on to the stage and sang it so beautifully, with such inimitable freshness and clarity, that it would have been easy to believe that she had just fallen in love with the song and was singing it for the first time.

In gratitude for the free concert, Bernard Miles had thought of a surprise gift for Elisabeth. At the end of the recital he presented her with a piece of brick cushioned on velvet in a glass case. It was part of the tiled stove on the first floor of a bombed house in Salzburg. Into this house Mozart had moved as a boy of four with his parents. It was a magical gift.

Elisabeth's future seemed to be decided by a strange quirk of fate.

Because she was to sing at Southsea Alec Sherman, who would be conducting, invited her to his home beforehand in order to go over some musical points.

Elisabeth found the maisonette in the semi-detached Regency house at 40 Hamilton Terrace, St John's Wood, quite delightful.[‡] The large drawing room at the back had bay windows giving onto

---

*By Schumann.

[†]*At the Piano* – Ivor Newton: *the world of an accompanist*, H. Hamilton, London, 1966.

[‡]Later to be lived in by Kathleen Ferrier and, after her death, by Gerald Moore.

a lovely garden which seemed to complement it perfectly. Innocently, and without any premonition of how her life was suddenly to be directed along a new path, she said how lovely this home was; whereupon her host said: "You can have it." And he was not joking. For professional reasons he was being forced to leave London and this home, much to his regret. Madame Schumann could move in. In an instant the conversation turned totally to the subject of the maisonette. The lease ran for another twelve years and it would cost her £44 per month (less than in New York).

Elisabeth hardly thought about the cost. She at once recognized the possibilities of a drawing room like this for teaching: it was large and not attached to another house. The rest of the maisonette was very pleasing, and the neighbourhood could not have been better. The garden would be perfect for the children. She would have them here as often as she could, and Schnuck and Biddy, always near; these separations should be over for ever.

Now she knew: she belonged here in England, in Europe. In America they would let her starve to death!

"Alec Sherman, I'll take it."

At first she kept it a secret from Winnie and from the family. She did not wish to raise their hopes in case everything fell through. For one thing she had to get a long-term work permit.

Before a recital which she was to give in Goldsmiths' Hall in the City of London Elisabeth had a cold she simply could not throw off, and she had a very uncomfortable boil on her hip; but luckily Dr Alexander declared her vocal cords unaffected, and the concert was not cancelled. It was a strain though; Elisabeth felt terribly tired and attributed it to the persistent cold.

By the time Elisabeth saw a skin specialist the boil had turned into a nasty carbuncle, for which she was prescribed penicillin and a few days in bed. Normally she would have quite enjoyed the luxury of days in bed, but, apart from the pain, she felt peculiarly ill and weak. Once again she seemed to be paying for her happiness. Yes, there was good news: the freeholder of 40 Hamilton Terrace had accepted Elisabeth as the next leaseholder and the work permit had come from the Home Office too.

Now the family could be told and could come to inspect her new home. What joy there was at her announcement that she was moving permanently to London. They had hoped so much that it could happen but never quite believed that it would. The day of the family inspection was great fun, not only for the boys who explored every corner, but also for Elisabeth who was already making plans for improvements here and there. That day seemed like a foretaste of what life would be like there: the boys playing in the garden, tramping through the house, filling it with happy voices, which would soon be joined by Joy's, for she was nearly three; Biddy here for a lesson or in order to give one herself; a cosy tea with her afterwards; and Schnuck could come from work for a drink or a meal.

"My child, you can always stay the night here if you finish work very late."

Gerd put his arm round her and they walked down the few steps and along the garden path to the waiting "Black Beauty". Elisabeth was just in the process of stooping into the low passenger seat when she groaned halfway down and could move no more. She was completely stuck and in terrible pain. "I've got awful lumbago, Schnuck." Luckily the acutest part of the pain only lasted a few seconds and Schnuck was supporting her under her arms by now. Gently he was able to lower her into the seat.

As they drove to Winnie's house in Barnes the pain grew less and less. How could lumbago be as painful as that though? she asked Schnuck. She hoped she would manage her last two concerts and a television programme she was due to do. And the journey back to New York! Well, if it got no better she'd just have to stay here for good!

In the event this might have been the best thing, but the "lumbago" did not provide this opportunity, only bothering her slightly after that attack. The concert in the delightful music club in South Audley Street, the IMA (International Music Association) took place. But listeners who knew the Elisabeth Schumann of old went away disappointed. The voice had sounded small and lustreless. Obviously Madame Schumann had not been on top form.

The TV programme sixteen days later turned out quite tolerably. She told lively stories about her life, the brick from Mozart's house was shown, two little songs were thrown in quite casually: little showpieces of a great art.

After that there was only one more concert, in Scarborough on November 21; on the 24th she would sail from Liverpool.

The recital in Scarborough was held in the Queen Street Central

Hall. The music critic of the *Scarborough Evening News* wrote:

> It is all too seldom nowadays that one can hear singing of such satisfying quality as that of Elisabeth Schumann. Madame Schumann is obviously still in love with her art. . . . Every song was a polished gem, shown up in a most appropriate setting by Hubert Greenslade, whose formidable and delicate task as accompanist was accomplished with considerable skill and complete accord.
>
> Beethoven, Haydn, Arne, Schubert, Strauss and Wolf were all represented in the programme, and in addition to the songs printed, Madame Schumann sang "Mausfallen-Sprüchlein" by Wolf, and "Die Forelle" by Schubert. She was equally at home in all of them.
>
> Her unerring sense of rhythm and nuance, her control of phrasing and inflexion, her lovely tone and faultless intonation, in fact her integrity as an artiste, succeeded in every case in recreating each song surely just as the composer would have wished. Here were no exaggerations, no miscalculations, no mannerisms, just perfect artistry, the spell-binding effect of which will, no doubt, have made a lasting impression on the great majority of last night's audience.

It was the last concert which Elisabeth Schumann ever gave.

The 24th arrived too soon for anyone's liking. Elisabeth had said her goodbyes to Biddy and the children in Ruislip. These goodbyes were frightful; it was a good thing they were to be no more.

Schnuck managed to get away from the BBC that morning for a quick meeting with his mother in a grand new boutique at 16 Brook Street. He found her in the first floor department up to which a wide, sweeping staircase led. She was wanting to buy presents there to take to New York. For a while they looked at things together, making jokes – although they felt anything but jovial – and cheerfully holding up scarfs and shawls against one another.

Suddenly Schnuck was serious: he had to get back to work. "No farewells, my child, just go quickly."

She gave him a swift kiss, as if they were to see each other again that evening. He went down the first few stairs, stopped and looked back. They waved to each other.

It was the last time she was ever to see him.

CHAPTER 22

The Last Months, 1951–1952

THE PASSAGE ON THE medium-sized *Parthia* was rougher than Elisabeth had ever experienced on the larger liners. She had to get dressed or undressed sitting down in order not to risk life or limb. But otherwise the stormy sea and the pitching and rolling ship bothered her not at all. She ate with a good appetite; she took exercise on deck, never letting go of the hand ropes; she bought her duty-free in the little shopping complex – a few Christmas gifts and presents for the "gang" who would be meeting her at the pier: Gustl, Trude el Bedell, Rosie and surely Burghauser too.

What the stormy sea had not managed to do to her, their stormy greeting did with a vengeance.

During their boisterous embraces she suddenly cried out in pain. She had turned deathly white, did not know how to stand or which position to maintain, in order to lessen the agony in her back. She was supported by her friends, no one spoke. Slowly, step by step, she was brought to the waiting car.

During the drive someone mentioned, almost as if to cheer her up, that Hans Krüger was dying. Elisabeth was not able to react much to the news, all she said was: let's hope he hasn't such terrible pain to bear. At home the pain was not quite so acute, but even lying in bed did not make her recover completely.

11th Dec. 51

My Schnuck, . . .

I'm rather knocked up – Burghauser's stormy greeting damaged a nerve in my back (these crazy men). I went to the doctor thinking I had broken a rib – but that wasn't it – it is only an injury to a nerve, very painful, and it will take 3 – 4 weeks. I'm getting pills for the pain, so it is much better, but for 5 days I was in a bad way.

It probably would have been more sensible to miss the recital given by Irmgard Seefried – her first in America. Her success was certainly deserved and Elisabeth was determined to tell her so after the concert, even if walking and standing was a problem at the moment. Seefried was thrilled to see her and especially when Elisabeth said how beautifully she had sung – "in a way that one rarely hears these days." She had hardly spoken when Seefried embraced her joyfully and began to turn her round on the spot. The pain in Elisabeth's back was excruiating and she had to stop her violently, explaining to the shocked young singer about her damaged nerve. Now she just wanted to get home as quickly as possible.

In the corridor a reporter asked her whether she would like to say something about the concert. "With pleasure. It was an oasis in present-day lieder-singing."

The pain did not get better. It always came back, sometimes worse, sometimes better. Sometimes she was completely unable to move for a minute or two.

Christmas was at the door. Should she cancel her by now traditional Christmas Eve celebrations with Trude, Gustl and others? She simply could not bear the thought of being alone, especially if she was in pain. Dr Kraus would just have to get her through it.

He came at midday on the 24th and gave her an injection. Supported by that and by an iron will Elisabeth played the jolly hostess. A lot of the time she sat in her armchair upright and well supported, and talked about London and the maisonette which was to be hers.

This frightful game of pretence had to be repeated on New Year's Eve, this time at friends'. Despite an injection Elisabeth could hardly climb into the taxi, but with the last reserves of her strength she managed to stay until midnight to drink to the New Year.

During the first days of 1952 she was still able to sit a little and walk a few steps indoors. From January 9 not even that was possible, for she was forced to lie motionless on her back. She felt as if she were paralysed: all her endeavours were now directed towards avoiding the terrible pain.

Then Desi von Saher arrived with her husband. She wanted to have some lessons again. When she saw how things stood with her poor teacher she took it upon herself to see what could be done for her. Elisabeth had no choice in the matter, she had to let Desi have her way.

So now, apart from Dr Kraus, the great orthopaedic surgeon

Professor Hass, who had once practised in Vienna, and a Dr Alexander Kelen, came to see her. They ordered tests and X-rays. After several days they still had not made a diagnosis; but they knew that a vertebra was damaged and prescribed a corset to immobilize the spine. They advised lying in bed as still as possible – Elisabeth was not even to write letters, she would have to dictate them to Gustl or other friends. Rosie nursed her devotedly from morning to evening; Gustl moved into the drawing room at night so that she would not be alone when Rosie had to go home to her husband.

Elisabeth was not unduly alarmed by her condition, she retained her cheerfulness and optimism. Nor did she make the slightest complaint. The financial situation worried her though: it seemed that this illness would not be over in a matter of days, and to be ill in America was an expensive business.

Gerd realized that money might be a problem now and wrote to her suggesting she might prefer a flat in London rather than the expensive maisonette, for which payments would be due from March 1. He also wrote that he no longer wished his mother to send him his monthly allowance, he would find extra work outside the BBC: translating and reading film commentaries, for example.

Meanwhile the doctors had ordered more tests, this time in hospital. Had they not done enough already? For the first time Elisabeth was slightly rattled; she confessed to Gustl that she feared that once she was in hospital it might not be easy to get out again, and a stay in hospital would cost a fortune. Why not pawn the diamond tiara? suggested Gustl. "I've already pawned it," was Elisabeth's reply.

So now Gustl too knew how things stood. Apart from C's brother, Kurt Pindar, and Burghauser, who had both readily lent her money, the only other people who knew were Rosie, Trude and Dr Adler, her gynaecologist – also a good friend.

When the ambulance men had gently placed Elisabeth on a stretcher and were carrying her carefully out, the procession with the slow, echoing steps of the silent men seemed to her so very solemn that she began to sing Elisabeth's prayer from *Tannhäuser*: "Almighty Virgin, hear my pleading! I cry to thee, extolled one! Let me die in dust before thee, oh take me from this earth! Make me enter, pure and angelic, thy blessed realm!"

She was in marvellous voice. Rosie, who had been running ahead to open the doors, was almost in tears. The stretcher-bearers tried to step more quietly. Even as they lifted their burden into the ambulance they hardly made a sound, only looking at each other in wonder.

The four days in hospital seemed to make her illness even more intolerable than it was. Elisabeth disliked the clinical atmosphere compared to the comfort of her home, and the tests were often unpleasant.

On the second evening Trude came with the news that Hans was dead.

Elisabeth was silent . . . the man whom she had once loved, so much that every concert tour, every absence from Vienna was unbearable, was no more – and she did not feel anything. It had all dissolved inside her, he had wiped it all out. His death did not even make her think back nostalgically to the time when they had loved. She merely said: "What a blessing that he is released from his torture."

When, on January 19, Elisabeth had been safely transported back to her home her optimism knew no bounds. The fact that she had left hospital so soon seemed to her to be proof that things were not serious even if they hurt a lot. She was delighted to see her friends around her again, and her room looked anything but a sick-room: the bed had been made to look more like a sofa, and there were flowers everywhere in the apartment, standing out beautifully against the snow outside in the yard. The refrigerator was full of gifts too: caviare, pâté, champagne.

On January 27 Elisabeth dictated a letter for Gerd to Gustl:

Well, my child . . . the tests have turned out to be negative. They can't find anything and I'm really upset that they want to do another blood test and a bone test. I think they ought to get on with some treatment. . . . Of course I must be patient . . . I estimate it might take about five or six months – but perhaps it will only be three or four. The fact that this all interferes with my great move is very much on my mind, but my decision to live in London is only strengthened. . . . In my mind's eye I can already see myself with you in my sweet house. . . . Don't imagine that I shall lose patience or courage, I shall get well, there is no doubt about that!!!!

I have now told Ibbs & Tillett too. I've cancelled the Bermuda concerts, and Brussels; and there's no question of 4th February with Bruno Walter [New York Town Hall]. Perhaps my first work again will be Bryanston.... The doctors are the best I could have – and sometimes they make me impatient with their thoroughness....

The next day Dr Kelen visited to do the further tests on Elisabeth with a local anaesthetic. Then it meant having patience and waiting again for results. In the meantime, two days later, Professor Hass arrived with the corset-maker to fit the corset, and they also brought crutches. Elisabeth was quite shocked. But the doctor explained that they were only for taking the weight off the spine.

When they had carefully sat her up and were lifting her onto the crutches, she let out a cry and fainted. The two men were just able to prevent her from falling to the floor and to get her back into bed; for that awkward procedure unconsciousness was a blessing.

What Professor Hass had decided not to tell the patient was that she was suffering from the disease she most dreaded: cancer – of the bone.

Two days later, having put the ill-fated attempt to stand behind her, Elisabeth wrote to the family:

My dear ones!
I'll come straight out with the diagnosis: it's osteoporosis ... I'm told that after a three-week course of hormones there will already be an improvement, and so I think that I'll be able to get up by then. I have no pain if I lie still and am living completely without drugs.... My pupils want me to teach from my bed at all costs (very American!) ... I am thinking of having the piano moved into the alcove of my bedroom and teaching again with an accompanist.
I'm beginning to feel like Sarah Bernhardt! But instead of the lions* which she always had with her, I have my friendly spaniel [Gustl's dog, Buddy]....

Gustl wrote Gerd a long letter to tell him the truth about the diagnosis, but it so happened that because he did not put enough stamps on the letter it was returned to New York before it reached its destination – many weeks later. In the meantime Gerd heard the shocking news from someone else.

Desi von Saher had flown home to Holland from New York and, having had strict instructions from Elisabeth to do so, she telephoned Gerd on February 19 to let him know how his mother was. Gerd was rehearsing a religious drama serial in a BBC studio when he was called out to the telephone. Hearing Desi's voice was an unexpected

*The famous French actress's pets included monkeys, a cheetah and lion cubs.

pleasure. He eagerly asked for news. "But haven't you heard? Haven't you had Gustl's letter?" She then had to tell him that his mother was suffering from a fatal disease. After this hurried, shocking telephone call Gerd had to return to the studio and carry on as if nothing had happened.

In moments of quiet, which were not very frequent because of her visitors, Elisabeth read the newly-published correspondence between Strauss and Hofmannsthal, a Christmas present from Schnuck. Through her work, and also socially, she had in the past felt very close to these two greats, and had had considerable insight into the Strauss – Hofmannsthal works. Now, in many places in their letters, the creative processes of their partnership were revealed with pleasing clarity. With joy she felt herself once again in communion with these artists whom she had so admired.

Although the diagnosis had been established, the doctors recommended asking the opinion of a most prominent medical man, the famous Snapper, who normally never made house visits and had his own research establishment.

Only after some hesitation did Elisabeth agree, and it was not only because of the huge extra expense. No, she, who all her life had circulated among the great, was afraid of this famous doctor, this great and unique expert. To be the healthy dinner partner of a well-known doctor at a banquet could be fun, often great fun; but to lie in ill health before such a genius was quite a different matter.

But in the event he was quite charming, pretended to agree with the diagnosis of osteoporosis, said he would make her better – although it could take six months – and would start reducing the pain. He was true to his promise. After only five days of treatment she was already more mobile and suffering less.

Steinway were called to move the piano into the bedroom, and she started to teach from her "couch". She did not teach more than three lessons a day, and she found it a wonderful distraction. In the afternoons queues of friends would come laden with gifts. Sometimes Rosie had tactfully to turn people away when it became too much. Lotte Lehmann telephoned from California and was amazed at how cheerful she was. Lotte sounded so sad and upset that Elisabeth was the one who had to do the comforting.

Elisabeth was very saddened by the news from London of King George VI's death. A friend lent her his television so that she was able to watch the funeral ceremony; she sometimes felt for whole minutes at a time that she was back in London.

Elisabeth's kind friend Dr Adler could see how worried she was about money. He contacted Mary Zimbalist, asking her to come to New York to see him. She came from Philadelphia at once and, without hesitation, offered personally to foot all medical bills and cover any other vital living expenses.

Mary Zimbalist must have been glad at last to be able to make up for the unjust treatment her husband had given Elisabeth, by helping her in this way. That same afternoon she visited the invalid and, without beating about the bush, broached the financial subject tactfully and sensitively.

Elisabeth accepted the generous offer, promising to pay the money back once she was settled in London.[*]

The pupils wanted more lessons. Surprisingly she had no trouble demonstrating to them: lying down absolutely still did not impair her voice in any way. Gradually she began to teach a little more.

But soon she realized that she was doing too much; she felt weak and listless. Dr Kelen found that she had a slight fever and prescribed penicillin which quickly cleared it up. Then the pills which Snapper had prescribed began to upset her stomach so that the dosage had to be reduced. What a relief to be able to enjoy her food again, especially breakfast, which was her favourite meal and her favourite time of day. Rosie could never come before nine o'clock, so Gustl would make the coffee and the boiled egg and serve it up on a tray covered with flowers: every morning there were new flowers, arranged differently; he tried each time to make it a "special breakfast". Often he had fresh rolls in a basket, or sometimes even a champagne cocktail to help wash down the pills.

While she was waiting for her breakfast her thoughts would often go back to the past. Gustl sometimes provoked this by asking her questions or her opinion. Once he asked her to name the three female singers whose voices she like most. The answer came at once: Emmy Destinn, Rosa Ponselle and Lotte. And male singers? Caruso, she supposed. She did not seem quite sure but admitted that his voice was a miracle. But how did she like him as a man? Not much.

---

[*]After Elisabeth's death Mary Zimbalist still refused to be paid back. Instead she asked Gerd for, and received, a lovely antique ring she had often seen on Elisabeth's hand.

"How can one fall in love with people who keep clearing their throats and coughing and spitting? I only ever found conductors fascinating. Singers were never a temptation. How they sweat on stage, and that nervousness and fear in their eyes before a high note! Mind you, to be a heroic tenor must be a terrible career, worse than mine. Often the success of an opera depends on him – a dreadful responsibility!"

"That's why they get such huge fees."

Elisabeth admitted that not even dramatic sopranos got anywhere near a tenor when it came to fees, let alone a soubrette like herself.*

On another occasion Elisabeth suddenly said: "Ten men in my life – do you think that's a lot?"† Gustl tried hard to keep a straight face. When she asked him what he found so amusing he replied: "Well, just that it is so few, ridiculously few." Elisabeth then maintained that it probably would not have been as many as ten if she had ever really found the right man. "I think that basically I'm a loyal person."**

On March 23 Gustl wrote to Gerd:

> She's been in bed now for 10½ weeks, and *never one* impatient word to anyone! Dr Kelen said, do you realize what a wonderful human being she is? (I really needed him to tell me that, I don't think!) . . . She has *unwavering*, enormously strong faith!

Yes, her belief that she would get better was determined; she said that miracles had been known in medicine and she was going to prove it by recovering far faster than the doctors predicted. To her friends and visitors, at any rate, she was quite the old, radiant Schumann, who enjoyed getting flowers and gifts, and laughed as far

---

*Perhaps she was remembering her 1914–15 season at the Met, when Caruso had earned $2,500 per performance against the mere $1,200 of Emmy Destinn, not to mention her own $300 as a newcomer.

†This is twice the number of men written about in this book; but so little, or nothing, is known about the other five that they have not been mentioned, even though Elisabeth considered marrying two of them (after the war: one in Norway and, later, one in South Africa).

**It seems that in a sense Klemperer remained the most important man in her life. During this time of her illness he telephoned. When Elisabeth replaced the receiver she said to Gustl with a sigh: "It was the red thread running through my life."

as her back would allow. But those who were constantly with her –
Rosie, Gustl and Trude el Bedell – saw that she was not always as
happy as she seemed at times; and Lene was told quite frankly in a
February letter: "Since 2nd December I've been very ill and bedridden
for five weeks, motionless, with the most terrible pain."

In a letter to another friend she confessed:

> I had excruciating pain. But the love and care of the children is the
> balm of my soul. They write a lot and can hardly wait to have me with
> them. Biddy has completely opened herself up to me, and we are both
> united for as long as I shall live.

When she wrote to Gerd and Biddy she hardly hinted at her
suffering: the last thing she wanted was for them to be worried. She
thanked them for their frequent letters, especially Biddy: "You write
so conscientiously, it's always like a ray of light. . . ." Once she
added by hand, right at the end of a letter typed by Gustl: "Keep
praying, I am too."

Biddy's mother, a convinced Christian Scientist, suggested that
Elisabeth should be treated by a Christian Science practitioner.
Through her own practitioner at home she knew of a lady who
practised in New York. Elisabeth replied to Biddy:

> Yes, my child, the same thing occurred to me too. But somehow I just
> haven't got that implicit faith . . . I don't find my illness a joke and
> I have such indescribable trust in Snapper that I cannot bring myself
> to follow up the address. I shouldn't wonder if a healer like that didn't
> affect Snapper's treatment.

The following day Gustl wrote to Gerd:

> We have talked together – not too intensively up to now – about
> Christian Science. *Deep down* she is not convinced by it –
> Catholicism interests her more, if anything; but basically she has her
> great big religion and her very strong, sincere belief – in something
> up there, whatever kind of god it is – and this belief is *much* stronger
> and more unshakeable than what most mortals can be given through
> church, Christian Science, etc.!

But by the end of March Elisabeth had had the practitioner, Miss
M. Gordon Fraser, come to see her twice, her philosophy being that
she wanted to leave nothing untried. She liked her very much but
found her rather superfluous since, as the lady herself noticed with
surprise, Elisabeth already possessed "faith and spirit" in such large
quantities.

If faith meant belief that she would get well, then Elisabeth had faith. If, as Miss Gordon Fraser did, one meant by faith the Christian Science belief that man, as a manifestation of God could, with his personality, express the purest godliness and thus become free of all impurities including illness, then Elisabeth did not have faith. Yet Miss Gordon Fraser proceeded with the instruction of the Science intelligently and discreetly because of the treatment which the doctors were giving. She sent a report to Biddy:

> She reads her textbook in secret because of those around her but I can feel her whole thought is changing. She loved the statement from *Science and Health** "you embrace your body in your thought" . . . I see a great strengthening in her.

And she really was getting better, almost by leaps if not by bounds. On March 30 she woke up, realized that it was little Christian's eleventh birthday, and half sat herself up. Gustl came in just at that moment with her early morning tea. They looked at each other with a start. She was almost sitting up!

April arrived, and with it the conviction that in four or five weeks she would be able to embrace her family in London "even if they have to be outwardly gentle embraces". Dr Kelen had great pleasure in announcing that he thought her body would have regained enough calcium to allow the journey in about the first week of May. He said, however, that it would be essential to make the journey in a lying position. From door to door on a stretcher? – Elisabeth was aghast.

Gerd, impatient for her arrival, wrote that travelling on a stretcher was no great problem. He described the endless journeys he had had to make in a horizontal position when he was wounded.

> Yes, my child, what you write about your journeys – what is one "stretcher" from New York – London compared to those! How often your wounding comforted me during the painful days. I told myself 100 times that I've got nothing to fuss about – but it is still sad that you had to suffer for it. One thing I would like, and that is that the little ones should not see me until I'm in Hamilton Terrace. I don't want them to get the wrong impression. I think in fact that only you two should be at the airport. No friends either. Oh children! It's unbelievable that we shall embrace each other in a few weeks.

It was as if the thought of seeing the family speeded the recovery.

---

*By Mary Baker Eddy, the founder of Christian Science, first published in 1875.

Soon Elisabeth could sit up completely. Every day the length of time she sat up in bed was increased. Now she could have more visitors again.

Bruno Walter and the soprano Delia Reinhardt, who were enjoying a love relationship, came to say farewell before leaving for Paris together. It seemed as if with him the great, wide musical world had suddenly come pouring into the room. Bruno seemed quite different. There was nothing of his usual slight reserve; he joked, told about concerts, and even illustrated a musical point of interpretation on the piano. They talked about the recital that he and Elisabeth had had to cancel in February. But next spring there would be one! He promised to keep a date free.

Fritz Reiner came and talked about the performance of *Die Meistersinger* which he had conducted and which she had partly heard on the radio. They agreed that the modern generation of singers sang without enough abdominal support. "That's what it sounds like, at any rate," said Elisabeth.

6. April 1952.

My dear ones . . . the visits and the flowers are just like "on the first day", my friends really are unshakeable. I know now just how many letters of condolence you'll get one day, for the letters of sympathy are coming in from far and wide and some of them sound as if I "were already on the other side". What a lot of work you'll have when you have to thank them all! I'm even looking at flowers from Africa, and Gustl has taken on his new job as gardener – I only ever see him with a watering can, one day he'll water me too. People don't seem to be able to imagine that I too can be allowed to take time off to be ill for once.

Now one could really feel that spring was coming. If Gustl opened the large glass door onto the yard, the air even here in New York had a silky feel with, at the same time, a tingling in it. It made Elisabeth feel hungry for fresh air after all the time she had been shut in.

She decided that once she had got everything sorted out in her new home she would enjoy the summer on the continent, in Gastein. Lisa Reitler wanted to come too, to the same hotel, and Erna and Jacques would be there. If only Schnuck and Biddy could come.

I would very much like to invite you there, even if only for a week. I must give myself a bit of a reward. After that I have great plans. Lene would say "Heavens! Wait a bit!! Don't go and start working again

337

yet." You see, the Zermatt Summer School, which is directed by Casals, has asked me to go there in August to take a course of lieder master classes and perhaps give a concert. The whole thing would be three weeks from mid-August. But before that I'll hear the dress rehearsal of Strauss's *Danaä* [*Danae*] in Salzburg. I think Zermatt will be a nice extra cure after Gastein and have accepted, because as you know I'm always an optimist and have been lying on one spot for long enough. . . .

Apart from some Easter cards for her grandchildren this was Elisabeth's last letter to her family for, a few days later, Dr Snapper declared himself satisfied with the patient's progress and gave permission for the journey. On April 21 Elisabeth received confirmation of her BOAC flight for May 3. The whole day she was in the happiest of moods. Every visitor heard her wonderful news: May 3! Late into the evening she talked and laughed with friends.

"Nurse" Gustl was giving a party in his apartment. Because of this he could not come downstairs to Elisabeth until nearly one o'clock in the morning. With a branch of blossoming cherry in his hand – a gift from one of his friends – he quietly entered the apartment, intending to place the branch at the window as a sign of spring. Then he saw a light in Elisabeth's room. He went to her, still carrying the branch.

Without even noticing the blossoms she said she had already been asleep, and now she had a dreadful headache. Gustl went to fetch some veganin. When he returned she groaned quietly and said: "Now its unbearable."

As he gave her the tablet with some water it was clear to him that he must call a doctor and he wanted to go to the telephone in the drawing room. She stretched out her hand a little way towards him and gasped: "Don't leave me alone now." So he used the 'phone by her bed. Luckily Dr Kelen was in and said he would come at once.

Elisabeth seemed to be drifting off. But suddenly she said: "You'll sort everything out, I know" and, a little later, in English, "it's fate . . . it's fate."

The doorbell rang. Gustl hurried to open it. As he returned with Dr Kelen Elisabeth was mumbling indistinctly. As the doctor gave her an injection she lost consciousness.

It was a brain haemorrhage.

Elisabeth was taken to the Memorial Hospital. An urgent telegram was sent to Gerd. Trude el Bedell sat by the patient's bedside for several hours, until she could bear the sights and sounds of dying no longer and ran weeping from the room. Elisabeth remained alone; only every now and then a nurse looked in briefly.

Without having regained consciousness Elisabeth Schumann died in the evening of April 23 1952.

Epilogue

Ibbs & Tillett lent Gerd the money to fly to New York. He was, however, just too late to see his mother alive.

The funeral in New York was held at noon on April 26. The Campbell Funeral Church was packed. There were no addresses but there was much music: the New York Quartet played the slow movement from Schubert's Quartet in G minor, and two of Elisabeth's pupils sang ("Bist du bei mir" and "Zur Ruh', zur Ruh'"). A Lutheran pastor read passages from the Bible and some prayers.

Gerd brought the ashes to England where they were buried in the graveyard of St Martin's Church, Ruislip. A memorial service was held at St Martin-in-the-Fields in London on what would have been Elisabeth's sixty-fourth birthday, June 13 1952. At this the Griller Quartet played the slow movement from Mozart's Quartet in B flat. The service was taken by the Vicar of St Martin-in-the-Fields, but the closing prayers were read by a Lutheran pastor in German. Inside the back of the order of service was printed a tribute by Lotte Lehmann, part of which follows this epilogue.

Biddy was invited by William Glock to teach at Dartington Summer School of Music (this was the Bryanston Summer School in a new location). She wrote a much acclaimed book on the teaching method of Elisabeth Schumann and continued to teach singing privately until ill health forced her retirement in 1977.

Gerd continued to work at the BBC until the early 1980s. He and Biddy now live in Sussex.

Christian is a mathematics teacher at a grammar school, and lives with his wife in Buckinghamshire. Rupert is married, with two daughters, and is a doctor in Bedfordshire. Joy works at a foreign-language bookshop in London and was a part-time professional singer for some years.

A tribute by Lotte Lehmann

Elisabeth Schumann's passing away makes me infinitely sad – I don't know how to find adequate words to express the deep sense of loss I feel. Not only the loss of a great singer, a wonderful colleague – but the loss of a friend with whom I shared a time in my life in which we were young together and went together on our paths, through failure and success, through laughter and tears, till we grew old and talked of the past whenever we met. The melody of our conversation seemed always to be: "Do you remember...?"

I shall remember her always; laughing, stepping lightly over obstacles, living with a song on her lips and in her heart; a generous and utterly noble heart, a heart which beat through her songs like the sound of a silver bell. Hers was not the tragic note of despair, not the dramatic outbreak. Hers was the infinitely fine and perfect glow of purity. Her concerts were a lesson in style and beauty.

She was the last great concert singer of noble tradition. Blessed the invention of the recording machine! Many of her lieder are captured forever and will delight many generations to come. Young singers will try to learn from her, will try to make the clarity of her singing their own. But will they ever learn the greatest secret of Elisabeth Schumann? Her charm? Her delicacy? Her inborn exquisiteness? I hope so....

This morning I found a little dead bird in our garden. I wept – but not about this little crushed life in my hand. I wept about a gay, birdlike song which is stilled forever. A happy heart which will not beat again. An exuberant laughter which will never ask again: "Do you remember...?"

Farewell, Elisabeth, I shall remember always.

THE RECORDINGS OF

ELISABETH SCHUMANN

by FLORIS JUYNBOLL *and* JAMES SEDDON

INTRODUCTION

The following basic recording list has been extracted from the complete discography of Elisabeth Schumann prepared by the above-named compilers, and published in Vol. 33, Nos. 3/5 of The Record Collector in March 1988. The list comprises all the commercial recordings she made between 1913 and 1950 arranged in chronological order, and the more important of her non-commercial recordings, derived mainly from English and American broadcasts by record collectors using amateur recording equipment.

Each commercial side recorded has been assigned a discography number. This is followed by the company's matrix number to which is hyphenated the 'take', the name given to repeat recordings of the same title. The published take is *set in italic type*. The title of the work and name of the composer follow, and the last line gives all known catalogue issue numbers.

The artist sings in German unless indicated otherwise by (E) English, (F) French, (I) Italian and (L) Latin. The indicator (G) signifies that she is singing a German translation of words set originally in another language.

In the listing the name of the conductor the artist married appears as Karl Alwin, as this spelling was in use in all pre-war catalogues and on record labels, and has continued in use for post-war long-playing and compact disc reissues. The correct spelling is, of course, Carl Alwin, as used in the biography.

KEY TO CATALOGUE NUMBERS

H.M.V. (U.K.)

International: DA series (10-inch/25 cm). DB series (12-inch/30 cm).

U.K.: E series (10-inch); D and VB series (12-inch)

Ireland: IR series (10-inch). IRX series (12-inch)

France: P series (10-inch). W series (12-inch)

Germany: EW series (10-inch). EJ and EH series (12-inch)

Austria, Hungary, Czechoslovakia: ER series (10-inch). ES and AN (12-inch series)

Spain: AA series (10-inch). AB series (12-inch)

Australia: EC series (10-inch). ED series (12-inch)

Victor (U.S.A.)

1400 and 2000 series (10-inch). 6800/8000 and 14/15000 series (12-inch)

Victor (Japan)

JE, JF, NF, VE series (10-inch). JD, ND, VD series (12-inch)

Private reissues on shellac (78 rpm)

International Record Collectors Club (IRCC): 3000 series (10-inch)

The Record Album (New York): RA series (12-inch)

Record Rarities (New York): RR series (12-inch)

Historic Masters (U.K.): HMB series (12-inch)

COMMERCIAL RECORDINGS, 1913 – 1950

I. THE ACOUSTIC RECORDINGS

Only the Edison recordings can be dated. Recording sheets for the Favorite, Odeon and Polydor issues are no longer available. Owing to the difficulty in tracing copies of the very rare Favorite Luxus records, discography Nos. 1, 2 and 3 are listed subject to correction.

FAVORITE LUXUS acoustic recordings, 25 cm, 1913

1. (3076 – b +)   (Title not traced)
                        1 – 16230

2. (3077 – b +)   MADAMA BUTTERFLY: Eines Tages seh'n wir (Un bel di
                        vedremo) (Act 2) (Puccini) (G)
                        1 – 16231

3. (3078 – b +)   LE NOZZE DI FIGARO: Ihr, die ihr Triebe des Herzens kennt
                        (Voi che sapete) (Act 2) (Mozart) (G)
                        1 – 16232

4. 3079 – b +   LE NOZZE DI FIGARO: Neue Freuden (Non so più cosa son)
                        (Act 1) (Mozart) (G)
                        1 – 16233

5. 3080 – b +   MIGNON: Kam ein armes Kind von fern (Je connais un pauvre
                        enfant) ('Styrienne') (Act 2) (Thomas) (G)
                        1 – 16234

6. 3081 – b +   MIGNON: Kennst du das Land? (Connais-tu le pays?) (Act 1)
                        (Thomas) (G)
                        1 – 16235

EDISON DIAMOND acoustic recordings, 25 cm, 1915

7. 3554   DER FREISCHÜTZ: Kommt ein schlanker Bursch' gegangen
                        (Act 2) (Weber)
                        82082

8. 3557   FIDELIO: Ach, wär ich schon mit dir vereint (Act 1)
                        (Beethoven)
                        73005, IRCC 3125

9. 3558   MIGNON: Kam ein armes Kind von fern (Je connais un pauvre
                        enfant) ('Styrienne') (Act 2) (Thomas) (G)
                        (82084) (not issued)

10. 3560   MIGNON: Kennst du das Land? (Connais-tu le pays?) (Act 1)
                        (Thomas) (G)
                        73004

Elisabeth Schumann

11. 3568   CARMEN: Je dis que rien ne m'épouvante, ('Air de Micaëla')
(Act 3) (Bizet) (F)
(not issued)

12. 3569   DER FREISCHÜTZ: Trübe Augen, Liebchen, taugen (Act 3)
(Weber)
82092

ODEON acoustic recordings, 30cm, 1917

13. xxB 6377   CARMEN: Ich sprach, dass ich furchtlos mich fühle (Je dis que
rien ne m'épouvante) ('Air de Micaëla') (Act 3) (Bizet) (G)
RXX 76724, RA-1

14. xxB 6378   FIDELIO: Ach, wär ich schon mit dir vereint
(Act 1) (Beethoven)
RXX 76725, RA-1

15. xxB 6379   HÄNSEL UND GRETEL: Wo bin ich? Wach ich? Ist es ein
Traum? (Act 3) (Humperdinck)
RXX 76728, UAA 79019

16. xxB 6380   DON GIOVANNI: Schmäle, schmäle, lieber Junge (Batti, batti,
o bel Masetto) (Act 1) (Mozart) (G)
RXX 76726

17. xxB 6381   DON GIOVANNI: Wenn du fein fromm bist (Vedrai carino)
(Act 2) (Mozart) (G)
RXX 76727

18. xxB 6382   DIE ZAUBERFLÖTE: Ach, ich fühl's, es ist verschwunden (Act
2) (Mozart)
RXX 76729, UAA 79020

19. xxB 6385   Morgen (Mackay-R. Strauss, Op. 27, No. 4) (pno & vln.)
UAA 57811, 0-6441 AA

20. xxB 6386   Frage und Antwort (Mörike-Wolf) (pno)
UAA 57812, 0-6441 AA

1919

21. xxB 6427   Die Forelle (Schubart-Schubert, D.550) (pno)
RXX 76749

22. xxB 6428   Blauer Sommer (Busse-R. Strauss, Op. 31, No. 1) (pno)
RXX 76750

POLYDOR (DEUTSCHE GRAMMOPHON) acoustic recordings, 30 cm, 1920

23. 269 as   LE NOZZE DI FIGARO: Neue Freuden, neue Schmerzen (Non
so più) (Act 1) (Mozert) (G)
B 24097, 65654

24. 270 as   LE NOZZE DI FIGARO: Ihr, die ihr Triebe des Herzens kennt
(Voi che sapete) (Act 2) (Mozart) (G)
B 24098, 65654

25. 271 as   DON GIOVANNI: Wenn du fein fromm bist (Vedrai carino)
(Act 2) (Mozart) (G)
B 24099, 65655

26. 272 as   DER WILDSCHÜTZ: Auf des Lebens raschen Wogen (Act 1)
(Lortzing)
B 24032, 65613

27. 273 as   FAUST: Jewelenarie (Air des Bijoux) (Act 3) (Gounod) (G)
043366, 65587

28. 274 as   DIE ENTFÜHRUNG AUS DEM SERAIL: Durch Zärtlichkeit
und Schmeicheln (Act 2) (Mozart)
043348, 65580, RR-4

29. 275 as   DIE ENTFÜHRUNG AUS DEM SERAIL: Welche Wonne,
welche Lust (Act 2) (Mozart)
043349, 65580, RR-4

30. 276 as   DON GIOVANNI: Schmäle, schmäle, lieber Junge (Batti, batti,
o bel Masetto) (Act 1) (Mozart) (G)
B 24100, 65655

31. 277 as   FRA DIAVOLO: Welches Glück (Quel bonheur) (Act 2)
(Auber) (G)
043365, 65587

32. 278 as   HÄNSEL UND GRETEL: Wo bin ich? Wach ich? Ist es ein
Traum? (Act 3) (Humperdinck)
B 24033, 65613

1922

33. 923 as   Die heiligen drei Könige (Heine-R. Strauss, Op. 56, No.6) (w.
orchestra)
B 24144, 65689

34. 924 as   EXSULTATE, JUBILATE: Part 1 – Allegro (Mozart, K.165)
(L)
B 24141, 65688, RR-1

35. 925 as   EXSULTATE, JUBILATE: Part 2 – Andante (L)
B24142, 65688, RR-1

36. 926 as   EXSULTATE, JUBILATE: Part 3 – Alleluia (L)
B 24143, 65689, RR-1

1923

37. 1258 as   LE NOZZE DI FIGARO: Endlich naht sich die Stunde ... O
säume länger nicht (Deh vieni, non tardar) (Act 4) (Mozart) (G)
B 24223, 65811

38. 1260 as   DIE ZAUBERFLÖTE: Ach, ich fühl's, es ist verschwunden (Act
2) (Mozart)
B 24224, 65811

Elisabeth Schumann

II. THE HMV ELECTRIC RECORDINGS

The entire list has been transcribed from the original recording sheets filed in the EMI Archive at Hayes. In this section the discography number is assigned at those sessions at which the published recording was obtained or, if the side was unpublished, at the session when the last recording was made. Unless otherwise indicated the recording speed is the standard 78 r.p.m. When not specified the recording venue is London.

30 April 1926: Studio A, Hayes. Orchestra cond. George W. Byng

(–) Cc 8377-1-2   LE NOZZE DI FIGARO: Voi che sapete (Act 2) (Mozart) (I). (See discog. No. 42)

(–) Cc 8378-1   LE NOZZE DI FIGARO: Deh vieni non tardar (Act 4) (Mozart) (I). (See 7 June 1926)

39 Cc 8379-1-2   DIE ENTFÜHRUNG AUS DEM SERAIL: Durch Zärtlichkeit (Act 2) (Mozart) (I). Not issued

(–) Cc 8380-1-2   IL RE PASTORE: L'amerò, sarò constante (Act 2) (Mozart) (I). (See 19 May 1926)

19 May 1926: Studio B, Hayes. Orchestra cond. George W. Byng

40 Bb 8403-*1*-2   EXSULTATE, JUBILATE: Alleluia (Mozart, K.165) (L) 7-53111, DA 845, 1454, IR 311, AA 148

41 Cc 8404-*1*   DON GIOVANNI: Batti, batti, O bel Masetto (Act 1) (Mozart) (I) 2-053265, DB 946, 7076, IRX 124

42 Cc 8377-*3*   LE NOZZE DI FIGARO: Voi che sapete (Act 2) (Mozart) (I) 2-053261, DB 946, 7076, IRX 124

(–) Cc 8380-3-4   IL RE PASTORE: L'amerò, sarò constante (Act 2) (Mozart) (I). (See discog. No. 44)

7 June 1926: Studio B, Hayes. Orchestra cond. George W. Byng

43 Bb 8504-*1*-2   DON GIOVANNI: Vedrai carino (Act 2) (Mozart) (I) 7-53095, DA 845, 1454, IR 311, AA 148. (77 rpm)

(–) Cc 8378-2   LE NOZZE DI FIGARO: Deh vieni, non tardar (Act 4) (Mozart) (I). (See discog. No. 52)

44 Cc 8380-*5*   IL RE PASTORE: L'amerò, sarò constante (Act 2) (Mozart) (I). (Vln. obb. Marjorie Hayward) 2-053266, DB 1011, AB 424. (77 rpm)

14 June 1926: Studio A, Hayes. Orchestra cond. George W. Byng

(–) Cc 8404-2-3   DON GIOVANNI: Batti, batti, o bel Masetto (Act 1) (Mozart) (I). (See Discog. No. 41)

1 February 1927: Studio C, Small Queen's Hall. Orchestra cond. Lawrance Collingwood

45 Bb 9871-*1*-1A-2A-3   LE NOZZE DI FIGARO: Non so più cosa son (Act 1) (Mozart) (I) 7-53109, DA 844, 1431, EW 34, AA 142

46 Cc 9872-1-2   DIE ZAUBERFLÖTE: Ach, ich fühl's (Act 2) (Mozart) (I) (2-053286). Not issued.

47 Bb 9873-*1*-2   LE NOZZE DI FIGARO: Venite, inginocchiatevi (Act 2) (Mozart) (I) 7-53110, DA 844, 1431, EW 34, AA 142

48 Cc 9874-1-2   DIE ENTFÜHRUNG AUS DEM SERAIL: Durch Zärtlichkeit (Act 2) (Mozart) (I) Not issued

49 Cc 9875-1   Du bist die Ruh' (Rückert-Schubert, D.776)
(2-043061) (See discog. No. 64)

4 February 1927: Studio C, Small Queen's Hall. Orchestra cond. Lawrance Collingwood
50 Cc 9857-1-2   Ständchen (Schack-R. Strauss, Op. 17, No. 2). In F
2-043062, DB 1010, 7210, AB 423, JD 386 (75 rpm)
51 Cc 9888-1-2   Morgen (Mackay-R. Strauss, Op. 27, No. 4)
2-043063, DB 1010, AB 423, JD 386 (75 rpm)
52 Cc 8378-3   LE NOZZE DI FIGARO: Deh vieni, non tardar (Act 4)
(Mozart) (I)
2-053288, DB 1011, AB 424 (75 rpm)
53 Cc 9889-1   EXSULTATE, JUBILATE: (Title not given) (Mozart, K.165) (L)
(2-053287). Not issued

24 May 1927: Studio C, Small Queen's Hall. Piano: Ivor Newton
54 Cc 10901-1-2   Freundliche Vision (Bierbaum-R. Strauss, Op. 48, No. 1)
2-043074, DB 1065, EJ 197
55 Cc 10902-1-2   Wiegenlied (Dehmel-R. Strauss, Op. 41, No. 1)
2-043074, DB 1065, 7210, EJ 197

11 November 1927: Small Queen's Hall. Orchestra cond. Karl Alwin
56 Cc 12007-1-2   CANTATA BWV 159: Es ist vollbracht (Picander-J.S. Bach
arr. Alwin) (Oboe, Leon Goossens)
2-043086, D 1410, 7275, W 980, EJ 243, ES 347 (77 rpm)
57 Bb 12008-1-2   DIE FLEDERMAUS: Mein Herr Marquis (Act 2) (J. Strauss II)
7-43097, E 545, EW 82, ER 319, P 853 (77 rpm)
58 Cc 12009-1   MATTHÄUS-PASSION: Aus Liebe will mein Heiland sterben
(J.S. Bach, BWV 244) (Flute, J. Amadio)
2-043087, D 1410, 7275, W980, EJ 243, ES 347 (77 rpm)

14 November 1927: Studio C, Small Queen's Hall. Piano: Karl Alwin
59 Cc 12011-1-2   (a) Die Post (Müller-Schubert, D.911) (Winterreise, No.13)
(b) Wohin? (Müller-Schubert, D.795) (Die schöne Müllerin,
No. 2)
2-043088, D 1411, 6837, W 957, EJ 260, ES 354, AB 447,
JD 16 (77 rpm)
(–) Bb 12012-1-2   DIE FLEDERMAUS: Spiel' ich die Unschuld vom Lande (Act
3) (J. Strauss II). (See discog. No. 63)
60 Cc 12013-1-2   (a) Im Abendrot (Lappe-Schubert, D.799)
(b) Die Vögel (Schlegel-Schubert, D.691)
2-043089, D 1411, 6837, W 957, EJ 260, ES 354, AB 447,
JD 16 (77 rpm)
61 Cc 12014-1-2   (a) Schlechtes Wetter (Heine-R. Strauss, Op. 69, No. 5)
(b) Ständchen (Schack-R. Strauss, Op. 17, No. 2)
2-043090, D 1951, 7707, EJ 557, ND 526, VD 8011 (77 rpm)
62 Bb 12015-1   Bird song imitations whistled by the artist (Private recording)

20 February 1928: Studio C, Small Queen's Hall. Piano: George Reeves
63 Bb 12012-3-4-5   DIE FLEDERMAUS: Spiel' ich die Unschuld vom Lande (Act
3) (J. Strauss II)
Not issued
64 Cc 9875-2   Du bist die Ruh' (Rückert-Schubert, D.776)
(2-043061). Not issued

15 October 1928: Vienna, Mittlerer Saal. Vienna State Opera Orchestra cond. Karl Alwin
65 CW 1909-1-2-3   Die heiligen drei Könige (Heine-R. Strauss, Op. 56, No. 6)
2-043108, D 1632, 7209, EJ 432, ES 555 (77 rpm)

66 BW 1910-*1*-2   Muttertändelei (Bürger-R. Strauss, Op. 43, No. 2)
7-43115, E 532, 1661, ER 304 (77 rpm)
67 BW 1911-1-2   Marienlied (Novalis-Marx)
7-43116, E 532, 1661, ER 304 (77 rpm)
68 CW 1912-1-2   JOSHUA: Oh! had I Jubal's lyre (Handel) (G) (77 rpm)
2-043109, D 1632, 7209, EJ 432, ES 555

29 April 1929: Vienna; Vienna Studio. Piano: Karl Alwin
69 BW 2482-1-2   Das Veilchen (Goethe-Mozart, K.476)
Not issued
70 BW 2483-1-2   Schlafe mein Prinzchen (Gotter-Flies, attrib. Mozart, K.350)
Not issued

29 May 1929: Kingsway Hall. London Symphony Orchestra cond. Albert Coates
MASS IN B MINOR, BWV 232 (J.S. Bach)
71
Cc 16643-1-1A-2-2A-3-3A   Christe eleison (Part 1) (L). With Margaret Balfour (contralto)
2-054315, C 1711, 9956, EH 434, AN 357 (78 rpm)
72
Cc 16644-1-1A-2-2A-3-3A   Christe eleison (Part 2) (L). With Margaret Balfour (contralto)
2-054316, C 1712, 9957, EH 435, AN 358
73
Cc 16645-1A-2-2A-3-*3A*   Et in unum (L). With Margaret Balfour (contralto)
2-054317, C 1720, 9965, EH 443, AN 366

31 May 1929: Kingsway Hall. London Symphony Orchestra cond. Albert Coates
MASS IN B MINOR, BWV 232 (J.S. Bach)
74
Cc 16647-*1*-1A-2-2A   Domine Deus (Part 1) (L). With Walter Widdop (ten.)
2-054313, C 1716, 9961, EH 438, AN 361 (77 rpm)
75
Cc 16648-*1*-2A-3-3A   Domine Deus (Part 2) (L). With Walter Widdop (ten.)
2-054314, C 1716, 9961, EH 439, AN 362 (77 rpm)

6 September 1929: Vienna. Mittlerer Saal. Vienna State Opera Orchestra cond.
Karl Alwin
76 BV 612-1-2-*3*   DER VOGELHÄNDLER: Wie mein Ahn'l zwanzig Jahr
(Act 3) (Zeller)
30-1471, E 554, EW 83, ER 338, DA 6037
77 BV 613-1-2   DER VOGELHÄNDLER: Wie mein Ahn'l zwanzig Jahr
(Act 3) (Zeller) (E)
(30-1472). Not issued
78 BV 614-1-2-*3*   DIE FLEDERMAUS: Spiel' ich die Unschuld vom Lande
(Act 3) (J. Strauss II)
30-1473, E 545, EW 82, ER 319, P 853
79 BV 615-1-2-3   Schlafe mein Prinzchen (Gotter-Flies, attrib. Mozart, K.350).
Not issued

3 January 1930: Vienna. Mittlerer Saal. Vienna State Opera Orchestra cond. K.
Alwin
80 BW 3104-1-2   DER VOGELHÄNDLER: Wie mein Ahn'l zwanzig Jahr (Act
3) (Zeller)
Not issued
81 BW 3105-1-2-3   DER OBERSTEIGER: Sei nicht bös' (Act 2) (Zeller)
Not issued
82 BW 3106-1-2-3   Schlafe mein Prinzchen (Gotter-Flies, attrib. Mozart, K.350)
Not issued

List of Recordings

6 January 1930: Vienna; Vienna Studio. Piano: K. Alwin

83 CW 3110-1-2   (a) All' mein Gedanken (Dahn-R. Strauss, Op. 21, No. 1)
(b) Hat gesagt, bleibt nicht dabei (Des Knaben Wunderhorn-R. Strauss, Op. 36, No. 3)
32-1191, D 1951, 7707, EJ 557, ND 526, VD 8011

17 February 1930: Kingsway Hall, Orchestra cond. Lawrance Collingwood

84 Bb 18665-1-2   DER OBERSTEIGER: Sei nicht bös (Act 2) (Zeller)
30-2818, E 552, E 554, EW 83, ER 338, ER 340, IR 281, DA 6037

85 Bb 18666-1-2-3   Schlafe mein Prinzchen (Gotter-Flies attrib. Mozart, K.350).
30-2819, E 555, EW 80, ER 339, DA 4435, DA 6006, JE 555, JE 259

86 Bb 18667-1-2   DER VOGELHÄNDLER: Wie mein Ahn'l zwanzig Jahr (Act 3) (Zeller) (E), 'Nightingale Song'
30-1472, E 552, ER 340, IR 282, B 32

18 February 1930: Studio C, Small Queen's Hall. Piano: George Reeves

87 Cc 18857-1-2   (a) Schneeglöckchen (Rückert-Schumann, Op. 76, No. 27)
(b) Der Nussbaum (Mosen-Schumann, Op. 25, No. 3)
32-1232, D 1824, ES 673, JD 110, JD 2009, ND 254

88 Cc 18858-1-2-3   (a) Er ist's (Mörike-Schumann, Op. 79, No. 23)
(b) Aufträge (L'Egru-Schumann, Op. 77, No. 5)
32-1233, D 1824, ES 673, JD 110, JD 2009, ND 254

89 Bb 18859-1-2   (a) Warnung (Männer suchen stets zu naschen) (Anon-Mozart, K.433)
(b) Wer hat dies Liedlein erdacht (Des Knaben Wunderhorn-Mahler)
30-2899, E 555, EW 80, ER 339, DA 6006, JE 555

16 May 1931: Kingsway Hall. London Symphony Orchestra cond. John Barbirolli

90 2B
543-1-1A-2-2A-3-3A   DIE MEISTERSINGER VON NÜRNBERG: Selig, wie die Sonne (Quintet) (Act 3) (Wagner). With Lauritz Melchior (ten.), Gladys Parr (contralto), Friedrich Schorr (bar.), Ben Williams (ten.)
32-2225, D 2002, 7682, EJ 693, ES 761, AB 715, AW 289

25 June 1931: Vienna Studios. Instrumental Sextet cond. K. Alwin. Piano: K. Alwin.

91 OL 293-1-2   Der Vogel im Walde (Taubert). With Sextet.
Not issued

92 OL 294-1-2   (a) Schweizerlied (Uf' im Bergli bin i g'sässe) (Goethe-Schubert, D.559). With piano.
(b) Liebhaber in allen Gestalten (Goethe-Schubert, D.558). With piano.
Not issued

4 April 1932: Studio No. 2, Abbey Road. Orchestra cond. Karl Alwin

93 OB 3060-1-2-3   Der Vogel im Walde (Taubert, arr. Alwin)
30-8593, DA 1274, 1606, JF 37

94 OB 3061-1-2-3   Was i' hab (Bavarian folksong arr. Bohm, Op. 326, No. 12)
30-8594, DA 1274, 1606, JF 37

7 November 1932: Studio No. 3, Abbey Road. Piano: Karl Alwin

95 2B 4472-1-2   (a) Traum durch die Dämmerung (Bierbaum-R. Strauss, Op. 29, No. 1)

	(b) Ich schwebe (Hanckell-R. Strauss, Op. 48, No. 2)
	32-3358, DB 1845, 14076
96 2B 4473-*1*	Mondnacht (Eichendorff-Schumann, Op. 39, No. 5)
	32-3359, DB 1845, 14076
97 2B 4474-1	(a) Die Lotosblume (Heine-Schumann, Op. 25, No. 7)
	(b) Über den Wellen (Wildgang-C. von Franckenstein, Op. 41, No. 1)
	(32-3360). Not issued
98 2B 4475-*1*-2	(a) Heidenröslein (Goethe-Schubert, D.257)
	(b) Das Lied im Grünen (Reil-Schubert, D.917)
	32-3361, DB 1844, 14077, JD 164
99 2B 4476-*1*	Du bist die Ruh' (Rückert-Schubert, D.776)
	32-3362, DB 1844, 14077, JD 164

20 September 1933: Vienna. Mittlerer Saal. Vienna Philharmonic Orchestra & Vienna State Opera Chorus, cond. Robert Heger (77 rpm throughout)
DER ROSENKAVALIER (abridged) (R. Strauss, Op. 59)
100 2WX 582-1-1A

    -2-2A   Mir ist die Ehre wiederfahren (Act 2). With Maria Olszewska (contralto) (Side 12)
32-4111, DB 2065, 7922

(–) 2WX 583-1-1A

    -2A   Wo war ich schon einmal (Act 2). With Maria Olszewska (contralto) (See discog. No. 109)

21 September 1933: DER ROSENKAVALIER (continued)
101 2WX 584-1-1A

    -2-2A   Sind halt aso (Act 3). With Maria Olszewska (contralto), Viktor Madin (bar.) (Side 26)
32-4123, DB 2072, 7929

    -3-3A   Sind halt aso (Act 3). With Lotte Lehmann (sop.), Maria Olszewska (contralto), Viktor Madin (bar.)
Not issued

102 2WX 585-1-1A-

    -2-2A   Heut' oder morgen (Act 3). With Lotte Lehmann (sop.),
    -3-3A   Maria Olszewska (contralto), Viktor Madin (bar.) (Side 23)
32-4120, DB 2071, 7928

103 2WX 586-1-1A

    -2-2A   Marie Theres'! Hab' mir's gelobt. With Lotte Lehmann (sop.), Maria Olszewska (contralto) (Side 24)
32-4121, DB 2071, 7928

104 2WX 593-1-*1A*   Weiss bereits nicht (Act 3). With Lotte Lehmann (sop.), Richard Mayr (bass) (Side 21)
32-4118, DB 2070, 7927

22 September 1933: DER ROSENKAVALIER (continued)
105 2WX 597-1-2-2A   In dieser feierlichen Stunde (Act 2). With Änna Michalsky (sop.) (Side 11)
32-4110, DB 2065, 7922

23 September 1933: DER ROSENKAVALIER (continued)
106 2WX 600-1-2

    -3-3A   Ich hab' halt schon einmal (Act 3). With Lotte Lehmann (sop.), Maria Olszewska (contralto), Richard Mayr (bass), Bella Paalen (contralto), William Wernigk (ten.) Hermann Gallos (ten.) (Side 22)
32-4119, DB 7070, 7927

107 2WX 602-*1*-1A-2 Zu ihm hätt' ich ein Zutraun (Act 2). With Maria Olszewska
        (contralto) (Act 2)
        32-4113, DB 2066, 7923 (Side 14)

108 2WX 604-1-*2A* Muss jetzt partout zu ihr (Act 3). With Lotte Lehmann (sop.),
        Maria Olszewska (contralto), Richard Mayr (bass), William
        Wernigk (ten.) Karl Ettl (bass) (Side 20)
        32-4117, DB 2069, 7926

24 September 1933: DER ROSENKAVALIER (continued)
109 2WX 583-3-3A
   -4-*4A* Wo war ich schon einmal. (Act 2). With Maria Olszewska
        (contralto) (Side 13)
        32-4112, DB 2066, 7923
(–) 2WX 584-4-*5A* Ist ein Traum (Act 3). With Maria Olszewska (contralto) (Side
        26) (See discog. No. 101)
110 2WX 606-1-1A Ist ein Traum . . . Sind halt aso! (Act 3) With Lotte Lehmann
        (sop.), Maria Olszewska (contralto), Viktor Madin (bar.)
        Not issued
    -2 Ist ein Traum (Act 3). With Maria Olszewska (contralto) (Side
        25)
        32-4122, DB 2072, 7929

27 November 1933: Studio No. 3, Abbey Road. Piano: George Reeves
111 OB 5471-*1* Wonne der Wehmut (Goethe-Beethoven, Op. 83, No.1)
        30-11515, DA 1357, 1836, JF 45 (78 rpm)
112 OB 5472-1-2 Mit einem gemalten Bande (Goethe-Beethoven, Op. 83, No.3)
        30-11516, DA 1357, 1836, JF 45 (77 rpm)
113 OB 5473-1 Das Veilchen (Goethe-Mozart, K.476)
        (30-11517)
        Not issued
114 OB 5474-1-2 (a) Loreley (Lorenz-Schumann, Op. 53, No. 2)
        (b) Ständchen (Reinick-Schumann, Op. 36, No. 2)
        30-11518, DA 1355, 1764, JF 49 (77 rpm)

29 November 1933: Studio No. 3, Abbey Road. Piano: George Reeves
115 OB 5476-*1* (a) An die Nachtigall (Claudius-Schubert, D.497)
        (b) Liebhaber in allen Gestalten (Goethe-Schubert, D.558)
        30-11519, DA 1355, 1764, JF 49 (78 rpm)

23 June 1934: Vienna. Mittlerer Saal. Orchestra cond. L. Rosenek
116 0WX 764-1-2 Sphärenklänge (Knepler-Mittler-Josef Strauss (Op. 235)
        30-12301, DA 1395, DA 4435, IR 281, JE 12 (77 rpm)
117 0WX 765-1-2 Auf Flügeln des Gesanges (Heine-Mendelssohn, Op. 34, No. 2)
        30-12302, DA 1395, 1837, JE 12 (77 rpm)
118 2WX 766-1-2-3 Ave Maria (Ellens Gesang III) (Scott trans. Storck-Schubert,
        D.839)
        32-4807, DB 2291, 8423, JD 49 (77 rpm)
119 2WX 767-1-2-3 Bist du bei mir (Stölzel, attrib. J.S. Bach, BWV 508)
        32-4808, DB 2291, 8423, JD 49 (77 rpm)

26 February 1935: No. 3 Studio, Abbey Road. Piano: George Reeves
120 0EA 1293-1-2 My lovely Celia (G. Monro arr. H. Lane-Wilson) (E)
        DA 1416
121 0EA 1294-1-2-*3* Flocks are sporting ('Pastorale') (H. Carey, arr. H. Lane-
        Wilson) (E)
        DA 1416, IR 283
122 0EA 1295-1-2 (a) Wiegenlied (Trad. ed. G. Scherer – Brahms, Op.49, No.4)

(b) Vergebliches Ständchen (Trad.—Brahms, Op. 84, No.4)
DA 1417, 1756, JE 61

(–) 0EA 1296-1-2-3 (a) Nachtigall (Reinhold-Brahms, Op. 97, No.1)
(b) Der Jäger (Halm-Brahms, Op. 95, No.4) (See discog. No. 127)

26 August 1934: No. 3 Studio, Abbey Road. Piano: Ernest Lush
123 0EA 2195-1-2 Schlafendes Jesuskind (Mörike-Wolf)
DA 1438, 1840

(–) 0EA 2196-1 HÄNSEL UND GRETEL: Abends will ich schlafen gehen (Act 2) (Humperdinck) (Part 1 of a self duet). (See discog. No. 124)

28 August 1935: No. 3 Studio, Abbey Road. Piano: Ernest Lush
124 0EA 2197-1-2 HÄNSEL UND GRETEL: Abends will ich schlafen gehen (Act 2) (Humperdinck)
DA 1439, 1948

125 0EA 2198-*1*-2 HÄNSEL UND GRETEL: (a) Ein Männlein steht im Walde (Volkslied) (Act 2). (b) Der kleine Sandmann (Act 2) (Humperdinck)
DA 1439, 1948

126 0EA 2199-*1*-2 Nun wandre, Maria (Heyse-Wolf)
DA 1438, 1840

19 November 1935: No. 3 Studio, Abbey Road. Piano: George Reeves
127 0EA 1296-4-*5* (a) Nachtigall (Reinhold-Brahms, Op. 97, No.1)
(b) Der Jäger (Halm-Brahms, Op. 95, No.4)
DA 1417, 1756, JE 61

128 2EA 2555-1 (a) Du denkst mit einem Fädchen (Heyse-Wolf)
(b) Mausfallen-Sprüchlein (Mörike-Wolf)
(c) Elfenlied (Mörike-Wolf)
Not issued

129 2EA 2556-1 (a) Ach, des Knaben Augen (Heyse-Wolf)
(b) Bedeckt mich mit Blumen (Geibel-Wolf)
Not issued

130 2EA 2557-1 (a) Frühlingsglaube (Uhland-Schubert, D.686)
(b) Die Forelle (Schubart-Schubert, D.550)
Not issued

131 2EA 2558-1 (a) Der Gang zum Liebchen (Wenzig-Brahms, Op. 48, No. 1)
(b) Der Tod, das ist die kühle Nacht (Heine-Brahms, Op. 96, No. 1)
Not issued

20 November 1935: Studio No.1, Abbey Road. Orchestra cond. Lawrance Collingwood
132 0EA 2804-1-2-*3* SISSY: Ich glaub' das Glück hält mich heute im Arm ('Caprice Viennois') (Act 3) (Kreisler)
DA 1455

133 0EA 2805-1-2-3 Vogellied (Mörike-von Weingartner, Op. 41, No. 4)
DA 1455

134 0EA 2806-*1* Last Night (Marzials-Kjerulf) (E)
DA 1457

135 0EA 2807-*1* Down in the Forest (H. Simpson-L. Ronald) (From: 'A Cycle of Life') (E)
DA 1457, IR 282

List of Recordings

7 September 1936: Studio No.2, Abbey Road. Piano: Gerald Moore Nos. 136, 137, 140,141), Elizabeth Coleman (Nos. 138, 139). Speed 77 rpm throughout

136 0EA 3759-*1*   Horch! horch! die Lerch' ('Ständchen') (Shakespeare trans. Schlegel, stanza two Reil. Schubert, D.889) DA 1526, 1933, VE 85, NF 4040

137 0EA 3760-*1*-2   An die Musik (Schober-Schubert, D.547). (DA 1525), 1932, VE 85

138 0EA 3761-*1*   Auf dem Wasser zu singen (Stolberg-Schubert, D.774) DA 1521, 1932, VE 1009

139 0EA 3762-*1*-2   (a) Der Jüngling an der Quelle (Salis-Schubert, D.300) (b) Geheimes (Goethe-Schubert, D.719) DA 1521, 1933, VE 1009

140 0EA 3763-*1*   Sandmännchen (Zuccalmaglio-Brahms, V.K.4) DA 1526, 1838, JE 130, NF 4184

141 0EA 3764-*1*   Der Tod, das ist die kühle Nacht (Heine-Brahms, Op. 96, No. 1) (DA 1525) 1838, JE 130, NF 4184

25 November 1936: Studio No.2, Abbey Road, Orchestra cond. Walter Goehr

142 0EA 3931-1-*1A*-2   DAS DREIMÄDERLHAUS: Was macht glücklich ('Lied aus Wien') (Act 1) (Willner-Reichert-Schubert, arr. H. Berté) DA 1541

143 0EA 3932-1-*1A*   Wien, du Stadt meiner Träume (Sieczynski) DA 1541

144 0EA 3933-1-*1A*   THE KISS (HUBICKA): Schlafe mein Kindlein (Act 1) (Smetana) (G) (Wiegenlied) DA 1544, 1839, JE 148

145 0EA 3934-1-*1A*
      -2A   PEER GYNT: Der Winter mag scheiden ('Solveig's Song') (Act 4) (Ibsen-Grieg, Op. 23, No. 11) (G) DA 1544, 1839, JE 148 NF 4040

26 November 1936: Studio No. 3, Abbey Road. Piano: Gerald Moore

146 0EA 4486-*1*   Des Fischers Liebesglück (Leitner-Schubert, D.933) DA 1545, 1934

147 0EA 4487-*1*   Der Musensohn (Goethe-Schubert, D.764) DA 1545, 1935

148 0EA 4488-*1*-2   Litanei auf das Fest aller Seelen (Jacobi-Schubert, D.343) DA 1546, 1934

149 0EA 4489-*1*   Liebesbotschaft (Rellstab-Schubert, D.957) Schwanengesang, No.1) DA 1546

150 0EA 4490-*1*-2   Fischerweise (Schlechta-Schubert, D.881) DA 1547, JE 99

151 0EA 4491-*1*   Gretchen am Spinnrade (Goethe-Schubert, D.118) DA 1547, 1935, JE 99

10 March 1937: Studio No.3, Abbey Road. Piano: Gerald Moore

152 2EA 4849-*1*-2   (a) Nähe des Geliebten (Goethe-Schubert, D.162) (b) Lachen und Weinen (Rückert-Schubert, D.777) DB 3184, 15168

153 2EA 4850-*1*-2   (a) Nacht und Träume (von Collin-Schubert, D.837) (b) Seligkeit (Hölty-Schubert, D.433) DB 3184, 15167

154 2EA 4851-*1*   Der Einsame (Lappe-Schubert, D.800) DB 3185, 15167, JD 1284

155 2EA 4852-*1*   Frühlingstraum (Müller-Schubert, D.911) (Winterreise, No.11) DB 3185, JD 1284

355

11 March 1937: Studio No.1, Abbey Road. Orchestra cond. Walter Goehr

156 0EA 4681-1A-*2A*   Immer leiser wird mein Schlummer (Lingg-Brahms, Op. 105,
    No. 2)
    DA 1562, 1837

157 0EA 4682-1A-*2A*   Wiegenlied (Trad. ed. G. Scherer-Brahms, Op. 49, No. 4)
    DA 1562

158 0EA 4683-1-*2A*   DER LANDSTREICHER: Sei gepriesen, du lauschige Nacht
    (Act 1) (Ziehrer)
    DA 1557

159 0EA 4684-1-*1A*   DER FREMDENFÜHRER: O Wien, mein liebes Wien (Act 2)
    (Ziehrer)
    DA 1557

29 June 1937: Paris; Théâtre des Champs Elysées. Vienna Philharmonic Orchestra,
Vienna State Opera Chorus, cond. Bruno Walter. With Kerstin Thorborg (mezzo-
sop.), Anton Dermota (ten.), Alexander Kipnis (bass)

160 2LA 2005-1 to   MASS NO. 19 IN D MINOR (REQUIEM) (Mozart, K.626)
2LA 2019-1   (L). Complete.

161 2LA 2020-1 to   TE DEUM IN C (Bruckner) (L) Complete
2LA 2025-1

21 September 1937: Studio No.3, Abbey Road. Piano: George Reeves. Clarinet:
Reginald Kell

162 2EA 5443-*1*   Der Hirt auf dem Felsen (Müller & von Chézy-Schubert,
    D.965). Part 1.
    DB 3317, 14815, VB 47, ED 115

163 2EA 5452-*1-2*   Der Hirt auf dem Felsen. Part 2
    DB 3317, 14815, VB 47, ED 115

22 November 1937: Studio No.1, Abbey Road, Orchestra cond. Lawrance
Collingwood

164 2EA 5899-*1-2-3*   Still wie die Nacht (C. Bohm, Op. 326, No. 27)
    DB 3641, 15735

165 0EA 5900-*1*   Zum Schlafen (Schellenberg-Reger, Op. 76, No. 59)
    DA 1619

166 0EA 5901-*1*   Mariae Wiegenlied (Boelitz-Reger, Op. 76, No. 52)
    DA 1619

167 2EA 5902-*1-2*   Oh, quand je dors (Hugo-Liszt, S.282/1) (F)
    Not issued

29 November 1937: Studio No.3, Abbey Road. Piano: George Reeves

168 0EA 6019-*1-2*   (a) O ihr Herren (Rückert-Schumann, Op. 37, No. 3)
    (b) Röselein, Röselein (von der Neun-Schumann, Op. 89,
    No. 6)
    DA 1620

169 0EA 6020-*1*   (a) Das Mädchen spricht (Gruppe-Brahms, Op. 107, No. 3)
    (b) Der Mond steht über dem Berge ('Ständchen') (Kugler-
    Brahms, No.106, No.1)
    DA 1620

170 2EA 6021-*1*   Des Baches Wiegenlied (Müller-Schubert, D.795) (Die schöne
    Müllerin, No.20)
    DB 3426, 15735

171 2EA 6022-*1-2*   (a) Schlafe, schlafe, holder, süsser Knabe ('Wiegenlied') (Anon-
    Schubert, D.498)
    (b) Der Schmetterling (Schlegel-Schubert, D.633)
    DB 3426, 15168

List of Recordings

1 June 1938: Studio No.3, Abbey Road. Piano: L. Rosenek

172 2EA 6652-*1*-2   Ruhe Süssliebchen im Schatten (Die schöne Magelone) (Tieck-Brahms, Op. 33, No. 9)
(DB 3598), DB 21572

173 2EA 6653-*1*-2   (a) Nachtviolen (Mayerhofer-Schubert, D.752)
(b) An die Geliebte (Stoll-Schubert, D.303)
(DB 3598), DB 21572

8 June 1938: Studio No.1A, Abbey Road. Orchestra cond. Walter Goehr

174 0EA 6353-1-2   Dors, mon enfant (Anon-Wagner) (G)
Not issued

175 0EA 6354-*1*-2   Ich muss wieder einmal in Grinzing sein (Benatzky)
DA 1651

(–) 2EA 6355-1-2   Night of Stars (Belle Nuit, O nuit d'amour) ('Barcarolle') (Act 3) (Offenbach) (E) (Part 1 of a self duet. See discog. No. 184)

176 2EA 6356-*1*   Dors, mon enfant (Anon-Wagner) (G)
DB 3654

11 June 1938: Studio No. 1A, Abbey Road. Orchestra cond. Walter Goehr

177 2EA 6361-1-2-(*3*)   Oh, quand je dors (Hugo-Liszt, S.282/1) (F)
DB 3654

178 0EA 6362-*1*-2   DER OPERNBALL: Im chambre séparée (Act 2) (Heuberger)
DA 1651

179 0EA 6363-1-2   Orpheus with his lute (Shakespeare-Sullivan) (E)
(DA 1662).
Not issued

180 0EA 6364-1   A memory (Goring Thomas) (E)
(DA 1662). Not issued

2 July 1938: Studio No.3, Abbey Road. Piano: L. Rosenek

181 2EA 6677-*1*   Der Jüngling und der Tod (von Spaun-Schubert, D.545)
DB 3600

182 2EA 6678-*1*   (a) Das Heimweh (Hell-Schubert, D.456)
(b) CLAUDINE VON VILLA BELLA: Hin und wieder fliegen Pfeile (Goethe-Schubert, D 239, No.3)
(c) CLAUDINE VON VILLA BELLA: Liebe schwärmt auf allen Wegen (Goethe-Schubert, D.239, No.6)
DB 3600

183 2EA 6679-1   An eine Äolsharfe (Mörike-Brahms, Op. 19, No. 5)
(DB 3599). Not issued

184 2EA 6680-*1*   LES CONTES D'HOFFMANN: Night of Stars (Belle Nuit, O nuit d'amour) ('Barcarolle') (Act 3) (Offenbach) (E)
DB 3641

6 July 1938: Studio No.3, Abbey Road. Piano: L. Rosenek

185 0EA 6681-*1*-2   (a) THE COUNTRY LOVER: The early morning (Belloc-Peel) (E)
(b) THE SHE-GALLANTS: So well Corinna likes the joy (Eccles transcr. A Bernard) (E)
DA 1668

186 2EA 6682-1   (a) Bitteres zu sagen (Daumer-Brahms, Op. 32, No. 7)
(b) Blinde Kuh (Anon Sicilian trans. A. Kopisch-Brahms, Op. 58, No.1)
(DB 3599). Not issued

187 0EA 6683-*1*   Lehn' deine Wang' (Heine-A. Jensen, Op. 1, No. 1)
DA 1663

188 0EA 6684-*1*   Wo du hingehst (Ruth I, 16-E. Hildach, Op.8)
DA 1663

8 July 1938: Studio No.3, Abbey Road. Piano: L. Rosenek
189 0EA 6685-1   (a) Erlaube mir, fein's Mädchen (Trad.-Brahms, D.V.2)
                        (b) Wie komm' ich denn (Trad.-Brahms, D.V.34)
                        (DA 1652). Not issued. HMB 73 (1991)
190 0EA 6686-1   In stiller Nacht (Spee-anon.-Brahms, D.V.42)
                        (DA 1652). Not issued
191 2EA 6687-*1*   (a) Mein Mädel hat einen Rosenmund (Zuccalmaglio-Brahms,
                        D.V.25)
                        (b) Da unten im Tale (Swabian-Brahms, D.V.6)
                        (DB 3597), DB 21605
192 2EA 6688-*1*-2   (a) Schwesterlein (Zuccalmaglio-Brahms, D.V.15)
                        (b) Och Moder, ich well en Ding han! (Trad.-Brahms, D.V.33)
                        (DB 3597), DB 21605
193 0EA 6689-1   Heimkehr (Schack-R.Strauss, Op. 15, No. 5)
                        Not issued. HMV 73 (1991)

16 August 1938: Studio No.3, Abbey Road. Piano: L. Rosenek
194 0EA 6700-*1*-2   THE TEMPEST: Where the bee sucks, there suck I
                        (Shakespeare-Arne) (E)
                        DA 1668

22 October 1938: Studio No.1, Abbey Road. Organ: Herbert Dawson
195 0EA 6816-*1*-2   O du fröhliche (Sicilian folksong arr. J. Falk)
                        DA 1666
196 0EA 6817-*1*-2   Stille Nacht, heilige Nacht (Mohr-Gruber)
                        DA 1666
197 0EA 6818-*1*   Silent night, holy night (Mohr-Gruber) (E)
                        DA 1667, 2013, IR 283
198 0EA 6819-1-2-3   The Coventry Carol (Trad.) (E)
                        DA 1667, 2013

10 October 1939: New York. Studio No.2 (Victor). String Quartet with M. Miller
(oboe), P. Sklar (dble bass), Yella Pessl (harpsichord), cond. Bruno Reibold
                        CANTATA BWV 202: Weichet nur, betrübte Schatten (Anon-
                        J.S. Bach). Complete
199 BS 042927-*1*-1A   Weichet nur, betrübte Schatten (Part 1)
                        DA 1757, 2069
200 BS 042928-*1*-1A   Weichet nur (Part 2): Die Welt wird wieder neu (Recitative)
                        DA 1757, 2069
201 BS 042931-*1*-1A   Das Glück es ist gefunden (Recitative); Zu freien im Maien
                        (Part 1)
                        DA 1759, 2071
202 BS 142932-*1*-1A   Zu freien (Part 2); So sei das Band (Recitative); Sehen in
                        Zufriedenheit ('Gavotta')
                        DA 1759, 2071

22 November 1939: New York. Studio No.2 (Victor). S. Shulman (vln) A. Shulman
('cello), Y. Pessl (harpsichord)
                        CANTATA BWV 202 (Bach) (Part 2)
203 BS 042929-*1*   Phoebus eilt mit schnellen Pferden
     -2-2A   DA 1758, 2070
204 BS 042930-1   Drum sucht auch Amor (Recitative): Wenn die Frühlingslüfte
     -2-2A   streichen
                        DA 1758, 2070

29 August 1945: Abbey Road Studios. Piano: Gerald Moore
205 0EA 10576-*1*-2   In der Frühe (Mörike-Wolf)
                        DA 1862 (76 rpm)

206 0EA 10577-*1*-2		(a) In dem Schatten meiner Locken (Heyse-Wolf)
		(b) Mausfallen-Sprüchlein (Mörike-Wolf)
		DA 1862
207 0EA 10578-*1*-2		She never told her love (Shakespeare-Haydn) (E)
		DA 1850, EC 150 (76 rpm)

30 August 1945: Abbey Road Studios. Piano; Gerald Moore (77 rpm)

208 2EA 10579-1		Abendempfindung (Campe-Mozart, K.523)
		Not issued
209 0EA 10580-*1*-2		Das Veilchen (Goethe-Mozart, K.476)
		DA 1854
210 0EA 10581-*1*-2		The sailor's song (Mrs. Hunter-Haydn) (E)
		DA 1850, EC 150
211 0EA 10582-*1*		Dass sie hier gewesen (Rückert-Schubert, D.775)
		DA 1854

26 November 1945: Abbey Road Studios. Piano: Gerald Moore (77 rpm)

212 0EA 10776-*1*-2		ROSAMUNDE VON CYPERN: Der Vollmond strahlt
		('Romanze') (von Chézy-Schubert, D.797, 3b)
		DA 1852, EC 152
213 0EA 10777-*1*-2		Die Forelle (Schubart-Schubert, D.550)
		DA 1852, EC 152
214 0EA 10778-*1*-2		Auch kleine Dinge (Heyse-Wolf)
		DA 1860

27 November 1945: Abbey Road Studios. Piano: Gerald Moore

(–) 0EA 10779-1-2		Wie glänzt der helle Mond (Keller-Wolf)
		(See 20th October 1947)
215 2EA 10780-1		Die junge Nonne (Craigher-Schubert, D.828)
		Not issued
216 0EA 10781-1		Nimmersatte Liebe (Mörike-Wolf)
		Not issued

17 June 1946: Abbey Road Studios. Piano; Gerald Moore

217 2EA 11072-1-2		Wie bist du, meine Königin (Daumer-Brahms, Op. 32, No. 9)
		Not issued
218 0EA 11073-1-2		Es träumte mir (Daumer-Brahms, Op. 57, No. 3)
		Not issued

18 June 1946: Abbey Road Studios. Piano: Gerald Moore

219 0EA 11074-1-2		(a) Therese (Keller-Brahms, Op.86, No.1)
		(b) Das Mädchen spricht (Gruppe-Brahms, Op.107, No.3)
		Not issued
220 0EA 11075-*1*-2		Das Mädchen (von Schlegel-Schubert, K.652)
		DA 1864
221 0EA 11076-*1*		Und willst du deinen Liebsten sterben sehen? (Heyse-Wolf)
		DA 1860
222 0EA 11077-*1*		An mein Clavier (Schubart-Schubert, D.342)
		DA 1864

9 October 1946: Abbey Road Studios. Piano: Gerald Moore

		FRAUENLIEBE UND – LEBEN (Chamisso-Schumann, Op.42)
(–) 2EA 11274-1		Seit ich ihn gesehen
		(See 20 October 1947)
223 2EA 11275-*1*		(a) Er, der herrlichste von allen'
		(b) Ich kann's nicht fassen, nicht glauben
		DB 9568 (77 rpm)

(–) 2 EA 11276-1-2	(a) Du Ring an meinem Finger (b) Helft mir, ihr Schwestern (See 20 October 1947)
224 2EA 11277-*1*	Süsser Freund, du blickest mich verwundert an DB 9569
225 2EA 11278-*1*	(a) An meinem Herzen, an meiner Brust (b) Nun hast du mir den ersten Schmerz getan DB 9568 (77 rpm)

20 October 1947: Studio No.3, Abbey Road. Piano: Gerald Moore
FRAUENLIEBE UND – LEBEN (continued)

(–) 2EA 11274-2-3	Seit ich ihn gesehen (See 2 October 1948)
(–) 2EA 11276-3-4	(a) Du Ring an meinem Finger (b) Helft mir, ihr Schwestern (See 2 October 1948)
(–) 0EA 10779-3	Wie glänzt der helle Mond (Keller-Wolf) (See discog. No. 226)

2 October 1948: Abbey Road Studios. Piano: Gerald Moore

226 0EA 10779-4-*5*	Wie glänzt der helle Mond (Keller-Wolf) Not issued FRAUENLIEBE UND – LEBEN (continued)
227 2EA 11274-4-*5*	Seit ich ihn gesehen DBS 9567 (77 rpm)
(–) 2EA 11276-5-6	(a) Du Ring an meinem Finger (b) Helft mir, ihr Schwestern (See Discog. No. 228)

20 June 1949: Studio No.3, Abbey Road. Piano: Gerald Moore
FRAUENLIEBE UND – LEBEN (concluded)

| 228 2EA 11276-7-8 | (a) Du Ring an meinem Finger
(b) Helft mir, ihr Schwestern
DB 9569 |

13 October 1949: Studio No.1A, Abbey Road. Piano: Gerald Moore

229 0EA 14255-1-2	Nur wer die Sehnsucht kennt (Lied der Mignon IV) (Goethe-Schubert, D.877) Not issued
230 0EA 14256-1	So lasst mich scheinen (Lied der Mignon III) (Goethe-Schubert, D.877) Not issued
231 0EA 14257-1	(a) Schweizerlied (Goethe-Schubert, D.559) (b) CLAUDINE VON VILLA BELLA: Hin und wieder (Goethe-Schubert, D.239, No.3) Not issued

III. THE ALLEGRO MICROGROOVE RECORDINGS

Recorded on tape in the artist's flat at 2 East 75th Street, New York. The songs by Mendelssohn and Franz were recorded on 6 and 27 February, and 3 April, 1950, and issued on a ten-inch long-playing record in mid-1950. The Wolf songs were recorded on 7, 8 and 18 December 1950 and issued on a twelve-inch long-playing record in early 1951.

232 Songs by Mendelssohn (piano: George Schick)
   a) Bei der Wiege (Klingemann), Op.47, No.6
   b) Das erste Veilchen (Ebert), Op.19a, No.2
   c) Frühlingslied (Robert), Op.8, No.6
   d) Die Liebende schreibt (Goethe), Op.86, No.3
   e) Der Mond (Geibel), Op.86, No.5
   AL 51 (USA), ALY 51 (UK), Festival CFR 10-222 (Australia)

233 Songs by Franz (piano: George Schick)
   a) Aus meinen grossen Schmerzen (Heine), Op.5, No.1
   b) Bitte (Lenau), Op.9, No.3
   c) Gute Nacht (Eichendorff), Op.5, No.7
   d) Liebchen ist da (Schröer), Op.5, No.2
   e) Mutter, o sing' mich zur Ruh' (Hemans), Op.10, No.3
   f) Stille Sicherheit (Lenau), Op.10, No.2
   g) Vöglein, wohin so schnell? (Geibel), Op.1, No.11
   h) Widmung (Müller), Op.14, No.1
   AL 51 (USA), ALY 51 (UK), Festival CFR 10-222 (Australia)

234 Songs by Wolf (piano: George Reeves)
   a) Als ich auf dem Euphrat schiffte (Goethe)
   b) Anakreons Grab (Goethe)
   c) Bedeckt mich mit Blumen (Span. Liederbuch)
   d) Blumengruss (Goethe)
   e) Du denkst mit einem Fädchen (Ital. Liederbuch)
   f) Gesegnet sei das Grün (Ital. Liederbuch)
   g) Ihr jungen Leute (Ital. Liederbuch)
   h) In der Frühe (Mörike)
   i) Nimmersatte Liebe (Mörike)
   j) Nun wandre, Maria (Span. Liederbuch)
   k) O wär' dein Haus durchsichtig (Ital. Liederbuch)
   l) Phänomen (Goethe)
   m) Sie blasen zum Abmarsch (Span. Liederbuch)
   n) Ein Ständchen Euch zu bringen (Ital. Liederbuch)
   o) Verborgenheit (Mörike)
   p) Wie glänzt der helle Mond (Keller)
   AL 98 (USA)

NON-COMMERCIAL RECORDINGS, 1936–1950

The Golden Age of Opera series (USA)
EJS 172: Potpourri No. 7
She never told her love (Haydn) (E) (1947)
Recorded from the BBC Light Programme 'Friday Concert' on 23 May 1947. The BBC Orchestra and Chorus were conducted by Walter Goehr.
EJS 213: Potpourri No. 12
L'amerò, sarò costante (Il Re Pastore) (Mozart) (I) (1942) Recorded from the radio show, 'America Preferred', broadcast on 28 February 1942. The orchestra is conducted by Alfred Wallenstein.
EJS 328: Two Lecture Recitals
The first lecture was pre-recorded on 13 October 1950 and transmitted on 22 February 1951 on the BBC Third Programme. The artist sang Das Veilchen (Mozart), Lachen und Weinen (Schubert), Mausfallen-Sprüchlein (Wolf) and Vergebliches Ständchen (Brahms). The second recital was pre-recorded on 16 November 1951 and transmitted on 31 January 1952, also on the BBC Third

Programme. The artist sang Morgen (R. Strauss), Die Forelle (Schubert), and In dem Schatten meiner Locken (Wolf). The accompanist was Ernest Lush.

EJS 332: Der Rosenkavalier (excerpts) (R. Strauss)

Not recorded from a single performance at the Vienna State Opera in 1936 as the label states, not conducted by Richard Strauss, but a composite of two performances, both conducted by Hans Knappertsbusch, the first on 22 April 1936 with Lotte Lehmann (Marschallin) and Eva Hadrabova (Octavian), and the second on 13 June 1937 with Hilde Konetzni (Marschallin) and Margit Bokor (Octavian). Elisabeth Schumann sang Sophie in both performances. Lotte Lehmann is heard only in the Trio. A fragment from Act 1, the 'Presentation of the Silver Rose' scene (with cuts) from Act 2, and the Trio and final duet from Act 3 make up the contents. The recordings were made in the opera house by a staff member.

EJS 444: Wagner Recital (Siegfried, Act 2)

The Woodbird scenes recorded during a performance given at the Vienna State Opera on 16 June 1937. The Woodbird's song which terminates Scene 2, Act 2, is omitted. The second and third songs are complete. The Siegfried is Max Lorenz.

EJS 532: Soprano Potpourri No. 23

An den Sonnenschein (Schumann); Therese (Brahms); Ich atmet' einen linden Duft (Mahler)

Recorded from the BBC Third Programme broadcast of 14 October 1945. The accompanist is John Wills.

Unique Opera Record Corporation (USA)

UORC 251: Requiem Mass, K.626 (Mozart). The Recordare and Confutatis are omitted. Taped from test pressings of the performance given on 29 June 1937 in Paris. See Discography No. 160 for details.

Discocorp (USA). IGI 274: Two Lecture Recitals

For the lecture recitals see EJS 328 above. Also included before the first lecture on side one, are performances of L'amerò, sarò costante (Il Re Pastore) and the Alleluia from the Exsultate, jubilate, K.165 by Mozart, recorded from the Promenade Concert at the Queen's Hall, London, on 8 September 1936, and broadcast by the BBC in their National Programme. Henry J. Wood conducted the BBC Symphony Orchestra. Neither aria is mentioned on the sleeve.

Perennial Records (USA): PER 1001: Elisabeth Schumann, soprano

The Contents include Ihr habt nun Traurigkeit from Ein deutsches Requiem (Brahms), and Blute nur from the St. Matthew Passion (Bach). Both are sung in English. The Bach aria was recorded from a CBS 'Invitation to Music' programme broadcast on 28 March 1944. The CBS Symphony Orchestra was conducted by Bernard Herrmann. The Brahms aria has not been traced.

Nippon Columbia (Japan). OW-7225-6-BS: Lieder Recital. Das Veilchen (Mozart); Die Liebende schreibt (Mendelssohn); Wonne der Wehmut, Mit einem gemalten Bande (Beethoven); Geheimes, Lied der Mignon III, Nachtlied, Hin und wieder fliegen Pfeile, Lied der Mignon IV, Liebe schwärmt auf allen Wegen, Schweizerlied, Liebhaber in allen Gestalten (Schubert); Phänomen, Anakreons Grab, Als ich auf dem Euphrat schiffte, Blumengruss (Wolf); Gefunden (R. Strauss); Singet nicht in Trauertönen (Schumann). Encore: In dem Schatten meiner Locken (Wolf). The pianist was Bruno Walter. Transferred from a Bruno Walter Society tape of the recital, which was given in Washington D.C., USA, on 2 April 1950.

List of Recordings

Rubini Records (UK): SJG 009 (BEV 1158/9)
Elisabeth Schumann Recital
O Wien, mein liebes Wien (Der Fremdenführer) (Ziehrer) (1947); Ruhe, Süssliebchen im Schatten, Der Jäger, Therese, Das Mädchen spricht, Vergebliches Ständchen (Brahms) (1949); Freundliche Vision (R. Strauss); Das Veilchen (Mozart); Glockenton, Der Vogel (Kienzl); Frieden, Gretel (Pfitzner) (1936/7); Der Gang zum Liebchen (Brahms), An den Sonnenschein (Schumann), Ich atmet' einen linden Duft (Mahler), An die Nachtigall (Brahms) (1945); Mausfallen Sprüchlein (Wolf) (1951).
All are recorded from BBC transmissions. The operetta aria is from the BBC Light Programme 'Friday Concert' of 23 May 1947, with Walter Goehr conducting the BBC Theatre Orchestra and Chorus. The five Brahms songs are from the Third Programme recital of 2 September 1949. The accompanist is Ernest Lush. The Strauss, Kienzl and Pfitzner songs are part of a Regional Programme recital of 6 September 1936. The accompanist was probably Berkeley Mason. Mozart's Das Veilchen was probably recorded from the Regional Programme broadcast of 19 September 1937, with Berkeley Mason at the piano. The final group of Lieder formed part of a Home Service recital given on 14 October 1945. The accompanist was John Wills. Wolf's Mausfallen-Sprüchlein (sung twice) was recorded from the BBC Television programme, 'Speaking Personally', transmitted at 8.15 p.m. on 18 November 1951. The accompanist was Clifton Helliwell.

Voce Recordings (USA). VOCE-117: Elisabeth Schumann
For the contents of the Washington D.C. Recital of 2 April 1950, which is included on this record, see Nippon Columbia OW-7225-6-BS. For An den Sonnenschein, An die Nachtigall and Ich atmet' einen linden Duft (1945); Ruhe, Süssliebchen im Schatten, Der Jäger, Therese and Das Mädchen spricht (1949); and Der Vogel and Gretel (1936) on side two see Rubini SJG 009 where full details are given.

Beledevere Teletheater 76.23589: Der Rosenkavalier (excerpts) Mir ist die Ehre widerfahren (Act 2), with Evan Hadrabova (Octavian). Hab' mir's gelobt (Trio) (Act 3), with Eva Hadrabova (Octavian), and Lotte Lehmann (Marschallin). Recorded during a performance at the Vienna State Opera on 22 April 1936. The Vienna State Opera Orchestra was conducted by Hans Knappertsbusch. See also EJS 332.

Belvedere Teletheater 76.23596/97: Pagliacci excerpt Wie die Vöglein schweben (Stridono lassu). Nedda's Bird Song. Recorded during a performance given at the Vienna State Opera on 10 May 1937. The Vienna State Opera Orchestra was conducted by Karl Alwin.

RECORDINGS INDEXED BY DISCOGRAPHY NUMBERS

367

INDEX

Der Musensohn

Goethe

Ziemlich lebhaft

1822

(*Poco vivace*)

Durch Feld und Wald zu schwei-fen, mein Liedchen weg zu pfei-fen, so geht's von Ort zu Ort, so geht's von Ort zu Ort! Und nach dem Tak-te re-get und nach dem Mass be-we-get sich al-les an mir fort, und nach dem Mass be-we-get sich al-les an mir fort.

Ich